THE WEST YORKSHIRE MOORS

THE WEST YORKSHIRE MOORS

2nd Edition

by Christopher Goddard

the beautiful dogs on Dog Hill

For Dolly, Eric and those before us who
trespassed as a matter of principle

Published by Gritstone Publishing Co-operative
Birchcliffe Centre, Hebden Bridge, West Yorkshire, HX7 8DG

www.gritstonepublishing.co.uk

Originally published by Northern Heritage Publications, 2013

Second Edition – 2019

Printed in Huddersfield by Had-Print

ISBN 978-0-9955609-7-0

ACKNOWLEDGEMENTS

I would like to thank those who have helped me along the
way and ultimately made this book possible:

Roger Goddard, Gill Corteen, Nick Goddard, Alison Ford, Phil
Cross, Amanda Daw, Joan Tindale, Tony Wright, Steve Archer,
Jayne Booth, John Billingsley, Steven Wood, Michael Stewart,
Kate, Jake and everyone at The Book Case and Book Corner
bookshops, my colleagues at Gritstone Publishing Co-
operative (Andrew Bibby, Andrew McCloy, Chiz Dakin and
Colin Speakman), everyone at Jeremy Mills Publishing,
and most of all the patience, support and invaluable
editing of my partner Caroline Hodgson.

THE WEST YORKSHIRE MOORS – CONTENTS

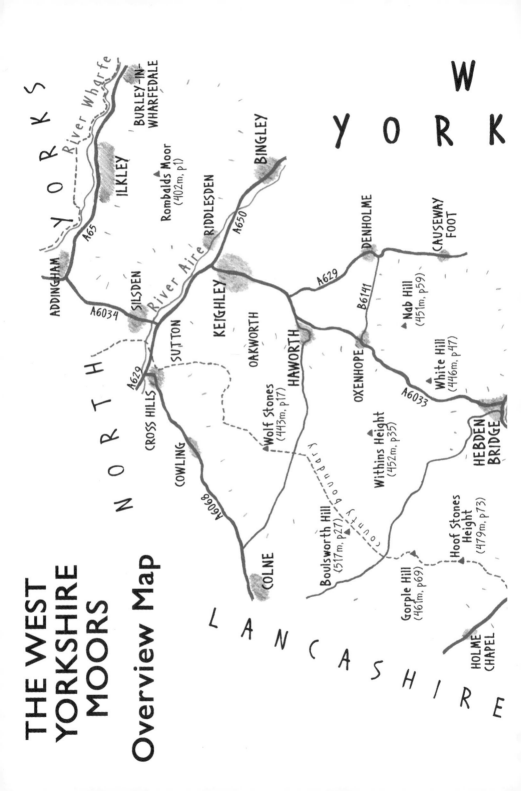

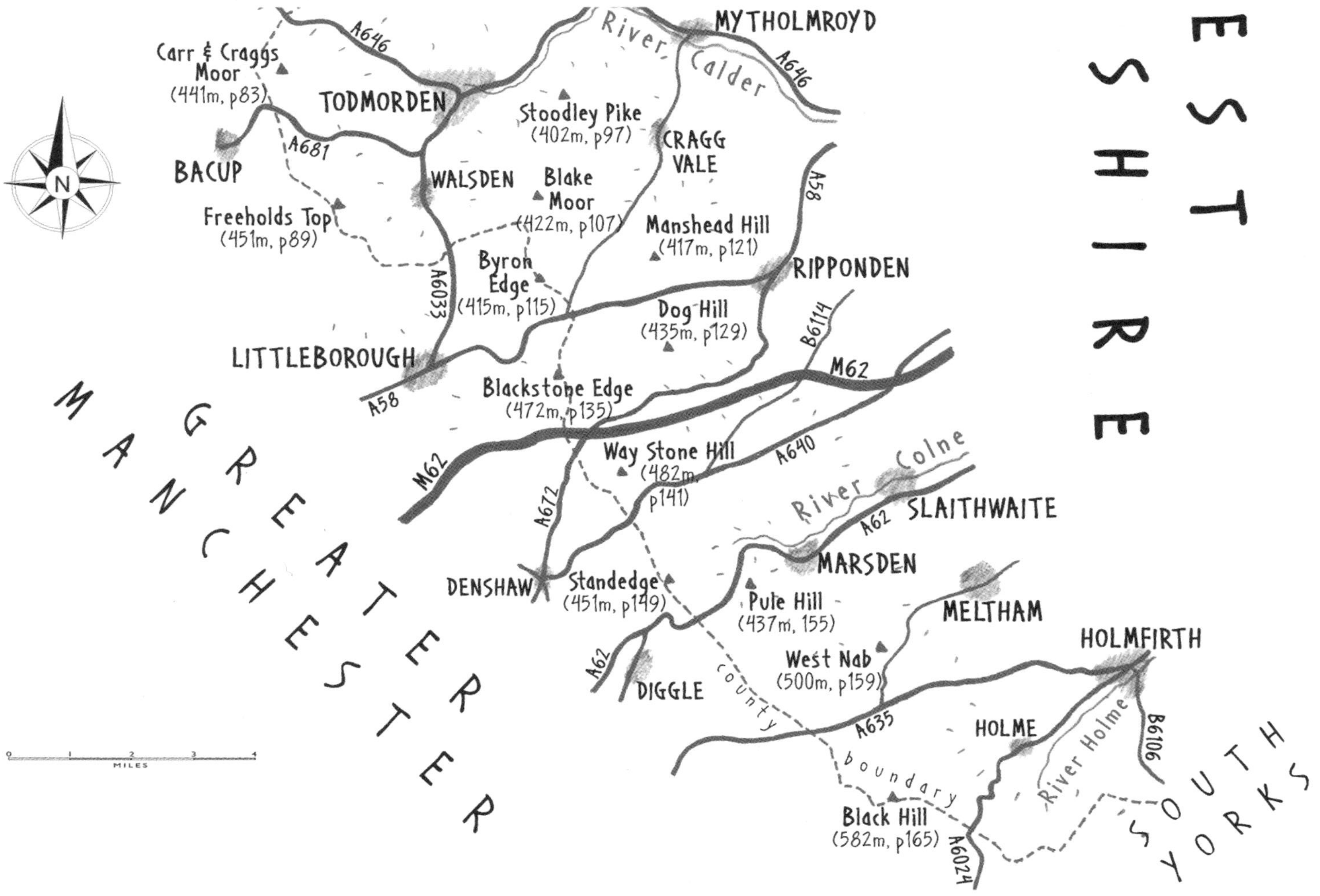

E S T

S H I R E

SOUTH YORKS

HOLMFIRTH

B6106

River Holme

MELTHAM

SLAITHWAITE

HOLME

A6024

boundary

Black Hill
(582m, p165)

MYTHOLMROYD

A646

River Calder

A58

RIPPONDEN

B6114

M62

River Colne

A62

MARSDEN

West Nab
(500m, p159)

A635

CRAGG VALE

Manshead Hill
(417m, p121)

Dog Hill
(435m, p129)

A640

Pule Hill
(437m, 155)

county

Stoodley Pike
(402m, p97)

Blake Moor
(422m, p107)

Byron Edge
(415m, p115)

Blackstone Edge
(472m, p135)

Way Stone Hill
(482m, p141)

Standedge
(451m, p149)

A672

DIGGLE

A62

WALSDEN

A6033

DENSHAW

TODMORDEN

A646

A681

Freeholds Top
(451m, p89)

M62

A58

LITTLEBOROUGH

G R E A T E R

M A N C H E S T E R

Carr & Craggs Moor
(441m, p83)

BACUP

N

0   1   2   3
MILES

List of High Points in West Yorkshire
(over 200m and with a prominence of at least 30m or 100ft)

PREFACE TO THE 2ND EDITION

I worked intermittently and inefficiently on the first edition of *The West Yorkshire Moors* between 2006 and 2013, unsure quite how it would be received but resolved that it would see the light of day. When I first started to show people the printed book I was blown away by the response, particularly to elements of the book I was most unsure about, like the sketches. People started seeing me as an artist and writer as well as a cartographer, despite my lack of credentials as either. Having vowed not to work on something so laborious again, I found myself starting work on the follow-up within months, buoyed by the pleasure my work seemed to give people.

The main criticisms of that first book were consistent and fair; the text was too small, the margins too tight, the photos too dark and the book difficult to navigate. And of course I had used 'feint' instead of 'faint'! The last was an intentional decision before printing, but one that I have heard commented on more than anything else about my books and I have come to admit that I was wrong. However, my own criticism of that first book is far greater than anyone else's and I have come to be slightly ashamed of it compared to the books I have produced since; most of all I find the maps themselves to be untidy and unappealing. For a long time, however, I couldn't face going back to look closely at it again. But when the publishing rights reverted to me last year I realised this was an opportunity to put right the wrongs of that first formative work.

In the five-plus years since publication and route-checking, much has changed on these apparently timeless moors. Most obviously, wind farms have been updated on Ovenden Moor and newly built above Todmorden, completely changing the face of both Carr and Craggs Moor and Shore Moor. New fencelines continue to divide up the moors to control grazing and restore the peat, particularly on Marsden Moors. Fell race routes have been altered, abandoned or newly devised, changing the lines of handy little paths my routes often made use of. Elsewhere gates have been locked, new drains dug, stiles removed, heather has grown or been burnt, and sheep have decided to wander elsewhere for their nutrition. When composing that first book, I had wondered whether my routes may become well-scored lines across the moors, but I have been surprised to find that on the whole it has had little effect. Indeed, on some routes, where there was once a faint path there is now nothing. The only exception is

Great Bride Stones on Hoof Stones Height

the once-intermittent line between Dog Hill trig and Cat Stones, which has quickly become a very clear path, although that may be the result of its use as part of a new race route. The consequence of all this is that, when I came to walk my routes again recently, I found myself flummoxed and pitying anyone else trying to decipher them. As well as improving and often simplifying these routes, I have devised two completely new routes, from Haworth and Ripponden (the first being a notable omission from the original book).

Even I have found the original book hard to navigate and have come to realise the error of organising the chapters alphabetically around moors whose names are often unfamiliar even to those who know the moors well (e.g. Blake Moor, White Hill, Way Stone Hill, Carr and Craggs Moor). This time I have ordered the chapters logically from north to south, with each map generally following geographically from the last. It has played havoc with my indexing, but hopefully the result is a far more coherent book.

I have also replaced the photos in the chapter introductions with new sketches of each moor, though it is hard in some cases to draw much shape from these flat tops (that's you Byron Edge!). I have widened the margins of each page and diligently increased the font size of every word on every map and page. This has necessarily resulted in the pages becoming more crammed and some text being removed. I have tried to keep what I thought most interesting or useful without losing the character of the original book, but I did come to realise how much waffle I had included originally. Most painfully though I have undertaken what I could term digital remastering of the maps themselves. This involves carefully editing of individual pixels to tidy up messy corners and remove the murk that covered parts of the maps. It is the only way to edit these maps in the first place, but as soon as I change one bit of the map I realise how much more needs working on nearby. It is a deep rabbit hole to go down, but I have emerged with something that I am now much prouder of.

I haven't found this an easy process compared to the excitement of working on something new and in many ways it felt as though it would have been easier to start again from scratch, but I do hope this new edition now sits more comfortably alongside *The West Yorkshire Woods* and *The South Yorkshire Moors* and whatever else there is to come.

Christopher Goddard

(January 2019)

THE WEST YORKSHIRE MOORS

'And the moors were always there, and the horizon never without its promise. No Bruddersford man could be exiled from the uplands and blue air; he always had one foot on the heather...'

(J.B. Priestley, *Bright Day*)

Think of West Yorkshire and you think of soot-blackened mills and grimy chimneys, and the moorlands whose dark features they echo; peat groughs, burnt heather and rough grit. The two have always been linked, the one providing plentiful water for the other, the towns that stretch as far up every watercourse as possible. For the people of West Yorkshire, the closeness of the moors has long been a chance to get out of the smoke and breathe fresh air. From towns across the South Pennines, you can walk straight up into the hills – it needn't be an expedition, a holiday, or a day off, the moors are always right there.

Though the days of the 'dark satanic mills' are gone, we're nostalgic for the atmosphere of the crumbling mills and lonely moorland ruins. We take to the moors in search of signs of the past, and so often when you get there it seems that you have the whole moor to yourself. Yet when you come back and talk to other people, you realise that they too wander the moors in the same spirit. But where were they? And whose feet have tramped such well-worn tracks across the hills? This is the enigma of the moors – the sense of isolation that pervades these apparently empty spaces, and yet the proximity of other people, both past and present. There are ancient settlements, boundary markers, abandoned farmsteads and industrial ley-lines at every turn, while all the time the thrum of modernity rises to these heights – valley life, pylons, the M62.

The endless grey horizons that stretch ahead of you at the top of the roads across Cock Hill, Holme Moss or Windy Hill are all that some people want to see. Sit in the car for a few minutes, perhaps get out for a blast of chill wind, then drive on. The moors, though, are harder work; the more you give, the more they return. Sometimes you have to walk all day to appreciate them, to get a sense of what it was you came out for. What I have tried to do with this book is give you more inspiration for exploring these moors and more ways of discovering their secrets.

Dove Stones on Boulsworth Hill

MY WEST YORKSHIRE MOORS

When I moved to Hebden Bridge in 2006, one of the first things I did was to yomp up the nearest hills so I could look out over the valley and get a sense of where I was; first High Brown Knoll, then Stoodley Pike. What I found remarkable on both Midgley Moor and Erringden Moor was the failure of the map to convey the paths across these moors. For anyone who holds Ordnance Survey maps in high esteem, as I do, it is a shock when they let you down. The map shows public footpaths where there are just swathes of heather and bog, and then you stumble across a fine path (like the one along Sheep Stones Edge) that is not shown at all. Although there is little the OS can do about the vagaries of the historical network of Public Rights of Way, I found the usually reliable black dashed lines[1] letting me down as well. The consequence is that in many places you are forced to navigate by base geographical features (contours, watercourses, crags, etc.) alone. While this may be a good navigational exercise, I felt there was an opportunity to map these moors more accurately.

So I set to work on Midgley Moor and Wadsworth Moor, following every last sheeptrack to see if it would reach a satisfactory conclusion or an interesting feature, and recording what I found. In truth, it is the kind of thing I have been doing since I was a boy. The woods around our house on the edge of Sheffield were mapped and remapped with names being given to every old quarry and mine-working. On holidays in Greece I was appalled at the standard of the maps and worked to create a decent plan of Kassiopi and its coastline. Finding a new path and committing it to the map was what drove me on in these endeavours. My mother said I was born a good century too late and should have been out exploring and mapping the world in the age of empire. Yet the exploring I like to do need not be particularly exotic, rather it just has to be somewhere new – and you can discover new things around the corner from your home every day. Exploring is also not linear, but nearly always leads me round in circles, as I am eager not to miss anything – indeed this is the only way to make a good map. So, after years of amateur map-making, it felt great to finally hit upon a project to which I could dedicate my passion for exploring the minutiae of the world outside my door.

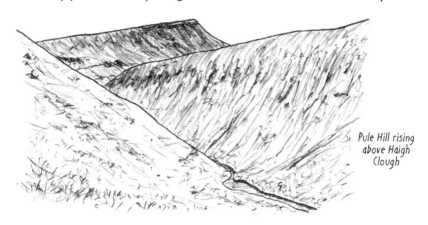

Pule Hill rising
above Haigh
Clough

---

[1] These faint black 'peck' lines are found on 1:25,000 maps, often underneath the thicker green dashes that mark Public Rights of Way. Forget the pretty colours all over the map, these black dashes and the solid black lines indicating fences and walls are often the only things you really need to find your way. These trusty companions have led me up obscure Lakeland fells and guided me through the other-worldly landscape of the Rhinogs in North Wales, as well as alerting me to the possibility of a Right of Way being purely notional (beware when there are no black dashes beneath the green line you are intending to walk!).

It is over twelve years later and those original maps of Wadsworth Moor have long been consigned to the dustbin, but they set in motion the work in this book, which has evolved as I have gone along. I squeezed in time between jobs surveying Public Rights of Way and National Trails, though there were many occasions when it felt like a busman's holiday. I was lucky, though, that my work included walking each of the 2,500km of paths in both Kirklees and Calderdale during this period, and slowly a fuller picture of West Yorkshire's moorland landscape emerged. Aware that obvious comparisons would be made with Wainwright's style, I never looked at his Lakeland books while producing my maps. When I finally did I was shocked at how much detail mine had in comparison, something that will hopefully be useful to anyone exploring the smaller paths and features of the moors; whether a fell-runner tracing a tiny path across a barren moor or an antiquarian seeking out a remote ancient stone. Yet the beauty of maps is that they are merely suggestive and there are always blank spaces yet to be explored.

The West Yorkshire Moors is not a commonly used designation, but for the purpose of this book it covers the large section of the South Pennines that falls within the modern county of West Yorkshire. West Yorkshire (as opposed to the West Riding of Yorkshire) was created only in 1974, though it makes a lot of sense in terms of both landscape and the natural watershed. Saddleworth was part of the old West Riding, but is on the other side of the Pennines and is now (administratively at least) part of Greater Manchester. The county boundary used to run through the middle of Todmorden, which is still home to the Lancashire 2nd XI cricket team. Yet it would make little sense to include the Saddleworth Moors or exclude the moors west of Todmorden, so I have decided to use the watershed as being the natural boundary[2] between West Yorkshire and Lancashire/Greater Manchester.

I have divided the moors of West Yorkshire by their high points, despite the fact that many of these are unmarked and little known. Perhaps tops like Way Stone Hill, Carr and Craggs Moor and Withins Height deserve to be better known; after all, the former is the highest top in Calderdale and the latter the highest in Bradford, yet all are largely unrecognised. I also decided that 400 metres made a natural cut-off point, meaning that the lower heaths of Norland Moor, Baildon Moor and the Chevin would not be included in this book, despite containing areas of open access land. All of these are actually very easy commons to explore and have few of the access and navigation problems associated with the higher grouse moors.

I have identified a total of fifty-one high points in West Yorkshire broadly using the Hewitt[3] classification (see list on page viii). The bulk of the lower tops (which are not included in this book) are either inaccessible or unremarkable (or both), but a few may be worth seeking out. Baildon Moor, Castle Hill and the Chevin are already well known, but Cheese Gate Nab, Gallows Pole Hill and Meltham Cop are also fine prominences (even if not all are legally accessible). Soil Hill, near Queensbury, is another anomaly – it is over 400 metres high, but contains no access land and has a scruffy quarried summit, so I have left it out. It can be easily reached by public footpaths if you wish to complete the set and offers fine views over Bradford.

Before the Victorians sought to conquer every corner of their world, the peaks were largely ignored, particularly in plateau country such as this. Consequently summits were rarely named, moors simply being known locally as the Great Moor, or else distinguished

---

[2] Hence the tops of both Boulsworth Hill and Blackstone Edge are assumed to stand on the true boundary, though they are stranded in Lancashire by the existing boundary (the latter admittedly by only a few metres).

[3] Hewitts are high points in England and Wales over 2,000 feet with a prominence of thirty metres (or 100 feet) from the surrounding ground. As there are no peaks in West Yorkshire that meet these criteria, I have simply dropped the minimum height to 200 metres.

by parish.[4] Where the moorlands had specific names they were often associated with local folklore, such as Rombalds Moor. The first detailed map of the area was Christopher Saxton's map of Yorkshire in 1577, in which he records only 'Blakeston Edge' and 'Gorpill Hill'. For years Saxton's maps were largely copied, until Thomas Jefferys' map of 1771 added far more detail, especially on the high ground; this saw the addition of 'Rombalds Moor', 'Wool Stones' (Wolf Stones), 'Crowell End' (Crow Hill), 'Hamilton Hill' (Black Hameldon), 'Alderman Stones' (Holder Stones), 'Standedge' and others.

Despite having been active in the south of England for fifty years, the Ordnance Survey's first one-inch (to the mile) map of Yorkshire was published in 1841, but included only the eastern part of the county. The western half of West Yorkshire followed in 1843, but it was not until 1858 that the one-inch map of the northern part of the county was published. By then, the remarkable six-inch (to the mile) maps of the whole country had been published – it is to these that we owe so much of our mapping information. While of tremendous value in preserving names we now have little other reference to (like Ogden Spa on Nab Hill, Cheetham Lad on Manshead Hill or Lads Grave on Blackstone Edge), these maps doubtless also erased or bastardised many others. Local names interpreted by surveyors became effectively fixed in stone and little has changed since – indeed these maps are instantly recognisable in a way that so many earlier maps aren't.

It is impossible to go back and restore many of the earlier names of these places as they were always so fluid, with pronunciations and spellings varying wildly from one valley to the next and one generation to the next. For example, Too To Hill on Warley Moor is thought to be a poor attempt to understand someone's pronunciation of Toad Hole Hill, but it would be foolish to reinstate this on a whim. Many names are also interchangeable, like *law* and *lowe* (and sometimes *lad*), or *hoar* and *hare*. What I have one is to restore local spellings of features such as *delf*, *dike* and *sike* (as opposed to *delph*, *dyke* and *syke*[5]). In many cases, names on the map have lost their original meaning and had suffixes like *-bridge*, *-dean* and *-gate* unnecessarily added when the dialect words *hebble*, *-den* and *rake* already suffice. The word *stoop*, originally a stone marking a track in bad weather, has come to refer to any vertical stone and is used as an abbreviation of gate-stoop.

As a consequence of all this, the accurate naming of the tops of West Yorkshire is fraught with difficulty, if not downright impossible, and I am happy to stand corrected for future editions. There are defined tops that appear never to have been satisfactorily named, such as that I have called Freeholds Top. From the Spodden Valley side, the top occurs above an area called Freeholds and at the end of Trough Edge, but neither Freeholds Top nor Trough Edge End would have been familiar to anyone from the Walsden Valley side, where it is the top of Inchfield Moor. And, on a 1786 map of Lancashire, it is marked as High Houses Moor, a name now entirely lost. So take your pick; I went with its name in Alan Dawson's list of Marilyns.[6] Gorple Hill is another top that is yet to be given a satisfactory name. I rejected Hameldon, Standing Stone Height and Birkin Clough Head, and had decided upon calling this high point Gorple Stones after a nearby feature, when I discovered Saxton's 1579 record of Gorpill Hill. Although this has long since fallen out of use, I have resurrected it in the absence of anything else.

---

[4] For example, Wadsworth Moor makes little topographical sense, comprising two separate moors on different sides of Crimsworth, unless taken in the context of the parish of Wadsworth.

[5] These versions were often created by early Ordnance Survey mapmakers, who preferred to use Greek and Latin inspired spellings of words that were thought more classy.

[6] The Marilyns are another classification for listing hills in the British Isles and includes only those peaks with a prominence of 150m. Of the West Yorkshire Moors, only Black Hill, Boulsworth Hill and Freeholds Top qualify.

Using this Book

This book, much like Wainwright's, is divided into chapters for each of the summits in West Yorkshire over 400m. For each there are detailed maps of all the moorland within its scope that is designated open access land. These maps are designed to be used as a base for inspiration and for exploring places and paths off the beaten track. I have striven for a high degree of relative accuracy (i.e. the features and paths marked should be useful in finding nearby marked features), but it should be noted that the Ordnance Survey's 1: 25,000 Explorer Maps still have both a greater absolute accuracy and more detail.[6]

The boundaries of my maps were initially defined by the boundaries of open access land, but I soon realised the need to extend the maps in places to reach roads or known places. These linking sections, as well as other pockets of land not designated open access, should not be assumed to be legally accessible. These maps should be used alongside OS 1:25,000 maps, which show the boundaries of access land and should be considered essential if you get into bother or need to call for help.

For those who like a guide, I have included a series of suggested routes, each exploring new pastures and ways opened up since the CRoW Act of 2000. Some of these routes intentionally follow faint sheeptracks or intermittent quad tracks, or cross rough pathless ground to reach summits or other places of interest. Particular care should be taken on these sections and, where possible, alternative routes are included for those who wish to stay on more obvious tracks. But above all the book should give you the confidence to freely explore these beautiful open spaces right on our doorstep.

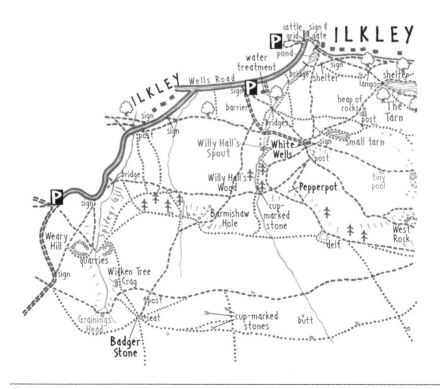

---

[6] There is nothing more detailed than the contour lines that portray every lump of ground, shallow slope and faint streambed. This was something I quickly acknowledged would have to be omitted, though I have tried to draw out the most striking slopes in pencil.

THE GEOLOGY OF THE WEST YORKSHIRE MOORS

Western Outlier (e.g. Freeholds Top)
Pennine Backbone (e.g. Blackstone Edge)
Coal Seams
Mudstone
COAL MEASURES
Walsden Valley
Rough Rock
MILLSTONE GRITS
LIMESTONE
faultline
faultlines

'Moors
Are a stage for the
    performance of heaven.
Any audience is incidental.'

(Ted Hughes, *Moors*)

The broad geology of the West Yorkshire Moors is no different from the rest of the Pennines. Running the length of the hills is a broad anticline, an upward fold in the earth's surface that has its oldest rocks at the centre. Different rocks are exposed in different areas, but the overall shape is the same. In the South Pennines the anticline is steeper in the west than the east, so the moorland plateaus tend to shelve gently down to the east and present steep faces like Blackstone Edge, Boulsworth Hill and Standedge to the west. The oldest rock is the limestone characteristic of both the White Peak and Yorkshire Dales, but in the South Pennines it is not exposed. Where it has been mined in the hushings across the north-western slopes of Boulsworth Hill and Wolf Stones, it represents glacial deposits brought down from the Dales. Elsewhere the limestone lies beneath the surface, covered by successive layers of shale, sandstone and, in places, coal measures.

Virtually all of the rock across the West Yorkshire Moors is of the Carboniferous period, formed between 300 and 360 million years ago. The limestone was formed on a sea floor from the accumulated shells of marine organisms. Subsequently the land was raised closer to the surface of the sea, with the consequence that sand and mud brought down by rivers were deposited on the shallower sea floor. As sea levels fluctuated over time these formed alternating layers of thick soft shale and dense hard sandstone. The sandstone in the Pennines is particularly coarse, containing quartz and feldspar, and is known as Millstone Grit. The numerous narrow layers of gritstone laid down across the area are of different ages and have different characteristics; from the oldest Pendle Grit, through Kinderscout Grit to Marsden Grit, there are many individual layers with local names (Gorpley Grit, Pule Hill Grit, Todmorden Grit and Warley Wise Grit), but the most common are the youngest beds, Huddersfield White Rock and Rough Rock. It is the latter, coarse and rough to the touch due to its higher feldspar content, that is most often quarried throughout the county because it weathers particularly slowly. In the faces of these quarries is revealed the layering of the rock; in between each narrow band of hard sandstone are the soft shales that end up stacked all around the quarries.

In the late Carboniferous period the area (and indeed much of Europe) became a warm, vegetation-rich swamp, with sea levels fluctuating enough that the vegetation was submerged every so often and covered with layers of mud and stone. It is this vegetation which formed the rich coal seams exposed on either side of the Pennines, and found in localised pockets on the moors themselves (particularly west of Todmorden). These coal-bearing strata are known as the coal measures and contain various types of stone other than coal. Some of the older coal measures formed ironstone and

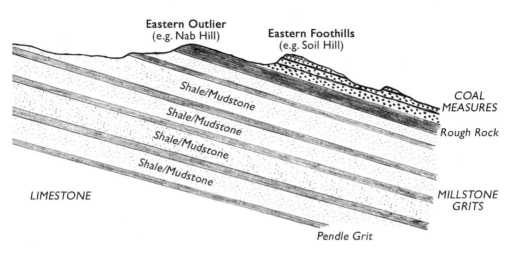

Elland flags, both of which have been quarried from an early time; the latter formed the building stone for most of West Yorkshire's towns.

The Pennine anticline was thrust upwards subsequent to all this activity and gradually eroded by ice and water to leave the great moorland plateaus and steep-sided valleys that we are familiar with today. The coal measures have long been eroded almost entirely from the surface of the land and the limestone left below even the deepest valleys. Hence the bulk of the West Yorkshire Moors is carved from a succession of shales and grits. And it is this geology that is responsible for the often perplexing distribution of water on the moors. In places, apparent basins can be completely dry, yet in others, innocuous slopes turn into unlikely quagmires. Beneath the tussocky grass is the answer to these apparent anomalies.

However, the region is not homogenous, faultlines having further complicated the picture. The Craven Faults (roughly along the line of the Aire Gap) form the divide between the gritstone-based South Pennine moors and limestone-based Dales. A significant faultline also runs through Todmorden, with the land to the west (including Freeholds Top and Carr and Craggs Moor) slipping far further than that to the east and bearing very different characteristics. These moors have more in common with the West Pennine Moors (of which they were once politically part), with coal deposits and shale lain on top of the Millstone Grit. However, numerous smaller faults here fractured the coal seams into such short sections that where exposed they were only suitable for small and often temporary mining operations.

The last Ice Age reshaped most of the surface features of northern England as glaciers advanced across the Pennines from the north-west. Although much of the high ground remained clear of ice except at the very height of the Ice Age, Rombalds Moor was entirely glaciated and the valleys of the South Pennines were defined by the glaciers and their subsequent retreat. While Airedale and Wharfedale were scoured by the glaciers themselves, Calderdale and the Colne and Holme Valleys were eroded as the bulk of the meltwater poured east, scouring deeper valleys and leaving a familiar terrace halfway up the moorsides at the level of the previous valley. Many of the odd lumps on the high ground in the north-west of the county (like Harbour Hill, Wycoller Ark and Hitching Stone Hill) were also formed by the glacial meltwater channels that poured across the watershed as the levels of glacial lakes to the west rose. Glacial moraine and erratics are very common in this part of the county, and have proved important sources of lime, chert and iron in areas where there was otherwise none.

THE HISTORY OF THE WEST YORKSHIRE MOORS

The moorland we see today – like much of our island – is certainly not 'natural' and this rare landscape is the product of thousands of years of climatic and human development. While the history of West Yorkshire, especially that associated with the Industrial Revolution, has been written many times over, the story of its moors is usually covered only in passing. I have tried to compose a historical account of the themselves and to chronicle humankind's interaction with this particular environment since we first stepped foot on it over ten thousand years ago.

Prehistory

Flint shards have been found across the high ground of the South Pennines from Ickornshaw Moor to West Nab, and the greatest concentration of microliths found anywhere in the country was near Pule Hill. People speak of finding flints by the handful in places where the layer of peat was removed and the earlier sandy soil was exposed. The oldest of these dates from the Mesolithic era (the Middle Stone Age from 8000-4500BCE), when most of the land was covered in dense forest and the peat had not begun to form. The wildwood had developed after the last Ice Age at altitudes up to approximately 1,300ft, leaving only the highest tops in this area covered in heathland – indeed the bracken across Ilkley Moor and other areas is an indication that there was previously woodland. The earliest settlements on the high ground are likely to have been the summer encampments of hunter-gatherers who migrated with the animals they hunted and the plants they gathered, and fragments of knapped flint from making blades are the only things they left behind.

Peat forms where decomposing plant matter becomes waterlogged and, rather than rotting, simply becomes piled upon itself. Its minerals are washed away, inhibiting further growth and turning strongly acidic. It is a process ideally suited to the soggy moorland plateau of the Pennines and was at its peak during a warm, wet era around 6000-4500BCE, soon covering the higher ground over 1,300ft. As the forest was subsequently removed elsewhere, further areas of the moors quickly developed into blanket bogs.

Deforestation probably began in earnest during the Neolithic era (4500-2200BCE), by which time sea levels had risen sufficiently for Britain to have become an island. People began to settle on land and domesticate plants and animals, at first in the form of small clearings in the forest that were abandoned after a few years. As the population began to increase, the uplands in particular were cleared to provide grazing land, as the thin topsoil would originally have been very rich. Throughout the Bronze Age (2200-800BCE) it is likely these moors were used for the widespread grazing of livestock, cultivation of cereals and small-scale family settlements. It has even been suggested that there was more land in Britain under cultivation during this period than at any time since. This is borne out by the range of prehistoric sites to be found across the West Yorkshire Moors, most notably on Rombalds Moor and Midgley Moor.

Ritual and funerary parts of the landscape were usually built apart from the settlements, often on a higher more exposed part of the moor. Ceremonial sites on Rombalds Moor include burial sites, ring cairns, stone circles, stone avenues and the cup-and-ring rock art for which it is most famed. The latter is thought to be associated with a particular Bronze Age cult that was active only for a short period. Ring cairns and stone circles are more widespread, Bronze Age features that may have had important geometric relationships with each other's locations, as well as that of solar alignments. Ring cairns are earthen circles that may or may not have had a ring of stones within and were associated with ceremonial rituals, as opposed to burial cairns (or barrows), whose stones or earth were heaped around a central burial chamber. Peat, soil and

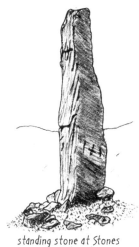

standing stone at Stones near Todmorden

grass development over subsequent millennia have obscured many of these sites, but when areas of heather are burnt back to the soil, subtle ancient features have been revealed.

There is also some evidence of Iron Age settlements and enclosures on the high ground, but the climate had become cooler and wetter (closer to that of today) by the late Bronze Age, and during the Iron Age (800-43BCE) people retreated from the high ground. By then the moorland landscape we are familiar with today would have been largely developed. Once the trees had been removed and the ground grazed, what nutrients there were quickly leached out of the soil. Continued grazing gave the soil little chance to recover and it became steadily more acidic with the wetter climate, leaving the denuded hilltops to develop into blanket bog. Although the moors may still have been suitable for summer grazing, the settlements moved further down the hillsides, causing further forest to be cleared for agriculture, pasture and timber harvesting for the smelting of iron. Only on Castle Hill in Huddersfield, which is significantly lower than the Pennine moors, is there evidence of the sort of hilltop forts typical of the Iron Age, and early ramparts and ditches for enclosing stock and dwellings are more commonplace.

The first trackways are likely to have followed the high ground, as it was the easiest to traverse – the valley bottoms were dense swamps that were often impassable. Eric Cowling coined the name Rombalds Way for an ancient trackway along the northern edge of Rombalds Moor, suggesting it may even have been part of an earlier trade route between Ireland and Europe while these lands were still connected. Roman roads in the area often followed the same routes, linking the fort at Ilkley (Olicana) and camps at Castleshaw (Saddleworth), Slack (near Outlane) and Littleborough with major centres like York, Manchester and Ribchester. A Roman road between Ilkley and Manchester famously crosses Blackstone Edge and continues across Ogden Reservoir near Halifax. Other roads ran along the Chevin from Ilkley to York, and across Standedge between the Castleshaw and Slack forts, the latter passing the likely site of a small fort or signal station at Worlow on Pule Hill.

For all that, the Romans had relatively little impact on the area, especially those living in the remote corners of the hills, who continued to speak a Brythonic tongue and worship Celtic deities. After the departure of the Romans, the kingdom of Elmet was established, stretching across the whole of the modern county of West Yorkshire (at its largest probably extending into South Yorkshire). Elmet was possibly defined by a tribal kinship that had survived through the Roman era and was something of an outlier from the surviving kingdoms of the Britons along the west coast.[7] Elmet had been at the heart of the earlier Celtic kingdom of Brigantia, which covered the whole of the north of England and worshipped the deity Brigid, which accounts for the many Bridestones in Yorkshire. Elmet fell in 617CE with the invasion of its stronghold in Barwick-in-Elmet by the Anglo-Saxons of Northumbria, but its native Celtic people probably survived long into the Middle Ages in enclaves in the more remote valleys. Names like Walshaw, Walsden, and Britland Edge Hill are likely to refer to these inhabitants (Walsh, like Welsh, meant foreigner), and British Camps are marked on many early maps. It is said that shepherds on the moors still used old Celtic numerals in the twentieth century when counting sheep.

---

[7] In fact Elmet was ruled by the kingdom of Gwynedd for a time, despite there being a significant Saxon kingdom in between the two.

The Middle Ages

Little is known of changes through the Middle Ages, though the placenames of the area reflect Anglo-Saxon, Norse and Norman occupation. After the Norman Conquest, large feudal estates were given control of the majority of the land and large swathes of West Yorkshire were designated royal hunting forests. The Forest of Sowerbyshire covered the majority of Erringden, Sowerby and Warley, and was the hunting ground of the Lords of Wakefield, as was the Forest of Holme. The area around Marsden was part of the hunting ground of the Lords of Pontefract, and there were numerous well-known hunting forests on the Lancashire side of the hills – Rossendale, Pendle, Trawden and Bowland. These areas were only partly forested, and the wild boar, deer, pheasants and grouse (known as moor game) within them could be hunted only by the Lord of the Manor or the King. Large parts of the moorland were enclosed from the thirteenth century as huge deer parks, most notably Erringden Moor near Hebden Bridge *(see p99 for more details on the Erringden Deer Park)*.

High ground was also used for cow pasture, with medieval vaccaries set up across the area, overseen by tenants of the Lord of the Manor. These large cattle ranches had demarcated summer and winter grazing grounds and many of their boundary ditches remain etched into the hillsides. Names ending in -tonstall are almost unique to Sowerbyshire and indicate the existence of a former vaccary (e.g. Heptonstall, Saltonstall, Rawtonstall and Cruttonstall), while the name booth often refers to the wooden hut the herdsman (or boothsman) lived in.

The Little Ice Age – the steady cooling of the European climate that began in the twelfth century – and the Black Death (as well as other diseases among livestock) are thought to have temporarily halted the settling and enclosure of new land. However, as the climate improved and the population recovered, this resumed apace from the sixteenth century onwards. The deer parks were dispaled as the owners of the estates realised there was more money in renting land for farming than using it for hunting. Rough ground was cleared of stones using graving spades, then limed and enclosed in fields for grazing. This 'winning from the moor' is evident in many of the place-names commonly seen across the high ground, such as Reaps, Intake, Hey and New Bricks. Impoverished squatters were also known to settle on the moorland fringes, before eventually being drawn into the manorial tithe system. As demand for land grew, enclosure reached further and further up the moorside; the soft water was good for bleaching fleeces and the alternating bands of shale and grit meant there were fresh springs at all levels up the hillsides.

Sheep farming and the wool and cotton trades were the main sources of income on the South Pennine hills. However, such was the paltry income to be made on these poor soils that wool was spun and cloth weaved in the same farms in order to make a decent living *(see p75 for information on traditional laithe houses and the dual economy)*. Small-scale quarrying was another way of supplementing incomes and led to the pattern of small delfs across the hillsides. In places the surface coal seams were mined, often on a very small scale, such was the fractured localised nature of many of these measures. Indeed, one is still operating at Greens Clough on the edge of Carr and Craggs Moor.

In poor hill communities peat was the primary source of fuel rather than wood or coal and commoners had turbary rights, allowing them to gather peat from designated parts of the moor. Peat is likely to have been used as a fuel from as early as the Neolithic era, and became widely relied on in areas like this for cattle bedding, as a basic fertiliser, constructing primitive buildings, insulating

peat stacks on Ickornshaw Moor

roofs and for use as charcoal in lime kilns. Usually undertaken during the summer months, peat-getting involved cutting peat turfs in rectangular blocks and carefully stacking them to dry, before carting or dragging them by sled from the moor. Many of the holloways down the moor edges were formed by this traffic and on Ickornshaw Moor some of the wooden huts used by families gathering peat remain in situ, now used largely for shooting. The scale of this industry over the past few millennia is likely to have seen millions of cubic metres of peat removed from West Yorkshire's moors and has greatly shaped them in the process.

The open moorlands tended to be the most disputed parts of parish boundaries and were often treated as shared commons with no defined boundaries. As a result, many boundary disputes centred on the moors, such as that between Haworth and Trawden, which resulted in the summit of Boulsworth Hill being entirely in Lancashire

Lanshaw Lad boundary stone on Rombalds Moor

(see p37 for more details). As there were few natural features, boundary stones became a particularly common sight in West Yorkshire during the 18th and 19th centuries after the Enclosure Acts parcelled up the remaining common land. Boundary perambulations became increasingly common too, though they had taken place in many parishes and manors during Rogationtide since the Middle Ages. The practice is thought to be based on ancient crop-blessing ceremonies and the term rogation relates to a divine blessing. As the term 'beating the bounds' suggests, these rituals increasingly became about asserting the parish's boundaries and defining its community.

The moorlands were often used for transporting goods, both out of the necessity to cross the hills and a desire to avoid the wetter ground in the valleys. The earliest packhorse routes across the Pennines were salters' ways from the Cheshire saltfields (like Salter Rake near Walsden) and limers' gates from Lancashire's lime hushings (such as the Limers' Gates above Hebden Bridge and Todmorden). Salt was needed to preserve food over the winter and lime was used to neutralise the acidic Pennine soils. The network of packhorse trails and drovers' roads had developed ever since animals were first used to cart goods along the prehistoric trackways, and the first Highways Act in 1555 required that roads be kept in a state of repair by each parish, initially using statute labour and later by payment of Highway Rates. The stone causey tracks that are familiar across the South Pennines were a way of negotiating the boggy ground that many of the routes crossed. Wealthy clothiers who relied on these routes sometimes left money for the provision of bridges, and fine arched examples are still to be found in many remote locations (like Lumb Bridge in Crimsworth Dean, Oxygrains Bridge in Booth Dean or Eastergate Bridge near Marsden).

Even with the arrival of turnpike roads in the mid-eighteenth century, many still chose to use the old free routes across the tops and the packhorse routes were actually at their busiest around this time. Early turnpikes often followed existing routes, but later roads forged new lines; on Standedge this involved creating Standedge Cutting on the line of what is now the A62 and, to prevent traffic using the nearby old coach road, ditches were dug across its line. In fact the era of turnpikes was very short lived due to the arrival of the railways; most never paid their way for subscribers, but they did lay out the routes of a lot of the modern trans-Pennine roads.

Parliamentary Enclosure & Grouse Shooting

The high-water mark for moorland occupation occurred during the Napoleonic Wars in the late eighteenth and early nineteenth century, when the high price of corn led to land being enclosed in the furthest reaches of the wastes. A 1793 Board of

Agriculture report recommended that common land in the West Riding of Yorkshire be enclosed and drained to improve the acreage and productivity of cropped land. A series of Parliamentary Enclosure Acts provided a legal framework for landowners to privatise what was previously common land in order to provide meat and grain, which were suddenly in great shortage. Most of the large regular fields, straight tracks and long drainage dikes on the moorside date from this era, though the Cotton Famine caused a further spate of enclosures in the 1870s in areas that relied on cotton.

Since the early medieval period, commoners had held rights to pasture livestock, cut peat, quarry stone and gather bracken and moss on the moorland wastes. Land was divided up by the commissioners of a parish or township based on existing land ownership. In some cases commoners were allocated thin strips of near-useless land on the extremities of the parish in exchange for their existing rights, in others their claims were dismissed and their previous rights declared illegal. Though the high moorland was never enclosed, the Lords and larger landowners themselves often acquired some of the largest lots on the high moor, as they had their eyes on establishing the sort of shooting estate that were already becoming popular in Scotland. Rombalds Moor illustrates the rather haphazard way the wastes ended up being designated. In places where the moor was part of an urban district (like Ilkley, Burley and Bingley), the wastes became urban common and commoners' rights were enshrined, but in rural districts they became private. The difference is still evident today, with Hawksworth and Morton Moors still given over to grouse shooting and for many years inaccessible, while Ilkley and Burley Moor are covered in paths and tourists.

The Industrial Revolution – the mechanisation of the spinning and weaving processes and the subsequent development of large steam-powered mills, canals and railways – brought more people down to the valleys and established the large towns of the area. It also led to a steady decline in the cottage weaving industry and consequently hill farming, as many remote farms could not survive on sheep farming alone. Further depopulation of whole valleys and hillsides was caused by building reservoirs to provide clean drinking water for the towns. Some farms were drowned, but most were forced out of business by a ban on grazing within the reservoirs' gathering grounds that was introduced in 1905. Areas like those around Widdop, Withens Clough, Stanbury Moor, Digley and Deanhead emptied completely. The fear of polluted drinking water, and in particular a typhoid epidemic, meant that the water corporations were as guilty as anyone of prohibiting access for many years (while all the time leasing their land to shooting interests). As long as reservoirs, tunnels and railways were being built, forests planted and power lines, conduits and roads laid, the moorsides were alive with activity and the shanty towns of the navvies who worked on them. Once they left, buildings lay abandoned across the moors and they reverted to being the playground of the wealthy.

Game has been hunted on these estates since the Norman Conquest, but it was only during the eighteenth century that the red grouse became popular over all other birds. Grouse shooting began as a form of hawking, with the birds caught in nets, but by the eighteenth century the shooting season was established from August 12th (the Glorious Twelfth) to mid December. Even then, the sport involved a long day's walking with a dog and a guide, who loaded the gun and carried the birds. Birds were shot as they flew away and both gun and guide ended the day covered in black powder from the gun. George Fisher, gamekeeper of Walter Spencer-Stanhope's Boardhill Moors near Penistone, is credited with introducing grouse shooting as we know it around 1805. As was done on the continent, the birds were driven by beaters towards a stationary shooter, originally hiding in a grough but later in constructed wooden or stone butts. Interestingly a similar method, called bow and stable, had been used in the

a red grouse

medieval deer parks, with herds of deer being driven towards archers.

Allied to improving shotguns and the royal approval bestowed on the sport by Queen Victoria, grouse shooting provided the moorland with its greatest commercial asset. In some places (such as Meltham and Warley) the Lords of the Manor held the hunting, hawking and fishing rights across the wastes; in others they were held by local freeholders (such as Marsden, Oxenhope and Haworth, the latter having been enclosed since the sixteenth century). In Ickornshaw, local freeholders have fiercely guarded their shooting rights on the moor to this day; in 1892, when butts were erected on Ickornshaw Moor by gamekeepers from an adjacent estate, shooting was interrupted on the Glorious Twelfth by villagers converging on the moor and tearing them down. But most freeholders (and many Lords) let out their shooting rights or sold them on to wealthy millowners or, later, the water corporations.

Gamekeepers were employed and the moorland managed exclusively to maximise red grouse numbers. Red grouse, a sub-species of the willow grouse, is found only in the UK and feeds almost exclusively on heather. This heather has to be carefully maintained by rotational burning over a period of seven to twenty-five years to prevent birch scrub woodland developing and provide a variety of ages of heather. Gamekeepers weren't the first to do this – it has been suggested that the original Mesolithic hunter-gatherers of the area used a similar system of regular burning on the high ground – but their actions have had a significant impact on the moorland landscape. Drains have been dug across the moors to encourage heather growth and limit sphagnum development. Many birds of prey were hunted to extinction locally to protect the vulnerable red grouse, including hen harriers, peregrine falcons and goshawks, a practice continued to this day despite the South Pennines being designated as a SSSI.

Initially there were numerous clashes between farmers or shepherds and gamekeepers where the same land was being used for different purposes, but eventually most moorland rights were acquired by those interested in shooting. Resentment existed among commoners no longer allowed even to collect bilberries on the moor; in Haworth, moorland was deliberately set on fire where grouse were nesting; and in Marsden two gamekeepers were killed in 1903. These battles continue to this day, with the Ban the Burn campaign seeking restrictions on heather burning and the drainage of blanket bogs after a number of serious floods in the Calder Valley in recent years.

The Leisure Age

The Victorians, who were notoriously fond of the benefits of the fresh air and natural spas provided by the moorlands of West Yorkshire, created the leisure industry as we know it today. Those areas that were publicly accessible – such as Ilkley Moor, Shipley Glen, and the Wessenden Valley – became increasingly popular with all classes and, by the late nineteenth century, horse-drawn bus services ran up onto the moors. During the Edwardian era, epic walking contests were a popular part of local galas, and long-distance cycling wagers were commonly settled.

As the twentieth century progressed, pony clubs, sailing clubs and fell races were established to capitalise on the area's natural resources. Although it would take until the 1970s for the landscape to be officially recognised, the Clean Air Acts from 1956 steadily improved the image of the South Pennines to the point today that it is a popular holiday destination. Its appeal lies in a mix of its much altered but still ostensibly 'natural' landscape and the preserved industrial heritage that weaves its way through every facet of modern West Yorkshire. Though much of it is hard to trace with any certainty, the moorland bears the scars of its history. Its haggard face is worn with many lines; tracks, ditches and ruins etched in its impenetrable expression for thousands of years, followed, altered and abandoned as history heaps upon itself.

ACCESS TO THE MOORS

'He called me a louse and said, Think of the grouse
Well I thought but I still couldn't see
Why old Kinder Scout and the moors round about
Couldn't take both the poor grouse and me'

(Ewan MacColl, *Manchester Rambler*)

It would not have been possible to publish a book such as this until recent years. Wainwright got away with it partly because it was in a different era and much of the Lakeland fells were already common land. Access to the moors of the South Pennines, though, has always been more contentious and their ownership and use by grouse-shooting interests make them more akin to the deer-hunting estates of the Scottish Highlands. While the Marsden Moors and parts of Rombalds Moor can be considered to be in public ownership, the bulk of West Yorkshire's moors are private estates and had limited access beyond a few Public Rights of Way before 2000. I grew up in Sheffield long after the age of the mass trespasses, and so was used to roaming freely across the moors of the Dark Peak. When I made it into West Yorkshire I scrambled up onto West Nab only to be faced with 'Private: No Access' daubed across rocks on the moor beyond. I found it odd that such attitudes to public access were still prevalent. So we in West Yorkshire have particular reason to be thankful for the Countryside and Rights of Way Act (CRoW), passed in 2000. It is far from perfect, but the 'right to roam' it created has given us the chance to legally explore many of the lost corners of the county.

Open Access Land

The main purpose of the CRoW Act was to open up over 900,000 hectares of land across England and Wales (over 6% of the total area) as open access land.[8] This included all registered common land and all land defined as 'open country' by a Countryside Agency survey. Anything considered mountain, moor, heath or down can now be identified by pale yellow shading on all new 1:25,000 Ordance Survey maps. There is little that can be defined as mountain in West Yorkshire and obviously no downland, but moor and heath are both prevalent. Moor refers to 'rough unimproved acid grassland', including areas of blanket bog, bare peat and rocky outcrops. Heath is 'characterised by natural ericaceous dwarf shrubs' such as heather, gorse, bilberry and bracken. Both are 'usually of an open character' and the bulk of the West Yorkshire Moors fits nicely into these categories. It is only around the fringes that definitions become stretched and anomalies crop up, often creating parcels of frustratingly excluded land that you need to cross to reach a road, path or further section of open access land. It is worth noting that 'agriculturally semi-improved grassland' is explicitly excluded, explaining why enclosures apparently covered in reeds and scrub are not always included on the map. In other places, however, there are clear errors where land has been incorrectly characterised. Reviews of the maps of open country are scheduled every ten years to allow these to be corrected, but the first review in England appears to have been deferred indefinitely.

Even within the land that has been mapped as 'open country', there are numerous exclusions; any land covered by buildings (including those under construction) or their immediate curtilage; land within 20m of a dwelling or building used for housing livestock; land used as a garden, golf course, aerodrome or railway; ploughed or cropped land; land

---

[8] Often called and indeed signed as Access Land, although this is not an official designation.

used for active quarrying; land classed as Military Lands. Landowners are also allowed to restrict access to any access land for up to twenty-eight days in a year by prior application (though this is not permitted on Christmas Day, Good Friday, or any Bank Holiday or summer weekend day). In other cases exclusions are imposed by the local authority or Secretary of State to protect flora, fauna, geological features or scheduled ancient monuments.

I have tried to sum up the access restrictions at the beginning of each chapter and, apart from the danger area on Shooters Nab, most of them relate to dogs *(see separate section on page xv)*. If you plan to go off the beaten track, you may want to check the website **www.countrysideaccess.gov.uk** for up-to-date information.

So what are we allowed to do on access land? The CRoW Act states that 'Any person is entitled to enter and remain on any access land for the purposes of open-air recreation, if and so long as he or she does so without breaking or damaging any wall, fence, hedge, stile or gate.' This sounds reasonable, though there are a number of further exclusions: driving a vehicle, riding a bike, using a boat, bathing, lighting fires, shooting, fishing, camping, para-gliding, playing organised games, intentionally damaging wildlife (including foraging), using a metal detector, or disrupting any legal activity *(see p134 for a full list of excluded activities)*. If you engage in any of these, you lose your rights of access and are treated as a trespasser – as a consequence you are not allowed on the same landowner's land within 72 hours. It is here that the CRoW Act has got some of its bad press; it fails to define 'open-air recreation' beyond this series of exclusions and creates a law by which pursuits such as swimming in mountain streams and collecting edible wild plants are considered trespass. However, we are talking about civil trespass rather than criminal trespass (which occurs only when illegally crossing railway lines or Military Lands); as such, costs can be claimed by the landowner only where damage can be proven. As always, one hopes that common sense prevails and, as long as you respect the owners and users of the land *(see Grouse Shooting section on page xv)*, you might reasonably be free to swim here or there.

As well as defining access land, the CRoW Act states that 'means of access' (gaps, stiles, gates, bridges) should be provided both onto and within areas of open access land where 'necessary for giving the public reasonable access to that land in exercise of the right conferred above'. This is a more contentious issue as it relies on the local authority to negotiate 'means of access' with landowners or give notice to them where obstructions are considered to have been created. With new fences springing up all the time and local authorities' resources stretched, it is becoming harder to ensure reasonable easement across open access land. This is particularly difficult when you think that you are considered a trespasser if you cause any damage to walls or fences; while no-one sets out to damage walls, there are times when you are left with no option but to climb them, and occasionally a stone or two may be loosened. It is obvious that one should use gates and stiles where they exist, but there are numerous places in this book where existing paths have been cut off by fences and ad hoc stiles have been erected by locals. If you come across these, I recommend you contact the appropriate local authority (Leeds, Bradford, Calderdale or Kirklees Metropolitan Borough Councils).

Public Rights of Way

All of the previous section on open access land has no relevance to Public Rights of Way, whose legal status is enshrined in separate legislation. Whatever anyone tells you, the legal right to 'pass and repass along the way' always exists on a Public Right of Way unless there is a local authority sign informing of a closure for a dated period – in which case an alternative route is usually suggested. I have not distinguished Public Rights of Way in my book, but they are clearly marked in green on all 1:25,000 Ordnance Survey maps. One of the problems, and a reason why I started creating this book in the first place, is that many of the mapped moorland Public Rights of Way are historical remnants (and in some cases complete anomalies). Try to trace many of them and you'll find nothing on the ground but rough tussocks; in other cases an old track may be long disused and densely overgrown, while there is a perfectly serviceable path 100m away. The law says you can walk along these notional Public Rights of Way across the heart of the moor even when there are open access land restrictions, yet you may not be permitted to use the well-frequented path nearby. Most walkers are probably happily unaware of these anomalies, and in the end common sense should prevail anyway. However, if challenged when on restricted access land, then use the existence of a nearby Public Right of Way to assert your legal right to pass (ask if they'd rather you walk on that line).

Dogs

Though Yorkshire could be considered 'Dog's Own Country', dogs present something of a problem when accessing its moorland expanses. I researched much of this book with dear Dolly who, as those who knew her will attest, was nothing if not always under close control, but there were many days and times of year when I had to reluctantly leave her at home. Most of the South Pennines is a SSSI (Site of Special Scientific Interest) because of its blanket bogs and important habitats for various nesting birds; while walkers' boots may have more impact on the former, rampaging dogs are very good at turfing birds out of their nests.

As a rule, unless clearly stated, dogs are allowed on all open access land, but must be kept on a 'short lead' (meaning of fixed length and not more than 2m) when in the vicinity of livestock and during the ground-nesting bird season (March 1st – July 31st). The same should be respectfully applied on Public Rights of Way, though the law states only that a dog should be 'on a lead or otherwise under close control' when in an enclosure with sheep. It is an offence to allow a dog to chase livestock, and the landowner may shoot the dog if it is the only reasonable way to prevent it from worrying or harming livestock.

There are large areas of open access land from which dogs are excluded at all times and others where they are excluded between March 1st and July 31st. In these cases dogs are still permitted on all Public Rights of Way but nowhere else. See the access restrictions at the beginning of each chapter for information on specific moors, and **www.countrysideaccess.gov.uk** for up-to-date access restrictions.

Grouse Shooting

As much of West Yorkshire's moorland is owned by various estates with grouse-shooting rights, this represents the most likely source of confrontation between landowner and walker. Certain estates very much begrudge the concession of access

the gamekeeper

rights to their treasured grounds, while there are plenty of nearby residents who can't stand the idea of shooting animals for sport. I'm not here to discuss the rights and wrongs of grouse shooting or associated moorland management practices, but rather the legalities and practicalities of sharing the moor when there is shot in the air.

Firstly I will restate that Public Rights of Way will never be closed for shooting – your legal right remains at all times. But that doesn't mean there won't be shooting near or even across Public Rights of Way, just that it will be the responsibility of those shooting to keep an eye on any users of these paths and ensure that they are not endangered by their activity. If necessary they should wait while you pass, but it may be diplomatic to wait for them if they are in the middle of a shoot.

In terms of open access land, the CRoW Act does allow the landowner to 'restrict access at their discretion in certain circumstances' for up to twenty-eight days a year (as explained earlier). Five day's notice will usually be required, but if only a small area of land is affected or the restriction is in place for less than four hours, then only two hours' notice is required. As a result it can often be impossible to ascertain whether an area of open access moorland is definitely accessible. It is worth noting that red grouse may only be shot between August 12th and December 10th and the shoots themselves are very brief. In my experience, encounters with shooting parties have been very civilised, even when I've had a dog with me. My advice is to respect all other users of the moor as long as they are being reasonable.

ACCESS SUMMARY

• Open Access land is not always legally accessible – restrictions and exclusions may be in place. Follow local signage as long as it is clear and dated.

• Unless a specific diversion is in force, Public Rights of Way are always legally accessible, even when open access land restrictions and exclusions are in place.

• Dogs are excluded from large areas of the West Yorkshire Moors, especially between March 1st and July 31st. Check before setting off and follow local signage.

• Dogs are always allowed on Public Rights of Way and are not required to be on leads, just under close control, but it is advisable to keep dogs on leads in the vicinity of livestock and during the ground-nesting bird season.

• Respect all other users of the moor, especially those with guns, but don't be intimidated.

A MOORLAND GLOSSARY

bar = steep hillside trackway
bents = ground covered in bent grass
biggin = building
booth (or **butt**) = temporary herdsman's shelter on summer grazing ground
bur (or **burgh**) = fortification
cairn = pile of stones (either waymarker, field clearance or ancient burial site)
carr = bog or wooded marshland
cote = cottage
dene (or **dean**) = valley
dun = hill
field = clearing
firth = wood or chase
glead = kite or other hawk
grain = fork of stream
grange = land belonging to a monastery
greaves = woodland grove
grough = deep peat channel
hag = peat bank
hagg = place cleared of trees
ham = homestead
hanging = land on steep slope
hare (or **hoar**) = boundary place
hey = hedged enclosure
hollin = holly trees grown for winter food
holme = island
hope = enclosed valley
hurst = wooded hill
ing = meadow
intake = land enclosed from moor
jagger = leader of packhorse train
laund = a narrow tongue of ground
ley (or **lea**) = woodland glade or clearing
low = hill or burial mound
mere = boundary place
owler = alder
rake = narrow hill path
reddle (or **ruddle**) = red-coloured, usually relating to ochre
rocher = steep rocky bank
rod (or **royd**) = clearing
shaw = copse
sick (or **sike**) = small ditch or stream
slack = a shallow valley or wet area below a slope
stoop = a stone post
storrs (or **storthes**) = plantation or coppice wood
thorp = outlying farmstead
ton = farmstead or village
wash = a watery place, or where sheep were washed
worth = enclosure or dwelling

CHAPTER 1 – ROMBALDS MOOR

Height: 402m
Grid Ref: SD971394
Map Sheet: Explorer 297 (Harrogate)
Access: No restrictions.
Public Transport: Keighley and Bingley are on main Airedale bus and train routes. Ilkley is on main Wharfedale bus and train routes.

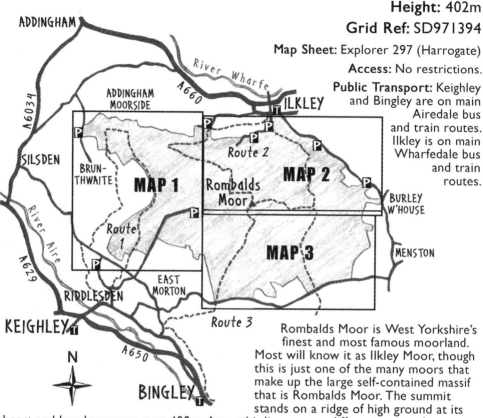

Rombalds Moor is West Yorkshire's finest and most famous moorland. Most will know it as Ilkley Moor, though this is just one of the many moors that make up the large self-contained massif that is Rombalds Moor. The summit stands on a ridge of high ground at its heart and barely scrapes over 400m. Around it lie so many different types of moorland scene that almost everything is contained within the moor's bounds; the sylvan beauty of Ilkley Moor; the rocky edges of Addingham Moor; the bogs of Morton Moor; and the grouse-shooting heath of Hawksworth Moor. Rombalds Moor is surrounded by the large settlements that have given these moors their names and is thus immensely popular and riddled with more paths than I can plot. It is an area that rewards any exploration and is unique in this book as the only non-Pennine moor.

The name Rombald is associated with the legend of a giant who is said to have lived on the moor, but most likely originated as a corruption of Romille, all of the moors around Skipton having been granted to Robert de Romille by William the Conqueror. In 1872, the War Office recommended using the whole of Rombalds Moor as a vast military camp, but the plan was eventually dropped after influential figures in Ilkley and Keighley voiced their concerns, as locals would have had to foot the bill.

the northern edges of Rombalds Moor overlooking Ilkley

1

MAP 1: ROMBALDS

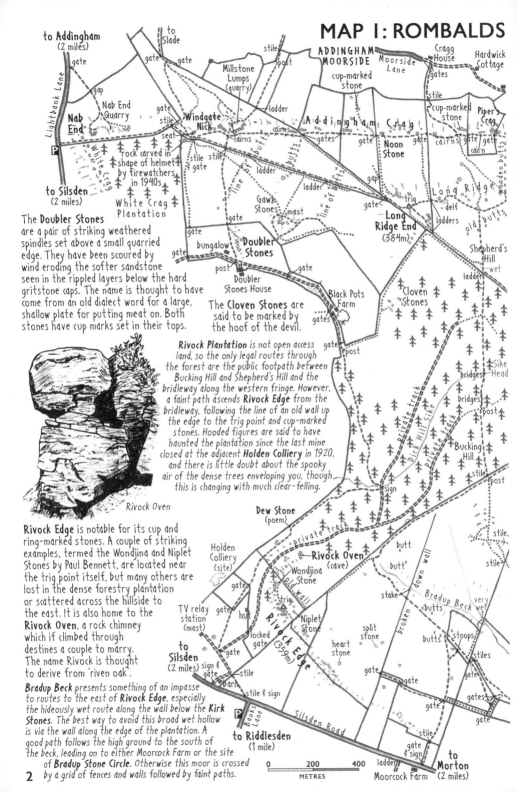

to Addingham
(2 miles)

to Slade

stile
post

ADDINGHAM
MOORSIDE

Moorside
Lane

Cragg
House

Hardwick
Cottage

gate

gate gate

Millstone
Lumps
(quarry)

cup-marked
stone

gates

gap

ladder

stile

Nab End
Quarry

gate
stile

Windgate
Nick

Addingham Crag

cup-marked
stone

Piper's
Crag

Lightbank Lane

Nab
End

seat

cairns

cairns

gates

gate

Noon
Stone

gate

cairns gate gate

cairn

rock carved in
shape of helmet
by firewatchers
in 1940s

stile stile
gate

butts

gap

Long Ridge

to Silsden
(2 miles)

White Crag

White Crag
Plantation

Gawk
Stones

mast

ladder

ladder

gate

trig

Long
Ridge End
(384m)

delf

ladders

old butts

The **Doubler Stones**
are a pair of striking weathered
spindles set above a small quarried
edge. They have been scoured by
wind eroding the softer sandstone
seen in the rippled layers below the hard
gritstone caps. The name is thought to have
come from an old dialect word for a large,
shallow plate for putting meat on. Both
stones have cup marks set in their tops.

gate

bungalow

Doubler
Stones

gate

gate

post

Doubler
Stones House

gate

Black Pots
Farm

gates

Shepherd's
Hill

wet

ladder

Cloven
Stones

The **Cloven Stones** are
said to be marked by
the hoof of the devil.

Rivock Plantation is not open access
land, so the only legal routes through
the forest are the public footpath between
Bucking Hill and Shepherd's Hill and the
bridleway along the western fringe. However,
a faint path ascends **Rivock Edge** from the
bridleway, following the line of an old wall up
the edge to the trig point and cup-marked
stones. Hooded figures are said to have
haunted the plantation since the last mine
closed at the adjacent **Holden Colliery** in 1920,
and there is little doubt about the spooky
air of the dense trees enveloping you, though
this is changing with much clear-felling.

gate
post

Sike
Head

bridges

bridges

private track

Dirk Hill Sike

private track

Bucking
Hill

stile

post

sign

Rivock Oven

Rivock Edge is notable for its cup and
ring-marked stones. A couple of striking
examples, termed the Wondjina and Niplet
Stones by Paul Bennett, are located near
the trig point itself, but many others are
lost in the dense forestry plantation
or scattered across the hillside to
the east. It is also home to the
Rivock Oven, a rock chimney
which if climbed through
destines a couple to marry.
The name Rivock is thought
to derive from 'riven oak'.

Dew Stone
(poem)

private track

butt

stile

stile

Holden
Colliery
(site)

Rivock Oven
(cave)

Wondjina
Stone

old wall

butt

butt

stake

down wall

Bradup Beck

very
wet

gate

trig

butts

TV relay
station
(mast)

gate

hut

Niplet
Stone

split
stone

broken

down wall

butts

stoops

to
Silsden
(2 miles)

sign &
gate

locked
gate

gate

Rivock Edge
(359m)

heart
stone

stiles

gate

gate

Bradup Beck presents something of an impasse
to routes to the east of **Rivock Edge**, especially
the hideously wet route along the wall below the **Kirk
Stones**. The best way to avoid this broad wet hollow
is via the wall along the edge of the plantation. A
good path follows the high ground to the south of
the beck, leading on to either Moorcock Farm or the site
of **Bradup Stone Circle**. Otherwise this moor is crossed
by a grid of fences and walls followed by faint paths.

barn

stile & sign

Banks Lane

P

to Riddlesden
(1 mile)

Silsden Road

stile

gate

gate
& sign

gate

gates

stile

gate
& sign

to
Morton
(2 miles)

0   200   400
METRES

ladders

Moorcock Farm

2

MOOR WEST (Addingham & Morton Moors)

Rombalds Moor sprawls westwards almost as far as Silsden, displaying a distinctive rocky scarp to the north and stretching down to the forested Rivock Edge overlooking Keighley. The further you get from Ilkley, the quieter the moor gets, even though there is still plenty to see, such as the renowned Swastika Stone carving, the Doubler Stones, the Buck Stones, and several cup and ring-marked stones scattered around Rivock Edge.

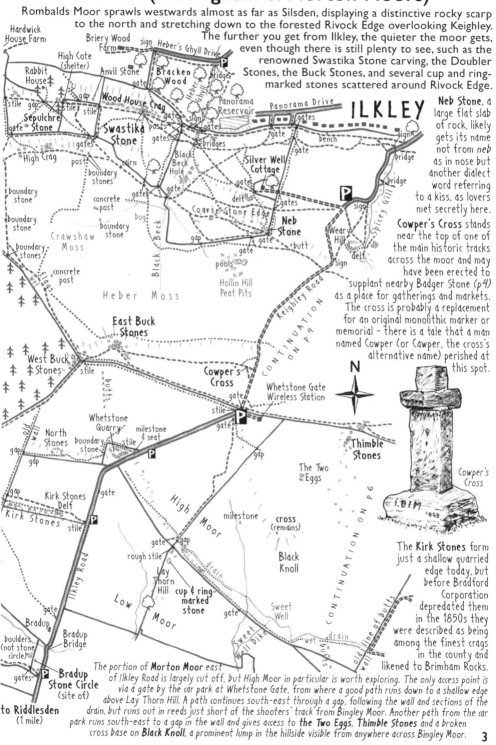

Neb Stone, a large flat slab of rock, likely gets its name not from *neb* as in nose but another dialect word referring to a kiss, as lovers met secretly here.

Cowper's Cross stands near the top of one of the main historic tracks across the moor and may have been erected to supplant nearby Badger Stone (*p4*) as a place for gatherings and markets. The cross is probably a replacement for an original monolithic marker or memorial – there is a tale that a man named Cowper (or Cawper, the cross's alternative name) perished at this spot.

The **Kirk Stones** form just a shallow quarried edge today, but before Bradford Corporation depredated them in the 1850s they were described as being among the finest crags in the county and likened to Brimham Rocks.

The portion of **Morton Moor** east of Ilkley Road is largely cut off, but High Moor in particular is worth exploring. The only access point is via a gate by the car park at Whetstone Gate, from where a good path runs down to a shallow edge above Lay Thorn Hill. A path continues south-east through a gap, following the wall and sections of the drain, but runs out in reeds just short of the shooters' track from Bingley Moor. Another path from the car park runs south-east to a gap in the wall and gives access to **the Two Eggs**, **Thimble Stones** and a broken cross base on **Black Knoll**, a prominent lump in the hillside visible from anywhere across Bingley Moor.

3

MAP 2: ROMBALDS MOOR NORTH (Ilkley Moor)

The northern section of Rombalds Moor is the well-known Ilkley Moor, rising steeply above Ilkley and the Wharfe Valley to a series of gritstone edges. Partly because the moor is quite so accessible from the town and partly because of its *baht 'at* fame, Ilkley Moor is by far the busiest hillside in West Yorkshire. It was bought by the Ilkley Local Board in 1893 for £13,500 as an amenity for the people of Ilkley and is now an urban common. The moor warrants this attention, such is its intricacy and beautiful little corners amid the bracken and heather. Whether it is a stone circle or prehistoric petroglyph, a tarn, waterfall or copse, Ilkley Moor is a Pandora's Box to be explored aimlessly.

The northern slopes of Ilkley Moor are a maze of paths through the bracken, criss-crossing between rocky outcrops, tarns and pockets of woodland. It is impossible to explain particular routes, but lower down all routes seem to lead to White Wells or the Tarn, while higher up the slopes you find yourself drawn to the large cairn on Cranshaw Thorn Hill (probably the best viewpoint over Ilkley) and the rocky ford across Backstone Beck.

The whitewashed buildings of **White Wells** are a dominant feature of the lower slopes of Ilkley Moor. They stand on an ancient spring that was discovered to have medicinal properties. A bath house was built here in 1791, making it Britain's first hydropathic spa. Though initially 'the Heather Spaw' was seen as rather rustic, the rigours of the Water Cure became fashionable in the Victorian era and turned Ilkley into the attraction it is today.

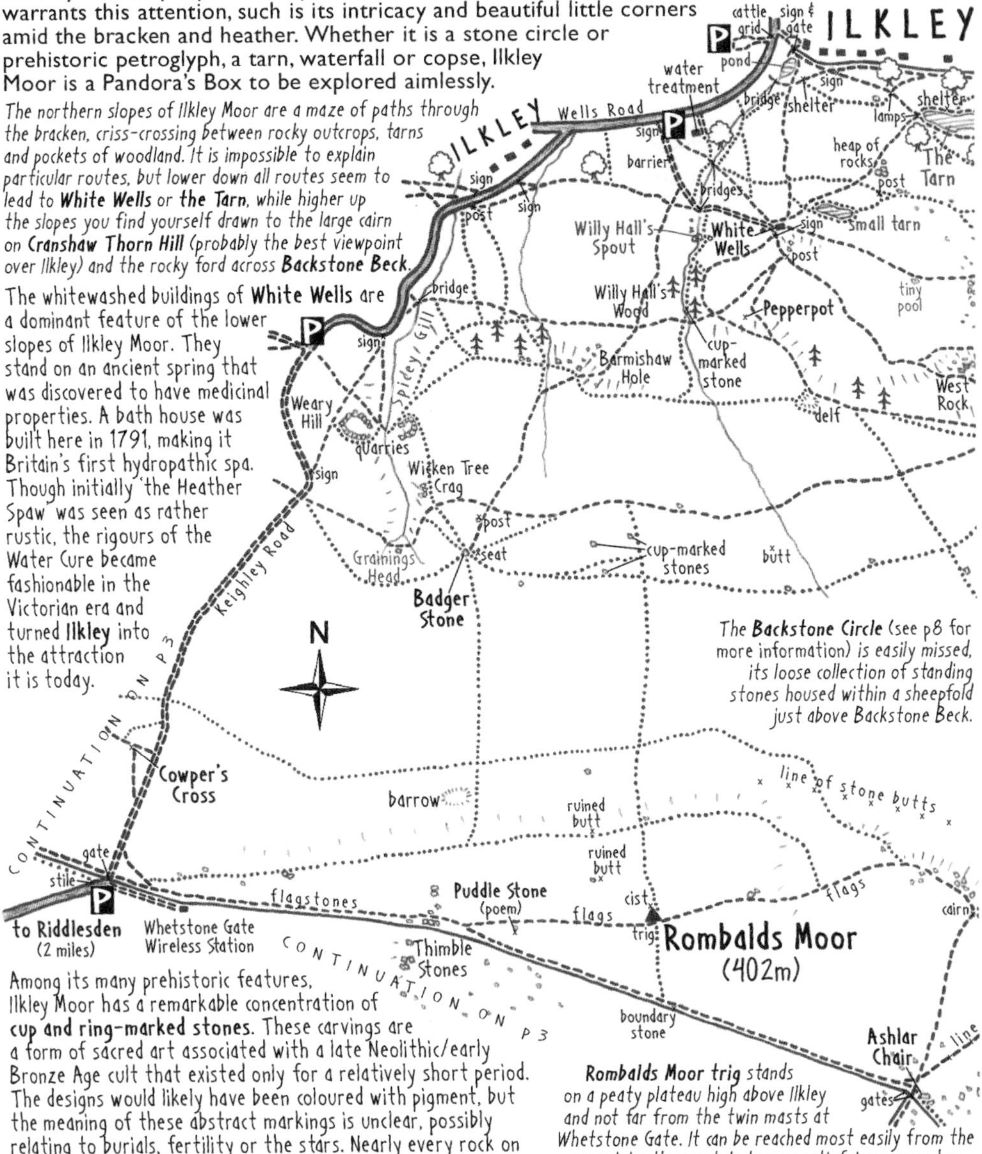

*The **Backstone Circle** (see p8 for more information) is easily missed, its loose collection of standing stones housed within a sheepfold just above Backstone Beck.*

Among its many prehistoric features, Ilkley Moor has a remarkable concentration of **cup and ring-marked stones**. These carvings are a form of sacred art associated with a late Neolithic/early Bronze Age cult that existed only for a relatively short period. The designs would likely have been coloured with pigment, but the meaning of these abstract markings is unclear, possibly relating to burials, fertility or the stars. Nearly every rock on the north side of the moor possesses some form of marking, though many are discernible only to those familiar with ancient carvings and others almost disappear in the wrong light. The carvings are best viewed when wet or in oblique (early or late) sunlight. Among the most remarkable examples are the **Swastika Stone** on the western moor (p3), the **Hanging Stones** near the Cow & Calf, the **Badger Stone**, the **Pepperpot**, the **Idol Stone** and **Haystack Rock**.

Rombalds Moor trig stands on a peaty plateau high above Ilkley and not far from the twin masts at Whetstone Gate. It can be reached most easily from the car park by the mast, but more satisfying approaches climb out of Ilkley. The main route across the moor climbs up **Ilkley Crags** from White Wells and then continues across Gill Head to reach the plateau at the **Lanshaw Lad** boundary stone. Turn right here to get to the summit. Alternatively a couple of smaller paths climb straight up the hillside, one directly from the **Badger Stone** and the other 400m to the east, leaving the path to Cranshaw Thorn Hill, shortly before a prominent boulder.

Map labels

ILKLEY

cattle sign & grid / gate · water treatment · pond · bridge · shelter · lamps · sign · shelter · heap of rocks · The Tarn · post · Wells Road · sign · barrier · bridges · post · sign · Willy Hall's Spout · White Wells · sign · Small tarn · post · tiny pool · ILKLEY · Ilkley Gill · Willy Hall's Wood · Pepperpot · cup-marked stone · Barmishaw Hole · West Rock · delf · bridge · Weary Hill · quarries · sign · Wicken Tree Crag · Grainings Head · seat · post · cup-marked stones · butt · Badger Stone · N · Cowper's Cross · barrow · line of stone butts · ruined butt · ruined butt · cist · flags · cairn · gate · stile · flagstones · Puddle Stone (poem) · trig · Rombalds Moor (402m) · to Riddlesden (2 miles) · Whetstone Gate Wireless Station · Thimble Stones · boundary stone · Ashlar Chair · line · gates

Keighley Road

CONTINUATION ON P 3

CONTINUATION ON P 3

4

The **Hanging Stones** refers to a small crag looking north from the huge quarry west of the Cow & Calf. The top of this crag is one huge canvas of Neolithic carvings, truly the most unusual of any across the moor and well worth a look. Remarkably this rock was saved from being engulfed within the quarry by a visitor who alerted the squire to its impending destruction. The hole beneath the crags is known as the Fairies' Parlour (or Fairies' Kirk).

The **Cow & Calf** is Ilkley Moor's most distinctive landmark, a gritstone promontory from which a large chunk has fallen to lie in its lee. According to legend, the Calf was broken from the Cow when the giant Rombald fled across the valley and stood on the rock. The name is thought to have come from an ancient beltane custom of driving cattle between old and new beacon fires that were traditionally lit on the moor. The Cow is also known as the Inglestone, *ingle* being a fire, and in it can be seen a face often called the Sphinx. There was once a giant Bull Stone too, but this was used to build the Crescent Hotel in Ilkley. Now the remaining rocks are covered in Victorian carvings, remarkable not for their antiquity but sheer density, covering every inch of the surface.

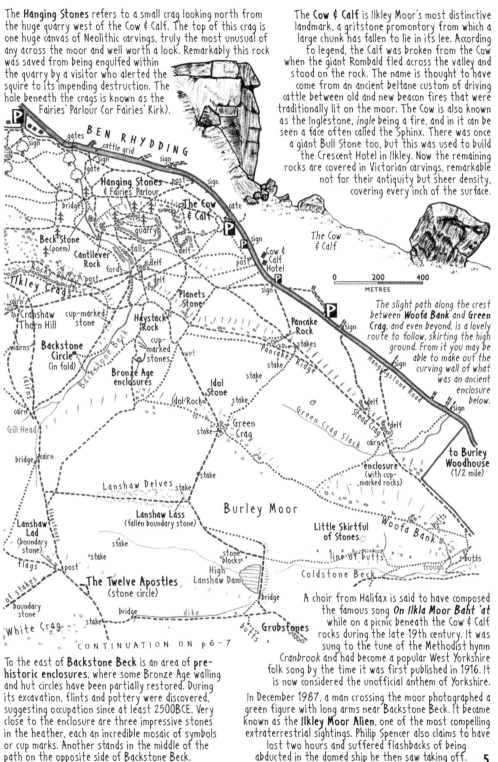

The slight path along the crest between **Woofa Bank** *and* **Green** *Crag, and even beyond, is a lovely route to follow, skirting the high ground. From it you may be able to make out the curving wall of what was an ancient enclosure below.*

A choir from Halifax is said to have composed the famous song *On Ilkla Moor Baht 'at* while on a picnic beneath the Cow & Calf rocks during the late 19th century. It was sung to the tune of the Methodist hymn Cranbrook and had become a popular West Yorkshire folk song by the time it was first published in 1916. It is now considered the unofficial anthem of Yorkshire.

In December 1987, a man crossing the moor photographed a green figure with long arms near Backstone Beck. It became known as the **Ilkley Moor Alien**, one of the most compelling extraterrestrial sightings. Philip Spencer also claims to have lost two hours and suffered flashbacks of being abducted in the domed ship he then saw taking off.

To the east of **Backstone Beck** is an area of **pre-historic enclosures**, where some Bronze Age walling and hut circles have been partially restored. During its excavation, flints and pottery were discovered, suggesting occupation since at least 2500BCE. Very close to the enclosure are three impressive stones in the heather, each an incredible mosaic of symbols or cup marks. Another stands in the middle of the path on the opposite side of Backstone Beck.

CONTINUATION ON p6-7

5

MAP 3: ROMBALDS MOOR SOUTH-EAST (Bingley,

The south side of Rombalds Moor appears rather empty, both of people and the rocky features that draw them to Ilkley Moor. Bingley and Hawksworth Moors are broad sweeps of heather given over to grouse shooting and crossed by just a few obvious paths. However, the high ground here is home to most of the cairn circles on the moor and the remarkable collection of cup and ring-marked rocks on Stanbury Hill.

CONTINUATION ON p 5

Stanbury Hill is barely noticeable on any map, yet this shoulder of land is home to one of the finest collection of cup and ring-marked stones on the moor. Study any of the stones near the far end of the ridge and you can't fail to find distinctive markings. The Lunar and Spotted Stones are the most striking, but look out too for Teaspoon Rock with a teaspoon shape engraved bottom left. The site is thought to have been a late Neolithic/early Bronze Age settlement.

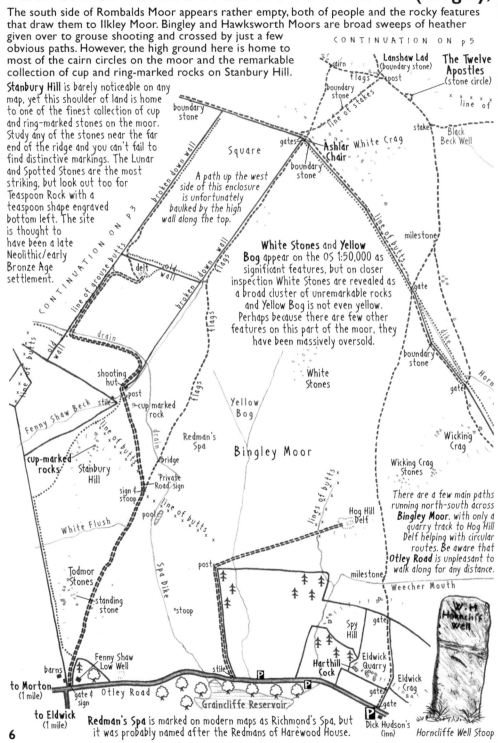

CONTINUATION ON p 3

Lanshaw Lad (boundary stone)

The Twelve Apostles (stone circle)

cairn
flags
post
boundary stone
line of stakes
stake
line of
Black Beck Well
White Crag
gates
Ashlar Chair
boundary stone
Square
A path up the west side of this enclosure is unfortunately baulked by the high wall along the top.

milestone

line of butts

White Stones and **Yellow Bog** appear on the OS 1:50,000 as significant features, but on closer inspection White Stones are revealed as a broad cluster of unremarkable rocks and Yellow Bog is not even yellow. Perhaps because there are few other features on this part of the moor, they have been massively oversold.

gate

boundary stone

White Stones

Yellow Bog

Horn
gate

Wicking Crag

Wicking Crag Stones

There are a few main paths running north-south across **Bingley Moor**, with only a quarry track to Hog Hill Delf helping with circular routes. Be aware that **Otley Road** is unpleasant to walk along for any distance.

delf
old wall
broken down wall
flags
flags
drain
shooting hut
post
stile
cup marked rock
Fenny Shaw Beck
line of butts
line of grouse butts
broken down wall
cup-marked rocks
Stanbury Hill
sign & stoop
line of butts
pool
White Flush
Redman's Spa
bridge
Private Road sign
drain
Bingley Moor
lines of butts
Hog Hill Delf
post
Spa Dike
stoop
Todmor Stones
standing stone
milestone
Weecher Mouth
Spy Hill
gate

barns
Fenny Shaw Low Well
to Morton (1 mile)
gate & sign
Otley Road
stile
Harthill Cock
Eldwick Quarry
Eldwick Crag
gate
to Eldwick (1 mile)
Redman's Spa is marked on modern maps as Richmond's Spa, but it was probably named after the Redmans of Harewood House.
Graincliffe Reservoir
Dick Hudson's (inn)

W. H. Horncliffe Well

Horncliffe Well Stoop

6

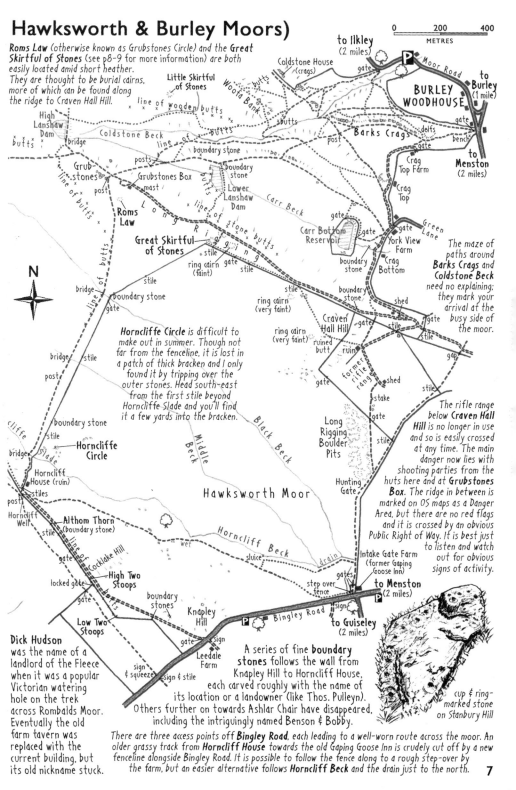

Hawksworth & Burley Moors)

Roms Law (otherwise known as Grubstones Circle) and the **Great Skirtful of Stones** (see p8-9 for more information) are both easily located amid short heather.
They are thought to be burial cairns, more of which can be found along the ridge to Craven Hall Hill.

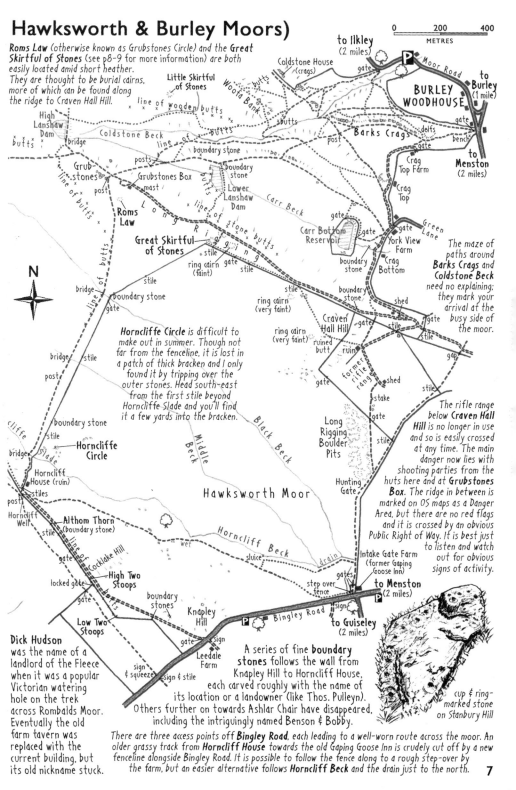

0 200 400
METRES

to Ilkley
(2 miles)

to Burley
(1 mile)

Moor Road

BURLEY WOODHOUSE

Coldstone House
(crags)

Little Skirtful
of Stones

Woofa Bank

line of wooden butts

butts

butts

High Lanshaw Dam

Coldstone Beck

line of butts

bridge

boundary stone

Barks Crags

delfs

bench

to Menston
(2 miles)

Crag Top Farm

Crag Top

post

Grub-stones

posts

Grubstones Box

mast

boundary stone

Lower Lanshaw Dam

Carr Beck

Long Rigging

Roms Law

line of stone butts

Great Skirtful of Stones

ring cairn (faint)

stile

gate stile

stile

Carr Bottom Reservoir

gate

gate

York View Farm

Crag Bottom

boundary stone

Green Lane

The maze of paths around **Barks Crags** and **Coldstone Beck** need no explaining; they mark your arrival at the busy side of the moor.

bridge

boundary stone

gate

ring cairn (very faint)

stile

boundary stone

shed

gate

stile

Craven Hall Hill

gate

gate

stile

bridge

stile

post

Horncliffe Circle is difficult to make out in summer. Though not far from the fenceline, it is lost in a patch of thick bracken and I only found it by tripping over the outer stones. Head south-east from the first stile beyond Horncliffe Slade and you'll find it a few yards into the bracken.

ring cairn (very faint)

ruined butt

ruin

former rifle range

gap

gate

shed

stile

stake

cliffe

boundary stone

stile

Horncliffe Circle

bridge

Slade

Horncliff House (ruin)

stiles

post

Horncliff Well

stile

Althom Thorn (boundary stone)

Black Beck

Middle Beck

Hawksworth Moor

Long Rigging Boulder Pits

Hunting Gate

gate

stile

The rifle range below **Craven Hall Hill** is no longer in use and so is easily crossed at any time. The main danger now lies with shooting parties from the huts here and at **Grubstones Box**. The ridge in between is marked on OS maps as a Danger Area, but there are no red flags and it is crossed by an obvious Public Right of Way. It is best to listen and watch out for obvious signs of activity.

line of Cocklake Hill

gate

locked gate

gate

High Two Stoops

boundary stones

Horncliff Beck

wet

sluice

drain

Knapley Hill

step over fence

gates

Intake Gate Farm (former Gaping Goose Inn)

to Menston (2 miles)

Low Two Stoops

sign

Leedale Farm

sign & squeeze

sign & stile

Bingley Road

sign

to Guiseley (2 miles)

Dick Hudson was the name of a landlord of the Fleece when it was a popular Victorian watering hole on the trek across Rombalds Moor. Eventually the old farm tavern was replaced with the current building, but its old nickname stuck.

A series of fine **boundary stones** follows the wall from Knapley Hill to Horncliff House, each carved roughly with the name of its location or a landowner (like Thos. Pulleyn). Others further on towards Ashlar Chair have disappeared, including the intriguingly named Benson & Bobby.

cup & ring-marked stone on Stanbury Hill

There are three access points off **Bingley Road**, each leading to a well-worn route across the moor. An older grassy track from **Horncliff House** towards the old Gaping Goose Inn is crudely cut off by a new fenceline alongside Bingley Road. It is possible to follow the fence along to a rough step-over by the farm, but an easier alternative follows **Horncliff Beck** and the drain just to the north.

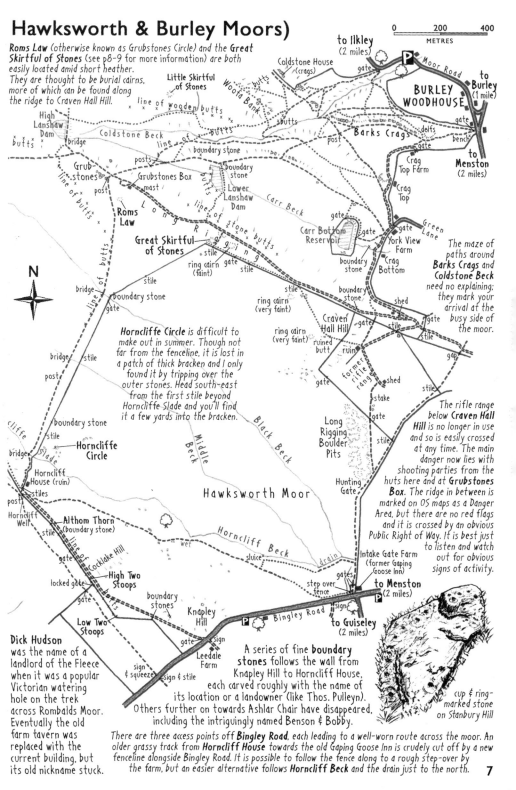

7

THE STONE CIRCLES & BURIAL

Stone circles are thought to have formed an important part of a mid Bronze Age ceremonial culture and to have come later than cup and ring markings. However, many of those referred to as stone circles on Rombalds Moor are actually ring cairns, built over Bronze or Iron Age burial chambers. Ring cairsn were originally built around stone cists, which were replaced by urns once cremation became standard.

BACKSTONE CIRCLE

Only rediscovered in 1994, the nature, and even authenticity, of this circle is very much unknown. Some have suggested it was a Victorian folly, others that was part of a greater complex. It has become associated with ghostly sightings in recent years.

BRADUP STONE CIRCLE

The story of Bradup Stone Circle (also known as Brass Castle or Kirkstones Circle) is remarkably sad. Though like others on Ilkley Moor it was most likely a burial cairn and not a stone circle, it was once referred to as 'Riddlesden's Stonehenge'. In 1885 there were apparently eighteen stones before the construction of Bradup Bridge used some of the stones. In 1929 it was recorded by Arthur Rastrick as having twelve stones left standing and he thought it the finest stone circle in the West Riding. These stones are said to have been present as late as the 1960s, but the laying of a gas pipeline in 1971 further disturbed the circle. Certainly by the 1990s all that remained was a solitary stone and an embankment clearly evident from above. However, it was declassified as a Scheduled Ancient Monument by English Heritage in 1994 and the field was ploughed up in 2004. Apparently, the archaeologist mistook the collection of boulders on the other side of the fence for the stone circle, with the consequence that any remaining stones are now among those heaped along the roadside. In just over a hundred years, human folly has completely obliterated this prehistoric site, leaving nothing but an empty field in its place.

THE GREAT SKIRTFUL OF STONES & ROMS LAW

Roms Law (or Rumbles Law) is a circle of around twenty small stones on Hawksworth Moor. It is recorded on OS maps as Grubstones Circle (this appears to be a corruption of Rum Stones), but is actually thought to represent the kerb of a ring cairn. It is recorded as an assembly place, particularly for freemasons (the Grand Lodge of All England is believed to have met here). Paul Bennett suggests it was used for burial rituals, associated with a stone avenue running along the ridge to the nearby Great Skirtful of Stones; Roms Law could have been used as a resting place for bodies on the way to the graveyard at the Great Skirtful.

CAIRNS OF ROMBALDS MOOR

The Great Skirtful of Stones is a vast ring of stones surrounding a central tomb that was excavated in the nineteenth century to reveal human bones. Legend has it that a Norse giant called Rawmr was buried here after being killed by the people of Elmet. Another suggests that the giant Rombald's wife dropped some of the stones she was carrying in her apron (hence its alternative name the Great Apronful of Stones). A large stone lies in the middle, a significant boundary marker that proclaims 'This is Rumbles Law'. For centuries the stone stood at Roms Law and the Rogation Day perambulation around the parish boundary of Hawksworth ended here with the declaration 'This is Rumbles Law'. However, after an eighteenth-century dispute, the boundary moved to the Great Skirtful of Stones and the stone was moved with it.

HORNCLIFFE CIRCLE

This is a rough double circle of stones on Hawksworth Moor that may be either a ring cairn with a central cist, but more likely an enclosure with a hearth – it was excavated in the nineteenth century and no bones or burial urn were found.

TWELVE APOSTLES STONE CIRCLE

The Twelve Apostles of Ilkley Moor is West Yorkshire's finest stone circle. Alone on the edge of a high ridge of heather moor, it is a fantastic vantage point. The twelve stones that usually (though not always) make up the circle are continually being re-erected. I very much like this idea of a constantly changing circle, a living entity as well as a remarkable part of the distant past, although the result is that none of the stones remains in its original position. The circle is thought to have had twenty or so stones originally set within a rubble bank, possibly with a single central stone, but its function is disputed. Eric Cowling suggested it was a symbolic neutral ground at the junction of two ancient trackways for trading between tribes. Paul Bennett thinks it was used as a druidical dial circle to observe the movement of celestial bodies. Others argue that it was a more straightforward burial cairn. Interestingly, on the summer solstice the sun rises directly above Kilburn White Horse on the edge of the North York Moors, even though this carved figure was only created in the nineteenth century.

WEECHER CIRCLE

A stone circle was removed or destroyed during the construction of Weecher Reservoir in the 1890s, though it stood just to the south of the reservoir. Although little is known about it, in 1905 Butler Wood spoke of it as 'the finest stone circle in the Rombalds Moor area'. It had a diameter of around 25m.

the Twelve Apostles stone circle

ROUTE 1: RIVOCK EDGE & ADDINGHAM CRAG FROM KEIGHLEY OR RIDDLESDEN

Distance: 9 miles (14.8km) from Riddlesden or 11 miles (17.6km) from Keighley

Ascent: 400m

Difficulty: Moderate

Parking: Keighley town centre car parks or various street parking in Riddlesden, including a small parking area by the Willow Tree pub.

Public Transport: Keighley is on major Airedale bus and train routes. Bus 662 from Bingley and Bradford to Keighley stops at Stockbridge Co-op near Riddlesden.

Character: Rivock Edge overlooks Keighley and this is the only natural moorland walk from this part of the Aire Valley. Starting in Riddlesden saves a tedious mile of main road walking at either end, but otherwise this is a very pleasant stroll that takes in Rivock Plantation, Doubler Stones, Addingham Crag and the Buck Stones.

4 Follow **Silsden Road** right up to the crest and turn left onto a bridleway. Follow the track past a large barn and round towards the TV relay mast. Leave the track where it splits, passing through a gate and following a grassy line into **Rivock Plantation**. At the first broken down wall, there is a potential diversion right up onto **Rivock Edge**. Follow the line of the wall up to a forestry track and then scramble up through the scrub onto the edge, passing the impressively cup and ring marked Wondjina Stone before reaching the trig. Easier to reach now is **Rivock Oven** (for more details see p2), whose narrow cleft is obvious in a crag further along the forestry track that can be seen from the main path below. Retrace your steps to rejoin the onward route.

5 Despite extensive felling, the track through **Rivock Plantation** is gloomy (and possibly haunted) in places, but is very easy to follow. Where it reaches a forestry track, turn left straight back into the forest to eventually emerge near **Black Pots Farm**. Follow the track leading away from the farm and onto the open ground on which stand the impressive weathered monuments of the **Doubler Stones** (for more details see p2). Follow the track to a post opposite Doubler Stones House, where you turn right past a bungalow and beneath the stones, which are most easily accessed from here. Reaching a gate, the path becomes clearer, climbing steadily to reach a large cairn on the rocky edge of the moor by **Millstone Lumps** quarry.

6 Turn right at the cairn above Millstone Lumps and follow the obvious path right along the top of **Addingham Crag**, overlooking Ilkley and the Wharfe Valley. After the third gate and just before the large boulder of the **Noon Stone**, turn right on a faint path up the wall. Follow the wall up the edge until it bends round left and joins a larger path leading to the trig point on **Long Ridge End**.

7 Fork right at the trig point, staying on the high ground towards the edge of the plantation. Join the boundary wall by a ladder stile and follow it all the way along to **West Buck Stones**. Turn right above the stones and cross a stile to continue following the edge of the plantation.

8 Follow the plantation edge for a mile to a depression at the head of **Bradup Beck**, then turn left on a path above the shallow valley. Cross one broken down wall and, by the second, fork diagonally right on a faint path across the open ground. Join another path to reach a gate in the next wall, then continue straight on to a stile and a path leading down the field to the road.

Map labels

Millstone Lumps (quarry)
line of butts
cairns
Addingham Crag
gate
Noon Stone
Long Ridge End
trig (384m)
ladder
ladder
Shepherd's Hill
boundary stones
wet
flags
Crawshaw Moss
East Buck Stones
stile
West Buck Stones
stile
stile post
Doubler Stones
cottage
post
Doubler Stones House
gate
Black Pots Farm
gate
Plantation
gate
sign
Dirk Hill Sike
post
Rivock Plantation
Dew Stone (poem)
old wall
Rivock Oven (cave)
Wondjina Stone
gate
trig
Rivock Edge (359m)
private track
gate
11DM p10
11DM p10
11DM p10
Bradup Beck
butts
11DM p10

N

0 200 400
METRES

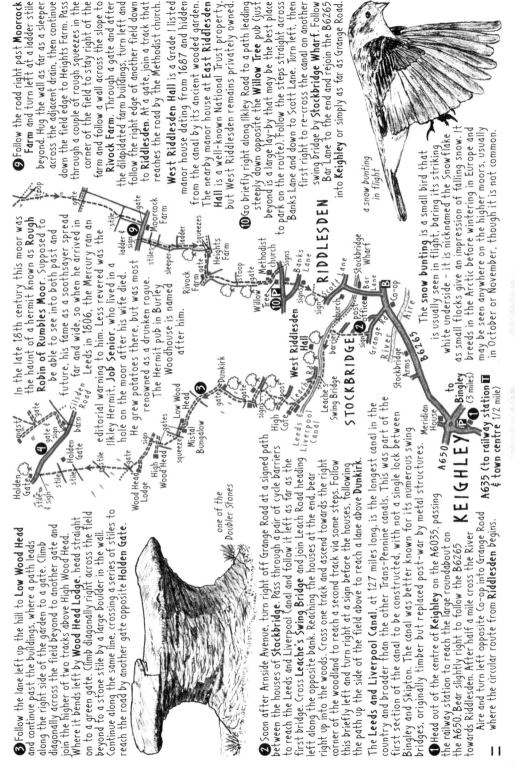

① Head out of the centre of **Keighley** on the A6035, passing the railway station to reach the large roundabout on the A650. Bear slightly right to follow the B6265 towards Riddlesden. After half a mile cross the River Aire and turn left opposite Co-op into Grange Road where the circular route from **Riddlesden** begins.

The **Leeds and Liverpool Canal**, at 127 miles long, is the longest canal in the country and broader than the other Trans-Pennine canals. This was part of the first section of the canal to be constructed, with not a single lock between Bingley and Skipton. The canal was better known for its numerous swing bridges, originally timber but replaced post-war by metal structures.

② Soon after Arnside Avenue, turn right off Grange Road at a signed path between the houses of **Stockbridge**. Pass through a pair of cycle barriers to reach the Leeds and Liverpool canal and follow it left as far as the first bridge. Cross **Leache's Swing Bridge** and join Leach Road heading left along the opposite bank. Reaching the houses at the end, bear right up into the woods. Cross one track and ascend towards the right corner of the woodland to reach a second track via some steps. Follow this briefly left and turn right at a sign before the houses, following the path up the side of the field above to reach a lane above **Dunkirk**.

③ Follow the lane left up the hill to **Low Wood Head** and continue past the buildings, where a path leads along the right side of the garden to a gate. Climb diagonally across the field beyond to another gate and join the higher of two tracks above High Wood Head. Where it bends left by **Wood Head Lodge**, head straight on to a green gate. Climb diagonally right across the field beyond to a stone stile by a large boulder in the wall. Continue along the same line, crossing a series of stiles to reach the road by another gate opposite **Holden Gate**.

In the late 18th century this moor was the haunt of a hermit known as **Rough Robin of Rumbles Moor**. Supposed to be able to see into both past and future, his fame as a soothsayer spread far and wide, so when he arrived in Leeds in 1806, the Mercury ran an editorial warning to him. Less revered was the Ilkley Hermit, **Job Senior**, who lived in a hole in the moor after his wife died. He grew potatoes there, but was most renowned as a drunken rogue. The Hermit pub in Burley Woodhouse is named after him.

⑨ Follow the road right past **Moorcock Farm** and turn left at a ladder stile beyond. Hug the wall as far as a sleeper across the adjacent drain, then continue down the field edge to Heights Farm. Pass through a couple of rough squeezes in the corner of the field to stay right of the farm and follow a wall across the slope to **Rivock Farm**. Through a gate and after the dilapidated farm buildings, turn left and follow the right edge of another field down to **Riddlesden**. At a gate, join a track that reaches the road by the Methodist church.

West Riddlesden Hall is a Grade I listed manor house dating from 1687 and hidden from the canal by its ancient wooded garden. The nearby manor house at **East Riddlesden Hall** is a well-known National Trust property, but West Riddlesden remains privately owned.

⑩ Go briefly right along Ilkley Road to a path leading steeply down opposite the **Willow Tree** pub (just beyond a large lay-by that may be the best place to park on the route). Follow the steps straight across Banks Lane and down to Scott Lane. Turn left, then first right to re-cross the canal on another swing bridge by **Stockbridge Wharf**. Follow Bar Lane to the end and rejoin the B6265 into **Keighley** or simply as far as Grange Road.

a snow bunting in flight

The **snow bunting** is a small bird that is usually seen in flight, baring its striking white underside - it is nicknamed the Snowflake as small flocks give an impression of falling snow. It breeds in the Arctic before wintering in Europe and may be seen anywhere on the higher moors, usually in October or November, though it is not common.

one of the Doubler Stones

11

ROUTE 2: THE PREHISTORIC STONES OF ILKLEY

Distance: 8½ miles (13.7km)

Ascent: 390m

Difficulty: Moderate

Parking: Wells Road car park (free), and street parking elsewhere in Ilkley.

Public Transport: Ilkley is the terminus for the Wharfedale train line. Buses also run regularly to Bradford and Leeds.

Character: A route that takes in the full array of Ilkley Moor's charms, combining the most impressive prehistoric markings and the trig point atop Rombalds Moor. Once descending from Haystack Rock, you may well want to pick your own route through the maze of paths back down to Ilkley, though the Hanging Stones are well worth a visit.

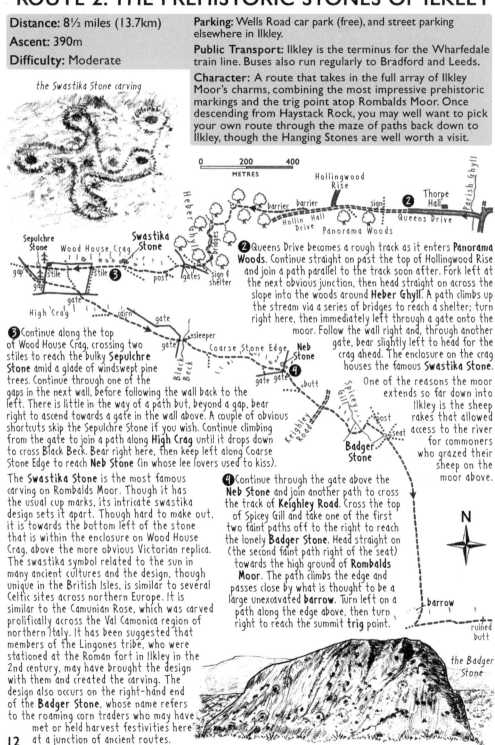

the Swastika Stone carving

2 Queens Drive becomes a rough track as it enters **Panorama Woods**. Continue straight on past the top of Hollingwood Rise and join a path parallel to the track soon after. Fork left at the next obvious junction, then head straight on across the slope into the woods around **Heber Ghyll**. A path climbs up the stream via a series of bridges to reach a shelter; turn right here, then immediately left through a gate onto the moor. Follow the wall right and, through another gate, bear slightly left to head for the crag ahead. The enclosure on the crag houses the famous **Swastika Stone.**

One of the reasons the moor extends so far down into Ilkley is the sheep rakes that allowed access to the river for commoners who grazed their sheep on the moor above.

3 Continue along the top of Wood House Crag, crossing two stiles to reach the bulky **Sepulchre Stone** amid a glade of windswept pine trees. Continue through one of the gaps in the next wall, before following the wall back to the left. There is little in the way of a path but, beyond a gap, bear right to ascend towards a gate in the wall above. A couple of obvious shortcuts skip the Sepulchre Stone if you wish. Continue climbing from the gate to join a path along **High Crag** until it drops down to cross Black Beck. Bear right here, then keep left along Coarse Stone Edge to reach **Neb Stone** (in whose lee lovers used to kiss).

The **Swastika Stone** is the most famous carving on Rombalds Moor. Though it has the usual cup marks, its intricate swastika design sets it apart. Though hard to make out, it is towards the bottom left of the stone that is within the enclosure on Wood House Crag, above the more obvious Victorian replica. The swastika symbol related to the sun in many ancient cultures and the design, though unique in the British Isles, is similar to several Celtic sites across northern Europe. It is similar to the Camunian Rose, which was carved prolifically across the Val Camonica region of northern Italy. It has been suggested that members of the Lingones tribe, who were stationed at the Roman fort in Ilkley in the 2nd century, may have brought the design with them and created the carving. The design also occurs on the right-hand end of the **Badger Stone**, whose name refers to the roaming corn traders who may have met or held harvest festivities here at a junction of ancient routes.

4 Continue through the gate above the Neb Stone and join another path to cross the track of **Keighley Road**. Cross the top of Spicey Gill and take one of the first two faint paths off to the right to reach the lonely **Badger Stone**. Head straight on (the second faint path right of the seat) towards the high ground of **Rombalds Moor**. The path climbs the edge and passes close by what is thought to be a large unexcavated **barrow**. Turn left on a path along the edge above, then turn right to reach the summit **trig** point.

the Badger Stone

MOOR FROM ILKLEY

Ilkley was still a village in the early 19th century when the hydropathic spas at Wheatley and White Wells transformed it into a Victorian resort that by-passed industrial development. Among its famous visitors, Charles Darwin recovered at Hillside House after *On the Origin of Species* was published, while the storm that ensued was raging elsewhere.

The **Panorama Stone** is the largest of three in a small enclosure off Queens Road. They were moved here from their original location in Panorama Woods to make way for development in 1890, having been bought for £10 by a local physician, Dr Little. The stone has deteriorated somewhat and its almost unique collection of ladders joining the rings are now hard to make out.

The Roman name of Olicana for the fort in the middle of Ilkley may have come from a local Celtic name *lecan*, meaning flat rocks.

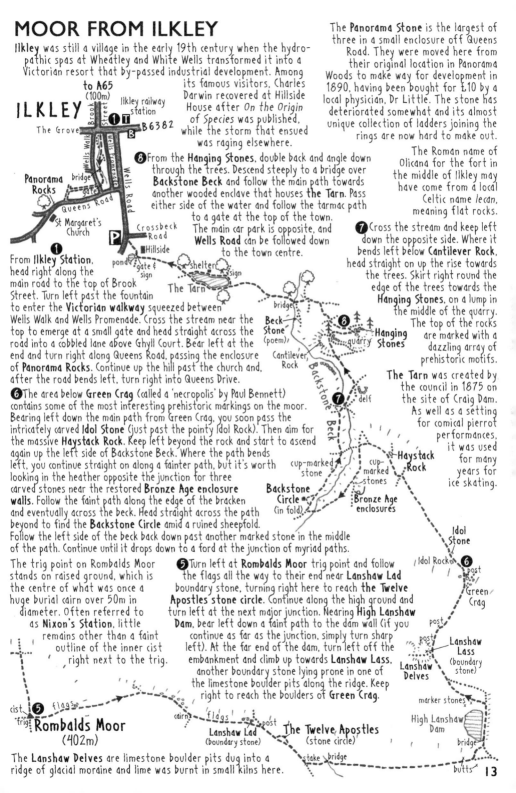

1 From **Ilkley Station**, head right along the main road to the top of Brook Street. Turn left past the fountain to enter the **Victorian walkway** squeezed between Wells Walk and Wells Promenade. Cross the stream near the top to emerge at a small gate and head straight across the road into a cobbled lane above Ghyll Court. Bear left at the end and turn right along Queens Road, passing the enclosure of **Panorama Rocks**. Continue up the hill past the church and, after the road bends left, turn right into Queens Drive.

6 The area below **Green Crag** (called a 'necropolis' by Paul Bennett) contains some of the most interesting prehistoric markings on the moor. Bearing left down the main path from Green Crag, you soon pass the intricately carved **Idol Stone** (just past the pointy Idol Rock). Then aim for the massive **Haystack Rock**. Keep left beyond the rock and start to ascend again up the left side of Backstone Beck. Where the path bends left, you continue straight on along a fainter path, but it's worth looking in the heather opposite the junction for three carved stones near the restored **Bronze Age enclosure walls**. Follow the faint path along the edge of the bracken and eventually across the beck. Head straight across the path beyond to find the **Backstone Circle** amid a ruined sheepfold. Follow the left side of the beck back down past another marked stone in the middle of the path. Continue until it drops down to a ford at the junction of myriad paths.

8 From the **Hanging Stones**, double back and angle down through the trees. Descend steeply to a bridge over **Backstone Beck** and follow the main path towards another wooded enclave that houses **the Tarn**. Pass either side of the water and follow the tarmac path to a gate at the top of the town. The main car park is opposite, and **Wells Road** can be followed down to the town centre.

7 Cross the stream and keep left down the opposite side. Where it bends left below **Cantilever Rock**, head straight on up the rise towards the trees. Skirt right round the edge of the trees towards the **Hanging Stones**, on a lump in the middle of the quarry. The top of the rocks are marked with a dazzling array of prehistoric motifs.

The **Tarn** was created by the council in 1875 on the site of Craig Dam. As well as a setting for comical pierrot performances, it was used for many years for ice skating.

The trig point on Rombalds Moor stands on raised ground, which is the centre of what was once a huge burial cairn over 50m in diameter. Often referred to as **Nixon's Station**, little remains other than a faint outline of the inner cist right next to the trig.

5 Turn left at **Rombalds Moor** trig point and follow the flags all the way to their end near **Lanshaw Lad** boundary stone, turning right here to reach **the Twelve Apostles' stone circle**. Continue along the high ground and turn left at the next major junction. Nearing **High Lanshaw Dam**, bear left down a faint path to the dam wall (if you continue as far as the junction, simply turn sharp left). At the far end of the dam, turn left off the embankment and climb up towards **Lanshaw Lass**, another boundary stone lying prone in one of the limestone boulder pits along the ridge. Keep right to reach the boulders of **Green Crag**.

The **Lanshaw Delves** are limestone boulder pits dug into a ridge of glacial moraine and lime was burnt in small kilns here.

13

ROUTE 3: ROMBALDS MOOR, BAILDON HILL & SHIPLEY GLEN FROM BINGLEY

Distance: 13½ miles (21.5km)

Ascent: 430m

Difficulty: Strenuous

Parking: Bingley town centre car parks, or various street parking in Bingley or Crossflatts. There are also several car parks and lay-bys on Glen Road above Shipley Glen.

Public Transport: Bingley is on the main Airedale bus and train routes.

Character: This is a long route, but follows good paths throughout and has an easy 3½-mile section along the Leeds and Liverpool Canal. The climb to Bingley Moor is long and steady, following Shipley Glen up from the edge of Saltaire via the top of Baildon Hill. The route takes in most of the interesting prehistoric sites on the south side of Rombalds Moor (three stone circles and the cup and ring-marked rocks on Stanbury Hill), before returning more directly via Micklethwaite.

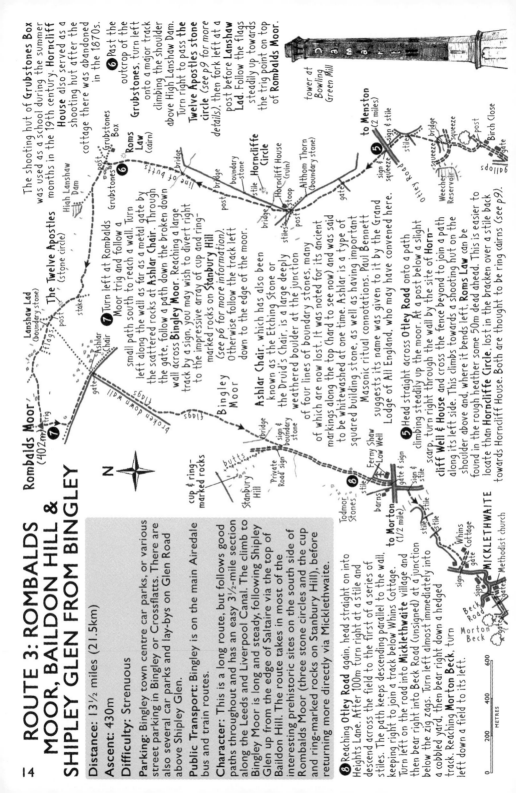

8 Reaching **Otley Road** again, head straight on into Heights Lane. After 100m turn right at a stile and descend across the field to the first of a series of stiles. The path keeps descending parallel to the wall, keeping right to join a track below Whins Cottage. Turn left on the road into **Micklethwaite** village and then bear right into Beck Road (unsigned) at a junction below the zig zags. Turn left almost immediately into a cobbled yard, then bear right down a hedged track. Reaching **Morton Beck**, turn left down a field to its left.

8 Reaching **Otley Road** again, head straight on into Heights Lane. After 100m turn right at a stile and descend across the field to the first of a series of stiles. The path keeps descending parallel to the wall, keeping right to join a track below Whins Cottage. Turn left on the road into **Micklethwaite** village and then bear right into Beck Road (unsigned) at a junction below the zig zags. Turn left almost immediately into a cobbled yard, then bear right down a hedged track. Reaching **Morton Beck**, turn left down a field to its left.

5 Head straight across **Otley Road** onto a path climbing steadily up the moor. At a post below a slight scarp, turn right through the wall by the site of **Horncliff Well & House** and cross the fence beyond to join a path along its left side. This climbs towards a shooting hut on the shoulder above and, where it bends left, **Roms Law** can be found in the rough heather some 50m dead ahead. This is easier to locate than **Horncliffe Circle**, lost in the bracken over a stile back towards Horncliff House. Both are thought to be ring cairns (see p.9).

Ashlar Chair, which has also been known as the Etching Stone or the Druid's Chair, is a large deeply weathered boulder at the junction of four lines of boundary stones, many of which are now lost. It was noted for its ancient markings along the top (hard to see now) and was said to be whitewashed at one time. Ashlar is a type of squared building stone, as well as having important Masonic ritual connotations. Paul Bennett suggests its name was given to it by the Grand Lodge of All England, who may have convened here.

7 Turn left at Rombalds Moor trig and follow a small path south to reach a wall. Turn left along the wall as far as **Ashlar Chair**. Through the gate, follow a path down the broken down wall across **Bingley Moor**. Reaching a large track by a sign, you may wish to divert right to the impressive array of cup and ring-marked rocks on **Stanbury Hill** (see p.6 for more information). Otherwise follow the track left down to the edge of the moor.

6 Past the outcrop of the **Grubstones**, turn left onto a major track climbing the shoulder above High Lanshaw Dam. Turn right to pass the **Twelve Apostles stone circle** (see p.9 for more details), then fork left at a post before **Lanshaw Lad**. Follow the flags steadily up towards the trig point on top of **Rombalds Moor**.

The shooting hut of **Grubstones Box** was used as a school during the summer months in the 19th century. **Horncliff House** also served as a shooting hut after the cottage there was abandoned in the 1870s.

Rombalds Moor (402m) trig

Lanshaw Lad (boundary stone)

The Twelve Apostles (stone circle)

flags

Ashlar Chair

gate

broken down wall

flags

cup & ring-marked rocks

Stanbury Hill

'Private Road' sign

butts

Bingley Moor

bridge

sign & boundary stone

Todmor Stones

barns

Ferny Shaw Low Well

gate & sign

sign & stile

stile

to Morton (½ mile)

stile

stile

Whins Cottage

gate

sign

MICKLETHWAITE

Methodist church

sign

gate

Beck Road

Morton Beck

gate

High Lanshaw Dam

Grubstones Box

Grubstones

post

line of butts

stake

post

bridge

Roms Law (cairn)

Horncliffe Circle

stile

stoop

Horncliff House (ruin)

Althom Thorn (boundary stone)

post

bridge

boundary stone

post

bridge

gate

Otley Road

sign & squeeze

sign & stile

squeeze bridge

Weecher Reservoir

squeeze

post

Birch Close

gallops

gate

to Menston (2 miles)

tower at Bowling Green Hill

N

METRES
0   200   400   600

Shipley Glen was a hugely popular Victorian playground. The restored 1895 tramway is the oldest working cable tramway in the country; it leads from Saltaire to the Shipley Glen Pleasure Grounds, with its notorious toboggan run, funfair and the Aerial Glide (which was only recently removed, despite being Britain's oldest functioning fairground ride).

Baildon Hill
(282m)

4 Turn sharply left at **Baildon Hill** trig and descend to the right of some curious weathered spoil. Fork left then right to descend to the road, always aiming for a prominent silver barn roof on the distant moor edge. Cross the road and keep left of the golf course to reach a gate by its far corner. Head straight across a dusty horse gallop and join a path following its left-hand side. Beneath the pylons, cross the gallop again to join a walled lane through **Birch Close**. Turn left at a tarmac track beyond and, where this reaches a T-junction, head through a squeeze in the wall ahead. Cross a small enclosure then aim for a stile in the far corner of the field and follow the wall up to the road.

3 The paths along **Bracken Hall Crag** run parallel to Glen Road. At a sign on the bend, you join a track that curves round to the left. Turn right at the end, then immediately left through a gate. At the far corner of the open ground, enter the woods of **Shipley Glen** and head straight on, following the main path to climb steadily up to the top of Bracken Hall Crag. The Iron Age enclosure at **Soldiers' Trench** can be found by heading right back along the edge for 200m (it has a lone tree in the centre).

2 Follow the **River Aire** as far as a boat house, where you join a track that curves round to the left. Aim for the left side of the caravan park and carry straight on to reach the trig point.

The **Leeds and Liverpool Canal** is noted for its staircase locks, the most famous of which is Bingley's **Five Rise Locks.** The Five Rise opened in 1774 to a crowd of some 30,000; the nearby Three Rise locks opened at the same time to rather less fanfare. It is said that Bingley folk enjoyed the pastime of offering their considerable wisdom to passing boats.

From the canal, the centre of Bingley is dominated by the A650 and the Italianate towers of **Bowling Green Mill,** in which Damart now make thermal underwear.

B I N G L E Y

Surrounded by high protecting hills, **Bingley** was once known as the Throstle's Nest of England.

The **Higher Coach Road** led from Salts Mill in Saltaire to the family's mansion at Milner Field. Built by Titus Salt Junior, Milner Field was demolished in the 1950s, though the drive, lodges and walled garden remain.

9 Cross **Morton Beck** at a footbridge and follow a path away from the stream, then turn left at the end to reach Morton Lane and the canal. Turn left along the towpath to return to Bingley, passing **Crossflatts** and the famous **Five Rise Locks.** A footbridge next to Three Rise Locks can be used to reach Main Street. Otherwise continue past **Bowling Green** Mill and return to the footbridge used on the way out of town at the beginning of the walk.

1 From the centre of **Bingley**, head for the canal which is squeezed in beyond the A650 dual carriageway that crudely slices the town in two. From the railway station or large central car park, head left past Aldi onto Ferncliffe Road. Turning left onto a feeder lane for the dual carriageway, a footbridge leads right across it. Turn right and head down steps before the second footbridge to join the canal towpath and follow it right out of Bingley. Cross the canal beyond **Dowley Gap Locks** to stay on the towpath. Soon after, the canal crosses the River Aire via the **Dowley Gap Aqueduct;** bear left just before this to drop down steps to the wooded river bank.

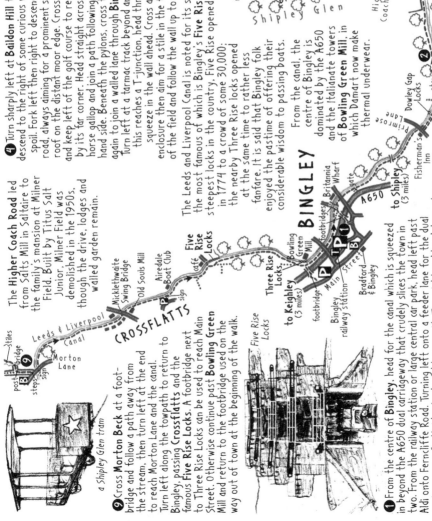

a Shipley Glen tram

15

Chickweed wintergreen is a delicate
small white flower found in woodland or
areas that once were woodland. It was
first discovered by the naturalist John
Ray on Ilkley Moor in the seventeenth
century, and this is now the only place it
can be found in West Yorkshire.

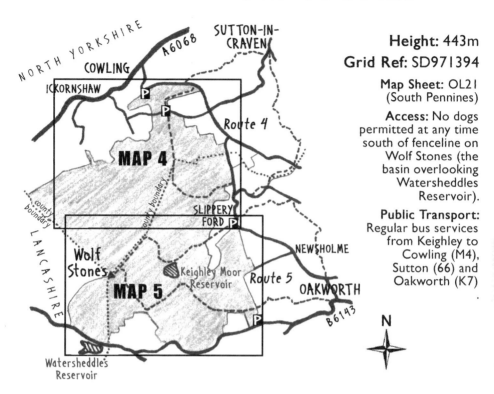

Height: 443m

Grid Ref: SD971394

Map Sheet: OL21 (South Pennines)

Access: No dogs permitted at any time south of fenceline on Wolf Stones (the basin overlooking Watersheddles Reservoir).

Public Transport: Regular bus services from Keighley to Cowling (M4), Sutton (66) and Oakworth (K7)

N

Wolf Stones crowns a vast moor that is straddles West Yorkshire, Lancashire and North Yorkshire. I have included a chunk of North Yorkshire on Ickornshaw and Sutton Moors in this chapter, as it represents the natural northward continuation of the county's peat moorland. Beyond Cowling, the landscape changes quickly and the Pennine backbone disappears at the Aire Gap before reappearing amid the limestone of the Yorkshire Dales.

Wolves were present in England until around the turn of the 16th century, but the moor's name may simply be inspired by the shape of the rocks. The Pennine Way crosses the moor near the summit outcrop, but much of the moor is left to shooting parties and peat-cutters. Only the Hitching Stone and Earl Crag command any real attention; the former being the largest boulder in Yorkshire and the latter's twin sentinels of Wainman's Pinnacle and Lund's Tower being familiar to travellers up the Aire Valley.

Wolf Stones from Combe Hill Cross

MAP 4: WOLF STONES NORTH (Ickornshaw &

Most of the northern flank of Wolf Stones is actually in North Yorkshire, the giant glacial boulder of the Hitching Stone representing the north-western corner of West Yorkshire. But I have included the dramatic edge of Earl Crag and its pair of distinctive follies as a natural extension of this gritstone moorland. Ickornshaw Moor is an empty swathe of vibrant heather and soggy mosses, while Sutton Moor is far more full of interest and consequently more well trodden.

Ickornshaw Moor is common land on which freeholders still hold fiercely defended shooting and turbary (peat-cutting) rights. Peat was cut for fuel and dried in large stacks designed to repel rain before being carted off the moors. The wooden huts found along the moorside are known as cowlings and were originally used by families when gathering peat. In some cases they were former garages carted up to the moor by villagers and used as basic holiday cottages. They remain in use largely for shooting; people traditionally sleep in the hut the night before the Glorious 12th.

The Pennine Way descends past **Further Dean Hole** to Ickornshaw, but the best route down to Cowling follows the edge of the moor round to **Moor Lodge**. The track up past Over Dean gives access to some faint paths along **Dean Brow** and to Mistress Moss. Heading straight up the shallow slope, you soon see the line of butts heading across to **Smallden Clough** and can pick up the only path across the moor.

The Scars are weathered limestone erratics perched on the side of this gritstone moor. Unfortunately you get only glimpses of them, as they sit on a chunk of private land. Similar glacial deposits of limestone at **Timothy Scaurs** and Lower Edge were mined by hushing (see p28).

The name **Ickornshaw** derives from an Old Norse word meaning squirrel.

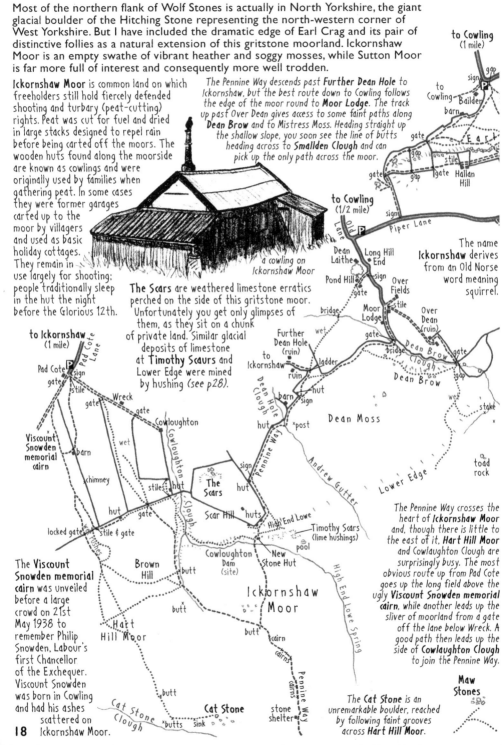

a cowling on Ickornshaw Moor

The Pennine Way crosses the heart of **Ickornshaw Moor** and, though there is little to the east of it, **Hart Hill Moor** and Cowlaughton Clough are surprisingly busy. The most obvious route up from Pad Cote goes up the long field above the ugly **Viscount Snowden memorial cairn**, while another leads up the sliver of moorland from a gate off the lane below Wreck. A good path then leads up the side of **Cowlaughton Clough** to join the Pennine Way.

The Viscount **Snowden memorial cairn** was unveiled before a large crowd on 21st May 1938 to remember Philip Snowden, Labour's first Chancellor of the Exchequer. Viscount Snowden was born in Cowling and had his ashes scattered on Ickornshaw Moor.

The **Cat Stone** is an unremarkable boulder, reached by following faint grooves across **Hart Hill Moor**.

to Cowling (1 mile)

to Cowling—Bailden

to Cowling (1/2 mile)

to Ickornshaw (1 mile)

to Ickornshaw

Pad Cote

Pad Cote Lane

Viscount Snowden memorial cairn

Wreck

Cowloughton

Cowloughton Clough

The Scars

Scar Hill

Brown Hill

Hart Hill Moor

Cat Stone Clough

Cat Stone

Dean Laithe

Pond Hill

Long Hill End

Over Fields

Over Dean (ruin)

Moor Lodge

Further Dean Hole (ruin)

Dean Hole Clough

Hallan Hill

Piper Lane

Old Lane

Dean Brow

Dean Brow Clough

Dean Moss

Andrew Gutter

Lower Edge

toad rock

stake

Ickornshaw Moor

High End Lowe

Timothy Scars (lime hushings)

New Stone Hut

Cowloughton Dam (site)

High End Lowe Spring

Pennine Way

Maw Stones

stone shelter

18 Ickornshaw Moor.

Sutton Moors)

When the county boundaries were redrawn in 1974, **Cowling** was initially included in Lancashire. The locals were incensed and eventually succeeded in having the village returned to its rightful place in Yorkshire.

The massive **Hitching Stone** dominates the moorland expanse between Earl Crag and Wolf Stones, but there were once more large boulders on this moor; though the Kid Stone and Winter Hill Stone remain, others have been quarried away, including the Quicken Stone, Buck Stone and Navaxstone (the latter two entirely lost from the moss north-east of the Hitching Stone.

*Reaching the **Hitching Stone** from Long Gate is not as straight-forward as it looks. The best path runs from a gate near the top of the road via **Kid Stone Hill** and Quicken Hole to a covered dam just short of the boulder. Another path sets off from a ladder stile further down the road and leads either up the side of **Slatesden Clough** or along the far side of the wall that leads to the stone.*

*The western end of **Earl Crag** is a maze of paths through the bracken, but further east there are few useful lines below the rocks and a couple of well-built walls obstruct progress. This leaves only the well-trodden route along the crag between the two monuments (see p26).*

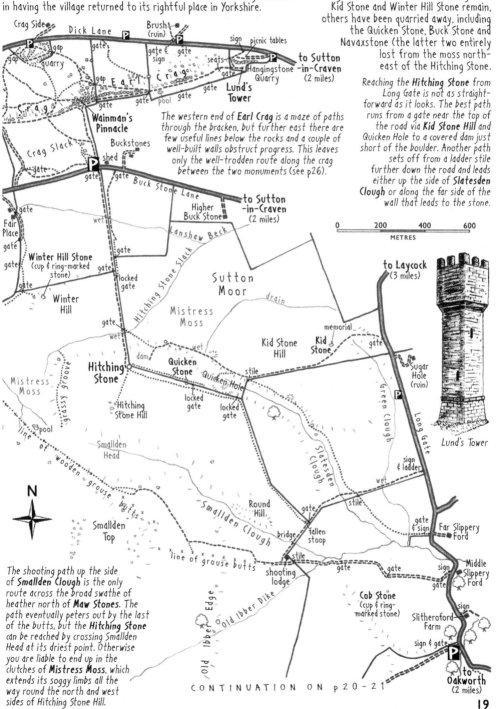

The shooting path up the side of **Smallden Clough** is the only route across the broad swathe of heather north of **Maw Stones**. The path eventually peters out by the last of the butts, but the **Hitching Stone** can be reached by crossing Smallden Head at its driest point. Otherwise you are liable to end up in the clutches of **Mistress Moss**, which extends its soggy limbs all the way round the north and west sides of Hitching Stone Hill.

CONTINUATION ON p 20-21

19

MAP 5: WOLF STONES SOUTH (Oakworth Moor)

The summit of Wolf Stones stands on a rocky crest overlooking the Keighley to Colne road, from where it has a definite hilltop appearance. From all other sides, it presents broad shoulders of heather. The southern part of the moor centres around Keighley Moor Reservoir and is well trodden, apart from the boggy ridge that runs from Combe Hill to Maw Stones via the summit.

Heath rush, or juncus squarrosus, is one of the most common plants across the South Pennines, its hardy tussocks thriving on the wettest acidic moorland. Its stems are circular and spongy inside, and have brown clusters of flowers near their sharp tips. It is favoured by grazing livestock during the winter when there is little else on offer.

*The summit trig of **Wolf Stones** stands on the undistinguished cluster of Little Wolf Stones. The real edge of Great Wolf Stones is beyond a stile to the south-west. The trig point is easily visible from the Pennine Way, though the path to it is rather faint at first, following the shallow ridge of high ground.*

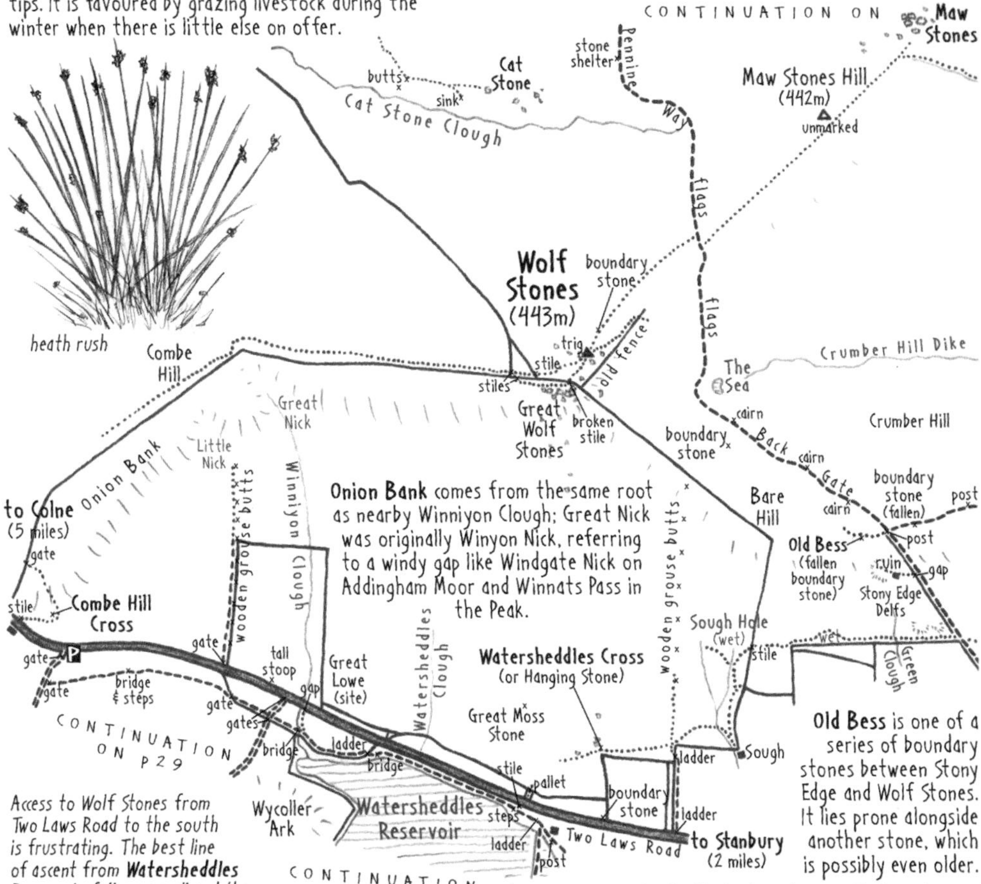

heath rush

CONTINUATION ON **Maw Stones**

stone shelter

Pennine Way

butts
sink
Cat Stone

Cat Stone Clough

Maw Stones Hill
(442m)
unmarked

flags

Wolf Stones
(443m)

boundary stone

Combe Hill

trig
stile
stiles

old fence

The Sea

Crumber Hill Dike

Great Nick

Little Nick

Great Wolf Stones

broken stile

cairn

boundary stone

Back

Crumber Hill

Winniyon Clough

wooden grouse butts

Onion Bank comes from the same root as nearby Winniyon Clough; Great Nick was originally Winyon Nick, referring to a windy gap like Windgate Nick on Addingham Moor and Winnats Pass in the Peak.

cairn

Bare Hill

gate

boundary stone

post

wooden grouse butts

Old Bess
(fallen boundary stone)
Stony Edge Delfs

ruin
gap
post

to Colne
(5 miles)

Onion Bank

gate

stile
Combe Hill Cross

gate
gate
bridge & steps

tall stoop
gate

gap
gates

Great Lowe
(site)

Watersheddles Clough

Watersheddles Cross
(or Hanging Stone)

Sough Hole
(wet)

stile

wet

Green Clough

Old Bess is one of a series of boundary stones between Stony Edge and Wolf Stones. It lies prone alongside another stone, which is possibly even older.

bridge
bridge

ladder

Great Moss Stone

stile
pallet

boundary stone

ladder

Sough

ladder

CONTINUATION ON P29

Wycoller Ark

Watersheddles Reservoir

steps

ladder

Two Laws Road

to Stanbury
(2 miles)

boundary stone
post

CONTINUATION ON P36

Access to Wolf Stones from Two Laws Road to the south is frustrating. The best line of ascent from **Watersheddles Reservoir** follows a wall and then a line of wooden grouse butts towards Combe Hill. When the path peters out, bear left up the shallow hollow of Little Nick to reach the fenceline along the ridge. There are no useful stiles to reach the faint path on the other side, but the ground is reasonably easy-going on both sides. The fence can also be reached via a stile and faint path up past **Combe Hill Cross**. The only other access points are via a short walled lane opposite the eastern end of the reservoir and the footpath across the field west of Sough.

*The Pennine Way is by far the best route up Wolf Stones because much of the rest of its south-eastern flank is rough and wet. The path from **Highfield House** looks appealing but crosses one of the wettest hollows in the South Pennines and is best avoided unless you have a keen interest in cotton and bog grasses. The continuation of this path towards **Watersheddles Cross** also crosses wet ground, but the worst can be avoided by dropping down towards the ruin at Sough.*

Combe Hill Cross is known locally as Camel Cross, a probable corruption of Gamel, the Saxon Lord who is thought to have erected it. It may have served as both a boundary stone and wayside cross along the medieval road, whose straight line is followed by the modern road. What remains is the base, inscribed 'Combe Cross', and a small stone set within the socket.

20

Combe Hill Cross

As it is a quiet area of moorland, nesting birds are common across Oakworth Moor; these include linnets, stonechats, peregrine, golden plover, wrens and goldeneye.

*The unmarked heathery top of Maw Stones Hill is just a metre lower than Wolf Stones. Its only feature is the collection of large flat rocks at **Maw Stones**, which are reached by a faint path along the ridge from the top of the Pennine Way. The only other satisfactory path to the stones follows a line of wooden grouse butts up from the corner of **Keighley Moor Reservoir**. Though it threatens to peter out, the route can be traced up the right side of the grough that bears left at the end of the butts.*

p 18 - 19

The enclosures around **Higher Intake** and **Clough Hey** are not open access land, with only Public Rights of Way to follow, but there are some attractive areas around them that are. **Blue Scar** is a dry ravine carved from an outcrop of limestone that can be reached from a gap in the wall above **Morkin Bridge**. Duck under the barbed wire and drop down across the smaller stream below to pick up a faint path following the slope above first Morkin Beck, then the dry valley itself. The path continues as far as the track to Clough Hey, though you'll have to jump the fence here.

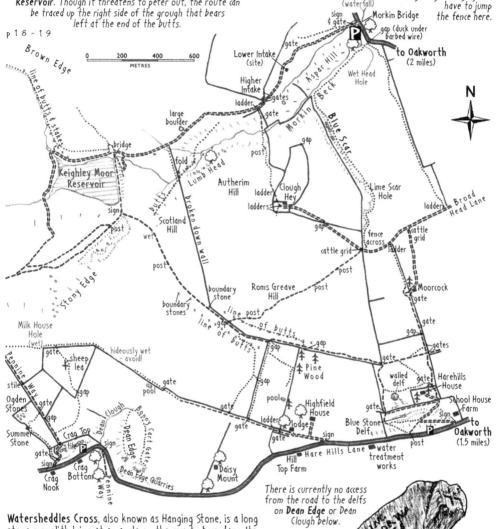

Watersheddles Cross, also known as Hanging Stone, is a long stone monolith lying at an angle on the county boundary. Its antiquity is unknown, although it was referred to in the 14th century simply as a standing stone. Following the boundary dispute over the Lad o' Crow Hill in the 17th century (see p37), it was carved with the inscription still present - 'Hanging Stone or Water Sheddles Cross' - and became a significant boundary marker. The cross on its top is thought to have been added later and it may well never have served as wayside cross, its name remaining something of a mystery. Another boundary marker, **Great Moss Stone**, stands in the heather to the west.

Watersheddles Cross **21**

ROUTE 4: EARL CRAG & HITCHING STONE FROM SUTTON-IN-CRAVEN

Distance: 7½ miles (11.9km)

Ascent: 330m

Difficulty: Easy

Parking: Street parking in Sutton-in-Craven, though this can be awkward on some of the narrow streets.

Public Transport: Sutton is on the 66 bus route between Keighley and Skipton, with further buses running through Cross Hills half a mile away.

Character: A very satisfying round that admittedly takes in more of North Yorkshire than West Yorkshire, but it links the gritstone moorland features of Earl Crag, the Hitching Stone and Grey Stones Hill with the sylvan charms of the Victorian walkways in Sutton Clough. The going is generally very good, though some of the paths are not well marked and there is a short pathless section across Smallden Head.

Sutton village may be in North Yorkshire, but it looks like a typical West Yorkshire textile village. One of its landmarks is the Jacobethan gatehouse that you pass under on Hall Drive. **Sutton Hall Lodge** was built in the late 19th century as the entrance to Sutton Hall, but is all that remains of the Hartleys' short-lived gothic mansion, which was demolished in the 1940s. The Hartleys operated High Mill in Sutton Clough and later Greenroyd Mill (also known as Hartley's Mill) which still dominates the centre of the village.

1 From **Sutton-in-Craven** High Street (running past the giant Greenroyd Mill and the Kings Arms and Black Bull pubs), head straight on where it bends left towards the Bay Horse. Hall Drive soon passes under the gatehouse of **Sutton Hall Lodge** and continues as a rough track through the houses beyond. The track leads straight into the estate woods of **Sutton Clough**. Follow the clear path all the way up the left bank of the stream. Reaching a walled track, turn right over an old clapper bridge and continue on the other side.

2 Follow the path up the right side of the clough to emerge into fields by a small waterfall. Stay with the stream and, beyond another stile, drop down left over a footbridge and follow a path up the right edge of the fields to **Gill Top**. Keep left through a couple of gateways in front of the farm, then bear right beyond the barn and aim for a gate in the far corner of the field. Follow the wall up to the steps below **America Farm**.

Follow the track downhill from **Crag** and, soon after it bends left, bear right down to a gate in the far corner. A narrow fenced path leads between houses to a road on the edge of **Sutton**. Head straight on, even where the road turns to the left, following a rough track called The Acres. At the far end turn left to reach the **High Street** and centre of the village again.

Sutton Clough and Lumb Clough are used somewhat interchangeably to refer to the ancient wooded valley running down into the village. Its walkways were laid out as a private Victorian garden by the owners of Sutton Hall; after the hall's demolition, it was gifted to the parish. At the confluence further up Lumb Clough, there was a small lead-smelting mill in the 18th century, making use of ore from mines on Glusburn Moor.

7 Retrace your route from **Lund's Tower** and follow the steps down and along the quarry edge to the road. 250m down the hill, turn right on a signed track that descends steadily to **High Jack Field**. Skirt round right in front of the house to a small gate beyond, then follow the field edge along to a stile just before a small wood. Cut diagonally down across the field to join a track to the left of the farm at **Crag**.

3 Join the track leading up between the buildings of **America Farm**; where it bends, use a couple of gates to the right to get into the field straight ahead and continue up to America Lane. 100m to the left, follow a sign pointing right towards Pole Stoop to reach a barely visible stone stile in the far corner of the field (look for the gap in the coping stones). The path continues along the bottom of the slope of Higher Edge to reach the road; **Pole Stoop** is angled out from the wall at the top of the field here. At the top of Pole Lane (opposite the stoop), go right through a gate and cross the heath, join a walled track leading down to **Greystones Lane**.

Pole Stoop leans at a remarkable angle from the base of a stone wall and is thought to be a medieval boundary stone. It is marked with a cross and a T, and is one of a series of stones lying along the current county boundary.

Pole Stoop

4 **Greystones Lane** can be followed right round to Long Gate, but a short diversion skirts along the wall over **Grey Stones Hill** before rejoining the road. At the end of the lane, turn right up Long Gate as far as a ladder stile to the left. Follow a faint path parallel to the wall, past two wet depressions and a gate off its hinges to reach a **shooting lodge**.

Estimated to weigh over a thousand tons, the **Hitching Stone** is the largest solitary boulder in Yorkshire. There is a chamber on one side known as the Priest's Chair, and a large sink in its palm that is filled with water up to six feet deep. Another small bore runs through the whole stone, thought to be where the remains of a fossilised tree have been worn away; it often plays a sound in the wind. Legend has it that a witch living on Rombalds Moor hitched the stone across the valley by inserting her broomstick in the hole. A Lammas Fair was held at the site on August 1st every year until 1870 and competitions between the villagers of Cowling and Sutton included fell racing, horse racing, quoits and treacle-pudding eating.

the Hitching Stone

6 Head downhill from the **Hitching Stone** and follow the wall all the way to the road. Head straight across to continue on to **Wainman's Pinnacle** and the dramatic viewpoint of Earl Crag. An obvious path leads along the edge to **Lund's Tower**, book-ending the crag to the east; this folly can be climbed by some stairs inside.

From the gate off its hinges shortly before the shooting lodge, the wall can be followed right all the way up to the **Hitching Stone**. There is a soggy path throughout, but I think it preferable to approach the stone from the other side of Smalden Clough and at least get a taste of the open moor.

5 Follow the track uphill from the **shooting lodge** until it joins a faint path following the line of wooden butts heading over the crest near the top of Smalden Clough. At butt number 7, turn right across the heather towards a small but prominent stone on the top of Hitching Stone Hill opposite. **Smalden Head** can be wet and Mistress Moss the other side even worse, so cross by the highest point of the pass before scrambling up to the stone. From a smaller stone just a few yards to the west of the one on top of Hitching Stone Hill, a faint path leads down to the giant **Hitching Stone** (which has remarkably remained hidden from view until this point).

23

ROUTE 5: WOLF STONES & NEWSHOLME DEAN FROM OAKWORTH

6 Double back to the right to divert to the **Maw Stones**, just 100m away but not visible from this side. Retrace your steps and follow this line on towards the trig point on Wolf Stones. Reaching the flags of the **Pennine Way**, turn right for about 20m to pick up a faint line aiming just to the right of the trig. This path soon becomes clear and curves round to the summit, with the **Great Wolf Stones** lying just beyond.

5 Turn right up the Yorkshire Water track from the parking area by **Morkin Bridge**. It leads past Higher Intake and up to **Keighley Moor Reservoir**. A simple shortcut crosses the dam wall here to join the return route the other side, but the onward route bears slightly right into a large open gravel area level with the dam wall and picks up a faint path heading roughly straight on (not the one going right) across the heather. This follows the line of a rough drain parallel to the reservoir until it joins a series of wooden grouse butts heading up the clough. At the end of the butts, follow the grough itself as it bends round to the left and pick up a faint path along its right bank. At the top of the grough, the path bends left to join a clearer route running in a straight line along the high ground of **Maw Stones Hill**.

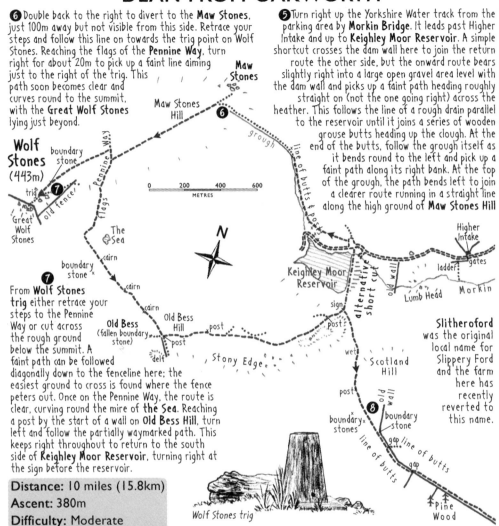

Wolf Stones trig

7 From **Wolf Stones** trig either retrace your steps to the Pennine Way or cut across the rough ground below the summit. A faint path can be followed diagonally down to the fenceline here; the easiest ground to cross is found where the fence peters out. Once on the Pennine Way, the route is clear, curving round the mire of **the Sea**. Reaching a post by the start of a wall on **Old Bess Hill**, turn left and follow the partially waymarked path. This keeps right throughout to return to the south side of **Keighley Moor Reservoir**, turning right at the sign before the reservoir.

Slitheroford was the original local name for Slippery Ford and the farm here has recently reverted to this name.

Distance: 10 miles (15.8km)

Ascent: 380m

Difficulty: Moderate

Parking: Street parking in Oakworth Lane End and next to Oakworth Cemetery. Small car park at Morkin Bridge (2 miles from Oakworth).

Public Transport: Oakworth is on the K7 and B2 bus routes from Keighley and Haworth.

Character: There are few paths on the east side of Wolf Stones, so this is the only natural round route to the summit. It can be shortened by parking at Morkin Bridge or skipping the moor tops. The route out of Oakworth follows the lush valley of Newsholme Dean up onto the moor, before making a loop of the high ground around Keighley Moor Reservoir and following the long ridge back down to Oakworth. The paths are generally easy to follow, except the short stretch up to Maw Stones and the summit.

8 The path soon joins the line of a wall between two files of large stone butts. Reaching another wall, the path goes through a gap to the left side of the wall and follows the other side past **Pine Wood** to a gate at the far end. Continue straight on to reach a narrow gate leading off the moor and follow the wall beyond. After a stile the wall bends left to reach a walled track, which you follow right past some woods. Where it bends sharply left towards **Tewitt Hill Farm**, continue straight on through a gate and turn left onto another track at the end. Beyond **Oakworth Cottage**, bear right where the track splits around a stone jutting out from the bank. Turnshaw Lane leads all the way back to Low Bank Lane and the Golden Fleece in **Oakworth**.

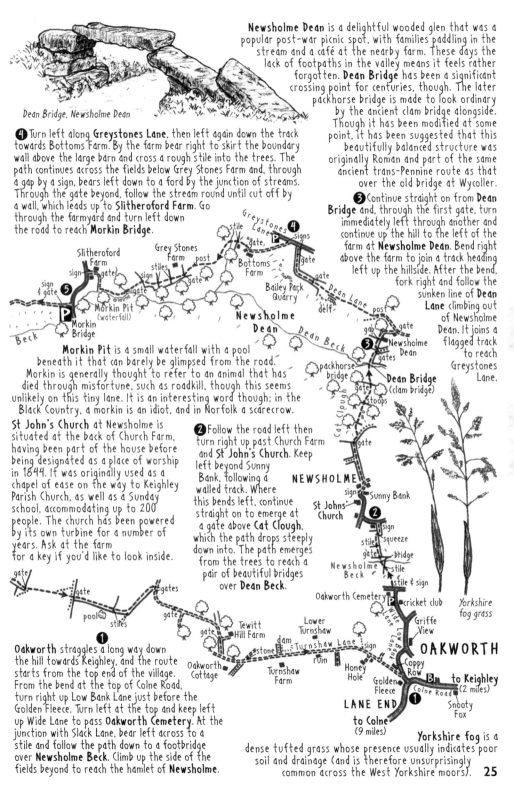

Newsholme Dean is a delightful wooded glen that was a popular post-war picnic spot, with families paddling in the stream and a café at the nearby farm. These days the lack of footpaths in the valley means it feels rather forgotten. **Dean Bridge** has been a significant crossing point for centuries, though. The later packhorse bridge is made to look ordinary by the ancient clam bridge alongside. Though it has been modified at some point, it has been suggested that this beautifully balanced structure was originally Roman and part of the same ancient trans-Pennine route as that over the old bridge at Wycoller.

Dean Bridge, Newsholme Dean

4 Turn left along **Greystones Lane**, then left again down the track towards Bottoms Farm. By the farm bear right to skirt the boundary wall above the large barn and cross a rough stile into the trees. The path continues across the fields below Grey Stones Farm and, through a gap by a sign, bears left down to a ford by the junction of streams. Through the gate beyond, follow the stream round until cut off by a wall, which leads up to **Slitheroford Farm**. Go through the farmyard and turn left down the road to reach **Morkin Bridge**.

3 Continue straight on from **Dean Bridge** and, through the first gate, turn immediately left through another and continue up the hill to the left of the farm at **Newsholme Dean**. Bend right above the farm to join a track heading left up the hillside. After the bend, fork right and follow the sunken line of **Dean Lane** climbing out of Newsholme Dean. It joins a flagged track to reach Greystones Lane.

Morkin Pit is a small waterfall with a pool beneath it that can barely be glimpsed from the road. Morkin is generally thought to refer to an animal that has died through misfortune, such as roadkill, though this seems unlikely on this tiny lane. It is an interesting word though; in the Black Country, a morkin is an idiot, and in Norfolk a scarecrow.

St John's Church at Newsholme is situated at the back of Church Farm, having been part of the house before being designated as a place of worship in 1844. It was originally used as a chapel of ease on the way to Keighley Parish Church, as well as a Sunday school, accommodating up to 200 people. The church has been powered by its own turbine for a number of years. Ask at the farm for a key if you'd like to look inside.

2 Follow the road left then turn right up past Church Farm and **St John's Church**. Keep left beyond Sunny Bank, following a walled track. Where this bends left, continue straight on to emerge at a gate above **Cat Clough**, which the path drops steeply down into. The path emerges from the trees to reach a pair of beautiful bridges over **Dean Beck**.

Oakworth straggles a long way down the hill towards Keighley, and the route starts from the top end of the village. From the bend at the top of Colne Road, turn right up Low Bank Lane just before the Golden Fleece. Turn left at the top and keep left up Wide Lane to pass **Oakworth Cemetery**. At the junction with Slack Lane, bear left across to a stile and follow the track down to a footbridge over **Newsholme Beck**. Climb up the side of the fields beyond to reach the hamlet of **Newsholme**.

Yorkshire fog is a dense tufted grass whose presence usually indicates poor soil and drainage (and is therefore unsurprisingly common across the West Yorkshire moors).

25

EARL CRAG MONUMENTS

The pair of follies at either end of Earl Crag are visible from many miles around and represent fine vantage points across the Aire Valley. The two striking structures, though, are unrelated and each has its own story to tell.

WAINMAN'S PINNACLE

Wainman's Pinnacle (also known as Cowling Pinnacle or 'salt pot') is the older of the two monuments, thought to have been built by Richard Wainman shortly after Wellington's victory at Waterloo in 1815. There are also stories dating it to the 17th century, when Lady Amcotts is said to have had it built to commemorate her husband who died in the Civil War. However, this is now thought spurious as Lady Amcotts' married Richard Wainman only in 1809. The Wainmans owned the sizeable Carr Head Estate in Cowling from the early 17th century, yet built the monument on private land on which they had to pay an annual ground rent. The monument was rebuilt in 1898 after being struck by lightning and falling into disrepair, and stands proudly on the highest boulder on the edge, very close to a natural trilithon (the sort of megalithic structure built at Stonehenge possibly used in sun worship).

LUND'S TOWER

Lund's Tower (also known as Sutton Pinnacle or 'pepper pot') was built by James Lund of Malsis Hall (near Sutton-in-Craven) in 1897. No-one knows for sure why it was built; some have suggested to commemorate Queen Victoria's Diamond Jubilee; others for Lund's daughter Ethel's 21st birthday (and indeed some refer to it as Ethel's Tower). The plaque on its face is mysteriously left blank. It is a very pure folly, a crenellated viewing tower plonked on the landscape as in a fairytale. Lund's folly can still be enjoyed, as a narrow stone staircase inside leads up to the viewing platform at the top.

CHAPTER 3 – BOULSWORTH HILL
(aka Lad Law)

Height: 517m

Grid Ref: SD930356

Map Sheet: OL21 (South Pennines)

Access: No dogs permitted at any time (except access to summit via Scotch Road or permissive routes from northwest or around Walshaw Dean Reservoirs & on public rights of way). Where permitted keep dogs on leads during grouse shooting season (between 12th August and 10th December).

Public Transport: With the bus to Widdop no longer running, the closest you can get to this moor is Heptonstall Slack (on the 596 bus from Hebden Bridge).

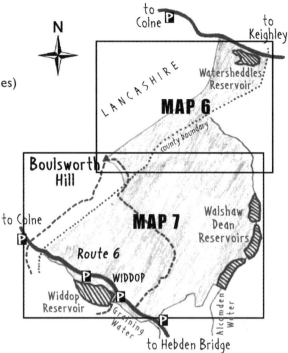

Though Boulsworth Hill is technically a Lancastrian peak, it probably shouldn't be (if we assume the Pennine watershed to be the boundary) and it caps a large area of moorland wilderness within West Yorkshire. Boulsworth Hill rears up impressively from the north-west (indeed the name is thought to mean 'bull's neck') and it dominates the moorland across the north-west of the county. Its summit ridge is studded with numerous rocky outcrops, among which are the legendary Elk and Bison carvings and Druid's Slaughter Stone, adding to the moor's forbidding air. Indeed it has been suggested that it is the dark yang to Pendle Hill's light yin.

Before the Right to Roam legislation of 2000, the whole of Boulsworth Hill was a private grouse moor and access had long been a source of contention. Attempts were made to open it up in the 1950s, but these were thwarted over rather ridiculous issues of drinking water purity. So make the most of the opportunity to explore the finest expanse of open heath in the county. Though you'll find little in the way of paths across much of the moor, this is great tramping country.

Boulsworth Hill and Dove Stones from the Scotch Road

MAP 6: BOULSWORTH HILL NORTH

Though the bulk of this map is in Lancashire, it includes the easiest routes onto Boulsworth from the Oakworth and Haworth side via Watersheddles Reservoir and Combe Hill Cross. This follows the ancient bridleway along the foot of the hills past Saucer Hill Clough, an area strewn with glacial drift and lime hushings. Apart from the busy northern fringe, this is wild open moorland with a scattering of interesting stone outcrops but little in the way of paths. Though its exploration can be a joy, beware of unexpected bogs.

Across the northern edge of Boulsworth Hill and Wolf Stones, there are various scars (similar to those at Sheddon Clough) where limestone was mined by **hushing**. The limestone here is not exposed, but is found in glacial deposits which also include erratics of grit, chert and ironstone. Hushing describes the effect that controlled torrents of water had on the soil, leaving the limestone exposed. These hillsides are cut by various disused dikes and dams for this purpose, and lime was burnt in kilns on site to produce quicklime, leaving conical mounds of waste.

There are several satisfying routes of ascent to **Boulsworth Hill** from the north. The obvious circuit follows a pair of earlier permissive routes, climbing via the **Abbot Stone** and descending via **Little Chair Stones** to Spoutley Lumb. Other routes are now accessible up Saucer Hill Clough, leaving the main track that skirts the foot of the moor opposite the cattle grid to Mean Moss. Beyond the first gate, the best route branches right to reach another gate (sadly locked) and follows a faint track up the west side of the clough to reach **Little Saucer Stones**. If you don't want to climb the gate, continue left to pick up a line of wooden grouse butts that climb nearly all the way to **Great Saucer Stones**.

Brink Ends Cairn is a small Bronze Age burial cairn in the bracken above Turnhole Clough. It is visible from a faint path leading up the bank from the sign above the oversized new bridge.

A faint path sets off across the moor from Robin Scar only to abandon you near the **Water Cut**, a disused dike that is even harder to avoid than it is to follow.

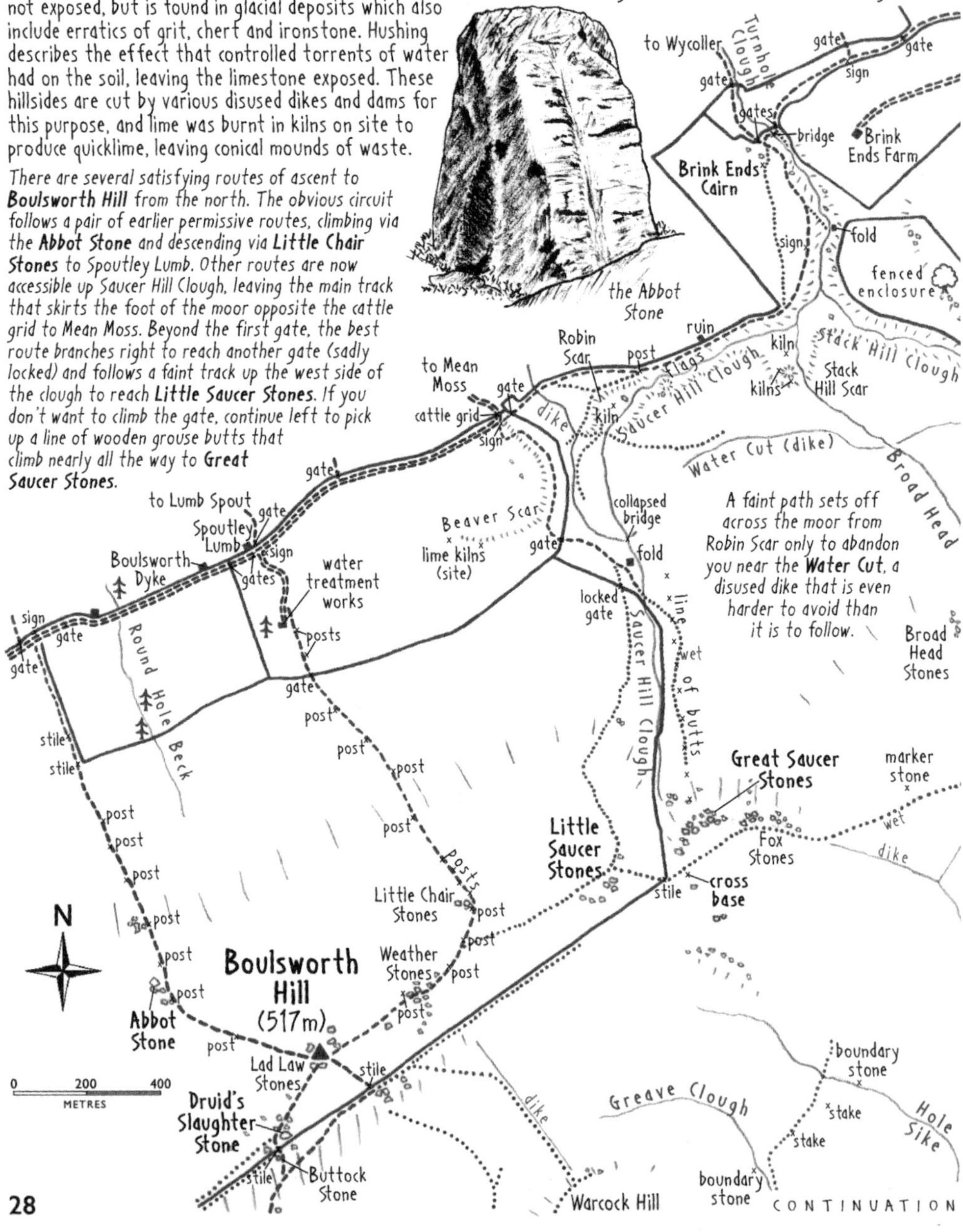

Brink Ends Cairn

the Abbot Stone

to Wycoller
Turnhole Clough
gate
gate
sign
gates
bridge
Brink Ends Farm
sign
fold
fenced enclosure

Robin Scar
post
ruin
Flags
kiln
Stack Hill Clough
Stack Hill Scar
kilns

to Mean Moss
gate
cattle grid
sign
dike
kiln
Saucer Hill Clough
Water Cut (dike)
Broad Head

to Lumb Spout
gate
Spoutley Lumb
sign
Boulsworth Dyke
gates
water treatment works
posts

Beaver Scar
lime kilns (site)
gate
collapsed bridge
fold
locked gate
wet
Saucer Hill Clough
line of butts

Broad Head Stones

sign
gate
gate
Round Hole Beck
gate
post
post
post
post
post
post
post

post
post
posts

Great Saucer Stones
marker stone
wet
Fox Stones
dike

Little Saucer Stones
stile
cross base

Little Chair Stones
post
Weather Stones
post
post

N

Boulsworth Hill
(517m)

Abbot Stone
post
Lad Law Stones
stile

0   200   400
METRES

Druid's Slaughter Stone

Buttock Stone

boundary stone
stake
stake

Greave Clough
Hole Sike

Warcock Hill
boundary stone
CONTINUATION

28

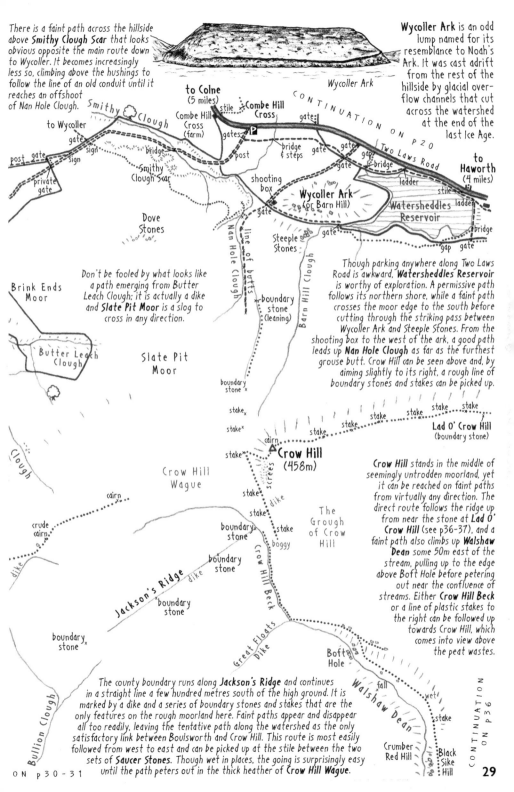

There is a faint path across the hillside above **Smithy Clough Scar** that looks obvious opposite the main route down to Wycoller. It becomes increasingly less so, climbing above the hushings to follow the line of an old conduit until it reaches an offshoot of Nan Hole Clough.

Wycoller Ark is an odd lump named for its resemblance to Noah's Ark. It was cast adrift from the rest of the hillside by glacial overflow channels that cut across the watershed at the end of the last Ice Age.

Wycoller Ark

to Colne
(5 miles)

S m i t h y   C l o u g h

to Wycoller

Smithy Clough Scar

Combe Hill Cross (farm)

stile

Combe Hill Cross

C O N T I N U A T I O N   O N   P 20

Two Laws Road

to Haworth (4 miles)

gate
post   gate
sign   sign
private gate
post
bridge

gates
P
post
bridge & steps
gate   gate   gap
gate   bridge
ladder
stile
ladder

shooting box

Wycoller Ark (or Barn Hill)

Watersheddles Reservoir

Dove Stones

gate

Steeple Stones

gate

gate
gap   gate
bridge

N a n   H o l e   C l o u g h

l i n e   o f   b u t t s

B a r n   H i l l   C l o u g h

Though parking anywhere along Two Laws Road is awkward, **Watersheddles Reservoir** is worthy of exploration. A permissive path follows its northern shore, while a faint path crosses the moor edge to the south before cutting through the striking pass between Wycoller Ark and Steeple Stones. From the shooting box to the west of the ark, a good path leads up **Nan Hole Clough** as far as the furthest grouse butt. Crow Hill can be seen above and, by aiming slightly to its right, a rough line of boundary stones and stakes can be picked up.

Brink Ends Moor

Don't be fooled by what looks like a path emerging from Butter Leach Clough; it is actually a dike and **Slate Pit Moor** is a slog to cross in any direction.

Butter Leach Clough

Slate Pit Moor

boundary stone (leaning)

boundary stone

stake
stake
stake   stake   stake
cairn   stake   stake   stake
stake   **Lad O' Crow Hill**
(boundary stone)

C l o u g h

Crow Hill Wague

cairn

crude cairn

dike

stake
stake
screes
stake
Crow Hill
(458m)

boundary stone
stake
boggy

dike

The Grough of Crow Hill

Crow Hill stands in the middle of seemingly untrodden moorland, yet it can be reached on faint paths from virtually any direction. The direct route follows the ridge up from near the stone at **Lad O' Crow Hill** (see p36-37), and a faint path also climbs up **Walshaw Dean** some 50m east of the stream, pulling up to the edge above Boft Hole before petering out near the confluence of streams. Either **Crow Hill Beck** or a line of plastic stakes to the right can be followed up towards Crow Hill, which comes into view above the peat wastes.

J a c k s o n ' s   R i d g e

dike
boundary stone
boundary stone

C r o w   H i l l   B e c k

boundary stone

G r e a t   F l o a t s   D i k e

Boft Hole

fall
wet
stake

B u l l i o n   C l o u g h

W a l s h a w   D e a n

Crumber Red Hill

Black Sike Hill

The county boundary runs along **Jackson's Ridge** and continues in a straight line a few hundred metres south of the high ground. It is marked by a dike and a series of boundary stones and stakes that are the only features on the rough moorland here. Faint paths appear and disappear all too readily, leaving the tentative path along the watershed as the only satisfactory link between Boulsworth and Crow Hill. This route is most easily followed from west to east and can be picked up at the stile between the two sets of **Saucer Stones**. Though wet in places, the going is surprisingly easy until the path peters out in the thick heather of **Crow Hill Wague**.

O N   p 3 0 - 3 1

C O N T I N U A T I O N   O N   P 3 6

29

The southern slopes of Boulsworth Hill form one of the finest moorland expanses in the county. Away from the shooting tracks that dominate Greave Clough, this is an entrancing expanse of heather and weathered rocks. With access restricted until 2000, the Access to Boulsworth Campaign fought for many years for public rights across this moor, so make the most of it.

The **Druid's Slaughter Stone** is said to have been used for sacrificial offerings. Beneath the rock is carved 'Lad Law The Hill Of Slaughter' and, on the top 'Llad Hloew', adjacent to a natural bowl that could be imagined to hold sacrificial blood. Though both are thought to be relatively modern carvings, the latter may refer to a Celtic word for kill or sacrifice, possibly to Taram, an equivalent of Thor (also found in the name of nearby Thursden valley).

Hidden away in steep Black Clough, **Robin Hood's House** may have been a hideaway of Barefoot Harry. He lived at Widdop and his gang of robbers, renowned across West Yorkshire, were said to hide out in Lancashire in times of danger.

The path following the line of **Dove Stones** towards Widdop becomes unclear as it crosses the peat groughs at the top of Tom Groove, but it is not far across the heather from here to the edge overlooking **Widdop Reservoir**.

to Colne (5 miles)

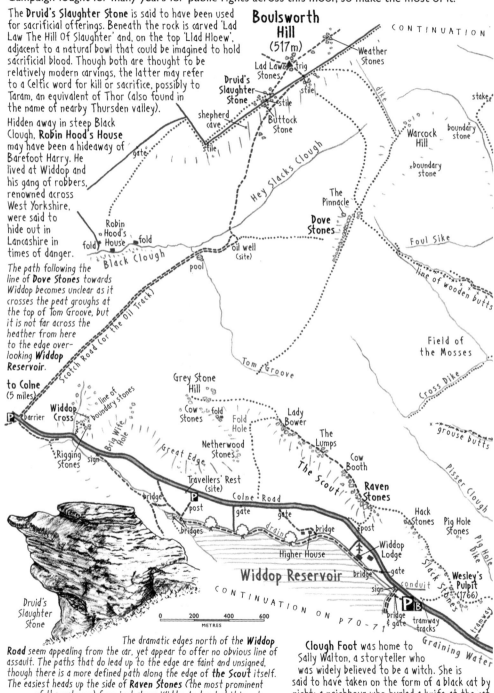

The dramatic edges north of the **Widdop Road** seem appealing from the car, yet appear to offer no obvious line of assault. The paths that do lead up to the edge are faint and unsigned, though there is a more defined path along the edge of **the Scout** itself. The easiest heads up the side of **Raven Stones** (the most prominent of the outcrops) from just above Widdop Lodge, but it is not far up from the car park to **Wesley's Pulpit** on Slack Stones.

Clough Foot was home to Sally Walton, a storyteller who was widely believed to be a witch. She is said to have taken on the form of a black cat by night; a neighbour who hurled a knife at the cat found Sally to have a bandaged arm the next day.

30

MAP 7: BOULSWORTH HILL SOUTH (Widdop Moor)

*A number of large shooting tracks lead up **Greave Clough**, the clearest of which follows the stream's east bank all the way up to the county boundary, where a faint path continues north-east across the heather. If you are heading for the summit of Boulsworth Hill, you may be as well to continue along the line of the stream contouring around **Warcock Hill** to pick up the path between Dove Stones and Boulsworth Hill. An alternative is to branch off the main track earlier, following a sunken shooting track and line of butts straight up towards **Dove Stones**. A faint path continues all the way to these rocks.*

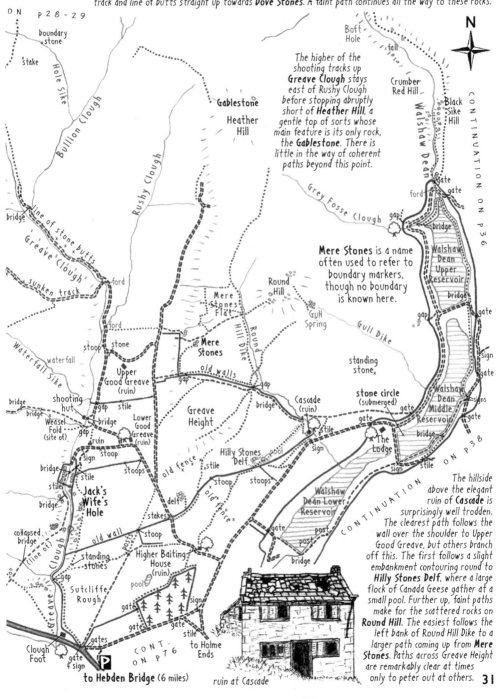

O N   p 28 - 29

boundary stone

stake

Hole Sike

Bullion Clough

Rushy Clough

bridge

line of stone butts

Greave Clough

sunken track

ford

Waterfall Sike

waterfall

stoop   stone

ford

Upper Good Greave (ruin)

bridge   shooting hut

bridge   gap   stile

Weasel Fold (site of)   bridge

gap   ruin

sign   stoop

bridge   stile

stile

Jack's Wife's Hole

bridge

collapsed bridge

(line of)   Clough

old wall

standing stones

Sutcliffe Rough

Clough Foot   gate & sign

to Hebden Bridge (6 miles)

Gablestone

Heather Hill

*The higher of the shooting tracks up **Greave Clough** stays east of Rushy Clough before stopping abruptly short of **Heather Hill**, a gentle top of sorts whose main feature is its only rock, the **Gablestone**. There is little in the way of coherent paths beyond this point.*

Boft Hole   fall

Crumber Red Hill

Walshaw Dean

Black Sike Hill

Grey Fosse Clough

gap

ford   gate   gate

bridge

Mere Stones is a name often used to refer to boundary markers, though no boundary is known here.

Walshaw Dean Upper Reservoir

bridge

Mere Stones Flat

Round Hill

Gull Spring

Gull Dike

Hill Dike

Round Hill Dike

gap   gate

Mere Stones

Lower Good Greave (ruin)

Greave Height

old walls   gap

gap   stile

Cascade (ruin)   bridge

sign

Hilly Stones Delf   pool

old fence   stile

delf

stoop   stoops

old fence

stakes

standing stones

Higher Baiting House (ruin)

pool

posts

gate   gate   gate   stile

to Holme Ends

CONT. ON P76

ruin at Cascade

standing stone

stone circle (submerged)   gate

stile

The Lodge

gate

sign

Walshaw Dean Lower Reservoir

gate

post   post

bridge

Walshaw Dean Middle Reservoir   signs

gate

bridge   x

stile

CONTINUATION ON P38

sign

stile

CONTINUATION ON P36

N

*The hillside above the elegant ruin of **Cascade** is surprisingly well trodden. The clearest path follows the wall over the shoulder to Upper Good Greave, but others branch off this. The first follows a slight embankment contouring round to **Hilly Stones Delf**, where a large flock of Canada Geese gather at a small pool. Further up, faint paths make for the scattered rocks on **Round Hill**. The easiest follows the left bank of Round Hill Dike to a larger path coming up from **Mere Stones**. Paths across Greave Height are remarkably clear at times only to peter out at others.*

31

ROUTE 6: BOULSWORTH HILL & GORPLE HILL FROM WIDDOP

Distance: 7½ miles (12.2km)

Ascent: 310m

Difficulty: Moderate

Parking: Car park below the dam of Widdop Reservoir on the Hebden Bridge to Colne road.

Public Transport: With the bus to Widdop no longer running, the closest you can get to this route is Heptonstall Slack (three miles away on the 596 bus route from Hebden Bridge).

Character: This route is unique in this book as the entire walk is on open moorland, forming a natural circuit of the hills overlooking Widdop Reservoir. Parts of the walk are ill defined (indeed any ascent of Boulsworth Hill from Greave Clough needs careful navigation), but the result is a joyous tramp across the lonely watershed tops of Boulsworth Hill and Gorple Hill. If necessary the route can be shortened before ascending Gorple Hill, by following the road then the reservoir shore back down to Widdop (see map on p70-71).

Note: No dogs are allowed on the section from Greave Clough to Dove Stones.

❸ The hills open up at **Dove Stones**, presenting an obvious arc round to the summit of Boulsworth Hill. Turn right at the stones, but fork left almost immediately to follow a good line heading round to the left of **Warcock Hill**. Keep left as you curve around the top of Hey Slacks Clough, then aim for the right-hand rocks on the edge of **Boulsworth Hill**. The path peters out here, but scramble up the slope to a stile above the rocks, from which a path leads across to the trig at **Lad Law Stones**.

❷ Join the vehicle track to pass the shooting hut and continue up **Greave Clough**. Fork left across a constructed ford and follow a sunken track up past a line of butts. At the end, bear left out of the grough and follow the butts up the left side of the grough. This faint line continues towards the **Dove Stones**, now apparent on the horizon. Where it bends right, continue straight on across the grough and follow its left side on up towards the rocks, the path becoming clearer as it nears them.

❹ From the summit of **Boulsworth Hill**, head back towards the fenceline in the direction of the distinctive prow of the **Druid's Slaughter Stone** (see p30 for more details). Cross another stile soon after the stone and descend diagonally down into **Hey Slacks Clough**. Across the stream, join the end of the **Scotch Road** and follow its gentle grassy crest for a mile to the top of the Widdop road.

Boulsworth Hill
(517m)

Lad Law Stones — trig

Druid's Slaughter Stone

line of dike

fenceline

stile

wet

stile

Warcock Hill

Hey Slacks Clough

The Pinnacle

Dove Stones ❸

cross grough here

pathless

line of grouse butts

butts

Field of the Mosses

ford

ford

pool

Scotch Road (or Oil Track)

Shuttleworth Rocks

The **Scotch Road** is thought to follow an ancient trackway along the high ground from the Iron Age settlement at Burwain's Camp near Thursden, later becoming a trade route between the Thursden and Worth valleys. The name may relate to an Old English word *scairtch*, meaning banked, a characteristic of the road. However, I suspect it refers to Scottish pedlars, who roamed the northern uplands in the 18th century selling fabrics, including a cheap cloth known as *Scotch-cloth*. There is also a Scots House in Holme Clough on Black Hill, and Scotchman's Arm on the moor above Ponden. More recently it has become known as the **Oil Track**: the track we see today was constructed in 1963, when it was thought there was oil beneath the shales of Hey Slacks Clough. A large drill was installed and a bore over 6,000ft deep sunk, but no oil was ever found.

1 From the car park by **Widdop Reservoir**, head back down the road towards Hebden Bridge for 1/4 mile. On a slight rise, turn left by some rocks at the roadside, from where a faint path runs away from the road. The narrow (and sometimes rather overgrown) path follows the line of a disused tramway past a collapsed but unnecessary bridge into the narrowest section of Greave Clough, known as **Jack's Wife's Hole**. A bridge crosses the clough at a small dam and concrete steps lead up to a stile. Turn left at a path just beyond, then continue straight across a larger track soon after, picking up a faint path that aims for a large shooting hut by the stream.

The **Boggart Stones** are named after a type of malevolent household spirit that crops up frequently in the folklore of Yorkshire and Lancashire. They were said to shapeshift and were blamed for many strange occurrences. Among other things, they were said to rearrange furniture, cause things to disappear, turn milk sour, make dogs go lame or even pull on a person's ears.

The **Dove Stones** are a great scar of gritstone in one long line facing the higher summit of Boulsworth Hill, with the Pinnacle cast adrift at its northern end. The name (previously Dave Stones) is thought to be a bastardisation of Dew Stones (from the gaelic *dubh*, meaning black).

to Colne & Burnley (5 miles)

5 Head straight across the road but, instead of following the obvious path leading away to the right, cross the bog straight ahead and pick up one of a number of faint quad tracks on top of the bank ahead and to the left of the narrow cleft. This bears slightly round to the left, climbing towards the corner of a fenceline. Follow the fence (or the quad track below) left all the way to the unmarked summit of **Gorple Hill** near a small boundary stone.

Gorple Hill (467m)

Birkin Clough

fenceline
boundary stone
Gorple Stones
old crags
cairn on rock
stake
stile
stile
stile
stile
gate
Little Gorple Hill
Gorple Gate
Gorple Stones
old walls
Shuttleworth Rocks

boundary stone near summit of Gorple Hill

6 From the boundary stone on **Gorple Hill**, you can follow the fenceline down to the packhorse route of **Gorple Gate** and double back to the left, or a well-worn quad track now offers a good shortcut. It passes a stake near the true top of the hill and descends the grassy shoulder of Little Hill to join Gorple Gate near the dramatic hanging stones of **Shuttleworth Rocks**.

to Hebden Bridge (6 miles)

Pisser Clough
Greave Clough
bridge
dam
bridge
bridge
collapsed bridge

Graining Water

Widdop Reservoir

sign
P B
bridge
sign
gate
1

N

METRES
0   250   500   750

Rocking The Cludders
Rocking Pig
Boggart Stones
Clough Head Stones
gate sign
post sign

7 Continue left down Gorple Gate from **Shuttleworth Rocks** to the first path branching off to the right, aiming for the first of a series of rocky outcrops on the high ground above Widdop Reservoir. If you reach a second 'Polite Notice' sign by a sharp bend in the track, you've gone too far, but can turn right here to rejoin the route at another post. The path continues along the high ground past the prominent **Rocking Pig** to the far end of **the Cludders**, where level with the dam wall a path drops steeply down between large rock parapets. Cross the dam and turn right to return to the car park.

Waterfall Sike
stone
gap
2
shooting hut
sign ruin
stoop
stile
Jack's Wife's Hole

a golden plover

The **golden plover** is an awkward-looking upright bird with a black breast and gold and black speckles down its back. It is common in the South Pennines, especially on areas of recently burned heather. It nests here during the summer before wintering on farmland and coastline.

33

THE ELK & BISON CARVINGS

In 1920, two boys playing in the stones scattered across Boulsworth Hill discovered a pair of carvings on the inside of one of the rocks; one of a running bison and the other of an elk's head. Many suggest that the only explanation for depictions of North American animals on this Pennine hillside are that they are the work of Native Americans who were touring the area as part of Buffalo Bill's Wild West show. Presented by Bill Cody himself, this mammoth extravaganza filled four trains and employed four hundred horses and a hundred Native Americans of various tribes. Having spent five months in Manchester in 1887, they later toured the whole country, performing in Keighley in 1903 and Burnley in 1904. However, it seems unlikely the Native Americans would have desecrated the sacred landscape in this way. It has also been suggested that it was the work of Reverend Percival Weldon, who owned part of Boulsworth Hill in the nineteenth century and may have been inspired by the age of scientific discovery to create his own piece of history.

The fact that their origin and age are unknown allows rumours of the carvings being prehistoric to persist. Eight thousand years ago, when Britain was connected to the continent, large aurochs (European bison) roamed the forested landscape and, alongside Irish elks (giant deer), were the principal large animals. It is quite feasible that our Mesolithic ancestors, whose flint tools have been found on Boulsworth Hill, carved these figures into the nearby rocks. This theory is best supported by the fact that the sun illuminates the carved rock only once a year, at midsummer sunrise. However, one look at the carvings is usually enough to say that they really don't look 8,000 years old, and it is thought unlikely they would have existed in isolation.

Another carving, that of a hawk (or possibly Horus, a hawk-headed Egyptian god), has been found on a rock near Upper Gorple Reservoir. This raises similar questions about its origin and, though it may have been the work of a navvy working on the dam, it is now thought to relate to an early twentieth-century Bradford-based occult group called the Temple of Horrors.

The Boulsworth carvings are located on the side of what could generously be described as a cave – it is possible for an individual to shelter in the hollow between the rocks here – but if you went looking for a cave you would never find it. The location is generally kept secret to protect the small carvings but, even with plenty of advice, it took me five trips to locate it, and only then with the aid of a guide.

So by all means go hunting, but prepare to be patient.

CHAPTER 4

WITHINS HEIGHT
(aka Stanbury Moor)

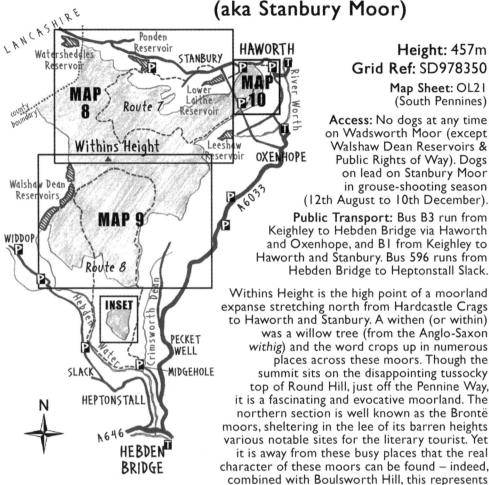

Height: 457m
Grid Ref: SD978350

Map Sheet: OL21
(South Pennines)

Access: No dogs at any time on Wadsworth Moor (except Walshaw Dean Reservoirs & Public Rights of Way). Dogs on lead on Stanbury Moor in grouse-shooting season (12th August to 10th December).

Public Transport: Bus B3 run from Keighley to Hebden Bridge via Haworth and Oxenhope, and B1 from Keighley to Haworth and Stanbury. Bus 596 runs from Hebden Bridge to Heptonstall Slack.

Withins Height is the high point of a moorland expanse stretching north from Hardcastle Crags to Haworth and Stanbury. A withen (or within) was a willow tree (from the Anglo-Saxon *withig*) and the word crops up in numerous places across these moors. Though the summit sits on the disappointing tussocky top of Round Hill, just off the Pennine Way, it is a fascinating and evocative moorland. The northern section is well known as the Brontë moors, sheltering in the lee of its barren heights various notable sites for the literary tourist. Yet it is away from these busy places that the real character of these moors can be found – indeed, combined with Boulsworth Hill, this represents the largest expanse of open moorland in the county. However, much of Wadsworth and Stanbury Moors is still dominated by grouse shooting interests who are possibly still struggling to come to terms with the notion of open access land.

Withins Height from Walhsaw Dean

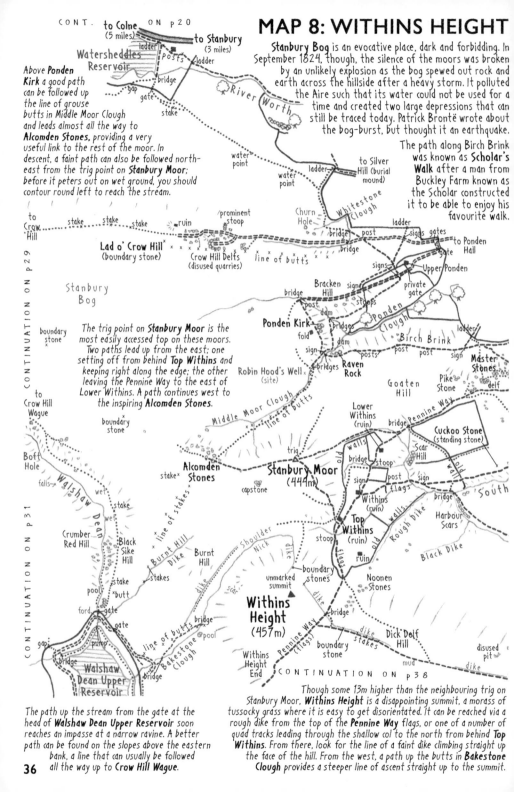

Stanbury Bog is an evocative place, dark and forbidding. In September 1824, though, the silence of the moors was broken by an unlikely explosion as the bog spewed out rock and earth across the hillside after a heavy storm. It polluted the Aire such that its water could not be used for a time and created two large depressions that can still be traced today. Patrick Brontë wrote about the bog-burst, but thought it an earthquake.

The path along Birch Brink was known as Scholar's Walk after a man from Buckley Farm known as the Scholar constructed it to be able to enjoy his favourite walk.

Above **Ponden Kirk** a good path can be followed up the line of grouse butts in Middle Moor Clough and leads almost all the way to **Alcomden Stones**, providing a very useful link to the rest of the moor. In descent, a faint path can also be followed north-east from the trig point on **Stanbury Moor**; before it peters out on wet ground, you should contour round left to reach the stream.

The trig point on **Stanbury Moor** is the most easily accessed top on these moors. Two paths lead up from the east; one setting off from behind **Top Withins** and keeping right along the edge; the other leaving the Pennine Way to the east of **Lower Withins**. A path continues west to the inspiring **Alcomden Stones**.

The path up the stream from the gate at the head of **Walshaw Dean Upper Reservoir** soon reaches an impasse at a narrow ravine. A better path can be found on the slopes above the eastern bank, a line that can usually be followed all the way up to **Crow Hill Wague**.

Though some 13m higher than the neighbouring trig on Stanbury Moor, **Withins Height** is a disappointing summit, a morass of tussocky grass where it is easy to get disorientated. It can be reached via a rough dike from the top of the **Pennine Way** flags, or one of a number of quad tracks leading through the shallow col to the north from behind **Top Withins**. From there, look for the line of a faint dike climbing straight up the face of the hill. From the west, a path up the butts in **Bakestone Clough** provides a steeper line of ascent straight up to the summit.

NORTH (Haworth & Stanbury Moors)

The north-eastern side of Withins Height leads down towards Haworth and Stanbury; these are the well-trodden moors popularised by the writing of the Brontë sisters. Away from the tourist trail up South Dean Beck though, the wild charm of the moors remains and there is much to be discovered.

The large boundary stone known as **Lad o' Crow Hill** (or Lancashire Lad) marks a corner of the county boundary on the ridge near Crow Hill Delfs. It is inscribed 'lad or scarr on crow hill' and is said to mark the place where a young lad died having been caught in a storm. Though he was Lancastrian, the authorities there disputed that he had perished on Yorkshire soil and, when eventually they did bury him in Trawden, Lancashire claimed this chunk of the moor as their own. Hence both the words *lad* and *scar* are taken to mean boundary stone. However, it was also known as Laddock Royle, which suggests it may have been an older site with Lad coming from the Celtic word *lladd*, meaning to destroy or slaughter.

Lad o' Crow Hill

The **Brontë Chair** is a distinctively shaped hunk of rock where it is said the young Brontë sisters used to sit and tell each other the stories that would later become part of their famous books. If the nearby **Brontë Bridge** comes as a disappointment, it is because the original stone clapper bridge was washed away by a flash flood in 1989.

There was a smallpox isolation hospital at **Upper Heights** in the late 19th century.

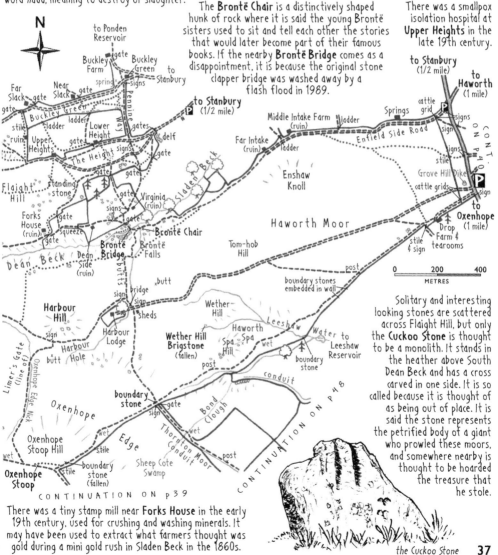

Solitary and interesting looking stones are scattered across Flaight Hill, but only the **Cuckoo Stone** is thought to be a monolith. It stands in the heather above South Dean Beck and has a cross carved in one side. It is so called because it is thought of as being out of place. It is said the stone represents the petrified body of a giant who prowled these moors, and somewhere nearby is thought to be hoarded the treasure that he stole.

the Cuckoo Stone

There was a tiny stamp mill near **Forks House** in the early 19th century, used for crushing and washing minerals. It may have been used to extract what farmers thought was gold during a mini gold rush in Sladen Beck in the 1860s.

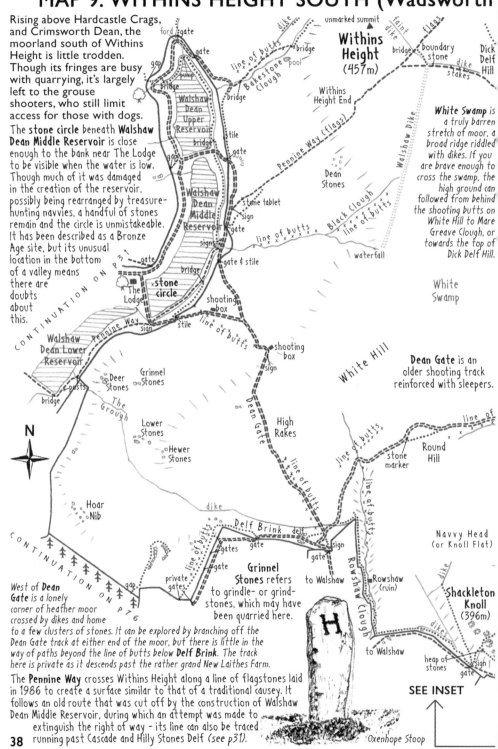

Rising above Hardcastle Crags, and Crimsworth Dean, the moorland south of Withins Height is little trodden. Though its fringes are busy with quarrying, it's largely left to the grouse shooters, who still limit access for those with dogs.

The **stone circle** beneath **Walshaw Dean Middle Reservoir** is close enough to the bank near The Lodge to be visible when the water is low. Though much of it was damaged in the creation of the reservoir, possibly being rearranged by treasure-hunting navvies, a handful of stones remain and the circle is unmistakeable. It has been described as a Bronze Age site, but its unusual location in the bottom of a valley means there are doubts about this.

White Swamp is a truly barren stretch of moor, a broad ridge riddled with dikes. If you are brave enough to cross the swamp, the high ground can be followed from behind the shooting butts on White Hill to Mare Greave Clough, or towards the top of Dick Delf Hill.

Dean Gate is an older shooting track reinforced with sleepers.

West of **Dean Gate** is a lonely corner of heather moor crossed by dikes and home to a few clusters of stones. It can be explored by branching off the Dean Gate track at either end of the moor, but there is little in the way of paths beyond the line of butts below **Delf Brink**. The track here is private as it descends past the rather grand New Laithes Farm.

Grinnel Stones refers to grindle- or grind-stones, which may have been quarried here.

The **Pennine Way** crosses Withins Height along a line of flagstones laid in 1986 to create a surface similar to that of a traditional causey. It follows an old route that was cut off by the construction of Walshaw Dean Middle Reservoir, during which an attempt was made to extinguish the right of way – its line can also be traced running past Cascade and Hilly Stones Delf (see p31).

38

SEE INSET

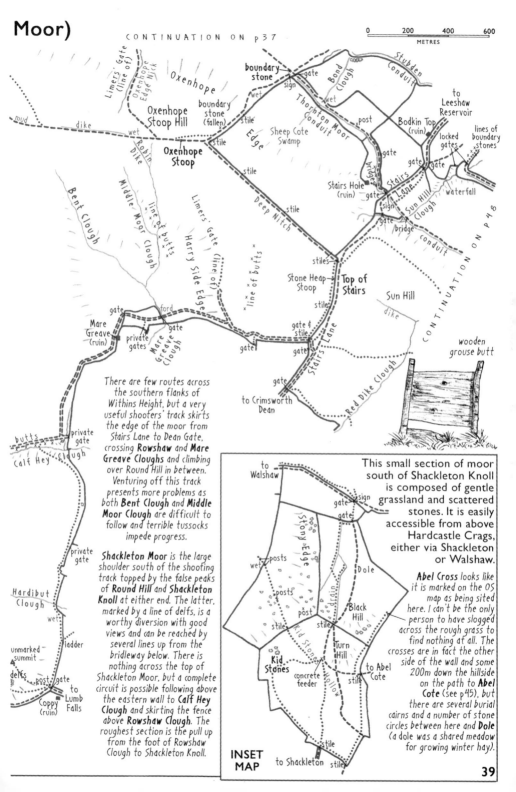

Moor)

CONTINUATION ON p37

There are few routes across the southern flanks of Withins Height, but a very useful shooters' track skirts the edge of the moor from Stairs Lane to Dean Gate, crossing Rowshaw and Mare Greave Cloughs and climbing over Round Hill in between. Venturing off this track presents more problems as both Bent Clough and Middle Moor Clough are difficult to follow and terrible tussocks impede progress.

Shackleton Moor is the large shoulder south of the shooting track topped by the false peaks of Round Hill and Shackleton Knoll at either end. The latter, marked by a line of delfs, is a worthy diversion with good views and can be reached by several lines up from the bridleway below. There is nothing across the top of Shackleton Moor, but a complete circuit is possible following above the eastern wall to Calf Hey Clough and skirting the fence above Rowshaw Clough. The roughest section is the pull up from the foot of Rowshaw Clough to Shackleton Knoll.

This small section of moor south of Shackleton Knoll is composed of gentle grassland and scattered stones. It is easily accessible from above Hardcastle Crags, either via Shackleton or Walshaw.

Abel Cross looks like it is marked on the OS map as being sited here. I can't be the only person to have slogged across the rough grass to find nothing at all. The crosses are in fact the other side of the wall and some 200m down the hillside on the path to Abel Cote (see p45), but there are several burial cairns and a number of stone circles between here and Dole (a dole was a shared meadow for growing winter hay).

INSET MAP

39

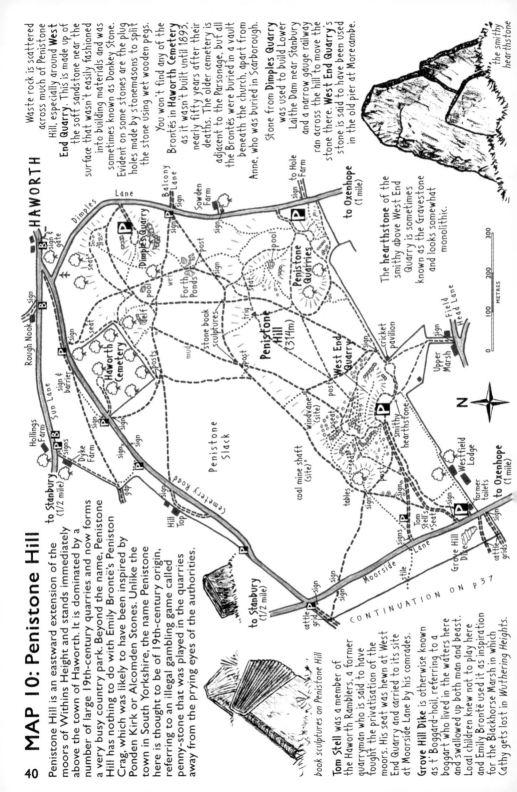

MAP 10: Penistone Hill

Penistone Hill is an eastward extension of the moors of Withins Height and stands immediately above the town of Haworth. It is dominated by a number of large 19th-century quarries and now forms a very busy country park. Beyond the name, Penistone Hill has nothing to do with Emily Brontë's Peniston Crag, which was likely to have been inspired by Ponden Kirk or Alcomden Stones. Unlike the town in South Yorkshire, the name Penistone here is thought to be of 19th-century origin, referring to an illegal gambling game called penny-stone that was played in the quarries away from the prying eyes of the authorities.

Tom Stell was a member of the Haworth Ramblers, a former quarryman who is said to have fought the privatisation of the moors. His seat was hewn at West End Quarry and carried to its site at Moorside Lane by his comrades.

Grove Hill Dike is otherwise known as t'Boggard-hoil, referring to a boggart who lived in the waters here and swallowed up both man and beast. Local children knew not to play here and Emily Brontë used it as inspiration for the Blackhorse Marsh in which Cathy gets lost in *Wuthering Heights*.

book sculptures on Penistone Hill

Waste rock is scattered across much of Penistone Hill, especially around **West End Quarry**. This is made up of the soft sandstone near the surface that wasn't easily fashioned into building materials and was sometimes known as Donkey Stone. Evident on some stones are the plug holes made by stonemasons to split the stone using wet wooden pegs.

You won't find any of the Brontës in **Haworth Cemetery** as it wasn't built until 1893, nearly fifty years after their deaths. The older cemetery is adjacent to the Parsonage, but all the Brontës were buried in a vault beneath the church, apart from Anne, who was buried in Scarborough.

Stone from **Dimples Quarry** was used to build Lower Laithe Dam near Stanbury and a narrow gauge railway ran across the hill to move the stone there. **West End Quarry**'s stone is said to have been used in the old pier at Morecambe.

The **hearthstone** of the smithy above West End Quarry is sometimes known as the Gravestone and looks somewhat monolithic.

the smithy hearthstone

HAWORTH

Dimples Lane
Balcony Lane
sign
seat
Sowden Farm
sign
sign to Hole Farm
Dimples Quarry
P
seat
wet
Forth Ponds
pool
post
sign
pool
Penistone Quarries
to Oxenhope (1 mile)
Self
pool
Stone book sculptures
sign
seat
trig
Rough Nook
sign
B
seat
Haworth Cemetery
posts
mud
post
Penistone Hill (314m)
West End Quarry
cricket pavilion
Upper Marsh
Field Head Lane
sign
Hollings Farm
Sun Lane
sign & barrier
P
sign
sign
gap
Penistone Slack
coal mine shaft (site) x
Windvane (site)
post
Smithy hearthstone
P
seat
Westfield Lodge
to Oxenhope (1 mile)
B
signs
Dyke Farm
sign
sign
to Stanbury (1/2 mile)
Cemetery Road
Hill Top
P
tables x
sign
seat
sign
former toilets
P
sign
to Stanbury (1/2 mile)
P
cattle grid
sign
sign
Moorside Lane
stile
Tom Stell's Seat
P
signs
Grove Hill Dike
cattle grids
CONTINUATION ON P37

N

0 100 200 300
METRES

TOP WITHINS & THE BRONTËS

It is impossible to overlook the Brontës' influence on Haworth and its surrounding moors. They are surely the single biggest reason that people venture out onto the West Yorkshire Moors, and their story is bound up with our imagination of these wild spaces. It has been suggested that the Brontës' associations with the eastern slopes of Withins Height was one of the reasons why pylons were not erected here and why there is still a footpath across Walshaw Dean, which now carries the Pennine Way but which the water board attempted to close with the construction of the reservoirs.

Though the Brontë sisters lives were tragically short, their ill health didn't stop them walking the moors above Haworth, most frequently visiting the bridge and falls on West Dean Beck to read and write each other stories. Their poetry is laden with images of the moorland and Emily Brontë's *Wuthering Heights* is the most famous description of life on the edge of the Pennine wilderness.

Top Withins is a proper Brontë pilgrimage site, so much so that the signs leading up there are marked in both Chinese and English. When the pilgrims reach their destination, they are faced with a concrete-reinforced shack and a plaque explaining that the building bears no resemblance to that described in *Wuthering Heights*. It is widely held that Emily Brontë took the Jacobean mansion at High Sunderland (near Halifax) and transported it here to the location of Top Withins to create her Wuthering Heights, home of the Earnshaws. Sure enough, wind howls through the walls and the wild moor presses closely in on Top Withins. However, there the romance ends.

There has been a building at Top Withins since the fourteenth century, though the current ruins are those of a seventeenth-century farmhouse. Top Withins was last lived in by a Haworth man, Ernest Roddy, who was advised by doctors to move to the country after being gassed in the war. He farmed poultry here until 1926, when he returned to Haworth. Yorkshire Water acquired Top Withins by chance as part of the catchwater for Lower Laithe Reservoir, and it has slowly decomposed since. It was listed as a historical building by English Heritage in 1974, apparently in error, but the concrete botch job on its restoration sealed its fate as little more than a remote picnic spot. Now de-listed, it is the least glorious ruin in all of the Pennines and one of the few places where it is hard to find solitude. Go to Coolam, Red Dikes, Rastrick Greave, or even Lower Withins, and imagine how atmospheric this spot might have been.

A far better Brontë pilgrimage is to wander the empty moorland spaces of Oxenhope Edge, Withins Height and Stanbury Moor, where the landscape will impress a far more convincing Wuthering Heights on your imagination, as it did for Emily Brontë. If you're very lucky you'll see her ghost wandering the moor as so many others have claimed, causing *The Yorkshire Post* mischievously to claim there was a need for 'a first-aid post to be set on the edge of the moors to revive people'.

Top Withins today

ROUTE 7: HAWORTH & STANBURY MOORS

Distance: 9½ miles (15.5km)

Ascent: 450m

Difficulty: Moderate

Parking: Various pay car parks in Haworth. Free car parks by Penistone Hill Country Park (off Moorside Lane).

Public Transport: Haworth is on the B1, B2 & B3 bus routes from Keighley, the B3 also coming from Hebden Bridge.

Character: An exploration of the wuthering moors that inspired Emily Brontë, but one that intentionally stays largely from the well-trodden tourist route to Top Withins. The route takes in the tops of Penistone Hill and Stanbury Moor, the outcrops of Alcomden Stones and Ponden Kirk, as well as the Brontë Parsonage and Ponden Hall, before returning via the attractive hilltop village of Stanbury.

❺ Turn right before the capstone at the heart of **Alcomden Stones** and follow a very faint path down into Middle Dean Clough. A better path is picked up there, following a line of butts down the right side of the stream. Cross a bridge, then continue down the stream until it steepens; fork left before a sign to stay along the top of the slope opposite Raven Rock. Pass the crag of **Ponden Kirk** before reaching a vehicle track which leads right around the head of Ponden Clough. At a sign, fork left down the side of an old wall, then carry straight on by further signs near **Upper Ponden** to reach another vehicle track.

Ponden Reservoir was built in the 1870s as a compensation reservoir for the millowners in the valley below, as all the water from Middle Moor Clough and Stanbury Bog was taken via an underground conduit to Watersheddles Reservoir to supply Keighley with drinking water.

❻ Follow the track to the right off the moor and down towards **Ponden Reservoir**. Turn right at a T-junction to pass **Ponden Hall** and follow the reservoir's shore round. Just beyond the dam wall, turn right at a sign onto a walled path leading up to Buckley Farm. Turn left at the top, following a track along the top of the hill. At its end, turn left along Back Lane, which soon joins the road heading into **Stanbury** village, beautifully perched on a ridge above Lower Laithe Reservoir.

Alcomden Stones (also known as Oakenden Stones) stand on the brink of the wilderness; though a cosy path leads here from Stanbury Moor, there is little beyond but Stanbury Bog. Despite suggestions of druidical sacrifices and the presence of a dolmen (with a capstone forming a small room), it is now widely acknowledged that these are entirely natural features. Ponden Kirk is usually thought to be the Peniston Crag in Emily Brontë's *Wuthering Heights*, though in many ways this isolated and far wilder setting makes more sense.

❹ Soon after **South Dean Beck**, you join the Brontë super-highway, a flagged path leading left up the hill past the ruins of Withins to **Top Withins**, the inspiration for Wuthering Heights (see p41 for more info). Behind the building, pick up a faint path bearing right up the slope above. Keep right along the edge to reach the trig point on **Stanbury Moor**. Bear left to continue to **Alcomden Stones**, an impressive collection of stones on the edge of the wilderness of Stanbury Bog.

the capstone at Alcomden Stones

FROM HAWORTH

The crag of **Ponden Kirk** rears up dramatically at the head of Ponden Clough, sheltering beneath it is a small gap in the rock long associated with marriage rituals. It was said that if a maiden crawled through she would be married before the year is out. There were also suggestions of sexual rituals, Halliwell Sutcliffe writing of 'this dark kirk of the wilderness, at which Pagan mothers once worshipped lustily'.

Robin Hood's Well is just one of three adjacent springs in Middle Moor Clough, the others being known as Little John's Well and Will Scarlett's Well. **Haworth Spa** is another well at the head of Leeshaw Water, and was the site of an annual church pilgrimage from Haworth on Spaw Sunday with a band playing sacred music there.

❶ From the car park by the Brontë Parsonage, follow a cobbled path left past the museum and church. Reaching the top of **Haworth**'s Main Street, turn sharp right on a path above the **Black Bull** (signed towards Penistone Hill). This passes above the other large central car park, before you turn right at a sign to head up past Balcony Farm. Across the road at the top, fork left as far as a sign, then turn left. Bear right straight after to climb up onto **Penistone Hill**, its trig point soon visible off to the right.

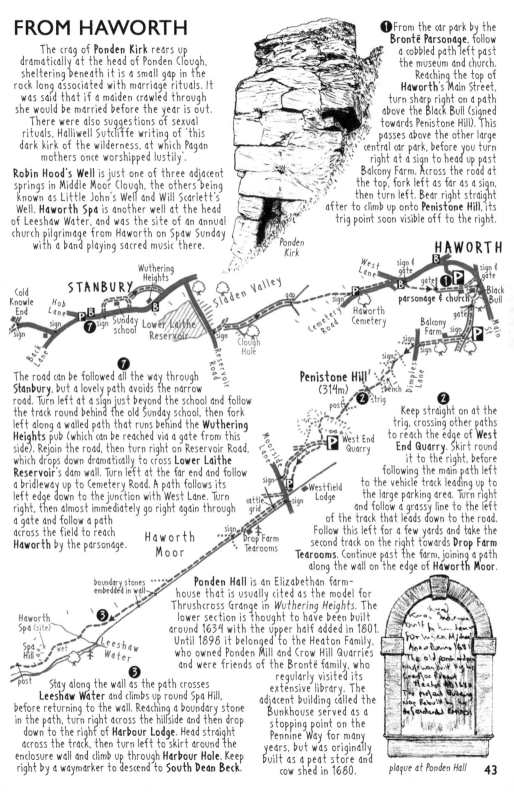

Ponden Kirk

❼ The road can be followed all the way through **Stanbury**, but a lovely path avoids the narrow road. Turn left at a sign just beyond the school and follow the track round behind the old Sunday school, then fork left along a walled path that runs behind the **Wuthering Heights** pub (which can be reached via a gate from this side). Rejoin the road, then turn right on Reservoir Road, which drops down dramatically to cross **Lower Laithe Reservoir**'s dam wall. Turn left at the far end and follow a bridleway up to Cemetery Road. A path follows its left edge down to the junction with West Lane. Turn right, then almost immediately go right again through a gate and follow a path across the field to reach **Haworth** by the parsonage.

❷ Keep straight on at the trig, crossing other paths to reach the edge of **West End Quarry**. Skirt round it to the right, before following the main path left to the vehicle track leading up to the large parking area. Turn right and follow a grassy line to the left of the track that leads down to the road. Follow this left for a few yards and take the second track on the right towards **Drop Farm Tearooms**. Continue past the farm, joining a path along the wall on the edge of **Haworth Moor**.

Ponden Hall is an Elizabethan farm-house that is usually cited as the model for Thrushcross Grange in *Wuthering Heights*. The lower section is thought to have been built around 1634 with the upper half added in 1801. Until 1898 it belonged to the Heaton Family, who owned Ponden Mill and Crow Hill Quarries and were friends of the Brontë family, who regularly visited its extensive library. The adjacent building called the Bunkhouse served as a stopping point on the Pennine Way for many years, but was originally built as a peat store and cow shed in 1680.

❸ Stay along the wall as the path crosses **Leeshaw Water** and climbs up round Spa Hill, before returning to the wall. Reaching a boundary stone in the path, turn right across the hillside and then drop down to the right of **Harbour Lodge**. Head straight across the track, then turn left to skirt around the enclosure wall and climb up through **Harbour Hole**. Keep right by a waymarker to descend to **South Dean Beck**.

plaque at Ponden Hall

43

ROUTE 8: WITHINS HEIGHT FROM MIDGEHOLE

Distance: 10½ miles (17.1km)

Ascent: 490m

Difficulty: Strenuous

Parking: National Trust pay car park at Midgehole.

Public Transport: Hebden Bridge, only a mile from Midgehole, is well served by trains and buses, but sadly the 906 bus no longer runs to Midgehole.

Character: This route combines the beautiful National Trust woodlands at Hardcastle Crags with some of the more remote corners of the moorlands above Hebden Bridge. While most of the navigation is straightforward, the section between Shackleton Knoll and Oxenhope Stoop has a couple of short pathless sections, but offers a more satisfying route than the traditional traipse up Stairs. The return route is simpler, following the well-used Hebden Bridge to Haworth walk in large part.

Note: No dogs allowed on most of the moorland section of this route.

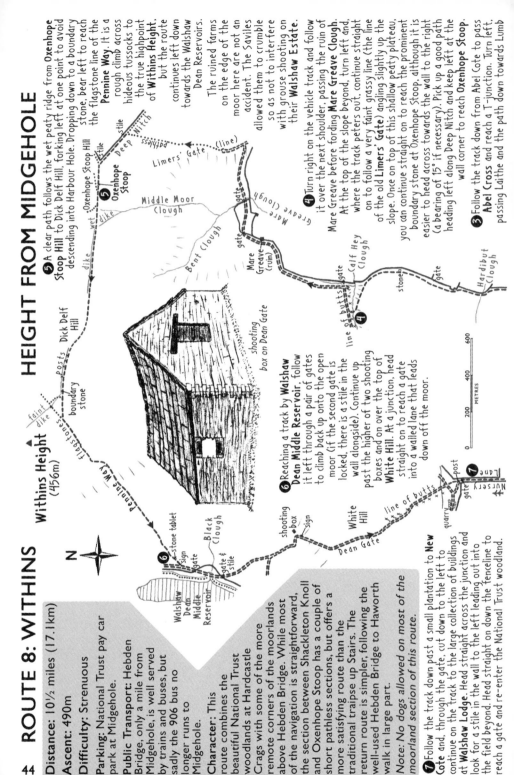

5 A clear path follows the wet peaty ridge from **Oxenhope Stoop Hill** to **Dick Delf Hill**, forking left at one point to avoid descending into Harbour Hole. Dropping down to a boundary stone, bear left to reach the flagstone line of the **Pennine Way**. It is a rough climb across hideous tussocks to the true highpoint of **Withins Height**, but the route continues left down towards the Walshaw Dean Reservoirs.

The ruined farms on the edge of the moor here are not an accident. The Saviles allowed them to crumble so as not to interfere with grouse shooting on their **Walshaw Estate**.

4 Turn right on the vehicle track and follow it over the next shoulder, passing the ruin of **Mare Greave** before fording **Mare Greave Clough**. At the top of the slope beyond, turn left and, where the track peters out, continue straight on to follow a very faint grassy line (the line of the old **Limers' Gate**) angling slightly up the slope. Once on top of this shallow peaty plateau, you can continue straight on to reach the prominent boundary stone at Oxenhope Stoop, although it is easier to head across towards the wall to the right (a bearing of 15° if necessary). Pick up a good path heading left along Deep Nitch and keep left at the wall corner to reach **Oxenhope Stoop**.

3 Follow the track down from Abel Cote to pass **Abel Cross** and reach a T-junction. Turn left, passing Laithe and the path down towards Lumb

6 Reaching a track by **Walshaw Dean Middle Reservoir**, follow it left through a pair of gates to climb back up onto the open moor (if the second gate is locked, there is a stile in the wall alongside). Continue up, past the higher of two shooting boxes and on over the top of **White Hill**. At a junction, head straight down to reach a gate into a walled lane that leads down off the moor.

7 Follow the track down past a small plantation to **New Cote** and, through the gate, cut down to the left to continue on the track to the large collection of buildings at **Walshaw Lodge**. Head straight across the junction and look for a stile in the wall to the left leading out into the field beyond. Head straight on down the fenceline to reach a gate and re-enter the National Trust woodland.

Abel Cross is actually a pair of stone crosses, nick-named Cain & Abel, or Mourning & Vanity. They probably served as wayside markers, but legend says they mark the graves of two rivals who fought over a woman. She was the White Lady who haunts Lumb Falls after jumping from the bridge there (see p54).

Bridge, before turning left up a walled lane by the ruined farm at **Nook**. Reaching the edge of the moor, turn immediately right on a faint path that hugs the wall. Beyond a ladder stile the path is less defined, but runs along the wall then parallel to it. Keep an eye out for snares, which the gamekeepers have cynically laid in the path here. Reaching **Calf Hey Clough**, the path angles gently down to the large grouse-shooting track.

2 Turn right into the cluster of farmhouses that make up **Shackleton** and look for a stile to the left of the far building. A path follows the wall then crosses an open field to a gateway. Stay on the right-hand side of the fence then old wall as it curves around the hillside with great views over Crimsworth Dean. A stone stile deposits you on the opposite side of the wall close to **Abel Cote**. Pass through a couple of gates to join a track immediately to the left of the farm.

1 From the end of the road at **Midgehole**, take the bridleway signed to the right from the entrance to the National Trust property. Where this reaches a track, continue straight across to follow a path along the edge of the woods. This soon turns right into a narrow walled walkway and the old causeway leads all the way up to the top of the woods past **Slurring Rock**. Keep right to reach a stile that leads into another narrow walled route up to the track by **Shackleton**.

Sitting outside the Blue Pig on a summer evening, it's hard to imagine **Midgehole** isn't named after the midges gnawing on you. However, it probably refers to a hollow where there was a manure dump or a boggy site. The **Blue Pig** itself is thought to have taken its name from the original colour of the Liberal Party in the 19th century, when pigs were a nickname for working men's clubs.

Walshaw Lodge was transformed from a small hamlet into the Saviles' shooting retreat in 1850 and has since become the family home.

The **Hardcastle Crags** (or Hills) themselves are a collection of landslipped rocky knolls further up the track from Gibson Mill. The river and the woods hold the real charm here, the latter being partially planted as a verdant entrance to the Saviles' shooting estate in the 19th century. Much of the woods were given to the National Trust in 1948.

Slurring Rock stands near the top of the woods below Shackleton and is marked with grooves where children slid (or slurred) down the rock.

Gibson Mill was an early 19th-century cotton mill, originally called Lord Holme Mill. In the early part of the 20th century it was used as a leisure facility with a dancing hall, roller skating rink, restaurants, boating lake and refreshment kiosks.

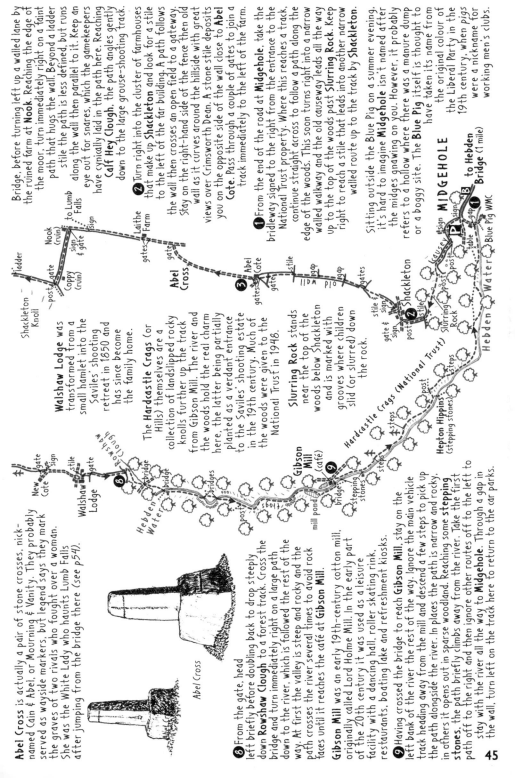

Abel Cross

8 From the gate, head left briefly before doubling back to drop steeply down **Rowshaw Clough** to a forest track. Cross the bridge and turn immediately right on a large path down to the river, which is followed the rest of the way. At first the valley is steep and rocky and the path crosses the river several times to avoid rock faces until it reaches the café at Gibson Mill.

9 Having crossed the bridge to reach **Gibson Mill**, stay on the left bank of the river the rest of the way. Ignore the main vehicle track heading away from the mill and descend a few steps to pick up a path alongside the river. In places the path is narrow and rocky, in others it opens out in sparse woodland. Reaching some **stepping stones**, the path briefly climbs away from the river. Take the first path off to the right and then ignore other routes off to the left to stay with the river all the way to **Midgehole**. Through a gap in the wall, turn left on the track here to return to the car parks.

45

THE RESERVOIRS OF WEST YORKSHIRE

Reservoirs are such an important part of the Pennine moorland landscape it is hard to imagine the scene without them. Yet, until the nineteenth century, drinking water came from the natural springs and wells that abounded in the area. The earliest dams on the moorland were usually small affairs constructed by groups of mill-owners who wanted to ensure a steady supply of water to their mills when the streams were low. Some of these can still be seen (Gaddings Dam, the Cold Edge Dams, Noah Dale Dam and Flints Reservoir); others were later buried under other reservoirs (Wessenden Old Reservoir, and Lingards Dam beneath Deer Hill Reservoir). The construction of the Rochdale and Huddersfield Narrow Canals in the 1790s required a number of reservoirs to be built to keep the water levels topped up, though most of these were still fairly small (indeed sometimes too small, as Thomas Telford observed about Brun Clough Reservoir near Standedge).

From the mid 19th century, towns became responsible for their own drinking water. Victoria Reservoir in Halifax was one of the first constructed by a water corporation, in 1848, and was known as 'the people's reservoir', though it was insufficient to meet the needs of the growing town. The corporations held powers of compulsory land purchase and set about clearing entire catchments in the hills to provide clean and safe drinking water. So paranoid were they about the possibility of pollution (and particularly the spread of typhoid), that they often sought to extinguish footpaths and remove *de facto* access agreements around these new reservoirs.

In the late 1890s and 1900s the demand for water increased dramatically and many reservoir projects were initiated. For the first time experienced labour was in short supply and navvies were known to move from project to project depending on weather, pay and conditions. Small wooden huts or alternative lodgings, often in mills that were due to be drowned, were usually provided and led to small shanties for a couple of hundred families springing up for a few years. The Navvy Mission Society was established in 1877 and built mission rooms at every site, and there was even a small church at the navvy settlement for Green Withens Reservoir above Oxygrains Bridge. There was usually a store and occasionally other facilities existed, such as a library, workshop or hospital. The latter was usually forced upon the contractor after a spate of accidents, as it was at Dawson City near Heptonstall, probably the largest and most notorious shanty, accommodating up to 540 people.

Tramways were often built around reservoir sites to move materials and men. Though stone could usually be quarried close by (think of the excavated faces above Blakeley and Deer Hill Reservoirs), puddle clay was often harder to come by. This watertight material was needed to fill the cut-offs at the foot of the dams and necessitated the construction of many of these tramways and often steep inclines into or out of the valleys. Initially trams were pulled by horses (as at Widdop) or even by hand (at Shiny Brook Clough), but steam locomotives were available by the time the Walshaw Dean Reservoirs were constructed in the 1900s, providing the most spectacular tramway of all as it crossed high above Blake Dean on a 100ft-high trestle bridge *(see p76 for more information)*.

Dams regularly leaked when they were first filled, necessitating further work by the contractors. Enoch Tempest was bankrupted by leaks on Walshaw Dean Lower and Middle Reservoirs and died of a stroke shortly before the work was completed nearly thirteen years after it began. Bilberry Reservoir never stopped leaking and burst in 1852, flooding Holmfirth and killing eighty-one people, and the collapse of Swellands Reservoir's dam killed six people in Marsden in 1810.

Over the years the natural flow of water has been so altered by human intervention that it is often hard to work out where it ends up. As well as the reservoirs, catchwaters, regulating drains and conduits take water from one side of a hill round (or sometimes through) to the other. Many reservoirs simply serve as compensation reservoirs for others, ensuring that as much water as possible can be stored for a dry spell, and there is such a maze of drains and culverts left over from the industrial boom that tracing any watercourse can often prove impossible.

CHAPTER 5 – WHITE HILL

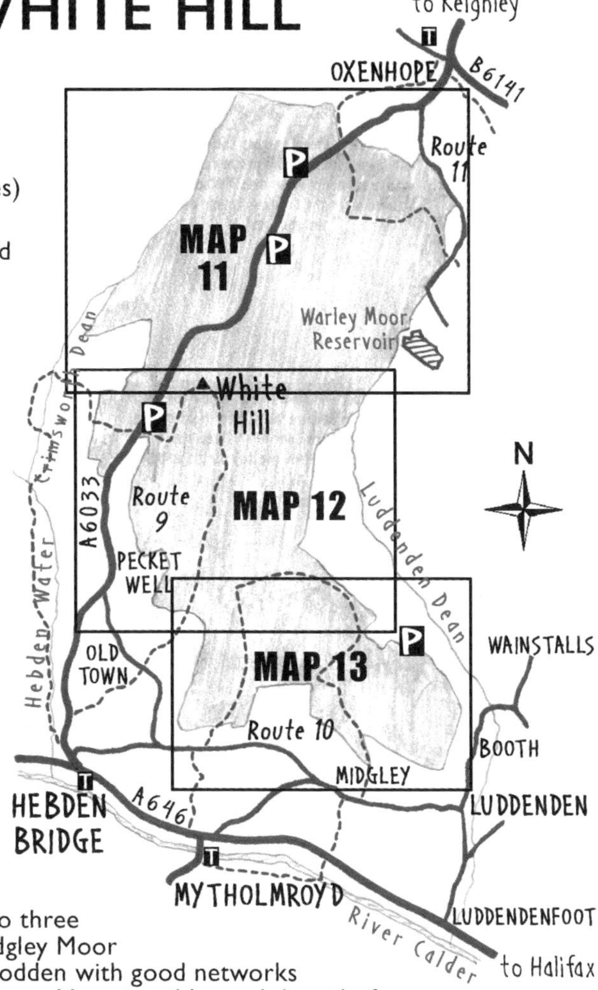

Height: 446m

Grid Ref: SE007313

Map Sheet: OL21 (South Pennines)

Access: No dogs on Oxenhope Moor (Map 11) during nesting bird season (1st March to 31st July).

Public Transport: Hebden Bridge & Mytholmroyd are on the main Caldervale train and bus routes. Other useful bus services include Halifax to Midgley (574), Hebden Bridge to Crimsworth turning circle (594), Hebden Bridge to Old Town (595), and Hebden Bridge to Keighley via Oxenhope (B3).

White Hill is the true summit of the expanse of moor that stretches north from the Calder Valley above Hebden Bridge, Mytholmroyd and Luddenden-foot, all the way over to Oxenhope and Warley Moor Reservoir. There are more natural hilltops at High Brown Knoll, Sheep Stones Edge and Crow Hill, but the broad grassy ridge above the A6033 outflanks them all. I have split the moor into three sections north to south. Both Midgley Moor and Wadsworth Moor are well trodden with good networks of tracks, whereas most of Oxenhope Moor is wilder and devoid of well-used paths. Each yields its own delights, whether the ancient burial mounds and imposing boundary stones of Midgley Moor, or the weathered rock caps and peat groughs of Oxenhope Moor.

to Keighley

OXENHOPE
B6141

Route 11

MAP 11

Warley Moor Reservoir

Crimsworth Dean

▲White Hill

Route 9

MAP 12

Luddenden Dean

PECKET WELL

A6033

Hebden Water

OLD TOWN

MAP 13

WAINSTALLS

Route 10

BOOTH

MIDGLEY

HEBDEN BRIDGE

A646

LUDDENDEN

MYTHOLMROYD

River Calder

LUDDENDENFOOT

to Halifax

N

White Hill and Wadsworth Moor from Withins Height

47

MAP 11: WHITE HILL NORTH (Oxenhope Moor)

The high moor north of High Brown Knoll and White Hill is a particularly bleak plateau of rough grass and peat bog. It is the only area from which one looks to the moor's summit as a natural high point. Even then, the Winny Stone steals the limelight on the tramp south from Cock Hill. This natural rampart is crested by beautifully weathered hunks of gritstone and is part of the same lump of land as White Hill, yet stands a foot or two lower. There are few other landmarks, yet it is an area worth exploring; faint sheeptracks appear and disappear, especially around the moor's fringes, where paths along the catchwater drains offer some respite from the undulating tussocks of the high moor.

the Winny Stone

The **Winny Stone** is one of the most striking features across the whole of White Hill, especially as it sits amid the most barren stretch of the moor. It was previously known as the **Hoyning Stone**, which is referred to as 'ancient' in 1594. It has been optimistically suggested Winny is a mispronunciation of Honing, yet *whin* is gorse and the Whinny Moor in Yorkshire folklore is the thorn-covered land across which the soul must travel after death. Whinstone is also a quarrying term, describing a hard rock that makes a particular sound when struck with a hammer, particularly chert, which is found in erratics on these moors and used for some of the earliest flints.

The A6033 over **Cock Hill** was built as the Hebden Bridge to Lees Turnpike in 1814, replacing an older route over Stairs. It was a notoriously dangerous route in bad weather. In 1831 Ben Foster, a yarn manufacturer from Denholme, lost his way on Cock Hill in a blizzard and stumbled across the moor to his frozen death. Subsequently 185 whitewashed stone stoops (with black tops that were visible in snow) lined the roadside, some of which can still be seen near the top (though now unpainted).

A useful but faint path skirts the edge of the moor above the A6033, becoming steadily more difficult to follow beyond **Clattering Edge**. It does link up with the track past the wonderfully named **Bedlam** and soldiers on below Leaning Grooves Edge to reach the stile at the top of **Cock Hill**.

The summit of **White Hill** is a broad grassy lump with a tiny cairn on top. No paths lead there, but it is easily reached from the faint paths along Clattering Edge or between the **Winny Stone** and High Brown Knoll.

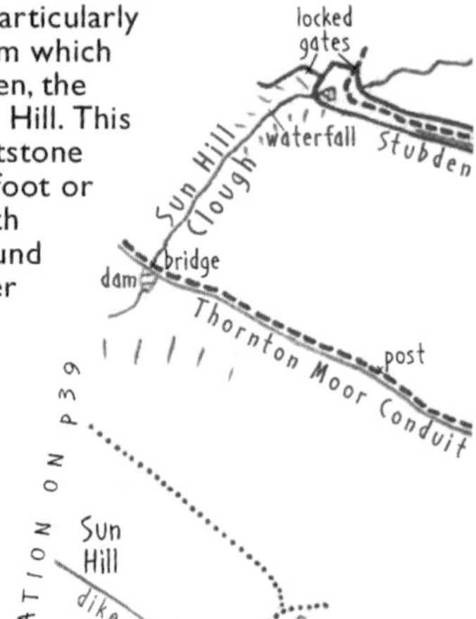

Map labels:

locked gates

Sun Hill Clough — waterfall — Stubden

bridge

dam

Thornton Moor Conduit

post

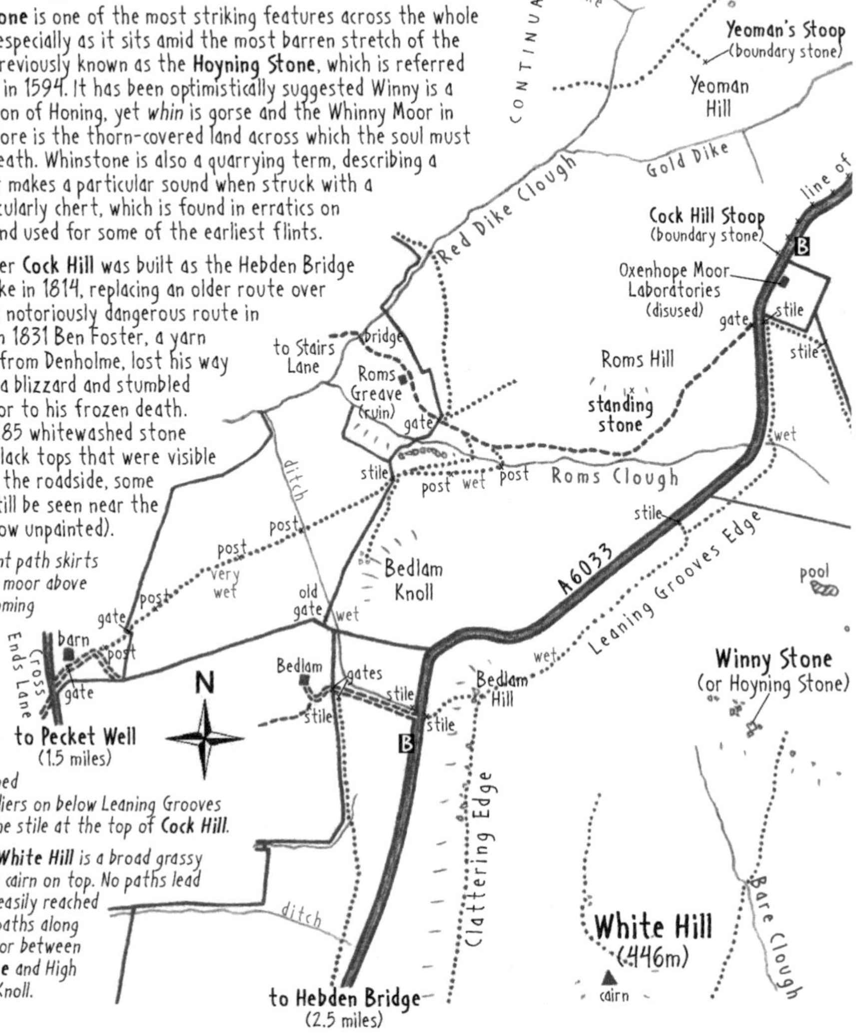

CONTINUATION ON P39

Sun Hill — dike

Yeoman's Stoop (boundary stone)

Yeoman Hill

Gold Dike

line of

Red Dike Clough

Cock Hill Stoop (boundary stone) — B

Oxenhope Moor Laboratories (disused) — gate — stile — stile

Roms Hill

to Stairs Lane — bridge

Roms Greave (ruin) — gate

standing stone

wet

stile — post wet — post — Roms Clough — stile

ditch

post — post — very wet — old gate — wet — Bedlam Knoll

post — post

A6033

Leaning Grooves Edge

pool

gate — barn — post — gate

Cross Ends Lane

Bedlam — gates — stile — Bedlam Hill — Bedlam Hill — wet

to Pecket Well (1.5 miles) — stile — stile — B

N

Winny Stone (or Hoyning Stone)

Clattering Edge

Bare Clough

ditch

to Hebden Bridge (2.5 miles) — cairn

White Hill (446m)

Oxenhope Moor Laboratories have been abandoned to the elements by the University of Bradford. The collection of buildings and satellite dishes originally served as a navigational aid station during WWII.

A permissive bridleway along **Thornton Moor Conduit** provides the only firm path on the north side of Oxenhope Moor and the easiest link with Withins Height. West of the road, the ridge from **Cock Hill** to **Yeoman Hill** and **Sun Hill** is crossed by long dikes and can be navigated using these and the boundary stones, though the ground is rarely easy.

The prominent cairn on **Stake Hill** draws you across the moor despite barely marking a rise in the plateau. The ground is not easy going, especially around **Great Grough Hole**, a mess of dark peat that lives up to its name. It is reached most easily from the top of **Near Peat Lane**, heading straight on over a stile and up the fenceline. From the **Waggon & Horses** a path heads up the hillside to the conduit. If you continue straight across then bear right over a stile you cross an enclosure towards the cairn (see p64 for detailed description of this route).

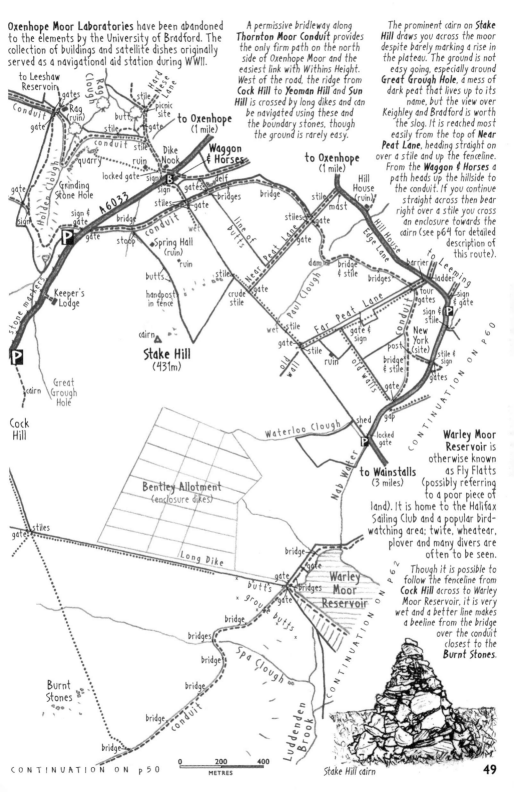

to Leeshaw Reservoir
Rag Clough
Hard Nese Lane
gates
stile
picnic site
Rag (ruin)
butts
stile
gate
to Oxenhope (1 mile)
Conduit
gate
conduit stile
Dike Nook
Waggon & Horses
quarry
ruin
to Oxenhope (1 mile)
locked gate
sign
B
delf
Hill House (ruin)
Grinding Stone Hole
A6033
sign
gates
bridges
bridge
stile
mast
gate
stiles
gate
line of butts
stiles
gate
Hill House Edge Lane
sign & gate
bridge
conduit
wet
P
stoop
Spring Hall (ruin)
ruin
Near Peat Lane
dam
bridge & stile
bridges
barrier
to Leeming
ladder
four gates
sign & gate
Keeper's Lodge
Stone markers
butts
handpost in fence
crude stile
stile
gate
Paul Clough
wet
stile
Far Peat Lane
gate & sign
Conduit
sign & stile
New York (site)
stile & sign
P
cairn
Stake Hill (431m)
gate
stile
old wall
ruin
post
old walls
bridge & stile
gate
gates
CONTINUATION ON P60
P
cairn
Great Grough Hole
shed
gap
Waterloo Clough
P
locked gate
Warley Moor Reservoir is otherwise known as Fly Flatts (possibly referring to a poor piece of land). It is home to the Halifax Sailing Club and a popular bird-watching area; twite, wheatear, plover and many divers are often to be seen.

Cock Hill
to Wainstalls (3 miles)
Nab Water
CONTINUATION ON P62
stiles
gate
Bentley Allotment (enclosure dikes)
Long Dike
bridge
gate
gate
Warley Moor Reservoir
butts
grou...
gate
bridges
bridge
butts
bridge
bridges
bridge
Spa Clough
conduit
bridge
Burnt Stones
bridge
Luddenden Brook
conduit
bridge

Though it is possible to follow the fenceline from **Cock Hill** across to Warley Moor Reservoir, it is very wet and a better line makes a beeline from the bridge over the conduit closest to the **Burnt Stones**.

0 200 400
METRES

Stake Hill cairn **49**

MAP 12: WHITE HILL CENTRAL (Wadsworth Moor)

Wadsworth Moor is the busy midriff between the barren grassy heights of Oxenhope Moor and the lower heather-clad Midgley Moor; the change in vegetation is pronounced, occurring between the knolls of Tom Tittiman Hill and Low Brown Knoll and the climb up to High Brown Knoll. The latter is the focal point of the moor, while the true summit of White Hill stands lonely and unrecognised half a mile to the north. This moor is easily accessible from Hebden Bridge and fringed on the west by the settlements of Pecket Well, Old Town and Chiserley, so it has plenty of well-worn routes and a plethora of tiny tracks. Unfortunately the beautiful head of Luddenden Dean (below the Dean Head Reservoirs) can be admired only from afar, as it is part of the Castle Carr Estate (see p58) and excluded from open access land.

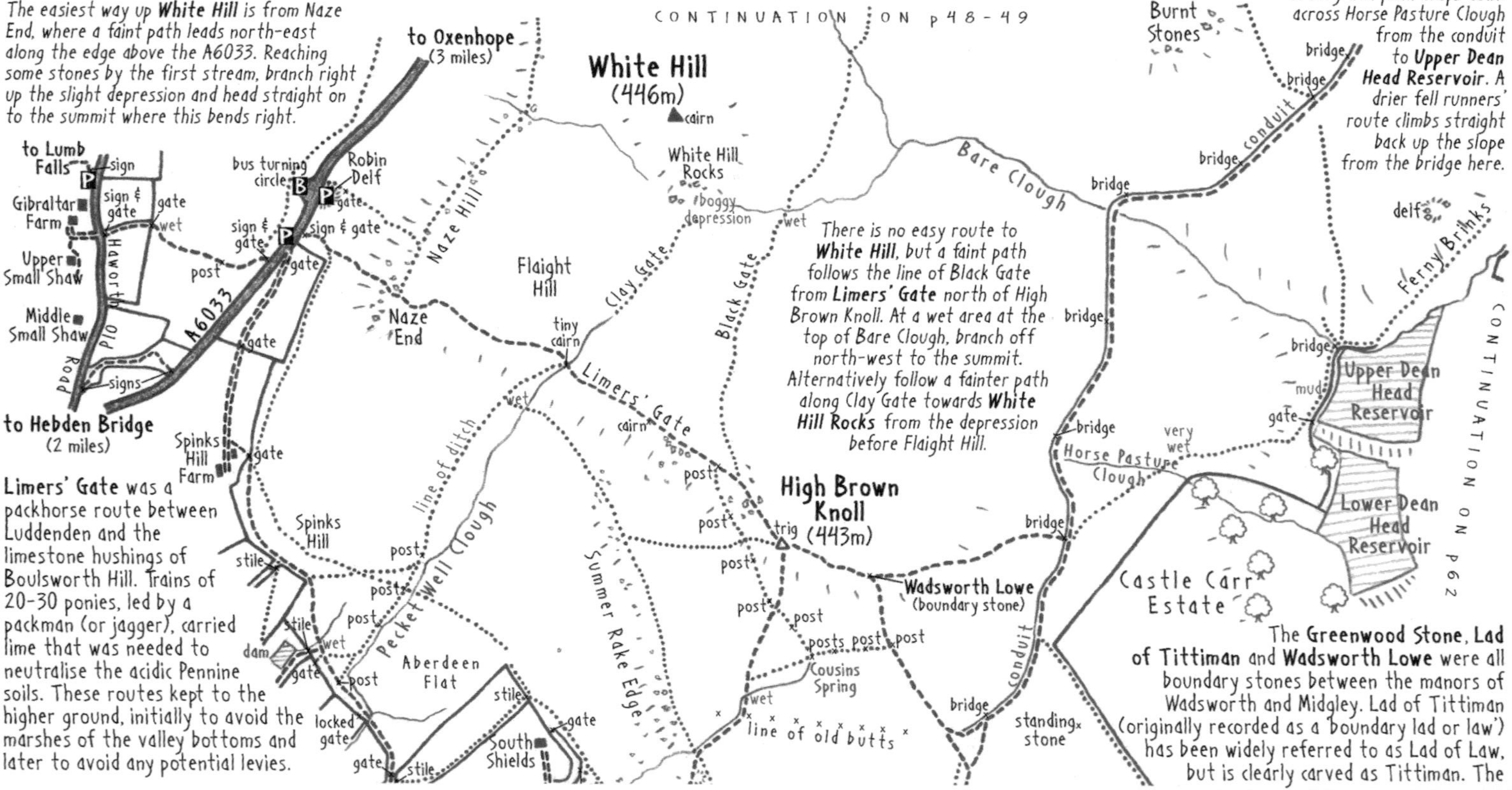

The easiest way up White Hill is from Naze End, where a faint path leads north-east along the edge above the A6033. Reaching some stones by the first stream, branch right up the slight depression and head straight on to the summit where this bends right.

CONTINUATION ON p62

A very wet path drops down across Horse Pasture Clough from the conduit to Upper Dean Head Reservoir. A drier fell runners' route climbs straight back up the slope from the bridge here.

Upper Dean Head Reservoir

Lower Dean Head Reservoir

Ferny Birks — delf

Burnt Stones

Castle Carr Estate

The Greenwood Stone, Lad of Tittiman and Wadsworth Lowe were all boundary stones between the manors of Wadsworth and Midgley. Lad of Tittiman (originally recorded as a boundary lad or law) has been widely referred to as Lad of Law, but is clearly carved as Tittiman. The

conduit — bridge — Horse Pasture Clough — very wet — gate — mud — standing stone

Bare Clough — bridge

CONTINUATION ON p48-49

There is no easy route to White Hill, but a faint path follows the line of Black Gate from Limers' Gate north of High Brown Knoll. At a wet area at the top of Bare Clough, branch off north-west to the summit. Alternatively follow a fainter path along Clay Gate towards White Hill Rocks from the depression before Flaight Hill.

Wadsworth Lowe (boundary stone)

High Brown Knoll (443m) — trig

posts, post, post — Cousins Spring — line of old butts

White Hill (446m) — cairn

White Hill Rocks — boggy depression

Black Gate — Clay Gate — Limers' Gate — cairn — tiny cairn

Flaight Hill

Summer Rake Edge

Naze Hill

Naze End

line of ditch — Pecket Well Clough

Aberdeen Flat

South Shields — stile — gate

Spinks Hill — stile — gate — post — wet — locked gate — dam

to Oxenhope (3 miles)

Robin Delf — bus turning circle — sign & gate — sign & gate — post — gate

A6033

Spinks Hill Farm

to Hebden Bridge (2 miles)

to Lumb Falls — sign — sign & gate — wet — signs

Haworth Old Road

Gibraltar Farm — Upper Small Shaw — Middle Small Shaw

Limers' Gate was a packhorse route between Luddenden and the limestone hushings of Boulsworth Hill. Trains of 20-30 ponies, led by a packman (or jagger), carried lime that was needed to neutralise the acidic Pennine soils. These routes kept to the higher ground, initially to avoid the marshes of the valley bottoms and later to avoid any potential levies.

The arc of moor above **Pecket Well** is most easily accessed via Delf Lane and through the quarry delfs below **Deer Stones Edge**. Fainter tracks lead up from near Spinks Hill Farm and cross the bare grassy slopes above South Shields, the most obvious following a rough ditch up to Limers' Gate.

The heathery heart of Wadsworth Moor is crossed by numerous small tracks between **Dimmin Dale** and the line of air shafts. The most obvious of these is very wet around the eastermost shaft. The route to the west is preferable and leads nicely up onto **Low Brown Knoll**, but can be hard to pick up on Old Hold Edge.

Tom Tittiman Hill and nearby **Lad of Tittiman** are thought to be named after an owner of the quarries on its slopes.

stones themselves were probably erected to settle a boundary dispute between the Saviles and Lacys in 1594. Carved into what is assumed to be the Greenwood Stone is the date 1775, when a beating of the boundary was likely carried out by Heptonstall Grammar School. It was re-erected in the 1970s, but stands off the old boundary line (a visible groove in the moor), so it may be the Greenwood Stone was originally one of the other nearby stones (which themselves have been re-erected). Other recorded boundary markers have disappeared; Middle Stoop (between Lad of Tittiman and Wadsworth Lowe) and Savile's Lowe or Law (across Midgley Moor towards Churn Milk Joan, see p.52.

the Greenwood Stone

The line of ventilation shafts across the heart of Wadsworth Moor stands above **Wadsworth Tunnel**, an underground conduit 500 feet below the hillside. It was built from 1869 to coincide with the construction of Widdop Reservoir. The tunnel passes from Well Holes (near the Pack Horse Inn, see p.71) to Alcomden Water and from there round Shackleton along the line of the tramway. It was originally planned to cross Crimsworth Dean by a large aqueduct, but it was never built and the route actually climbs two hills on its way to the treatment works in Halifax. Pressure forces the water uphill as air is pushed out of these vents and, if you put your ear to the grill, you can hear the water far below.

If you look closely at the ground around **Bog Eggs Edge**, moss gathers in a series of small lumps where the grass is short. I like to think of these as bog eggs, though John Billingsley has suggested that the term might have referred to witches and demons that sucked children's blood because of its similarity to boggart and hedges.

ventilation shaft near Tom Tittiman Hill

Map labels:

to Luddenden Dean · Shore End Gate (no access) · Gaping Stones · Pasture Nook · Back Clough · wet · very wet · rough drain · Limers' Gate · post · shaft · **The Greenwood Stone** (boundary stone) · stone · CONTINUATION ON P52 · line of grouse butts · Dimmin Dale · Dimmin Dale Edge · line of stone butts · **Lad of Tittiman** (fallen boundary stone) · **Low Brown Knoll** · Weavers' Gate · Collon Flat · shed · stile · Collon Hall (site) to Lane Ends · post · Deer Stones Edge · stake · cairn · Delph End Stiles · Delf Lane End gates · Slack House · Delf End Quarry · ruin · Weather House · Stone shelter · **Tom Tittiman Hill** (408m) · Old Hold Edge · Old Hold · vane · gate · Latham · Latham Slack · Bog Eggs Edge · Bog Eggs Farm · Old Town Reservoir · Old Laithe · post · post office · to Pecket Well · Moor Side · reservoir · squeeze · stiles · signs · Rock Edge · Rock (ruin) · Billy Lane · sign · **CHISERLEY** · to Hebden Bridge (1 mile) · Wall Stones Edge · Parrock Lane · barn · Wainsgate Lane · Wainsgate Farm · chapel · Waterloo Bank · **OLD TOWN** · to Pecket Well (½ mile)

to Pecket Well

0   200   400
METRES

N

Robin Hood's Penny Stone is a large boulder composed of Huddersfield Rough Rock; though it is thought to be a glacial erratic, it appears to have been moved into position subsequently. At the winter solstice, the sun appears to rise right out of the heart of nearby Miller's Grave, suggesting it may have served a function in Bronze Age burial rituals. Its name is often considered to refer to its use as a plague stone – coins were left by plague victims in a vinegar-filled depression on top of the stone in exchange for food. But the name may equally relate to the game of penny-stone, a quoits-like gambling game often played in remote places (see p68). A larger stone of the same name stood near Wainstalls until it was broken up in the 19th century; in an obvious echo of the game, Robin Hood is said to have flung this stone across the valley from there.

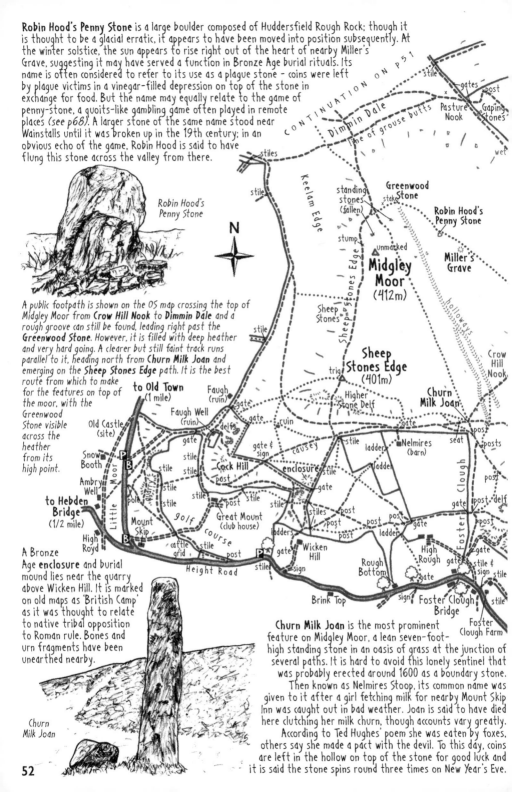

Robin Hood's Penny Stone

N

A public footpath is shown on the OS map crossing the top of Midgley Moor from **Crow Hill Nook** to **Dimmin Dale** and a rough groove can still be found, leading right past the **Greenwood Stone**. However, it is filled with deep heather and very hard going. A clearer but still faint track runs parallel to it, heading north from **Churn Milk Joan** and emerging on the **Sheep Stones Edge** path. It is the best route from which to make for the features on top of the moor, with the **Greenwood Stone** visible across the heather from its high point.

A Bronze Age **enclosure** and burial mound lies near the quarry above Wicken Hill. It is marked on old maps as 'British Camp' as it was thought to relate to native tribal opposition to Roman rule. Bones and urn fragments have been unearthed nearby.

Churn Milk Joan

Churn Milk Joan is the most prominent feature on Midgley Moor, a lean seven-foot-high standing stone in an oasis of grass at the junction of several paths. It is hard to avoid this lonely sentinel that was probably erected around 1600 as a boundary stone. Then known as Nelmires Stoop, its common name was given to it after a girl fetching milk for nearby Mount Skip Inn was caught out in bad weather. Joan is said to have died here clutching her milk churn, though accounts vary greatly. According to Ted Hughes' poem she was eaten by foxes, others say she made a pact with the devil. To this day, coins are left in the hollow on top of the stone for good luck and it is said the stone spins round three times on New Year's Eve.

52

(Map labels: CONTINUATION ON P51, Dimmin Dale, line of grouse butts, Pasture Nook, Gaping Stones, stile, gates, post, x, wet, stiles, Keelam Edge, standing stones (fallen), stake, Greenwood Stone, Robin Hood's Penny Stone, stile, stump, unmarked, Sheep Stones Edge, Midgley Moor (412m), Miller's Grave, holloways, Sheep Stones, Crow Hill Nook, trig, Sheep Stones Edge (401m), Churn Milk Joan, to Old Town (1 mile), Faugh (ruin), gate, Higher Stone Delf, post, Faugh Well (ruin), delf, ruin, gate, Old Castle (site), gate, gate & sign, causey, stile, ladder, Nelmires (barn), seat, posts, Snow Booth, P, B, stile, stile, Cock Hill, post, enclosure, stile, ladder, Foster Clough, Ambry Well, pole, stile, stile, post, stile, gate, stile, gate, post, delf, to Hebden Bridge (1/2 mile), Little Moor, QUARRY, golf course, Great Mount (club house), stiles, post, post, post, ladder, gate, post, delf, High Royd, B, Mount Skip, cattle grid, stile, ladders, post, post, ladder, High Rough, gate, gate, stile & sign, Wicken Hill, Rough Bottom, gate, stile, P, gate, Height Road, stile, sign, Brink Top, sign, Foster Clough Bridge, Foster Clough Farm, stile, Foster Clough)

MAP 13: WHITE HILL SOUTH (Midgley Moor)

Midgley Moor is surrounded on all sides by the hillside villages of Chiserley, Midgley and Booth, as well as the larger valley towns, so it is well trodden and easily accessed. The moor's highest point is unmarked, but both Sheep Stones Edge trig and the small knoll of Crow Hill are natural vantage points, while Churn Milk Joan, Robin Hood's Penny Stone and Miller's Grave burial mound are among the many archaeological sites that are part of the moor's fascinating history.

The curious enclosure of **Bracken's Folly** is a useful navigational aid, an area of grassland surrounded by a broken down wall that seems to be home to most of the sheep on Midgley Moor. A Luddenden mill-owner, Jonathan Bracken, suggested this area of moorland could be cultivated to provide work and food for the unemployed poor, but the crops' failure seems inevitable.

*The two small unnamed reservoirs at **High House Pasture** are Yorkshire Water property, though a broken stile gives access to a path around them. The smaller has never held any water, having leaked from the outset and caused its builder to go bankrupt.*

Miller's Grave is thought to be the remains of a Bronze Age burial cairn; though much of it has been removed over the years, a bank of earth and stones encloses a large split earthfast stone (see sketch on p56). Its name comes from the end of the 18th century when a miller from Hebden Bridge committed suicide and was condemned to be buried on the rough. Initially buried on the outskirts of Midgley, his presence haunted the locals until a mob decided to inter him by an old cairn on the moor. Even then, their imaginations were not appeased and his body had to eventually be removed to a churchyard.

The Bronze Age **ring cairn** on the grassy area to the east of Foster Clough Delfs is the most easily observed of a number of ancient features across the south side of Low Moor. Even without a heather covering, the broad circular embankment is best seen from the slopes above. The **cairn circle** to the east, and the rest of what Paul Bennett has suggested is a significant Bronze Age settlement or burial ground, are harder to find amid the heather.

The heathery plateau of **Low Moor** is crossed by little more than sheeptracks, but a single path makes out from the stile above **High Lee Head** and follows a groove most of the way across the moor towards the corner of the wall of **Bracken's Folly**. Other notional Rights of Way do not fare so well.

Workhouse Slack refers to the 18th-century workhouse sited at New Earth Head (now New Heath Head), a name that signifies land newly enclosed from the moor.

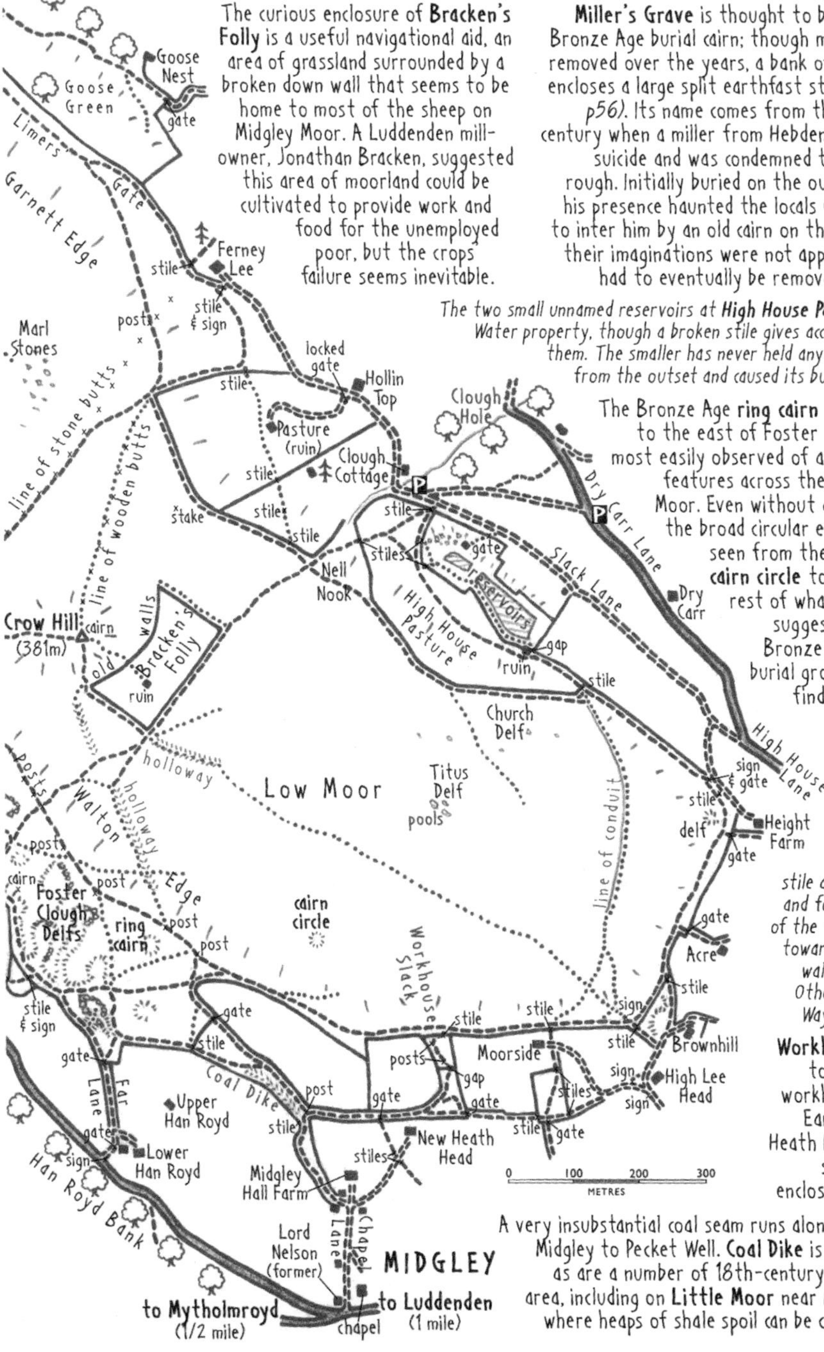

A very insubstantial coal seam runs along the hillside from Midgley to Pecket Well. **Coal Dike** is a remnant of this, as are a number of 18th-century drift mines in the area, including on **Little Moor** near Mount Skip, where heaps of shale spoil can be clearly seen.

Map labels:

Goose Green · Goose Nest · gate · Limers Gate · Garnett Edge · stile · Ferney Lee · stile · post · stile & sign · Marl Stones · line of stone butts · line of wooden butts · locked gate · stake · stile · stile · Hollin Top · Pasture (ruin) · Clough Cottage · Clough Hole · Nell Nook · stiles · gate · Reservoirs · High House Pasture · Slack Lane · Dry Carr Lane · Dry Carr · gap · ruin · stile · Crow Hill cairn (381m) · old walls · Bracken's Folly · ruin · holloway · holloway · Walton Edge · posts · post · cairn · Foster Clough Delfs · ring cairn · post · post · Low Moor · Titus Delf · Church Delf · pools · cairn circle · Workhouse Slack · line of conduit · High House Lane · sign · gate · stile · delf · Height Farm · gate · gate · Acre · stile · stile · stile · sign · Brownhill · stile & sign · gate · gate · posts · Moorside · gap · gate · stiles · sign · High Lee Head · sign · Coal Dike · post · gate · gate · stiles · stile · gate · Upper Han Royd · stile · New Heath Head · Lower Han Royd · stiles · Midgley Hall Farm · Far Lane · gate · sign · Han Royd Bank · Lord Nelson (former) · Chapel Lane · **MIDGLEY** · chapel

to Mytholmroyd (1/2 mile) · to Luddenden (1 mile)

0   100   200   300
METRES

53

ROUTE 9: HIGH BROWN KNOLL & LUMB HOLE FROM HEBDEN BRIDGE

Distance: 8 miles (12.8km)

Ascent: 420m

Difficulty: Moderate

Parking: Various pay car parks in Hebden Bridge town centre, or National Trust car park at Hardcastle Crags.

Public Transport: Hebden Bridge is on the main Caldervale train & bus routes.

Character: High Brown Knoll is one of Hebden Bridge's natural vantage points and this route makes straight for its summit via Nutclough Woods. It returns via Lumb Hole waterfall and the beautiful valley of Crimsworth Dean. The true summit of White Hill is only a short diversion from Limers' Gate and, though this additional loop is largely untrodden, the paths otherwise are all obvious and generally easy-going.

Lumb Bridge is an 18th-century packhorse bridge on the Limers' Gate route that is followed over High Brown Knoll. *Lumb* refers to a wooded section of a clough, but the bridge used to be known as Horse Bridge and the valley as Horse-bridge Clough. On a misty night, Lumb Bridge is said to be haunted by a White Lady, the ghost of a woman who committed suicide by jumping from the bridge into the falls. Ignoring the fact that it is impossible to reach the falls from the bridge, you only have to watch the kids jumping into the pool from the rocks high above **Lumb Hole** to know that this is hardly a way to certain death.

❼ Cross **Wheat Ing Bridge** and turn right through a gate beyond the house. Follow a clear path across three fields and into **Purprise Wood**. Fork right at the first waymark post and follow the waymarkers through the heart of the wood. Eventually you reach a gate on the right, from which a path leads

❻ Cross **Lumb Bridge** and follow the track up to the bend, where you fork left on a path through the bracken above Crimsworth Dean. This crosses some old walls to reach a high stone stile behind **Outwood**. Skirt to the right of the building and then head straight across the track beyond, descending steeply to a stile at the edge of **Abel Cote Wood**. Continue through the wood to **Wheat Ing Bridge**.

❺ At **Naze End** join the main path to drop steeply down to the main road. Follow the road left for 100m before taking a bridleway right down to **Haworth Old Road**. Turn right past Gibraltar Farm to another bridleway leading down to the left. Follow the rough setts of Lumb Lane to emerge by the waterfall at **Lumb Hole**, where you can scramble down to the pool for a dip on a hot day.

❹ From **High Brown Knoll**, bear left on the main path (NNW) along the high ground. To stay on the beaten track, follow the old packhorse route of **Limers' Gate** all the way to Naze End. To reach the true summit of White Hill, bear right on a faint path 50m before an obvious waymark post. This becomes clearer, following the line of **Black Gate** towards the outcrop of the Winny Stone. After crossing a wet hollow, turn left off the path and climb through short grass to the tiny cairn on top of **White Hill**. From here, aim due west (towards the Gorple Reservoirs) to reach the rock-strewn edge of Naze Hill. Follow the edge left to rejoin the main route at **Naze End**.

Flight Hill was the planned site for a 44-turbine wind farm in 1993 that would have covered most of Oxenhope Moor. It was eventually dropped on ecological grounds after significant local opposition.

Flaight (or *flait*) is a dialect word for a thin section of peat for burning. It was also cut with a *flait-spade*, which was also used for removing the surface turf.

Nutclough Woods is named after the hazelnut as the woods were used for traditional

Hirst Bridge, Nutclough

to Keighley (8 miles)

N

down the field. Descend to join the packhorse route of Jockey Gate, which winds down past Lane Ends to the road and public toilets at Midgehole.

8 Follow the road right for 50m, then turn left on a track before the entrance to Hardcastle Crags. Over the bridge, turn left and pass the Blue Pig. Soon after the barrier, fork right and climb up to join a tarmac track higher up the woods. Follow this left for 300m to a waymark post directing left down some narrow steps. At the bottom, go left then immediately right on a track above Lower Lee, before skirting round to the left of Tenter Croft.

9 The track descends to a bowling club, where a path to the left of the building leads on along the river bank. This leads into Hebden Bridge past the cricket pitch, emerging at Foster Mill Bridge. Cross the bridge and follow the road to the first junction; turn right into Grove Road, then left at the end. Follow Victoria Road round as it crosses the river again and becomes Valley Road. At the end, turn left to reach the centre of Hebden Bridge.

Hebden Bridge (originally Hepton Bridge) was a late developer as industrial Pennine towns go and so is largely Victorian in its make up. It grew quickly as a centre for fustian, a dense cotton fabric of which corduroy is a type. The mills crammed the flat land in the valley bottom, leaving the terraces to climb precariously up the adjacent hillsides.

3 Keep left above Bog Eggs Farm and join a larger path running around the hillside. By a stile in the wall on the left, fork right and climb steadily up past some ruined walls to the top of Deer Stones Edge. Follow the edge left towards the high ground of High Brown Knoll, bending right around Cousins Spring before pulling up to the trig point.

Dominating the skyline in Old Town and Chiserley is Old Town Mill (also known as Mitchell's Mill). Until recently it possessed an even larger neighbour, the infamous Acre Mill. A giant woollen mill, Acre Mill was unused at the start of World War II, when it was seen as an ideal location for manufacturing gas mask filters made from asbestos. The mill continued producing asbestos until shortly before it was demolished in the 1970s. It is estimated that over 700 people have died of asbestos-related diseases from working at Acre Mill, and this slowly evolving tragedy is talked of as being possibly Britain's biggest industrial disaster.

hazel coppicing until the industrial revolution. It was then an ancient oak woodland, but the planting of fast-growing beech and sycamore to power the mills in Hebden Bridge led to a decline in biodiversity and left it a dingy, litter-strewn hole. Since 2003 the area has been managed as a Local Nature Reserve by a volunteer organisation, the Friends of Nutclough Woods, and has quickly become a pleasant sanctuary once again.

2 Climb steeply across the fields to join a walled path by an old gate. At the end turn left up the road through Chiserley. At the T-junction at the top, go straight across, following a walled path up towards Rock Edge. This bends right to join a larger track, which curves around the hill and leads up past the equestrian centre at Bog Eggs Farm to a gate onto the edge of the moor.

Built in the late 18th century, Nutclough Mill is the largest remaining mill in Hebden Bridge. It was home to the Nutclough Fustian Manufacturing Society, a notable workers co-operative with as many as 356 workers receiving a share of the profits. One of its members, Robert Halstead, went on to co-found the Workers' Educational Association.

1 Follow the A6033 Keighley Road north out of Hebden Bridge past the White Lion Hotel. As the road bends left at a set of lights, turn right onto a track just before the former Nutclough Tavern. Through the gates into Nutclough Woods, keep left to climb steeply above the millpond and reach a packhorse track at the top. Turn left, away from Hirst Bridge, then almost immediately right up some rough steps.

Tom Tittiman Hill

Moor Side — stile — sign — gate — Bog Eggs Farm — post

Rock Edge — Rock (ruin) — Billy Lane — Walker Lane — sign — old gate

CHISERLEY

to Old Town (1/4 mile)

playing field — Club Houses

squeeze — Ibbot Royd Clough — Hirst Bridge — steps — posts

Nutclough Woods — mill pond — gate — sign — Nutclough Tavern

White Lion — Keighley Road — A6033 — Victoria Road — Valley Road

Shoulder of Mutton — to Todmorden (4 miles)

HEBDEN BRIDGE — A646 — to Mytholmroyd (1 mile) — railway station

Hebden Water — Foster Mill Bridge — cricket pitch — bowling club — Tenter Croft — Lower Lee — Lee Wood — Blue Pig — barrier

Jockey Gate — Lane Ends — sign & gate — toilets — **MIDGEHOLE**

Old Town Mill

ROUTE 10: MIDGLEY MOOR FROM MYTHOLMROYD & MIDGLEY

Distance: 6½ miles (10.4km)

Ascent: 400m

Difficulty: Easy

Parking: Car parks at Mytholmroyd Community Centre (small charge) and St Michael's Church.

Public Transport: Mytholmroyd is on the main Caldervale train and bus routes.

Character: A fairly short and straightforward route that climbs steeply up the hillside straight out of Mytholmroyd, before taking in the two natural summits of Sheep Stones Edge and Crow Hill, as well as the historic sites of Miller's Grave and Churn Milk Joan. The only rougher section can be skipped, though it does lead to the three interesting sites at the heart of the moor; Miller's Grave, Robin Hood's Penny Stone and the Greenwood Stone.

The **Northern Eggar** is the northern form of the Oak Eggar moth. It eats heather and bilberry and is associated with heath and bog, hence it is often seen on Midgley Moor. It has a two-year life cycle and is most likely seen as a large hairy caterpillar during July and August before it pupates in September. The moth itself is large, brown and with a distinctive yellow line and single white spot on each wing.

a Northern Eggar caterpillar

Miller's Grave

④ From **Sheep Stones Edge** trig, continue straight on along the lovely heather-clad slope. The finest features on Midgley Moor are set off the main paths, but easily reached from a junction at the far end of Keelam Edge. Bear right up through the heather here and after a few yards the prominent **Greenwood Stone** is visible ahead. A faint path runs past the boundary stone towards the large glacial boulder of **Robin Hood's Penny Stone**, just visible across the heather. Keep left of the stone to continue to the burial cairn of **Miller's Grave** (see pp.51-53 for more information on these features). Tempting as it may be to drop straight down to the onward route below Garnett Edge, the ground is far easier going if you retrace your steps.

⑤ Rejoin the main path and descend to **Dimmin Dale**, a broad saddle between Midgley and Wadsworth Moors. Beyond the line of grouse butts, turn right at a large junction and descend to **Pasture Nook**, overlooking the Luddenden Valley. Bear right before the gate here and follow the hillside below Garnett Edge, keeping right around a particularly wet section. Some way before the trees by **Ferney Lee** fork right on a grassy line that soon starts to climb away from the fence.

⑥ Reaching another wall corner, turn right up through **Crow Hill Nook** (another shallow saddle), following the right-hand line of butts to reach **Churn Milk Joan**. Turn sharp left at this famous marker stone (see p.52 for more details) and ascend the gentle knoll of **Crow Hill**. Turn right at the cairn and follow a faint path down to the corner of **Bracken's Folly** (an old enclosure surrounded by broken down walls). Continue straight on here; the faint path soon bends left and follows the line of a grassy groove through the heather. Though the path is indistinct, stay with the

③ Turn right on **Height Road** for 100m before turning left up a track towards **Wicken Hill**. Before reaching the farm,

as it crosses a larger path and continues all the way down to a post on the **Calderdale Way**.

The **sweet dock** is just one of many (often local) names for bistort; elsewhere it is snakeweed, red legs, pink pokers, passions, dragonwort or Easter-ledge. A number of these names refer to the puddings traditionally made throughout northern England from the plant's young leaves, usually fried in lard and served with bacon and eggs. In Cumbria Easter-ledge pudding and elsewhere passion pudding (as the dish was eaten on Passion Sunday, the fifth in Lent). While the tradition has lapsed elsewhere, the **World Dock Pudding Competition** has been held in Mytholmroyd Community Centre every March since 1971.

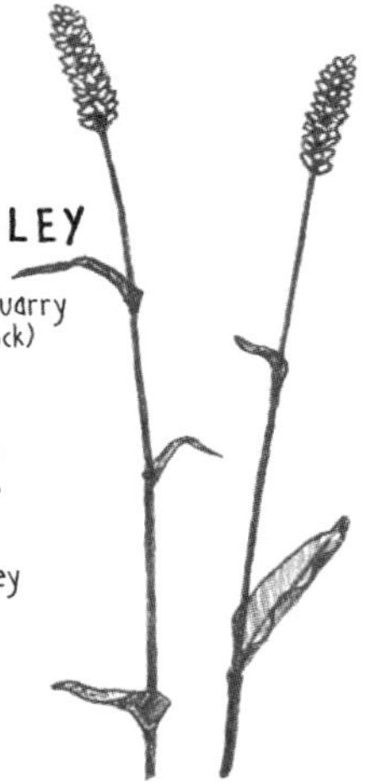

the sweet dock in flower

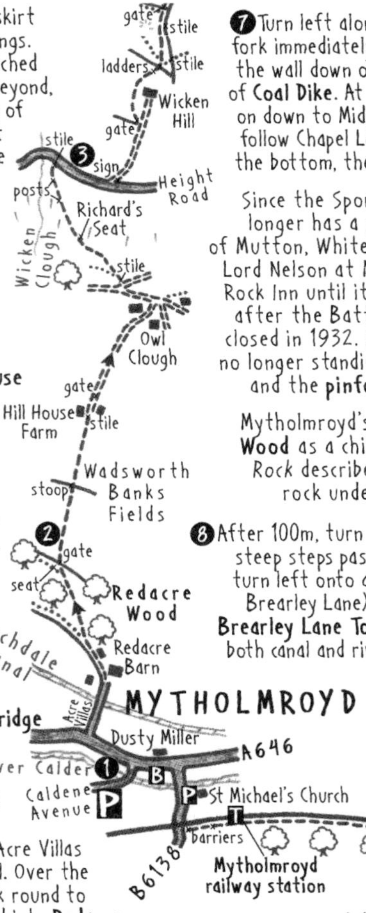

7 Turn left along the **Calderdale Way**, then fork immediately right and join a path following the wall down off the moor above the cutting of **Coal Dike**. At a larger track, continue straight on down to Midgley Hall Farm, keeping right to follow Chapel Lane into **Midgley**. Turn right at the bottom, then fork left down Midgley Road.

Since the Sportsman closed in 1990, **Midgley** no longer has a pub, but at one time it had a Shoulder of Mutton, White Lion, Weaver's Arms and Lord Nelson. The Lord Nelson at Midgley was a coaching inn known as Black Rock Inn until it was renamed, like its twin in Luddenden, after the Battle of Trafalgar. It was built in 1755 and closed in 1932. A Blue Bell Inn stood nearby on a terrace no longer standing. Chapel Lane was formerly Pinfold Lane and the **pinfold** can still be seen below Green Royd.

Mytholmroyd's most famous son, Ted Hughes, played in **Redacre Wood** as a child and his poem *The Ancient Briton Lay Under His Rock* describes how he and his brother tried to dig beneath a rock under which legend told there was a body buried.

8 After 100m, turn left off **Midgley Road** by a seat and descend some steep steps past the face of Scout Head Quarry. At the bottom, turn left onto a narrow walled path (the continuation of the old Brearley Lane), which winds steeply down to the main road at **Brearley Lane Top**. Head straight on into Brearley Lane and, beyond Bridge Barn. After **Brearley Chapel**, follow the cycle path as it leads over the railway and keeps right through the birch woods alongside it. This emerges on the B6138 by **Mytholmroyd railway station**: turn right to return to the main road and car parks.

A 'mytholm' is a river mouth or confluence: in the case of **Mytholmroyd**, it is where the Calder and Turvin meet.

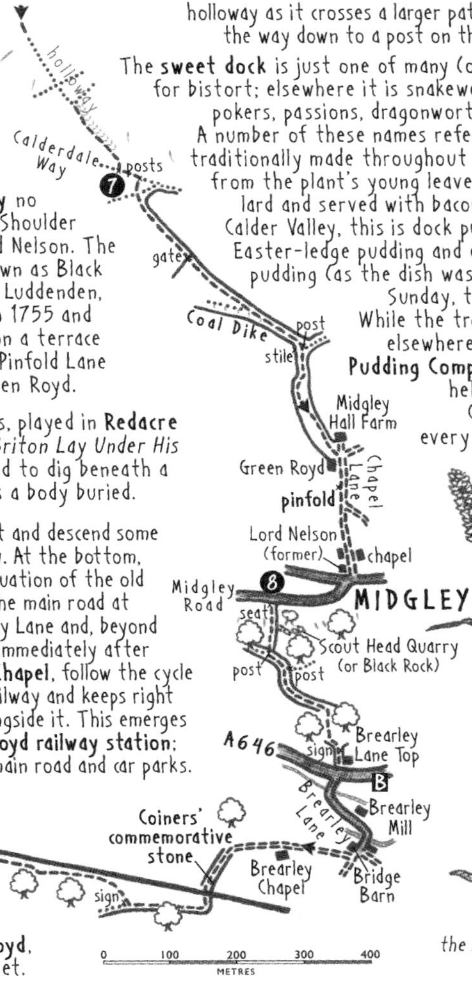

go left through a gate and skirt round the edge of the buildings. The edge of the moor is reached at a couple of ladder stiles beyond, where you follow the middle of three paths heading straight up the heather-strewn slope to join the left side of a fenceline. Follow a path along the fenceline up to a wall corner below **Sheep Stones Edge**, bearing slightly left to climb up the edge to reach the trig point.

2 The path rises steeply across the fields to **Hill House Farm**, which is perched on a spur with great views over Mytholmroyd. Continue straight on up a track to **Owl Clough**, turning sharp left at a junction of several tracks. At the next junction, head right over a stile and climb steeply across the gorse-covered hillside, keeping right to reach a stile onto **Height Road**.

1 Follow the A646 west through **Mytholmroyd** (in the direction of Hebden Bridge) and turn right into Acre Villas just before the junior school. Over the canal bridge, follow the track round to the left of Redacre Barn and into **Redacre Wood**. Fork right to climb steeply up to a gate out of the top of the woods.

to Hebden Bridge (1 mile)

MIDGLEY

MYTHOLMROYD

THE CASTLE CARR ESTATE

The Castle Carr Estate is a sealed private enclave at the head of Luddenden Dean, one of the most picturesque valleys in the county. The name Castle Carr existed before there was ever a castle on the site and referred to a homestead rather than a traditional castle. The area was part of the grazing land of the Saltonstall vaccaries (cattle ranches) in the thirteenth century, as evidenced by buildings called Winter Booth Lee and Summer Booth Fold within the estate (booths were the farmers' temporary seasonal shelters). Castle Carr was just one of twenty-one farms in the area by the time the estate was assembled in the nineteenth century, first by George Bischoff and then by Captain Joseph Priestley Edwards. 'A gentleman of independent means', Edwards previously rented a shooting estate in Scotland and decided to replicate it closer to his home at Fixby Park, Huddersfield. He acquired much of the moorland wastes in the Warley Enclosure Act of 1852 and was subsequently granted the right to hunt, fish and hawk across the moors and reservoirs of Warley, Saltonstall and Oxenhope parishes.

The castle itself was built from 1859 on the site of an earlier house and took over twelve years to complete, employing as many as a hundred people on the site. Built from local stone, the castle was a mix of Norman and Elizabethan styles, complete with battlements, towers and a courtyard with a grand fountain in the centre flanked by Talbot hounds (to commemorate the Priestley family name). Inside, the castle housed a grand hall, banqueting hall, gallery, ante-hall, billiard room and library, and featured paved corridors, giant arches and a sprung oak floor for dancing. In the park, there was a croquet lawn, pheasantry, kennels and plantations, overseen by the Castle Carr Commissioner of the Woods and Forests.

Captain Priestley never saw the castle completed, as he died in the Abergele rail disaster in 1868, though one of his sons oversaw its completion. Its primary purpose had been as a shooting lodge and retreat, but it was only briefly in use. Through a succession of owners, it fell into ruin and was largely dismantled due to dry rot, with its component parts sold off in 1962. The fountain ended up in Trevelyan Square in Leeds and the remains that are visible from Midgley Moor and Warley Moor are part of the crumbling gatehouse and adjacent heaps of embellished stone.

When land within the estate was acquired by Halifax Corporation to build the Dean Head and Castle Carr Reservoirs in the 1860s, a fountain and ornamental water garden were created by way of compensating the owners. The gravity-powered fountain was over 100ft high and renowned for being higher than those in Versailles. It functions to this day and occasionally the estate is opened to the public for a display. Otherwise access is vigorously opposed and has been since the two roads up the valley were closed in 1868. Following legal disputes in the 1890s, a London judge ruled that the current right of way across Warley Moor to Slade was sufficient compensation for the routes lost through the estate. And that was that. Until 2000, you couldn't get anywhere near the estate; now you can peer in from the moorsides and bemoan the lack of access to this exclusive manor slowly rotting in its damp glade.

the ruined gatehouse at Castle Carr today

CHAPTER 6 – NAB HILL

Height: 451m

Grid Ref: SE037323

Map Sheet: OL21
(South Pennines)

Access: No restrictions.

Public Transport: Buses
502 & 504 run along A629
through Causeway Foot
between Halifax and
Keighley. Bus 20A runs from
Halifax to Wainstalls. Bus
B3 runs through Oxenhope
between Hebden Bridge
and Keighley. Bus 69 runs
from Bradford to
Oxenhope via B6141.

The summit of Nab Hill stands on the boundary between Bradford and Calderdale, facing proudly north-west overlooking Oxenhope. This steep escarpment is responsible for its name, *nabbi* being Norse for a prominent hilltop. It would be easy to say that Nab Hill has been ruined, as its summit is churned up by over a hundred years of quarrying and the remaining plateau is dominated by the wind farms across Ovenden Moor, yet the trig point perches on a satisfying crest between the two and the moor has plenty of character. Rising in the south-east from Ogden Reservoir, the south-west from Luddenden Dean, the north-west from Oxenhope and the north-east from Denholme, Nab Hill provides a natural high point from all directions. Its accessibility from so many towns makes it a busy moor, yet never have I seen another soul on the summit.

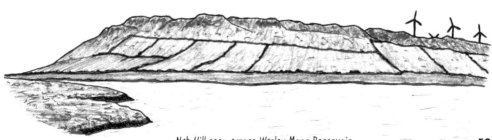

Nab Hill seen across Warley Moor Reservoir

59

MAP 14: NAB HILL NORTH (Thornton Moor)

The northern fringe of Nab Hill is marked by a series of stone castellations, equally intriguing up close as from the hillside below. They are combination of cairns and shelters, each different from the next, formed of the waste stone from the adjacent quarries. Most prominent is a towering cairn shelter shaped like a question mark and nearby there is a mosaic tapped into the peat that reads 42, a Douglas Adams reference.

Between **Leeming** and Nab Hill is a busy moorland slope that was once well populated. Once the reservoirs were built, their catchments ensured were cleared, leaving only bare ruins and grouse-rearing enclosures. **Sawood Lane** crosses the middle of this slope but can be very muddy and wet. Better options are paths along the two conduits, the lower weaving a particularly pleasant way across the hillside from near Whitehill Farm to **Nan Scar**.

N

Nan Scar was home to a rifle range in the 1880s. Its name comes from the Welsh word *nant*, for a small river.

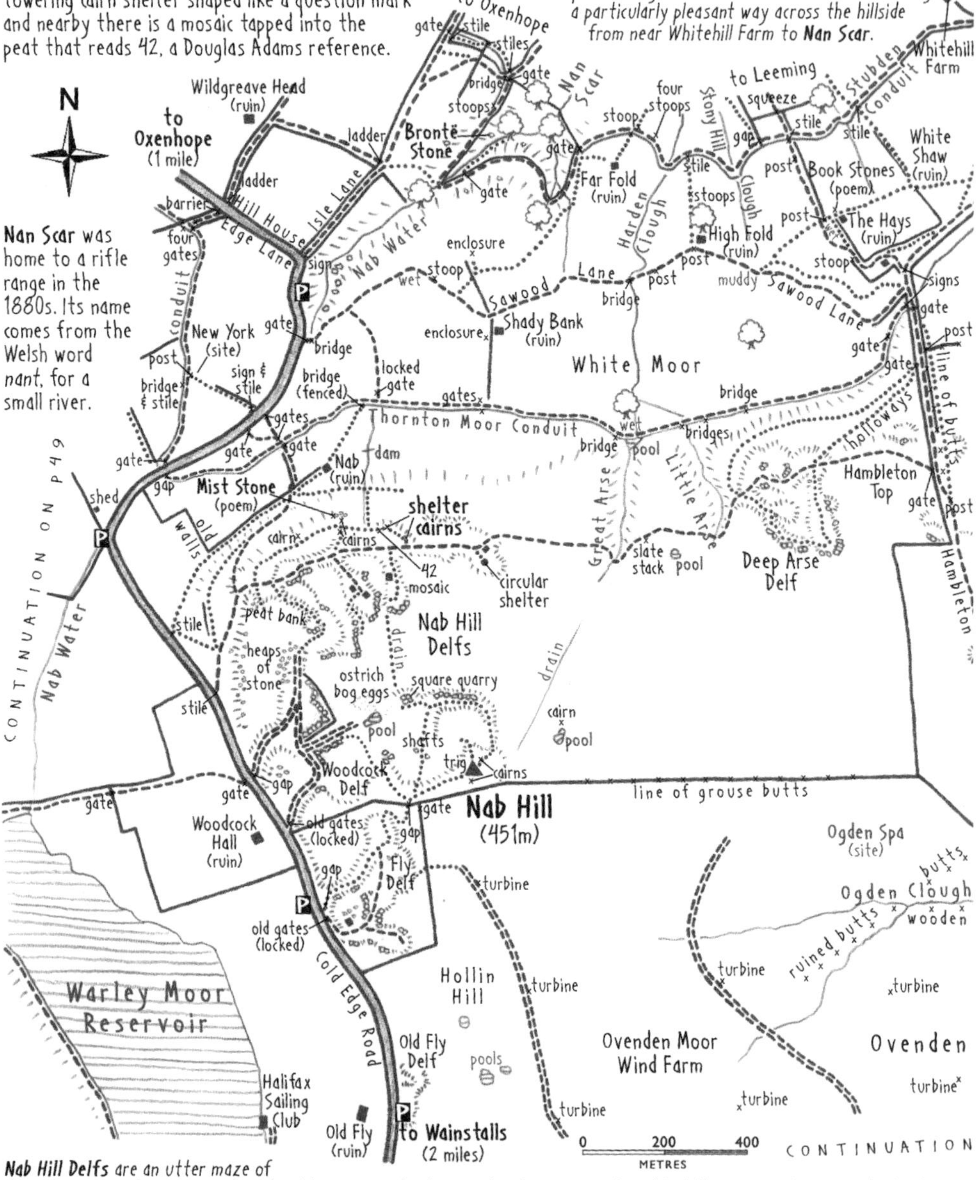

to Oxenhope (1 mile)

Wildgreave Head (ruin)

to Oxenhope

gate stile stiles

Nan Scar

to Leeming

Whitehill Farm

Stubden Conduit

ladder **Brontë Stone**

Far Fold (ruin)

bridge gate

four stoops

stoop

squeeze stile

Stony Hill

gap stile stile

White Shaw (ruin)

ladder

barrier

four gates

Mill House

Isle Lane

Edge Lane

sign

Nab Water

Harden Clough

stile

post **Book Stones** (poem)

stoops

High Fold (ruin)

post

The Hays (ruin)

stoop

signs

enclosure

wet stoop

Sawood

Lane

post

bridge

muddy Sawood Lane

gate

post

New York (site)

gate

bridge

sign & stile

bridge & stile

enclosure **Shady Bank** (ruin)

locked gate

gates

White Moor

bridge

gate

line of butts

CONTINUATION ON P49

conduit

old walls

post

gate gate

gates

Thornton Moor Conduit

wet

bridge pool

bridges

hollow ays

Hambleton Top

gate post

gate

Mist Stone (poem)

Nab (ruin) dam

shelter /cairns

cairn

cairns

42 mosaic

circular shelter

Great Arse

slate stack pool

Little Arse

Deep Arse Delf

Hambleton

shed

gap

tile

peat bank

heaps of stone

Nab Hill Delfs

Nab Water

stile

ostrich bog eggs

square quarry

pool

shafts

trig

cairns

cairn pool

Woodcock Delf

line of grouse butts

gate

gap

Nab Hill (451m)

gate **Woodcock Hall** (ruin)

old gates (locked)

gap

gate

Ogden Spa (site)

gap

Fly Delf

turbine

Ogden Clough

ruined butts wooden

butts

old gates (locked)

Cold Edge Road

Warley Moor Reservoir

Hollin Hill

turbine

turbine

turbine

Old Fly Delf

pools

Ovenden Moor Wind Farm

turbine

Ovenden

turbine

Halifax Sailing Club

Old Fly (ruin)

to Wainstalls (2 miles)

turbine

0   200   400
METRES

CONTINUATION

Nab Hill Delfs are an utter maze of disused quarries whose geography is hard to explain. The trig point makes a logical target but there is no obvious route to it. One possible route leads through **Fly Delf** from a gap just north of the southernmost gates off the road. Emerging from the quarry, the fence is trodden down and a path leads across to the trig. Another follows the quarry track (partly filled in to dissuade motorbikes) from a gap in the fence opposite the top of the track down to the reservoir. Bear right into the vast open area of **Woodcock Delf** then left up a track to a pool, from where the trig is visible. Other faint tracks lead out of the northern delfs and across the short stretch of open moorland to the 'ostrich bog eggs', a distinctive area of scattered giant moorland sods that is difficult to avoid. But most likely you'll end up like me wandering aimlessly through this maze.

The area around **Sawood** is littered with shallow coal-pits and trial holes, but the seams here were so fractured that little coal was ever dug.

The moorland above **Denholme** was enclosed in the 15th century as a deer park by the Tempest family. The name Denholme Gate refers to one of its entrances and parts of the boundary wall are still visible above Stubden Reservoir – the boundary roughly followed the line of Thornton Moor Road. Ultimately the estate was gambled away to the Saviles of Halifax.

*Stubden Reservoir is a little gem, with a path running around it carved from the rock of the hillside. A further path climbs up the rocky slope opposite a delf above the reservoir and wanders across the bracken-covered slopes to a rickety gate at the end of the dam wall. Unfortunately access from Denholme is possible only via a private track to Stubden House, but a couple of paths drop down from the moorland above by gates off **Thornton Moor Road**. The easiest way onto the moor from Denholme is via the footpath from the A629 south of the village up to Thornton Moor Road.*

Stubden
Reservoir
valve
tower

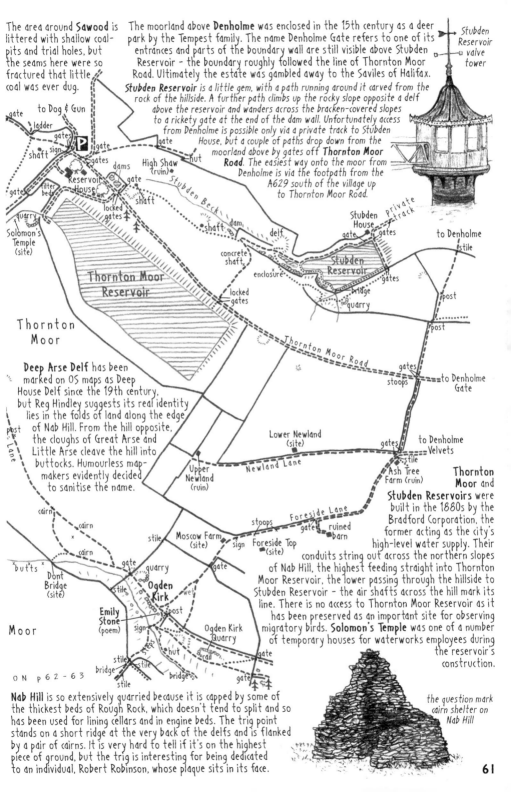

to Dog & Gun
gate
ladder
gates
sign
shaft
P
gate
gates
dams
High Shaw
(ruin)
hut
Stubden Beck
Reservoir
House
gate
filter
beds
gate
shaft
locked
gates
shaft
concrete
shaft
enclosure
dam
delf
shaft
quarry
Solomon's
Temple
(site)

Stubden
House
gate
gates
private track
to Denholme
stile

Stubden
Reservoir
gates
bridge
quarry
post

Thornton Moor Reservoir

Thornton
Moor

locked
gates

post

Thornton Moor Road

gates
stoops
to Denholme
Gate

Deep Arse Delf has been marked on OS maps as Deep House Delf since the 19th century, but Reg Hindley suggests its real identity lies in the folds of land along the edge of Nab Hill. From the hill opposite, the cloughs of Great Arse and Little Arse cleave the hill into buttocks. Humourless map-makers evidently decided to sanitise the name.

post
Lane

Lower Newland
(site)
gates
to Denholme
Velvets
stile
Upper
Newland
(ruin)
Newland Lane
Ash Tree
Farm (ruin)

Thornton Moor and **Stubden Reservoirs** were built in the 1880s by the Bradford Corporation, the former acting as the city's high-level water supply. Their conduits string out across the northern slopes of Nab Hill, the highest feeding straight into Thornton Moor Reservoir, the lower passing through the hillside to Stubden Reservoir – the air shafts across the hill mark its line. There is no access to Thornton Moor Reservoir as it has been preserved as an important site for observing migratory birds. **Solomon's Temple** was one of a number of temporary houses for waterworks employees during the reservoir's construction.

cairn
cairn
x
cairn
x
butts
x
Dont
Bridge
(site)
stile
stile
Moscow Farm
(site)
sign
quarry
gate
Ogden Kirk
wet
Emily Stone (poem)
sign
post
Ogden Kirk
Quarry
Moor
stoops
gate
ruined
barn
Foreside Lane
Foreside Top
(site)

Foreside Top
(site)

stile
hut
rail
gate
gate
Moor
O N p 62 - 63
stile
bridge
stile
bridge
stile
gate

Nab Hill is so extensively quarried because it is capped by some of the thickest beds of Rough Rock, which doesn't tend to split and so has been used for lining cellars and in engine beds. The trig point stands on a short ridge at the very back of the delfs and is flanked by a pair of cairns. It is very hard to tell if it's on the highest piece of ground, but the trig is interesting for being dedicated to an individual, Robert Robinson, whose plaque sits in its face.

the question mark
cairn shelter on
Nab Hill

61

From Cold Edge Road, **Warley Moor** looks bleak and uninspiring, but actually yields a series of scattered stone edges crowned by the **Rocking Stone**. This lies just off the only obvious path crossing the moor, though it can also be reached from the conduit to the west by pick up a grassy track along the line of butts near a fenced water gauge.

During the construction of Warley Moor Reservoir in the 1860s there was a Reservoir Inn at **Slade**, a building that has only recently been salvaged from the moor. There was also a Delvers Arms near **Old Fly** at the height of the quarrying on Cold Edge. **Ovenden Moor** is one of the ten windiest inland sites in the UK.

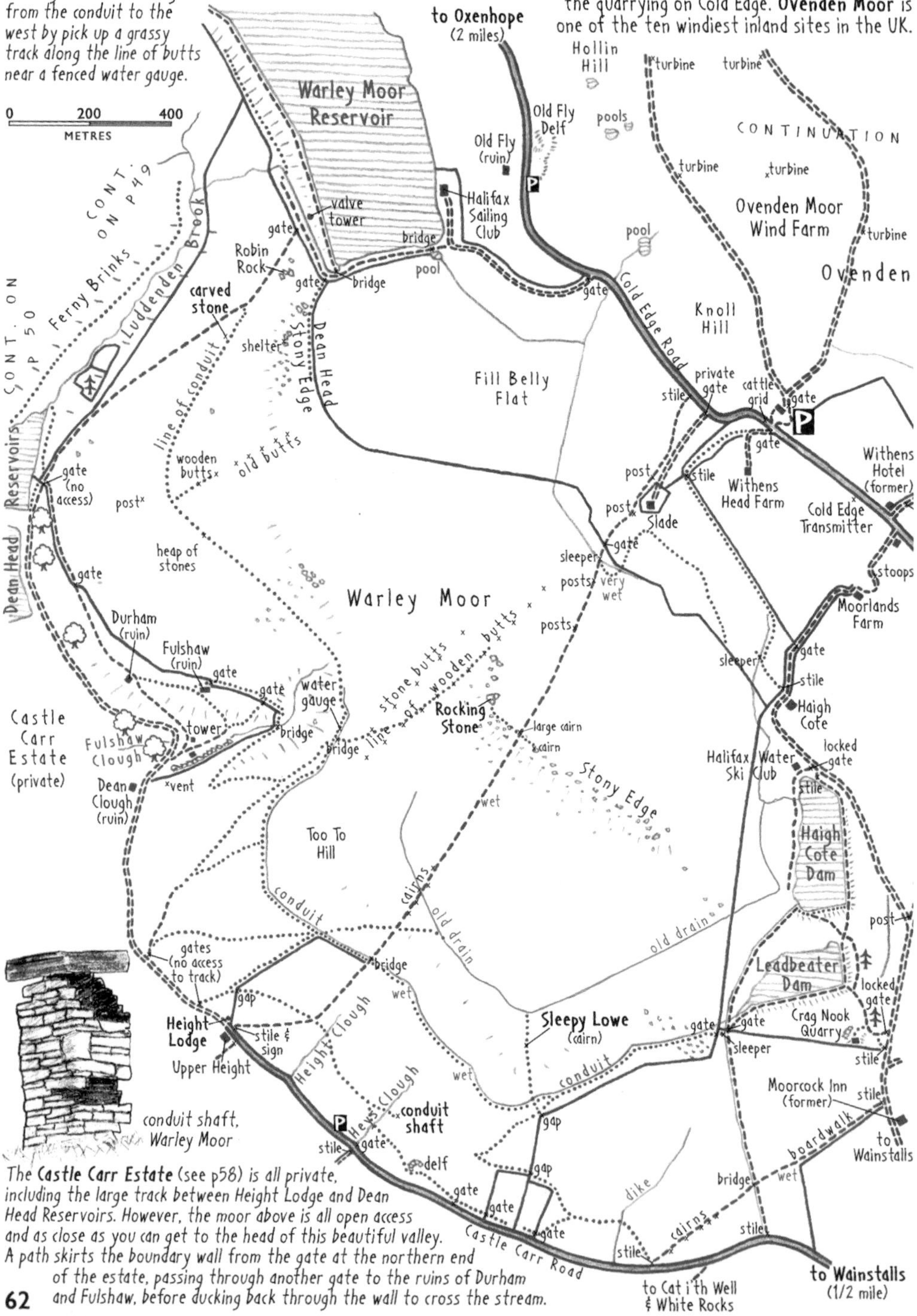

MAP 15:

to Oxenhope
(2 miles)

Hollin
Hill

turbine   turbine

CONTINUATION

**Warley Moor
Reservoir**

Old Fly
Delf

pools

Old Fly
(ruin)

P

turbine   turbine

Ovenden Moor
Wind Farm

turbine

0   200   400
METRES

CONT. ON P.49

valve
tower

gate

bridge

Halifax
Sailing
Club

pool

O v e n d e n

Robin
Rock

gate

pool

bridge

gate

Knoll
Hill

CONT. ON P.50

Ferny Brinks

Luddenden Brook

**carved
stone**

Dean Head Stony Edge

shelter

private
gate

stile

cattle
grid

gate

P

Withens
Hotel
(former)

Fill Belly
Flat

post

stile

Withens
Head Farm

Cold Edge
Transmitter

Dean Head Reservoirs

gate
(no
access)

wooden
butts

old butts

post

heap of
stones

post

post

Slade

gate

sleeper

posts very
wet

gate

stoops

Moorlands
Farm

Durham
(ruin)

Fulshaw
(ruin)

gate

water
gauge

W a r l e y   M o o r

posts

posts

sleeper

gate

stile

Castle
Carr
Estate
(private)

Fulshaw
Clough

tower

gate

bridge

bridge

stone butts

line of wooden butts

**Rocking
Stone**

large cairn

cairn

**Haigh
Cote**

locked
gate

Halifax Water
Ski Club

stile

Dean
Clough
(ruin)

vent

Too To
Hill

Stony Edge

wet

Haigh
Cote
Dam

conduit

cairn

old drain

old drain

post

gates
(no access
to track)

bridge

wet

Leadbeater
Dam

locked
gate

Crag Nook
Quarry

gap

Sleepy Lowe
(cairn)

gate

gate

sleeper

stile

**Height
Lodge**

stile &
sign

Height Clough

Heys Clough

wet

conduit

Moorcock Inn
(former)

stile

Upper Height

P

**conduit
shaft**

gap

boardwalk

to
Wainstalls

conduit shaft,
Warley Moor

stile

gate

delf

gap

gate

dike

bridge

wet

gate

cairns

stiles

Castle Carr Road

stile

to Wainstalls
(1/2 mile)

The **Castle Carr Estate** (see p58) is all private, including the large track between Height Lodge and Dean Head Reservoirs. However, the moor above is all open access and as close as you can get to the head of this beautiful valley. A path skirts the boundary wall from the gate at the northern end of the estate, passing through another gate to the ruins of Durham and Fulshaw, before ducking back through the wall to cross the stream.

to Cat i'th Well
& White Rocks

62

NAB HILL SOUTH (Warley & Ovenden Moors)

Ogden Plantation is full of surfaced paths, though the most useful links with Ovenden Moor are a couple of grassy paths, one leading up from the Giant's Tooth and the other crossing the rough unplanted ground above the Spice Cake Hills to head up Skirden Clough.

Nab Hill's southern slopes lead down to the heads of the Luddenden and Hebble Brooks and represent the closest moorland to Halifax, rising immediately above Mixenden, Causeway Foot and Wainstalls. Ovenden Moor is dominated by wind turbines and Ogden Water Country Park, while Warley Moor is quieter but worthy of closer inspection. The two are divided by the rough road across Cold Edge.

Halifax Golf Club lies in a pleasant green basin above Mixenden and is crossed by two well waymarked paths. The whole course is open access but is probably not worth exploring off the paths for fear of flying balls. The exception is the eastern corner along the Hebble Brook and above, where there is an area of intriguing walled delfs and a maze of paths.

ON p 60-61

Map labels:
Ogden Kirk · wet · post · sign · Ogden Kirk Quarry · steps · hut · gate · bridge · bridges · gate · stiles · Ogden Clough · large cairn · cairns · stile · turbine · stile · Moor · gate · Giant's Tooth · sign · stile · Great Scar · post · seat · seat · gate · stile · bridge · stile · dam · stile · Skirden Clough · Boggart's Grave · gate · stile · Round Hill Quarry · stile · bridge · bridge · gate · Rock Hollow · to Causeway Foot (200m) · Round Hill · Spice Cake Hills · Ogden Water · gate · gate · gate · The Saffery (or Ogden Dribbling Well) · Ogden Plantation · sign & gate · café · gate · gate · stile · Withens New Road · stiles · sign · stile · to Ogden · Upper Ings (site) · posts · sign · to Ogden · Middle Grain Beck · post · gate & sign · gate · Lower Ings (ruin) · post · bridge · post · sign · bridge · gate & sign · stile · post · post · post · sign · stone · Carrs Beck · delfs · sign · gate & sign · Wamesley Scar · ladder · stile · post · Lower Ings Lane · Halifax Golf Course · hut · bridge · Halifax Golf Club · gate · Iron Age enclosure · hut · post · Hebble Brook · gate · stile · ruin · Brookhouse · post · sign · Spring Mill Fold · to Wainstalls (1 mile) · gap · gate · to Mixenden · Hunter Hill (ruin) · Brookholes · N

A reservoir at Ogden was originally planned by a group of millowners along the Hebble Brook before it was taken on by the Halifax Corporation. **Ogden Reservoir**, once known as 'Little Switzerland', has been Halifax's primary country park for over a century, though it has recently rebranded itself as **Ogden Water**, with the Victorian Promenade restored. The most dubious element of this is the invention of a series of local myths; the Boggart's Grave (a stone spring that gurgles with air as it emerges), Giant's Tooth (a white stone supposedly pulled from the giant Ogden's mouth with the aid of a windmill), and Ogden Dribbling Well (another spring with alleged healing powers).

A rocking stone (or logan) was traditionally a large stone that required little effort to rock slightly. However, no amount of leaping will make Warley Moor's **Rocking Stone** move. In fact, the real rocking stone was probably a short distance away from the main stone, but Reverend Watson records that it was unmoveable in 1775. It has been suggested that only those with special powers could move such stones and that they were venerated by the druids.

The southern edge of **Warley Moor** is crossed by lots of sheeptracks but little else. It is possible but rough and wet to follow the conduit round beneath the cairned mound of **Sleepy Lowe**, but the best paths are lower down the slope, passing a striking conduit shaft

the Rocking Stone, Warley Moor

The **Waggon & Horses** was originally on the opposite side of the road, but the licence is thought to have been transferred to new premises around 1850. It is the start of the annual Oxenhope Straw Bale Race in July, when the locals don fancy dress and run, walk or stumble the three-mile course while carrying a bale of straw and downing pints in every pub along the way.

1 From the Bay Horse pub in the middle of **Oxenhope**, follow the A6033 south towards Hebden Bridge. Turn first right into Shaw Lane and, after 50m, turn left on a footpath behind some houses and up the side of a field past St Mary's Church. Turn right at the top and pick your way between the houses of **West Croft Head**.

2 Reaching the edge of the common, head straight across a track and follow the path along the top of **Stones**, a rough edge with good views over the valley. This eventually drops down to join Hard Nese Lane, a walled track that passes Hardnaze Farm and climbs up to the road near the **Waggon & Horses**.

3 Head straight across the road above the pub to join a fenceline up onto the moor. At **Thornton Moor Conduit**, the alternative route turns left and follows the conduit all the way to Far Peat Lane. However, you can continue straight on up a rough line to Stake Hill. Across the bridge, go right over a stile then follow the fenceline up the wet slope. Veer right to avoid the worst of the wet ground and make for a small cluster of stones ahead. Follow the shallow edge right to reach a fenceline, which you can climb with the aid of a helpful handpost. Bear left slightly towards the prominent cairn on **Stake Hill**.

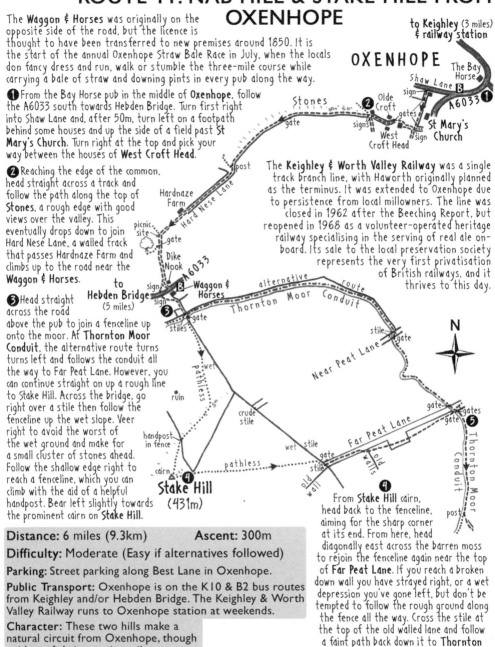

The **Keighley & Worth Valley Railway** was a single track branch line, with Haworth originally planned as the terminus. It was extended to Oxenhope due to persistence from local millowners. The line was closed in 1962 after the Beeching Report, but reopened in 1968 as a volunteer-operated heritage railway specialising in the serving of real ale on-board. Its sale to the local preservation society represents the very first privatisation of British railways, and it thrives to this day.

4 From **Stake Hill** cairn, head back to the fenceline, aiming for the sharp corner at its end. From here, head diagonally east across the barren moss to rejoin the fenceline again near the top of **Far Peat Lane**. If you reach a broken down wall you have strayed right, or a wet depression you've gone left, but don't be tempted to follow the rough ground along the fence all the way. Cross the stile at the top of the old walled lane and follow a faint path back down it to **Thornton Moor Conduit**.

Distance: 6 miles (9.3km)   **Ascent:** 300m

Difficulty: Moderate (Easy if alternatives followed)

Parking: Street parking along Best Lane in Oxenhope.

Public Transport: Oxenhope is on the K10 & B2 bus routes from Keighley and/or Hebden Bridge. The Keighley & Worth Valley Railway runs to Oxenhope station at weekends.

Character: These two hills make a natural circuit from Oxenhope, though neither of their tops is easily accessible. If the obvious alternative routes are followed, this is a very straightforward stroll on good paths. If the tops are sought, prepare for short rough sections and an exploration of the maze that is Nab Hill Delfs.
Note: no dogs on Stake Hill March-July.

the top of Nab Hill

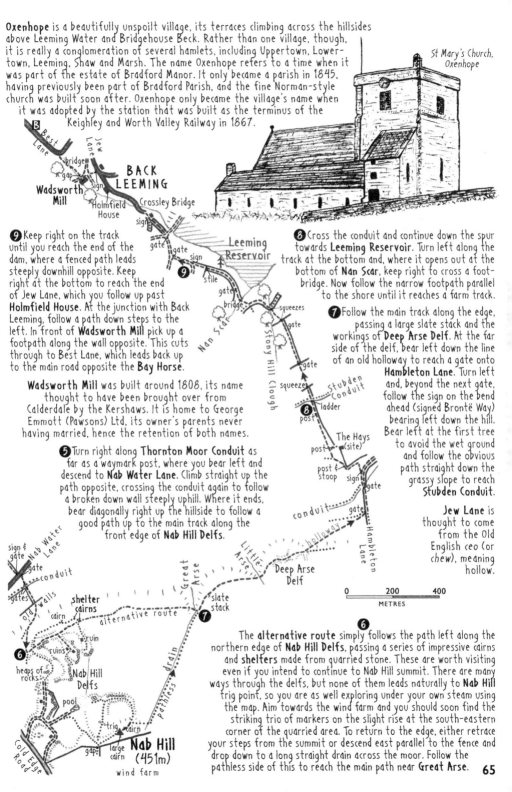

Oxenhope is a beautifully unspoilt village, its terraces climbing across the hillsides above Leeming Water and Bridgehouse Beck. Rather than one village, though, it is really a conglomeration of several hamlets, including Uppertown, Lowertown, Leeming, Shaw and Marsh. The name Oxenhope refers to a time when it was part of the estate of Bradford Manor. It only became a parish in 1845, having previously been part of Bradford Parish, and the fine Norman-style church was built soon after. Oxenhope only became the village's name when it was adopted by the station that was built as the terminus of the Keighley and Worth Valley Railway in 1867.

St Mary's Church, Oxenhope

B

Best Lane

Jew Lane

bridge

gap

Wadsworth Mill

sign

BACK LEEMING

Holmfield House

Crossley Bridge

sign

gate
gate
sign

9 Keep right on the track until you reach the end of the dam, where a fenced path leads steeply downhill opposite. Keep right at the bottom to reach the end of Jew Lane, which you follow up past **Holmfield House**. At the junction with Back Leeming, follow a path down steps to the left. In front of **Wadsworth Mill** pick up a footpath along the wall opposite. This cuts through to Best Lane, which leads back up to the main road opposite the **Bay Horse**.

Wadsworth Mill was built around 1808, its name thought to have been brought over from Calderdale by the Kershaws. It is home to George Emmott (Pawsons) Ltd, its owner's parents never having married, hence the retention of both names.

5 Turn right along **Thornton Moor Conduit** as far as a waymark post, where you bear left and descend to **Nab Water Lane**. Climb straight up the path opposite, crossing the conduit again to follow a broken down wall steeply uphill. Where it ends, bear diagonally right up the hillside to follow a good path up to the main track along the front edge of **Nab Hill Delfs**.

Leeming Reservoir

stile

gate

bridge

Nan Scar

Stony Hill Clough

squeezes

gate

gate

squeeze

Stubden Conduit

ladder

post

The Hays (site)

post

post & stoop

sign

gate

conduit

gate

holloway

Hambleton Lane

8 Cross the conduit and continue down the spur towards **Leeming Reservoir**. Turn left along the track at the bottom and, where it opens out at the bottom of **Nan Scar**, keep right to cross a footbridge. Now follow the narrow footpath parallel to the shore until it reaches a farm track.

7 Follow the main track along the edge, passing a large slate stack and the workings of **Deep Arse Delf**. At the far side of the delf, bear left down the line of an old holloway to reach a gate onto **Hambleton Lane**. Turn left and, beyond the next gate, follow the sign on the bend ahead (signed Brontë Way) bearing left down the hill. Bear left at the first tree to avoid the wet ground and follow the obvious path straight down the grassy slope to reach **Stubden Conduit**.

Jew Lane is thought to come from the Old English ceo (or chew), meaning hollow.

sign & gate

Nab Water Lane

gate

conduit

gates

old walls

shelter cairns

cairn

alternative route

Great Arse

slate stack

7

Little Arse

Deep Arse Delf

6

0   200   400
METRES

6

ruin
ruins

heaps of rocks

Nab Hill Delfs

pool

trig cairn

Nab Hill
large cairn
(451m)

gap

Cold Edge Road

wind farm

The **alternative route** simply follows the path left along the northern edge of **Nab Hill Delfs**, passing a series of impressive cairns and **shelters** made from quarried stone. These are worth visiting even if you intend to continue to Nab Hill summit. There are many ways through the delfs, but none of them leads naturally to **Nab Hill** trig point, so you are as well exploring under your own steam using the map. Aim towards the wind farm and you should soon find the striking trio of markers on the slight rise at the south-eastern corner of the quarried area. To return to the edge, either retrace your steps from the summit or descend east parallel to the fence and drop down to a long straight drain across the moor. Follow the pathless side of this to reach the main path near **Great Arse**.

ROUTE 12: OGDEN KIRK, NAB HILL & WARLEY MOOR FROM CAUSEWAY FOOT

④ From the trig point on **Nab Hill**, pick up a faint path west along the high ground to a junction of fences. Bear right away from the fenceline and skirt round to the right of a large quarry on a rough track. Beyond, bear right then left to follow the line of a depression down to the road. Hopefully there will be a gap in the fence by the lay-by here, but if not there is a stile 100m to the right. From the gate opposite the lay-by, a clear track leads on around the head of **Warley Moor Reservoir**.

⑤ At the corner of **Warley Moor Reservoir**, continue round the reservoir along its low grassy dam wall (though technically you should follow the grassy line along the fence at its foot). Towards the far end, drop down to a valve tower and join a vehicle track leading away through a gate opposite. Where this bends right, bear left onto a faint path leading past a **stone** carved 'A Sinner Saved By Grace'. The path contours round the hillside along the line of an underground conduit, eventually aiming for the prominent Rocking Stone (the only feature on the moor above) only to bend right away from it. Straight after a fenced water gauge, turn left over a small bridge and follow a faint path up past some butts that gives up shortly before the **Rocking Stone** is reached.

⑥ Cross the pathless high ground from the **Rocking Stone** to reach the main path across **Warley Moor** by a large cairn. Turn right down across the wet plateau below to reach a series of small cairns. In the middle of these, turn left along the line of an old drain and follow its rough grassy line around the hillside. Eventually you near the large cairn of **Sleepy Lowe** away to the right, which you cut across to at the drain's closest point. At Sleepy Lowe, pick up a faint path that leads straight down the slope to a more functional conduit.

③ Follow the clear path along the hillside towards the prominent cairns on the edge of **Nab Hill Delfs**. The path continues all the way to the road, though the trig point on **Nab Hill** is located on a hump across the delfs to the south. It is clearly visible from the first cairn, near which a path of sorts winds through the quarries and across the moor to this true high point.

Leadbeater Dam was constructed in 1835 as one of three dams built by the Cold Edge Dam Company to supply ten mills in the Wainstalls and Luddenden area, who each paid a levy for the water. It is topped up by a conduit from Warley Moor Reservoir and the name comes from Leadbeater and Stansfield, the company who constructed the dams.

Sleepy Lowe is a large modern cairn on a barren shoulder of Saltonstall Moor, its name possibly a corruption of 'slippery'. It is likely that it was built on top of an earlier burial cairn that was excavated by Reverend Watson, when cremation remains were discovered.

⑦ Follow the conduit left towards **Leadbeater Dam** and drop down through a gate to the right just before the wall around the reservoirs. Over a crude sleeper bridge, turn left through a gate and follow the dam's embankment right. At the corner of the dam, turn right down past a small plantation to reach a stile in the corner (to the right of a locked gate).

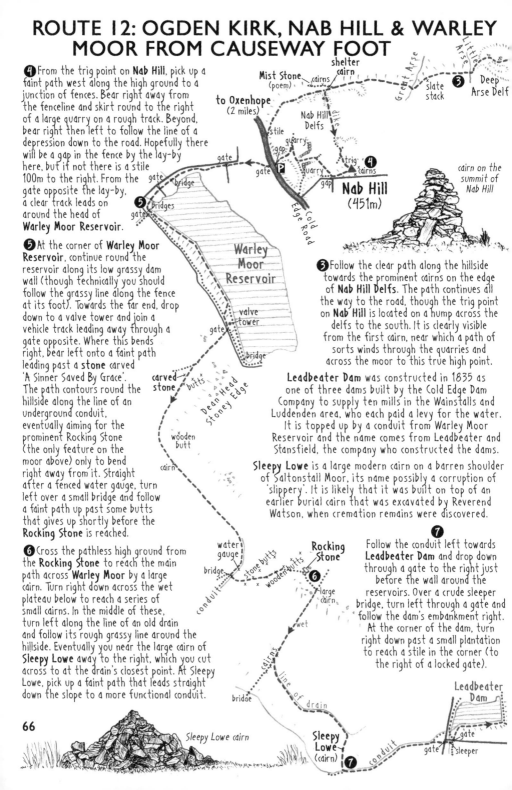

shelter
cairn

Mist Stone
(poem)
cairns

to Oxenhope
(2 miles)

Nab Hill
Delfs

stile

quarry

gap

gate

gate P

bridge

gate

bridges

gate

Warley
Moor
Reservoir

valve
tower

gate

bridge

carved
stone

butts

Dean Head
Stoney Edge

wooden
butt

cairn

water
gauge

bridge

stone butts

wooden butts

Rocking
Stone

Great Arse

Little Arse

slate stack

③ Deep
Arse Delf

Cold Edge Road

trig **④**
cairns

quarry

gap

Nab Hill
(451m)

cairn on the
summit of
Nab Hill

⑥

large cairn

wet

conduit

line of drain

cairns

bridge

Sleepy Lowe cairn

Sleepy
Lowe
(cairn) **⑦**

conduit

gate

Leadbeater
Dam

gate

sleeper

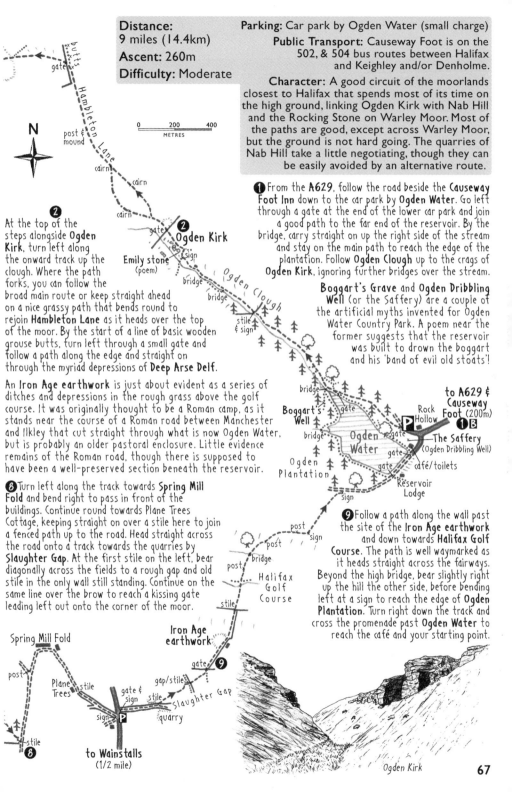

Distance: 9 miles (14.4km)
Ascent: 260m
Difficulty: Moderate

Parking: Car park by Ogden Water (small charge)
Public Transport: Causeway Foot is on the 502, & 504 bus routes between Halifax and Keighley and/or Denholme.
Character: A good circuit of the moorlands closest to Halifax that spends most of its time on the high ground, linking Ogden Kirk with Nab Hill and the Rocking Stone on Warley Moor. Most of the paths are good, except across Warley Moor, but the ground is not hard going. The quarries of Nab Hill take a little negotiating, though they can be easily avoided by an alternative route.

❶ From the A629, follow the road beside the Causeway Foot Inn down to the car park by Ogden Water. Go left through a gate at the end of the lower car park and join a good path to the far end of the reservoir. By the bridge, carry straight on up the right side of the stream and stay on the main path to reach the edge of the plantation. Follow Ogden Clough up to the crags of Ogden Kirk, ignoring further bridges over the stream.

Boggart's Grave and Ogden Dribbling Well (or the Saffery) are a couple of the artificial myths invented for Ogden Water Country Park. A poem near the former suggests that the reservoir was built to drown the boggart and his 'band of evil old stoats'!

❷ At the top of the steps alongside Ogden Kirk, turn left along the onward track up the clough. Where the path forks, you can follow the broad main route or keep straight ahead on a nice grassy path that bends round to rejoin Hambleton Lane as it heads over the top of the moor. By the start of a line of basic wooden grouse butts, turn left through a small gate and follow a path along the edge and straight on through the myriad depressions of Deep Arse Delf.

An Iron Age earthwork is just about evident as a series of ditches and depressions in the rough grass above the golf course. It was originally thought to be a Roman camp, as it stands near the course of a Roman road between Manchester and Ilkley that cut straight through what is now Ogden Water, but is probably an older pastoral enclosure. Little evidence remains of the Roman road, though there is supposed to have been a well-preserved section beneath the reservoir.

❽ Turn left along the track towards Spring Mill Fold and bend right to pass in front of the buildings. Continue round towards Plane Trees Cottage, keeping straight on over a stile here to join a fenced path up to the road. Head straight across the road onto a track towards the quarries by Slaughter Gap. At the first stile on the left, bear diagonally across the fields to a rough gap and old stile in the only wall still standing. Continue on the same line over the brow to reach a kissing gate leading left out onto the corner of the moor.

❾ Follow a path along the wall past the site of the Iron Age earthwork and down towards Halifax Golf Course. The path is well waymarked as it heads straight across the fairways. Beyond the high bridge, bear slightly right up the hill the other side, before bending left at a sign to reach the edge of Ogden Plantation. Turn right down the track and cross the promenade past Ogden Water to reach the café and your starting point.

Ogden Kirk

67

DELVING IN THE QUARRIES

The quarrying of stone in West Yorkshire is recorded as early as the fourteenth century, although early quarrying was generally of earthfast stones or exposed edges – pick marks can be found on some of the stones remaining on the moor. Stones gathered either from the open moor or from areas that had been cleared for grazing were used largely for building. The Elland Flags, which occur in a narrow band east of Halifax and Keighley, were used as crude roofing tiles known as thackstones (thatch-stones), with moss-packs gathered from the moor used to stuff joints for waterproofing. Also known as York Stone, the Elland Flags had a market across the whole country and can still be seen in many London pavements.

Later, Rough Rock *(see pages xvi-xvii for more details on the local geology)* was used for building, with quarries appearing across the moors in ever greater number to meet the demand for stone needed for the construction of reservoirs, churches, mills, roads and houses, which reached a peak towards the end of the nineteenth century. Quarries were often dug into the sides of the moor where access was easier, and then worked steadily across the plateau, as at Nab Hill. Some of this quarrying activity decimated impressive natural features (like the Kirk Stones on Morton Moor, or Jackson Rock at Withens Gate), but others created dramatic features (at Shooters Nab, Gaddings Hole or Hell Hole Rocks near Heptonstall). As part of the enclosure acts, township delfs (quarries) were created, where people could take free stone for enclosure walls and repairing buildings, though these would usually be shallow pits dug into the poorer rock.

As well as peat, the useless broken surface stone (or rag) had to be removed to reach the workable layers, often being built into large judd walls (like those in the Shibden Valley near Halifax, *see page 18 in The West Yorkshire Woods: Part I*). No explosives were used; instead steam cranes with hooks were fixed beneath a layer of the stone by the delvers (quarrymen). The stone was then dressed on site and removed by horse-drawn carts. Rough Rock was used for flags, jambs and kerbs, while the older grits served as setts, building stone, pulping stones (for the paper industry) and were crushed for gravel or sand. The roughest serviceable stone was used for dry stone walling and at one time there were gangs of itinerant wallers constantly employed. Many farmers also supplemented their income by working as wallers or quarrymen.

During the nineteenth century, peat pits (those places where peat had been dug for fuel) and quarries like those across Nab Hill became popular sites for gambling activities on Sundays. Men with little to do gathered to bet on games like penny-stone, pitch and toss, and knurr and spell. Penny-stone was a boules-type game from which Penistone Hill gets its name, and knurr and spell involved striking a large marble (the knurr) with a wooden bat (the spell) as far as possible. For this, courses as long as 200 yards were marked out, so the moorland was perfect ground to play on – indeed it was invented on these moors and is often called Northern spell. Lookouts were posted to keep an eye out for policemen (a possible source of the name Sentry Hill near Sawood) and there are accounts of gatherings being broken up by large operations on Nab Hill and at Widdop, following a concerted effort by the Halifax, Keighley and Bradford police forces. The delfs on Nab Hill were quarried until 2000, since when they have been used only for occasional raves, keeping up this centuries-old tradition of illicit activities.

heaps of waste stone

CHAPTER 7 – GORPLE HILL

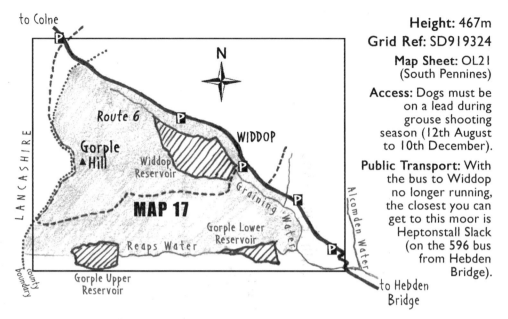

Height: 467m

Grid Ref: SD919324

Map Sheet: OL21 (South Pennines)

Access: Dogs must be on a lead during grouse shooting season (12th August to 10th December).

Public Transport: With the bus to Widdop no longer running, the closest you can get to this moor is Heptonstall Slack (on the 596 bus from Hebden Bridge).

Gorple Hill is the wedge of moor squeezed between Widdop and Gorple Reservoirs and straddling the Lancashire-Yorkshire boundary. Here the Pennines seem like an undulating ridge of hills, with Hoof Stones Height and the Black Hameldon ridge rising impressively to the south and Boulsworth Hill to the north. Seen from the east, Gorple Hill is the shapely dome in the middle of the ridge. Though its summit is something of a boggy plateau above the crags of Gorple Stones, it has dramatic rock-scarred faces on many sides and some of the best climbing and bouldering sites in the South Pennines, with the parapets of the Cludders towering above the beautiful moorland road between Hebden Bridge and Colne. Gorple Hill is a long way from any real settlement and it is a full day's walk to take in these heights without using the bus or a car up to Widdop. Once here though there is plenty of easy moorland walking, and the potential for satisfying round routes makes it worthy of a day out.

The name Gorple has been suggested to mean 'upper pile' or even 'bloody pile' (from Anglo-Saxon, possibly referring to the scattered mass of Gorple Stones on the southern face of the hill), but may also come from the Celtic *gor* (moor) and *pwl* (pool) – indeed 'gorcock' is another name for the red grouse. Gorpill Hill was one of the few Pennine hills marked on Saxton's map of 1579 and it is from here that I've revived this old name for an otherwise unnamed high point.

Gorple Hill and the Pennine watershed from Heptonstall Moor

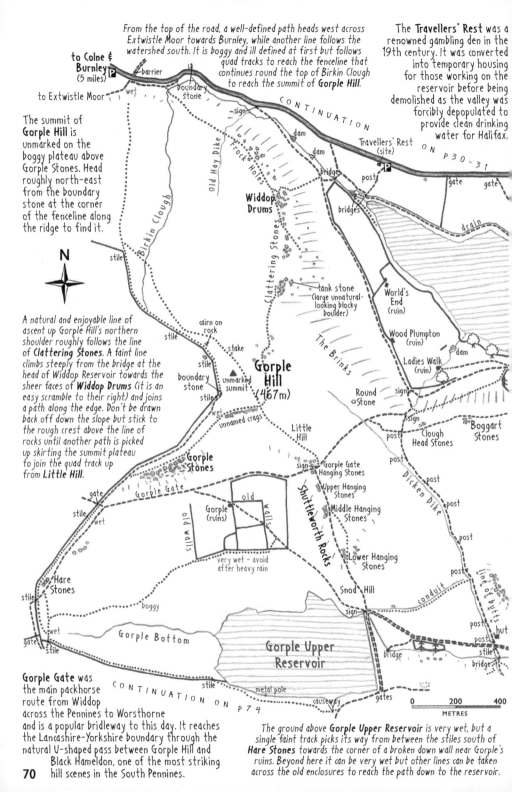

From the top of the road, a well-defined path heads west across Extwistle Moor towards Burnley, while another line follows the watershed south. It is boggy and ill defined at first but follows quad tracks to reach the fenceline that continues round the top of Birkin Clough to reach the summit of **Gorple Hill**.

The **Travellers' Rest** was a renowned gambling den in the 19th century. It was converted into temporary housing for those working on the reservoir before being demolished as the valley was forcibly depopulated to provide clean drinking water for Halifax.

The summit of **Gorple Hill** is unmarked on the boggy plateau above Gorple Stones. Head roughly north-east from the boundary stone at the corner of the fenceline along the ridge to find it.

A natural and enjoyable line of ascent up Gorple Hill's northern shoulder roughly follows the line of **Clattering Stones**. A faint line climbs steeply from the bridge at the head of Widdop Reservoir towards the sheer faces of **Widdop Drums** (it is an easy scramble to their right) and joins a path along the edge. Don't be drawn back off down the slope but stick to the rough crest above the line of rocks until another path is picked up skirting the summit plateau to join the quad track up from **Little Hill**.

Gorple Gate was the main packhorse route from Widdop across the Pennines to Worsthorne and is a popular bridleway to this day. It reaches the Lancashire-Yorkshire boundary through the natural U-shaped pass between Gorple Hill and Black Hameldon, one of the most striking hill scenes in the South Pennines.

The ground above **Gorple Upper Reservoir** is very wet, but a single faint track picks its way from between the stiles south of **Hare Stones** towards the corner of a broken down wall near Gorple's ruins. Beyond here it can be very wet but other lines can be taken across the old enclosures to reach the path down to the reservoir.

MAP 16: GORPLE HILL

Though its summit is off the beaten track, Gorple Hill is a well-trodden moor, with its rocky fringes above Widdop and Gorple Reservoirs easily accessed. Most of the moor is strewn with interesting rock features; beyond the well-known Cludders and Shuttleworth Rocks, it is worth seeking out the Widdop Drums, Gorple Stones and two different Round Stones.

Widdop is a contraction of 'wide hope', a *hope* being a hollow in the hills, but the scattered hamlet was abandoned after the construction of the reservoir. Despite being so remote, there was obviously enough of a population for John Wesley to deem it worth visiting twice, the latter commemorated on a rock by the dam marked 'J.W. 1766' and known as **Wesley's Pulpit** (p30). Construction began on the dam in 1871, utilising a horse-drawn tramway along the hillside from Shackleton (a remnant of which can be seen on the raised area opposite the car park). Some 200 navvies worked on the project and were housed in a wooden shanty town, which was known as Navvyopolis and located by Well Hole. The Mayor of Halifax opened the reservoir in 1878, though it is smaller than originally planned, as a dam could not satisfactorily be constructed across the narrow Notch just downstream.

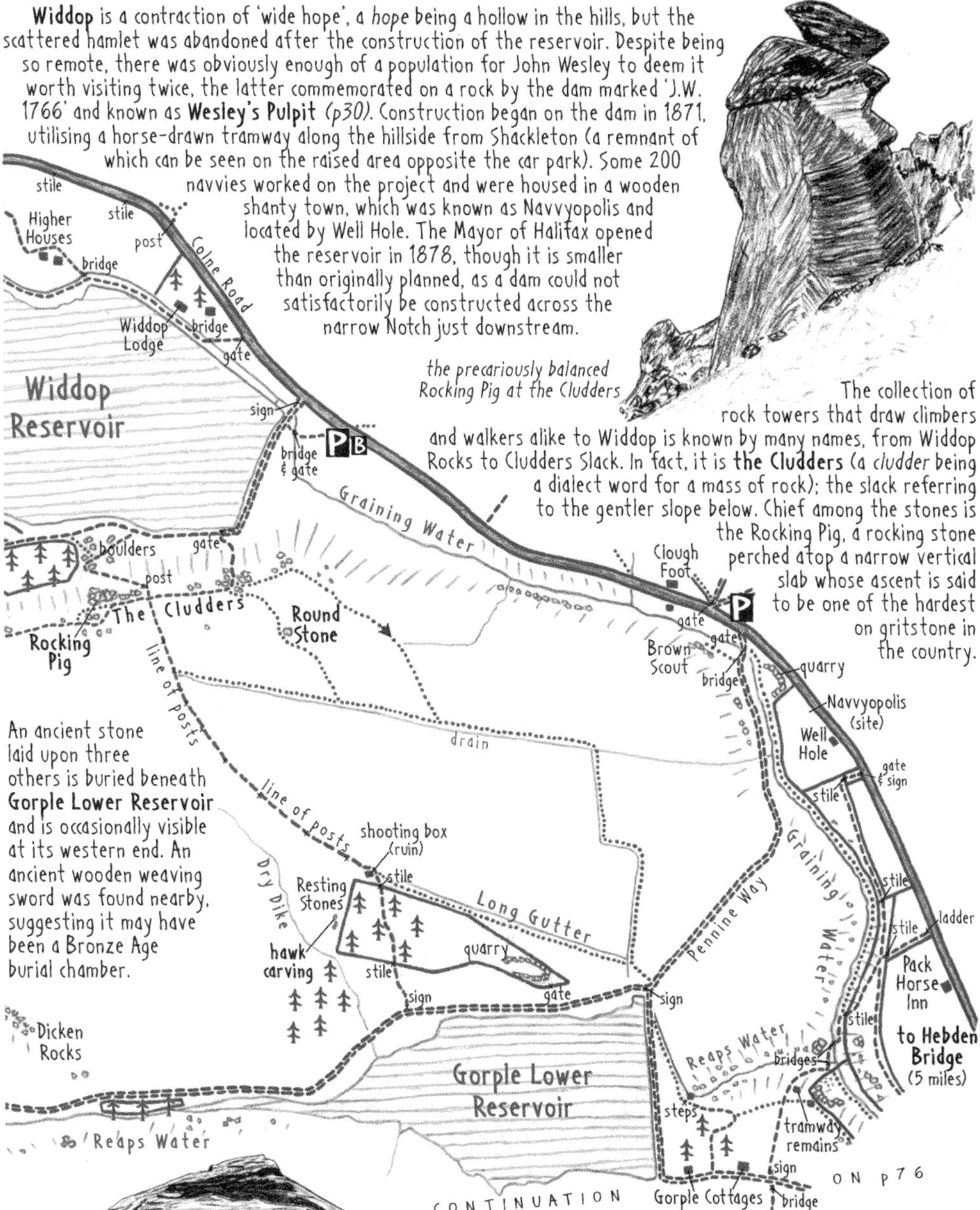

the precariously balanced Rocking Pig at the Cludders

The collection of rock towers that draw climbers and walkers alike to Widdop is known by many names, from Widdop Rocks to Cludders Slack. In fact, it is **the Cludders** (a *cludder* being a dialect word for a mass of rock); the slack referring to the gentler slope below. Chief among the stones is the Rocking Pig, a rocking stone perched atop a narrow vertical slab whose ascent is said to be one of the hardest on gritstone in the country.

An ancient stone laid upon three others is buried beneath **Gorple Lower Reservoir** and is occasionally visible at its western end. An ancient wooden weaving sword was found nearby, suggesting it may have been a Bronze Age burial chamber.

Map labels

stile
Higher Houses
stile
post
bridge
Colne Road
Widdop Lodge
bridge
gate
Widdop Reservoir
sign
P B
bridge & gate
Graining Water
boulders
gate
post
The Cludders
Round Stone
Rocking Pig
line of posts
line of posts
Dry Dike
drain
shooting box (ruin)
stile
Resting Stones
hawk carving
stile
Long Gutter
quarry
sign
gate
sign
Dicken Rocks
Reaps Water
Gorple Lower Reservoir
CONTINUATION
Clough Foot
gate
P
Brown Scout
bridge
quarry
Navvyopolis (site)
Well Hole
gate & sign
stile
Graining
Pennine Way
Water
stile
stile
ladder
Pack Horse Inn
stile
to Hebden Bridge (5 miles)
Reaps Water
bridges
steps
tramway remains
sign
Gorple Cottages
bridge
ON p76

The **Round Stone** sits alone on a squelchy bit of moor – indeed after rain it sits within a moat. It is aptly named (more so than the other Round Stone above the Gorple Gate track) and a striking boulder, whether seen from across the moor or from the road above the Pack Horse Inn. From certain angles it looks like a giant curling stone.

the Round Stone near the Cludders

FELL RUNNING & RACING

Among those who make fullest use of the moorland spaces opened up since 2000 are the fell runners you often see filing across the skylines that are usually left to the sheep and grouse. While it is of course not a new sport, it is as popular now as ever. Many faint paths that I have been hard pushed to account for turn out to have been worn by hundreds of fell runners as part of obscure race routes. It is something I have been drawn to since moving to the area; once you reach the moorland (the difficult bit!), it offers lovely, springy ground and gently undulating slopes and a real sense of escape from the clutter of the valleys far below. It often feels that these moors were made for running on.

Fell running grew out of the Guides Races that were held in the Yorkshire Dales and the Lake District from the early nineteenth century. These races were just some of the trials of strength competed in at local shows and, in hilly country, it made sense to race to the top of the nearest hill and back. Initially, like all sports, it was closely linked to gambling and there are plenty of tales of locals obstructing the leader to influence the outcome. Similar races doubtless took place at local events in West Yorkshire as well, though none has survived to this day. A fell race is recorded as part of the Lammas Fair that took place at the Hitching Stone in the mid nineteenth century. Men from the villages of Cowling and Sutton charged across the moss and back between the Hitching and Navax Stones.

Fell running only became a sport in the twentieth century with the formation of amateur running clubs and races officially sanctioned by the Amateur Athletic Association. Holmfirth Harriers is the oldest fell running club in the area, having continued since 1907 (although Halifax Harriers is over 125 years old and has a fell running arm). It dwindled like many other clubs in the 1950s and 60s, but kept going and now has a booming 700-strong membership. Other lapsed clubs re-formed in the 1970s, such as the Harriers of Ilkley, while many new clubs have sprung up since, including my own Todmorden Harriers.

West Yorkshire now boasts a very full fell running calendar as more and more people want to take part in events, the average field numbering in the hundreds. The Stoodley Pike Fell Race is possibly the oldest established in the area, a short haul up and down the pike from, Lumbutts established in the 1970s. Many others have been running for 25 years, like the Holme Moss Fell Race, the Easter Bunny Runs around Penistone Hill, while the Auld Lang Syne from Haworth on December 31st was established in the early 1990s. The area even has its own version of the Bob Graham Round; the South Pennine 39 Trigs is 105 miles long and includes some 20,000ft of ascent, though it has yet to be completed in under 24 hours. The Haworth Hobble (or Wuthering Hike) has been shortened from 44 to 32 miles, but is still an ultra-marathon, likewise the Calderdale Hike. The ultimate test of endurance though is The Spine, a seven-day race along the length of the Pennine Way in January each year that brands itself 'Britain's most brutal race'.

a Todmorden Harrier in action

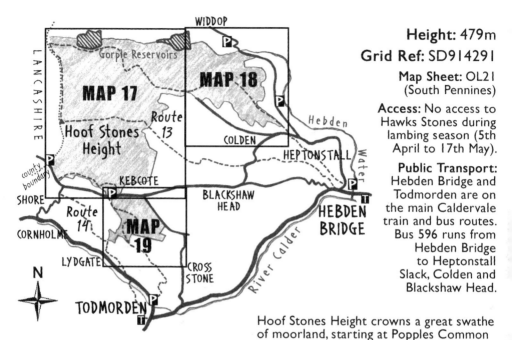

Height: 479m
Grid Ref: SD914291

Map Sheet: OL21
(South Pennines)

Access: No access to Hawks Stones during lambing season (5th April to 17th May).

Public Transport: Hebden Bridge and Todmorden are on the main Caldervale train and bus routes. Bus 596 runs from Hebden Bridge to Heptonstall Slack, Colden and Blackshaw Head.

Hoof Stones Height crowns a great swathe of moorland, starting at Popples Common near Heptonstall and arcing right round to Bride Stones Moor and Whirlaw Rocks just above Todmorden. The name would appear to be a corruption of Hoar Stones Height – it is marked as Hoat Stones Height on the 1843 map and Hoar Side Moor lies on its east flank. Hoar (sometimes spelt Hoor) Stones, like Hare Stones just to the north, comes from an Old English word *har* relating to a boundary and appears frequently in the South Pennines. The summit ridge, a wall of dark peat that is also referred to as Black Hameldon (evocatively meaning 'black-scarred hill'), forms the county boundary and remains a remote corner of West Yorkshire. Unlike the busy fringe of the moor, its heart is by-passed by the Pennine Way and many other major routes across the moors, yet it represents one of the most defined summits in Calderdale, with grand views towards Pendle Hill and the Yorkshire Dales.

Hoof Stones Height rising above Gorple Upper Reservoir from Shuttleworth Rocks

73

CONTINUATION ON p70-71

MAP 17: HOOF STONES HEIGHT WEST (Stansfield Moor)

Hoof Stones Height is the high point of a ridge running south from Gorple Gate to the Long Causeway. It is a sparse landscape with scattered stones, abandoned dams and crumbling ruins in its lee.

The broad ridge of **Black Hameldon** has a fenceline running along its crest with rough lines either side. The surrounding moor is raw peat and streaks of heather broken only by occasional fir trees that have taken root and sometimes give the impression of a walker bent into the westerly wind. Faint quad tracks lead up towards the ridge past the Whinberry Stones and from Noah Dale Dam site only to peter out near these lone trees.

Rush Candle Clough refers to the widespread use of rushes for candles. The white pith burned well (though quickly) and candle wax was too expensive for most people.

Lead Mine Clough, like Cat Hole near Orchan Rocks (p82), was mined for lead in the 18th century as the Heptonstall Lead Mines. Both proved unsuccessful ventures as the cost of extracting and transporting the ore was too great. **Noah Dale Dam** (originally called Broad Holme Dam) was a later project.

Grey Stones' name comes from the same root as that of Hoar and Hare Stones, the Old English word har, referring to a boundary.

Of the paths that strike out west from **Reaps Cross**, a path runs faintly along an old dike along Reaps Edge before dropping out of the edge and heads boldly into the empty spaces of **Raistrick Greave Hill**. However, this and the pleasant path leading north-east from the stone post at the top of **Clegg Clough** do not happily meet – a short adjustment is needed near a cut that feeds Flaight Clough.

On 21st January 1943, a Halifax bomber crashed into **Hoar Side Moor** during an operation, killing two of its crew and scattering across the moor.

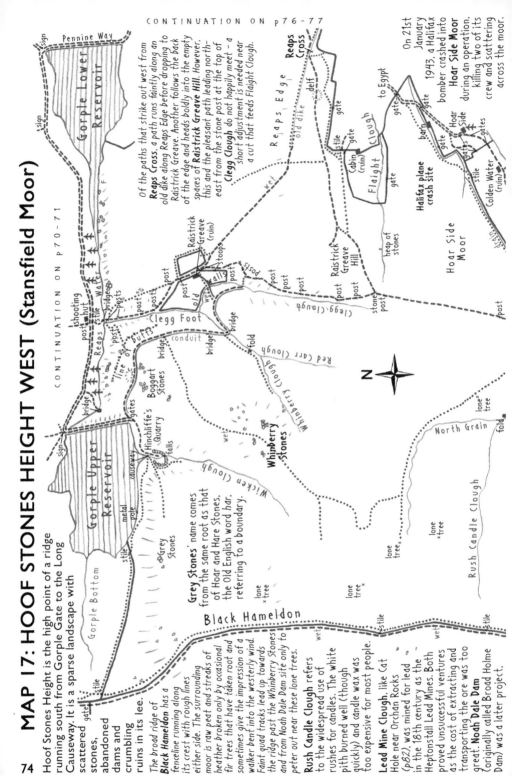

Map labels: Pennine Way · sign · Gorple Lower Reservoir · Reaps Water · Reaps Cross · Reaps Edge · old dike · delf · gate · stile · Flaight Clough · Cabin (ruin) · gate · barn · gate · to Egypt · Hoar Side · Colden Water · stile · gates · Halifax plane crash site · heap of stones · Raistrick Greave Hill · Raistrick Greave (ruin) · Stoop · walls · old well · post · posts · (Clegg Clough) · stone post · Hoar Side Moor · shooting hut · post · Clegg Foot · line of butts · conduit · bridge · fold · Red Carr Clough · Boggart Stones · bridge · Whinberry Clough · Whinberry Stones · Hinchliffe's Quarry · falls · gates · Gorple Upper Reservoir · metal pole · causeway · stile · Grey Stones · Gorple Bottom · Wicken Clough · wet · Black Hameldon · well · stile · N · North Grain · lone tree · Rush Candle Clough · fold · lone × tree

74

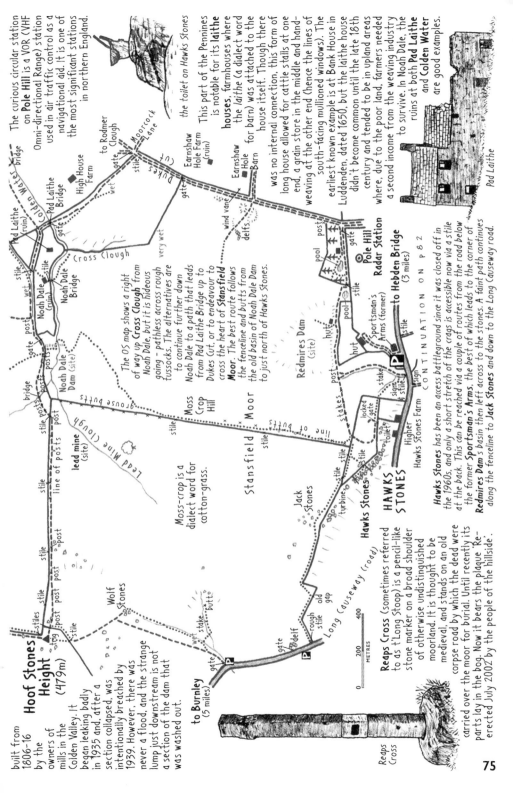

The curious circular station on **Pole Hill** is a VOR (VHF Omni-directional Range) station used in air traffic control as a navigational aid. It is one of the most significant stations in northern England.

the toilet on Hawks Stones

This part of the Pennines is notable for its **laithe houses**, farmhouses where the *laithe* (a dialect word for barn) was attached to the house itself. Though there was no internal connection, this form of long house allowed for cattle stalls at one end, a grain store in the middle and hand-weaving at the other end (hence the lines of south-facing mullioned windows). The earliest known example is at Bank House in Luddenden, dated 1650, but the laithe house didn't become common until the late 18th century and tended to be in upland areas where, due to the poor land, farmers needed a second income from the weaving industry to survive. In Noah Dale, the ruins at both **Pad Laithe** and **Colden Water** are good examples.

Pad Laithe

to Rodmer Clough

High House Farm — Moorcock Lane — Pad Laithe Bridge — Pad Laithe (ruin) — Colden Water bridge — stile — gate — wet gate

Earnshaw Hole Farm (ruin) — Earnshaw Hole Barn — Dukes Cut — wind vane — delfs

Cross Clough — very wet — wet — stile — gate — posts — Noah Dale (ruin) — Noah Dale Bridge — post — bridge — Noah Dale Dam (site) — stile posts — grouse butts — stile — post — line of posts — lead mine (site) — Lead Mine (Clough)

Moss Crop Hill

Moss-crop is a dialect word for cotton-grass.

Stansfield Moor — line of butts — stile

The OS map shows a right of way up **Cross Clough** from Noah Dale, but it is hideous going - pathless across rough tussocks. The alternatives are to continue further down Noah Dale to a path that leads from Pad Laithe Bridge up to Dukes Cut, or to endeavour to cross the heart of **Stansfield Moor**. The best route follows the fenceline and butts from the old basin of Noah Dale Dam to just north of Hawks Stones.

Redmires Dam (site) — hut — hut — Sportsman's Arms (former) — pool — stile

to Hebden Bridge (3 miles)

Pole Hill Radar Station — pool — post — gate — stile — delfs

Jack Stones — turbine — stile — stile — Hawks Stones (road) — **HAWKS STONES** — Higher Hawks Stones Farm — toilet — stile — locked gate — sign — stile — stakes — post

Hoof Stones Height (479m)

built from 1806-16 by the owners of mills in the Colden Valley. It began leaking badly in 1935 and, after a section collapsed, was intentionally breached by 1939. However, there was never a flood, and the strange lump just downstream is not a section of the dam that was washed out.

to Burnley (5 miles)

Wolf Stones — stile — post — post — stile — stiles — trig — stile

Hawks Stones has been an access battleground since it was closed off in the 1960s, and only a short stretch of the crags is accessible now via a stile at the back. This can be reached via a couple of routes from the road below the former **Sportsman's Arms**, the best of which leads to the corner of **Redmires Dam**'s basin then left across to the stones. A faint path continues along the fenceline from left across to **Jack Stones** and down to the Long Causeway road.

CONTINUATION ON p 82

Reaps Cross (sometimes referred to as t'Long Stoop) is a pencil-like stone marker on a broad shoulder of otherwise undistinguished moorland, and stands on an old corpse road by which the dead were carried over the moor for burial. Until recently its parts lay in the bog. Now it bears the plaque 'Re-erected July 2002 by the people of the hillside'.

Reaps Cross

Long Causeway (road) — old gap — rough stile — delf — stake — butts — wet — gate — gate

0   200   400   METRES

MAP 18: HOOF STONES HEIGHT EAST (Heptonstall Moor & Blake Dean)

Standing Stone Hill, the highest point on Heptonstall Moor, is a proud lump crowned by a trig point that feels quite separate from Hoof Stones Height, but is not quite high enough to warrant its own chapter in this book. On its north side the picturesque ravine of Blake Dean is one of the most recognisable corners of the South Pennines and frames this easily accessible side of the moor.

The lower section of Blake Dean, between the hostel and the top of the Hardcastle Crags woodland, is busy with paths and well worth exploring. The higher section, along Graining Water, is more remote but the south bank can be followed fairly easily; only one short section beneath King Common Brinks is at all rough.
Although the north bank looks a better bet from the bridge near Reaps Water, a wall soon squeezes the bank in too tightly to follow any further.

Blake Dean Scout Hostel is part of what remains of a Baptist chapel built in 1820 and used until 1959. The chapel itself has been demolished, but not the cottages that served as a Sunday school nor the tiny graveyard squeezed in the elbow of the hairpin bend. It is said to be haunted by the ghost of the green lady, a young woman who fell from the trestle bridge in Blake Dean.

The Gorple Reservoirs were built from 1927-34, employing fourteen steam locomotives on various tracks and inclines (the lines of which can still be seen). Quarries like Reaps Level were dug for stone for the dams and the scattered remains below the Lower Reservoir include those of the navvies' huts.

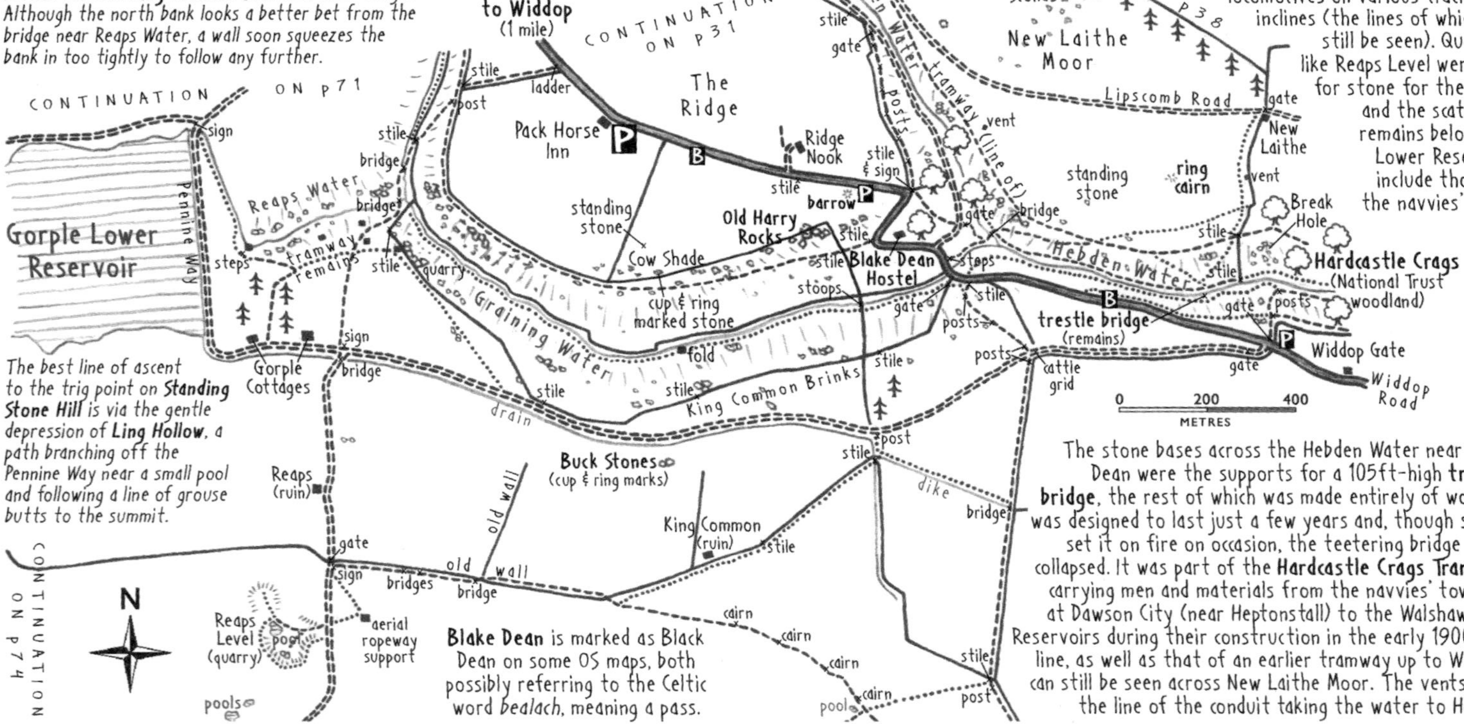

The stone bases across the Hebden Water near Blake Dean were the supports for a 105ft-high trestle bridge, the rest of which was made entirely of wood. It was designed to last just a few years and, though sparks set it on fire on occasion, the teetering bridge never collapsed. It was part of the Hardcastle Crags Tramway, carrying men and materials from the navvies' township at Dawson City (near Heptonstall) to the Walshaw Dean Reservoirs during their construction in the early 1900s. Its line, as well as that of an earlier tramway up to Widdop, can still be seen across New Laithe Moor. The vents show the line of the conduit taking the water to Halifax.

Blake Dean is marked as Black Dean on some OS maps, both possibly referring to the Celtic word bedlach, meaning a pass.

The best line of ascent to the trig point on Standing Stone Hill is via the gentle depression of Ling Hollow, a path branching off the Pennine Way near a small pool and following a line of grouse butts to the summit.

CONTINUATION ON p71

CONTINUATION ON p74

CONT. ON p 38

C O N T. O N p 71

C O N T I N U A T I O N O N p 31

to Widdop (1 mile)

Hardcastle Crags (National Trust woodland)

Widdop Road

Widdop Gate

New Laithe

Break Hole

Hoar Stones

New Laithe Moor

Lipscomb Road

ring cairn

Hebden Water

standing stone

trestle bridge (remains)

cattle grid

Alcomden Water

tramway (line of)

Holme Ends

Ridge Nook

barrow

Blake Dean Hostel

The Ridge

Old Harry Rocks

stoops

Cow Shade

cup & ring marked stone

fold

King Common Brinks

King Common (ruin)

Buck Stones (cup & ring marks)

Pack Horse Inn

standing stone

Graining Water

drain

old wall

aerial ropeway support

Reaps (ruin)

Reaps Water

tramway remains

Gorple Cottages

Reaps Level pool (quarry)

pools

Pennine Way

Gorple Lower Reservoir

ladder

METRES
0   200   400

N

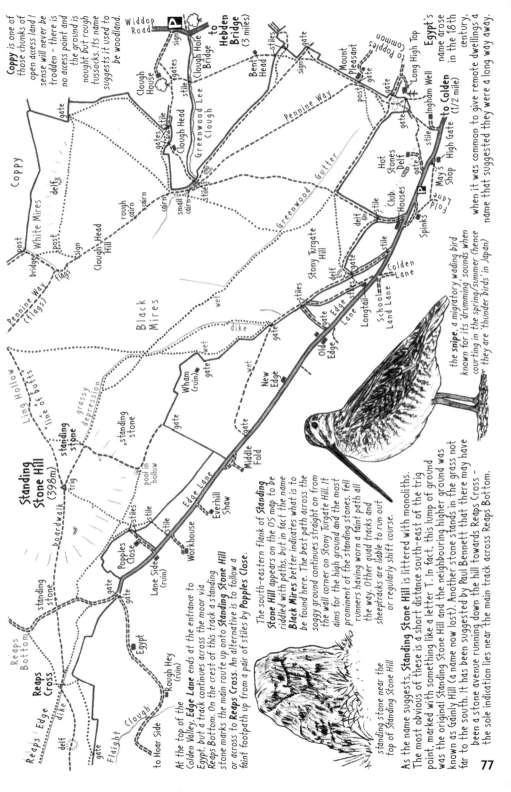

Coppy is one of those chunks of open access land I sense will never be trodden - there is no access point and the ground is nought but rough tussocks. Its name suggests it used to be woodland.

Widdop Road

to **Hebden Bridge** (3 miles)

to Popples (common)

Egypt's name arose in the 18th century, when it was common to give remote dwellings a name that suggested they were a long way away.

to Colden (1/2 mile)

Clough House
Clough Hole Bridge
Clough Head
Greenwood Lee Clough
Clough Head Hill
Bent Head
Mount Pleasant
Long High Top
Ingham Well
May's Shop
High Gate
Pennine Way
Greenwood Gutter
Hot Stones Delf
Club Houses
Spinks
Fold Lane
Colden Lane
Coppy
White Mires
Clough Head Hill
Pennine Way (flags)
Black Mires
Stony Turgate Hill
School Land Lane
Longtail
Old Edge
New Edge
Wham (ruin)
Ling Hollow
line of butts
grassy depression
standing stone
pool in hollow
Middle Fold
Everhill Shaw
Edge Lane
boardwalk
trig
Standing Stone Hill (398m)
standing stone
Popples Close
Lane Side (ruin)
Workhouse
Reaps Bottom
standing stone
Egypt
Rough Hey (ruin)
Reaps Cross
Reaps Edge
delf
Flight Clough
to Hoar Side

the **snipe**, a migratory wading bird known for its 'drumming sounds when courting in the spring/summer (hence they are 'thunder birds' in Japan).

The south-eastern flank of **Standing Stone Hill** appears on the OS map to be riddled with paths, but in fact the name **Black Mires** better indicates what is to be found here. The best path across the soggy ground continues straight on from the wall corner on Stony Turgate Hill. It aims for the high ground and the most prominent of the standing stones, fell runners having worn a faint path all the way. Other quad tracks and sheeptracks are liable to run out or regularly shift course.

standing stone near the top of Standing Stone Hill

As the name suggests, **Standing Stone Hill** is littered with monoliths. The most obvious of these is a short distance south-east of the trig point, marked with something like a letter T. In fact, this lump of ground was the original Standing Stone Hill and the neighbouring higher ground was known as Gadnly Hill (a name now lost). Another stone stands in the grass not far to the south. It has been suggested by Paul Bennett that there may have been a stone avenue running down the hill towards Reaps Cross - the sole indication lies near the main track across Reaps Bottom.

At the top of the Colden Valley, **Edge Lane** ends at the entrance to Egypt, but a track continues across the moor via Reaps Bottom. On the crest of this track a standing stone marks the main route up onto **Standing Stone Hill** or across to **Reaps Cross**. An alternative is to follow a faint footpath up from a pair of stiles by **Popples Close**.

77

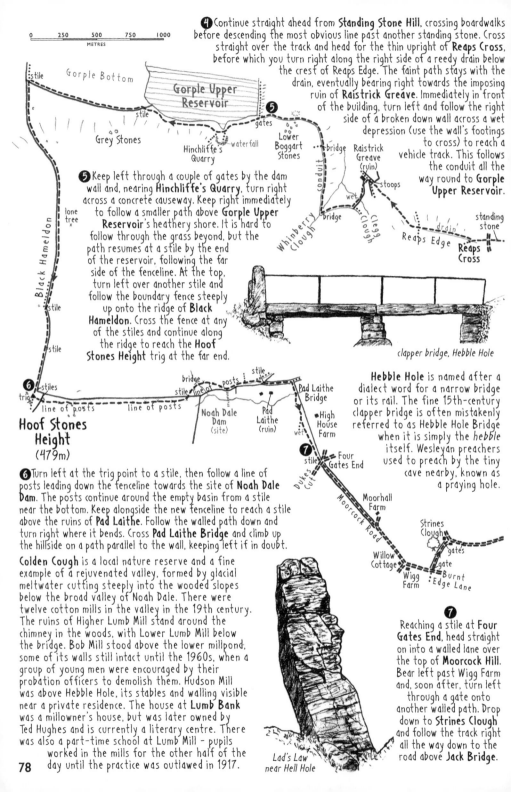

④ Continue straight ahead from **Standing Stone Hill**, crossing boardwalks before descending the most obvious line past another standing stone. Cross straight over the track and head for the thin upright of **Reaps Cross**, before which you turn right along the right side of a reedy drain below the crest of Reaps Edge. The faint path stays with the drain, eventually bearing right towards the imposing ruin of **Raistrick Greave**. Immediately in front of the building, turn left and follow the right side of a broken down wall across a wet depression (use the wall's footings to cross) to reach a vehicle track. This follows the conduit all the way round to **Gorple Upper Reservoir**.

⑤ Keep left through a couple of gates by the dam wall and, nearing **Hinchliffe's Quarry**, turn right across a concrete causeway. Keep right immediately to follow a smaller path above **Gorple Upper Reservoir**'s heathery shore. It is hard to follow through the grass beyond, but the path resumes at a stile by the end of the reservoir, following the far side of the fenceline. At the top, turn left over another stile and follow the boundary fence steeply up onto the ridge of **Black Hameldon**. Cross the fence at any of the stiles and continue along the ridge to reach the **Hoof Stones Height** trig at the far end.

clapper bridge, Hebble Hole

Hebble Hole is named after a dialect word for a narrow bridge or its rail. The fine 15th-century clapper bridge is often mistakenly referred to as Hebble Hole Bridge when it is simply the *hebble* itself. Wesleyan preachers used to preach by the tiny cave nearby, known as a praying hole.

Hoof Stones Height
(479m)

⑥ Turn left at the trig point to a stile, then follow a line of posts leading down the fenceline towards the site of **Noah Dale Dam**. The posts continue around the empty basin from a stile near the bottom. Keep alongside the new fenceline to reach a stile above the ruins of **Pad Laithe**. Follow the walled path down and turn right where it bends. Cross **Pad Laithe Bridge** and climb up the hillside on a path parallel to the wall, keeping left if in doubt.

Colden Cough is a local nature reserve and a fine example of a rejuvenated valley, formed by glacial meltwater cutting steeply into the wooded slopes below the broad valley of Noah Dale. There were twelve cotton mills in the valley in the 19th century. The ruins of Higher Lumb Mill stand around the chimney in the woods, with Lower Lumb Mill below the bridge. Bob Mill stood above the lower millpond, some of its walls still intact until the 1960s, when a group of young men were encouraged by their probation officers to demolish them. Hudson Mill was above Hebble Hole, its stables and walling visible near a private residence. The house at **Lumb Bank** was a millowner's house, but was later owned by Ted Hughes and is currently a literary centre. There was also a part-time school at Lumb Mill – pupils worked in the mills for the other half of the day until the practice was outlawed in 1917.

⑦ Reaching a stile at **Four Gates End**, head straight on into a walled lane over the top of **Moorcock Hill**. Bear left past Wigg Farm and, soon after, turn left through a gate onto another walled path. Drop down to **Strines Clough** and follow the track right all the way down to the road above **Jack Bridge**.

Lad's Law near Hell Hole

78

Map labels:
0 250 500 750 1000 METRES
Gorple Bottom, stile, Gorple Upper Reservoir, Grey Stones, Hinchliffe's Quarry, waterfall, Lower Boggart Stones, gates, bridge, Raistrick Greave (ruin), stoops, conduit, Whinberry Clough, bridge, wet, Clegg Clough, Reaps Edge, drain, standing stone, Reaps Cross, lone tree, Black Hameldon, stile, stile, bridge, line of posts, stile, posts, stile, Pad Laithe Bridge, Noah Dale Dam (site), Pad Laithe (ruin), wet, High House Farm, stiles, trig, line of posts, line of posts, stile, Four Gates End, Dukes Cut, Moorcock Road, Moorhall Farm, Willow Cottage, gate, Wigg Farm, Burnt Edge Lane, Strines Clough, gates

ROUTE 13: HOOF STONES HEIGHT & STANDING STONE HILL FROM HEBDEN BRIDGE

Distance: 14½ miles (23.2km)

Ascent: 540m

Difficulty: Strenuous

Parking: At the railway station or pay car parks in Hebden Bridge town centre.

Public Transport: Hebden Bridge is on the main Caldervale train & bus routes. Bus 596 runs from Hebden Bridge to Blackshaw Head via Popples Common and Jack Bridge and can be used to shorten the route.

Character: A substantial walk out of Hebden Bridge, steadily climbing to the summit of Hoof Stones Height on the county boundary via Heptonstall Crags and Standing Stone Hill. The return route takes in Noah Dale Dam and Colden Clough. Much of the route is necessarily on narrow tussocky paths and rough ground, but the navigation is not too challenging.

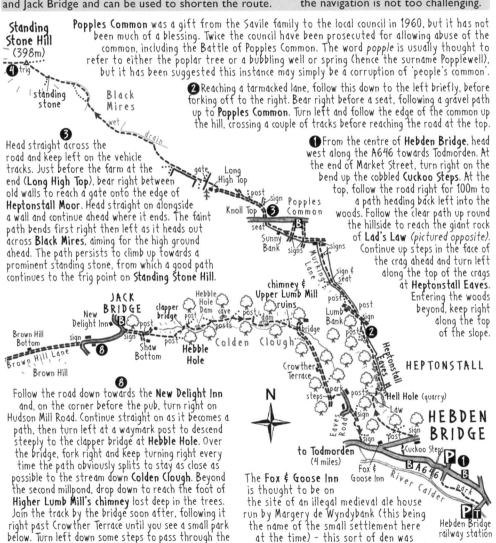

Popples Common was a gift from the Savile family to the local council in 1960, but it has not been much of a blessing. Twice the council have been prosecuted for allowing abuse of the common, including the Battle of Popples Common. The word *popple* is usually thought to refer to either the poplar tree or a bubbling well or spring (hence the surname Popplewell), but it has been suggested this instance may simply be a corruption of 'people's common'.

❷ Reaching a tarmacked lane, follow this down to the left briefly, before forking off to the right. Bear right before a seat, following a gravel path up to **Popples Common**. Turn left and follow the edge of the common up the hill, crossing a couple of tracks before reaching the road at the top.

❶ From the centre of **Hebden Bridge**, head west along the A646 towards Todmorden. At the end of Market Street, turn right on the bend up the cobbled **Cuckoo Steps**. At the top, follow the road right for 100m to a path heading back left into the woods. Follow the clear path up round the hillside to reach the giant rock of **Lad's Law** (*pictured opposite*). Continue up steps in the face of the crag ahead and turn left along the top of the crags at **Heptonstall Eaves**. Entering the woods beyond, keep right along the top of the slope.

❸ Head straight across the road and keep left on the vehicle tracks. Just before the farm at the end (**Long High Top**), bear right between old walls to reach a gate onto the edge of **Heptonstall Moor**. Head straight on alongside a wall and continue ahead where it ends. The faint path bends first right then left as it heads out across **Black Mires**, aiming for the high ground ahead. The path persists to climb up towards a prominent standing stone, from which a good path continues to the trig point on **Standing Stone Hill**.

Standing Stone Hill (398m)

Black Mires

❽ Follow the road down towards the **New Delight Inn** and, on the corner before the pub, turn right on Hudson Mill Road. Continue straight on as it becomes a path, then turn left at a waymark post to descend steeply to the clapper bridge at **Hebble Hole**. Over the bridge, fork right and keep turning right every time the path obviously splits to stay as close as possible to the stream down **Colden Clough**. Beyond the second millpond, drop down to reach the foot of **Higher Lumb Mill's chimney** lost deep in the trees. Join the track by the bridge soon after, following it right past Crowther Terrace until you see a small park below. Turn left down some steps to pass through the park and follow the road right beyond. On the bend fork left up a track and join the path into the woods at its end, keeping right to reach the main road, which can be followed left back into **Hebden Bridge**.

The **Fox & Goose Inn** is thought to be on the site of an illegal medieval ale house run by Margery de Wyndybank (this being the name of the small settlement here at the time) – this sort of den was known as a *tiddlywink*. There was also a brewhouse here in the 17th century as part of Litt House, which spanned the road as a gatehouse to the Sutcliffe Estate before the turnpike necessitated its removal.

JACK BRIDGE

New Delight Inn

Brown Hill Bottom

Brown Hill

Hebble Hole Dam

Shaw Bottom

Hebble Hole

Colden Clough

chimney & Upper Lumb Mill ruins

Lumb Bank

Crowther Terrace

HEPTONSTALL

Hell Hole (quarry)

Eaves Road

Law

HEBDEN BRIDGE

to Todmorden (4 miles)

Cuckoo Steps

Fox & Goose Inn

River Calder

Hebden Bridge railway station

Sunny Bank

Knoll Top

Popples Common

Long High Top

Heptonstall Eaves

N

79

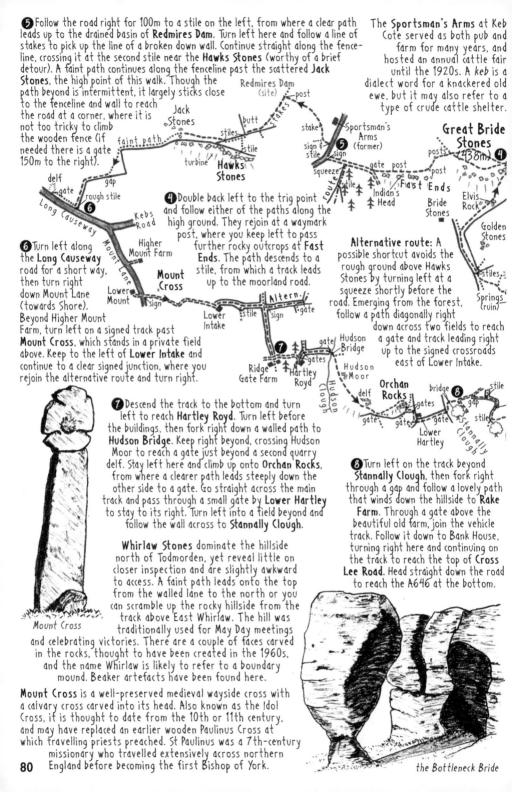

⑤ Follow the road right for 100m to a stile on the left, from where a clear path leads up to the drained basin of **Redmires Dam**. Turn left here and follow a line of stakes to pick up the line of a broken down wall. Continue straight along the fence-line, crossing it at the second stile near the **Hawks Stones** (worthy of a brief detour). A faint path continues along the fenceline past the scattered **Jack Stones**, the high point of this walk. Though the path beyond is intermittent, it largely sticks close to the fenceline and wall to reach the road at a corner, where it is not too tricky to climb the wooden fence (if needed there is a gate 150m to the right).

The **Sportsman's Arms** at Keb Cote served as both pub and farm for many years, and hosted an annual cattle fair until the 1920s. A *keb* is a dialect word for a knackered old ewe, but it may also refer to a type of crude cattle shelter.

④ Double back left to the trig point and follow either of the paths along the high ground. They rejoin at a waymark post, where you keep left to pass further rocky outcrops at **Fast Ends**. The path descends to a stile, from which a track leads up to the moorland road.

⑥ Turn left along the **Long Causeway** road for a short way, then turn right down Mount Lane (towards Shore). Beyond Higher Mount Farm, turn left on a signed track past **Mount Cross**, which stands in a private field above. Keep to the left of **Lower Intake** and continue to a clear signed junction, where you rejoin the alternative route and turn right.

Alternative route: A possible shortcut avoids the rough ground above Hawks Stones by turning left at a squeeze shortly before the road. Emerging from the forest, follow a path diagonally right down across two fields to reach a gate and track leading right up to the signed crossroads east of Lower Intake.

⑦ Descend the track to the bottom and turn left to reach **Hartley Royd**. Turn left before the buildings, then fork right down a walled path to **Hudson Bridge**. Keep right beyond, crossing Hudson Moor to reach a gate just beyond a second quarry delf. Stay left here and climb up onto **Orchan Rocks**, from where a clearer path leads steeply down the other side to a gate. Go straight across the main track and pass through a small gate by **Lower Hartley** to stay to its right. Turn left into a field beyond and follow the wall across to **Stannally Clough**.

Whirlaw Stones dominate the hillside north of Todmorden, yet reveal little on closer inspection and are slightly awkward to access. A faint path leads onto the top from the walled lane to the north or you can scramble up the rocky hillside from the track above East Whirlaw. The hill was traditionally used for May Day meetings and celebrating victories. There are a couple of faces carved in the rocks, thought to have been created in the 1960s, and the name Whirlaw is likely to refer to a boundary mound. Beaker artefacts have been found here.

Mount Cross is a well-preserved medieval wayside cross with a calvary cross carved into its head. Also known as the Idol Cross, it is thought to date from the 10th or 11th century, and may have replaced an earlier wooden Paulinus Cross at which travelling priests preached. St Paulinus was a 7th-century missionary who travelled extensively across northern England before becoming the first Bishop of York.

⑧ Turn left on the track beyond **Stannally Clough**, then fork right through a gap and follow a lovely path that winds down the hillside to **Rake Farm**. Through a gate above the beautiful old farm, join the vehicle track. Follow it down to Bank House, turning right here and continuing on the track to reach the top of **Cross Lee Road**. Head straight down the road to reach the A646 at the bottom.

Mount Cross

the Bottleneck Bride

ROUTE 14: THE BRIDE STONES & OTHER ROCKS FROM TODMORDEN

Distance: 8 miles (12.8km)

Ascent: 420m

Difficulty: Moderate

Parking: At Todmorden railway station, or the car park just off Stansfield Road.

Public Transport: Todmorden is on the main Caldervale train & bus routes.

Character: A very satisfying and varied route that climbs straight out of Todmorden to the various rocky outcrops that fringe the hills to the north. It is largely easy walking on clear paths and tracks, except for the rough section along Hawks Stones and Jack Stones, which can be avoided by a shortcut if necessary.

Bottleneck Bride
trig

3 A line of causey leads past the ruins of West Whirlaw and on round the foot of **Whirlaw Stones** to join the walled track of **Stony Lane**. At the next junction turn right through a gate and follow an overgrown track up the slope. Continue straight ahead where the track bends right towards some quarry delfs and soon join the main path up to the stile below the **Bride Stones**. Fork left and follow the fenceline round towards a prominent quiff-like balanced rock. The most obvious path leads above Elvis Rock and through the stones below the trig point to reach the famous **Bottleneck Bride**.

2 The path climbs to a pond, where you keep left to head towards the walk's first prominent rocky outcrop, the **Butt Stones**. You can climb up to the rocks, but the onward route follows the path round to the left, joining the walled track of **Broad Gate**. Continue straight on at Wickenberry Clough, following Scrapers Lane up through the woods. At a sharp bend just beyond East Whirlaw Farm, turn left and follow a path above the farm, then continue straight on below **Whirlaw Stones**.

delfs

Stony Lane

gate gate gate

gate

causey gate

Whirlaw Stones

Springs Farm, now a ruin, was renowned for selling stingo, a crude and strong beer.

West Whirlaw (ruin)

3 East Whirlaw

Scrapers Lane

Bents Clough

Wickenberry Clough

sign

post

Broad Gate

Butt Stones

sign

Stony Lane was a packhorse route across the side of the moor between Cross Stone and Mount Cross. Lines of causey are visible on several sections and are particularly well preserved below Whirlaw Stones. A Packhorse Inn existed at either East or West Whirlaw before the packhorse routes were usurped by turnpike roads.

gates

Rake Farm

post

cattle grid

Bank House

cattle grid

sign

railway

Cross Lee Road

Hare & Hounds

to Burnley (8 miles)

9

North Lodge

B

Todmorden High School

gate

P

leisure centre

0 200 400
METRES

N

Hole Bottom

sign

Chimney House

dam

2

Fountain (former)

Stansfield Hall Road

railway

bridge

1 From the centre of **Todmorden**, head out towards Burnley on the A646. Beyond the railway arches, turn right at a mini roundabout into Stansfield Road and follow it to the top. Turn right to cross a bridge over the other railway line, then turn left down Stansfield Hall Road. At the corner, turn right up Meadow Bottom Road. Soon after the prominent **Chimney House**, the track splits; curve round to the right, and follow a path into the trees.

Bog asphodel, a deep yellow lily seen in early summer in wet areas of acid bog

Meadow Bottom Rd

Centre Vale Park

statue

Buckley Wood

steps

Lovers' Walk

A646

P

Stansfield Road

fire station

railway

TODMORDEN

B to Hebden **B** Bridge (4 miles)

Town Hall

Well Lane

Ridge Steps

1

A646

railway station

T

P

to Rochdale (7 miles)

9 Turn left on the main road, then turn right into **Centre Vale Park** soon after Ewood Lane. Follow the main track round the park as far as the statue of John Fielden; turn right here, then immediately bear left up the slope into **Buckley Wood**. Turn left at the top, then immediately right up some rough steps. Head left again through the heart of the wood, soon joining the tarmac of **Lovers' Walk**. This emerges on Well Lane above the town centre. Follow the steep Ridge Steps down to reach the railway arches near **Todmorden** railway station.

Ewood Lane

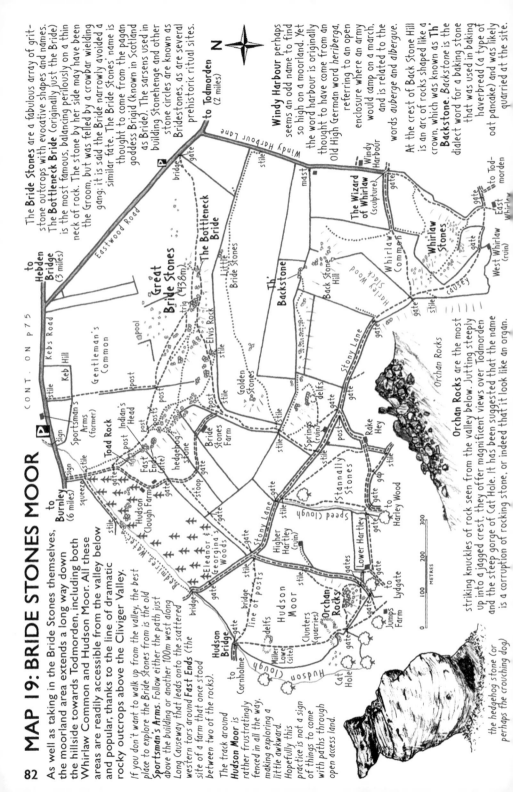

MAP 19: BRIDE STONES MOOR

As well as taking in the Bride Stones themselves, the moorland area extends a long way down the hillside towards Todmorden, including both Whirlaw Common and Hudson Moor. All these areas are readily accessible from the valley below and popular, thanks to the line of dramatic rocky outcrops above the Cliviger Valley.

If you don't want to walk up from the valley, the best place to explore the Bride Stones from is the old Sportsman's Arms. Follow either the path just above the building or another 100m west along Long Causeway that leads onto the scattered western tors around Fast Ends (the site of a farm that once stood between two of the rocks).

The track around Hudson Moor is rather frustratingly fenced in all the way, making exploring a little awkward. Hopefully this practice is not a sign of things to come with paths through open access land.

The Bride Stones are a fabulous array of grit-stone outcrops with evocative shapes and names. The Bottleneck Bride (originally just the Bride) is the most famous, balancing perilously on a thin neck of rock. The stone by her side may have been the Groom, but was felled by a crowbar wielding gang; it is said the Bride narrowly avoided a similar fate. The Bride Stones' name is thought to come from the pagan goddess Brigid (known in Scotland as Bride). The sarsens used in building Stonehenge and other stone circles are known as Bridestones, as are several prehistoric ritual sites.

Windy Harbour perhaps seems an odd name to find so high on a moorland. Yet the word harbour is originally thought to have come from an Old High German word *heriberga*, referring to an open enclosure where an army would camp on a march, and is related to the words *auberge* and *albergue*.

At the crest of Back Stone Hill is an arc of rocks shaped like a crown, which was known as Th' Backstone. *Backstone* is the dialect word for a baking stone that was used in baking haverbread (a type of oat pancake) and was likely quarried at the site.

Orchan Rocks are the most striking knuckles of rock seen from the valley below. Jutting steeply up into a jagged crest, they offer magnificent views over Todmorden and the steep gorge of Cat Hole. It has been suggested that the name is a corruption of rocking stone, or indeed that it look like an organ.

the hedgehog stone (or perhaps the crouching dog)

Orchan Rocks

CONT. ON P75

to Hebden Bridge (3 miles)

to Burnley (6 miles)

to Todmorden (2 miles)

to Cornholme

to Harley Wood

to Todmorden

Map labels:
Eastwood Road · Kebs Road · Keb Hill · Gentleman's Common · Sign · Sportsman's Arms (former) · Toad Rock · Indian's Head · Fast Ends · Hudson Clough Farm · hedgehog stone · Bride Stones Farm · Eleanor & Georgina's Woods · Hudson Moor · Hudson Bridge · Miller Lowe (site) · Clunters (quarries) · Orchan Rocks · Cat Hole · Hudson Clough · delfs · Jumps Farm · Lydgate · Lower Hartley · Higher Hartley (ruin) · Stony Lane · Stannally Stones · Springs (ruin) · Rake Hey · Golden Stones · Elvis Rock · Great Bride Stones (438m) · trig · pool · Little Bride Stones · The Bottleneck Bride · Th' Backstone · Back Stone Hill · Hartley Slack · Harley Wood Wood · Speed Clough · Whirlaw Common · The Wizard of Whirlaw (sculpture) · Windy Harbour Lane · Windy Harbour · mast · Whirlaw Stones · West Whirlaw (ruin) · East Whirlaw · bridges · gate · stile · post · squeeze · stoop · gap

0 100 200 300 METRES

N

CHAPTER 9 – CARR & CRAGGS MOOR
(aka Todmorden Moor)

Height: 441m

Grid Ref: SD894252

Map Sheet: OL21
(South Pennines)

Access: No restrictions.

Public Transport:
Todmorden is on the
main Caldervale
train and bus
routes. Bus 466
runs from Todmorden
to Bacup via Clough
Foot. Buses 589 & 592
run from Todmorden to
Burnley via Cornholme
and Portsmouth.

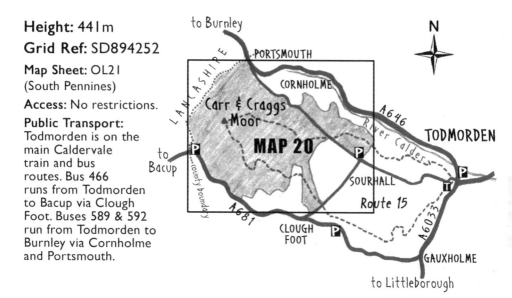

Carr & Craggs Moor is the highest grassy lump on Todmorden Moor, its unmarked summit lying north of Flower Scar Road, which cleaves the moor in two. Like neighbouring Freeholds Top, the moor is littered with the scars of opencast coal mining and fire clay extraction, which were particularly concentrated along Dulesgate (the A681). It is now marred by by landfill, fly-tipping and the new wind farm, but without the marks of spoil heaps, trial holes, quarries and subsidence, Carr and Craggs Moor would be largely uninteresting. To the north, overlooking Cornholme and Portsmouth, the moor finally comes into its own with the rocky promontories of Eagle's Crag and the Old Woman.

The name Carr is likely to come from the Old Norse word *kjarr*, meaning swamp or wet hollow (indeed in Lancashire dialect carr-water was peaty water). This combination of carr and craggs seems to sum up the character of the moor, but is confused somewhat by its recording as 'Carn Crags Moor' on the 1848 map – a mis-spelling or perhaps the suggestion of a Celtic link?

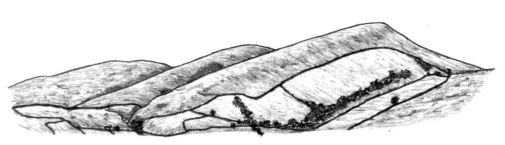

Carr and Craggs Moor from Gorpley

Though the top of Carr and Craggs Moor is rather dull, the routes up from **Portsmouth** and **Cornholme** are anything but. A good path starting opposite the Roebuck Inn climbs above the dramatic scar of **Beater Clough** via a former tramroad to reach the mine and landfill site at its head. Various paths also climb up **Tower Clough** above Bearnshaw Tower, the most substantial going through the plantation. The others all lead to the ruins of **Flower Scar Farm**, though some are tough going – the best starts at a stile on the first bend above the tower and follows the stream below the plantation before zig-zagging up to the ruins.

Above the rocky scar of Beater Clough, **Greens Clough** is very obviously polluted, predominantly by iron oxides from the coal mine workings all across the moor above. Though Hill Top Colliery closed in the 1960s, there is still a small working mine in the clough, a jumble of rusty prefab buildings that represents a one-man drift mine operation. A landfill site once occupied the fenced-off former colliery site above.

Portsmouth was so named by the son of the first landlord of the Roebuck Inn; he was a mariner who had been recently stationed on the south coast.

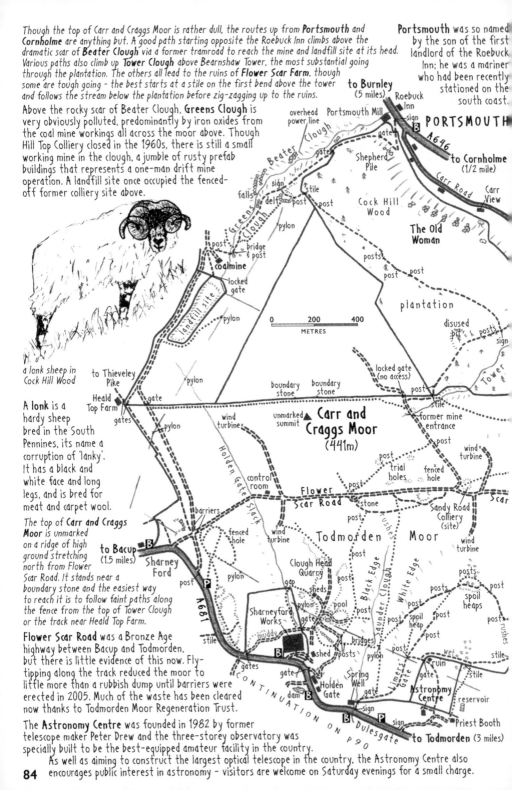

a lonk sheep in Cock Hill Wood

A **lonk** is a hardy sheep bred in the South Pennines, its name a corruption of 'lanky'. It has a black and white face and long legs, and is bred for meat and carpet wool.

The top of **Carr and Craggs Moor** is unmarked on a ridge of high ground stretching north from Flower Scar Road. It stands near a boundary stone and the easiest way to reach it is to follow faint paths along the fence from the top of Tower Clough or the track near Heald Top Farm.

Flower Scar Road was a Bronze Age highway between Bacup and Todmorden, but there is little evidence of this now. Fly-tipping along the track reduced the moor to little more than a rubbish dump until barriers were erected in 2005. Much of the waste has been cleared now thanks to Todmorden Moor Regeneration Trust.

The **Astronomy Centre** was founded in 1982 by former telescope maker Peter Drew and the three-storey observatory was specially built to be the best-equipped amateur facility in the country.

As well as aiming to construct the largest optical telescope in the country, the Astronomy Centre also encourages public interest in astronomy – visitors are welcome on Saturday evenings for a small charge.

MAP 20: CARR AND CRAGGS MOOR

As is evident, **Bearnshaw Tower** no longer has a tower; it apparently collapsed in 1860 following frenzied digging beneath it for a pot of gold rumoured to be buried there. In the 17th-century it was renowned as the home of a witch who was said to roam in the form of a white doe or cat. While in doe form, Lady Sybil was hunted by her future husband on horseback and cornered on **Eagle Crag**. The doe disappeared before he could shoot, but the vision is still said to haunt the crag (also known as the Witches' Horse Block) on Hallowe'en. Denied a Christian burial, she was laid beneath Eagle Crag. Previously known as Bill Knipe, the name Eagle Crag is thought to have been given it by a passing traveller.

Todmorden Moor is an urban common, its landscape shaped by mining, quarrying, landfill, and most recently wind turbines. There is little wild peat or heather, just a barren surface that has been subjected to industrial forces. Restoration schemes are underway to encourage regeneration of the heath moor, though when waste paper pulp was spread across neighbouring Heald Moor as a soil 'improver' in the 1990s, it formed a hard crust that took years to break down. Flower Scar Hill forms the most prominent part of Todmorden Moor, but it is a false top that leads gently up to the true summit of Carr and Craggs Moor.

The Old Woman is the most prominent of the crags jutting out of the woods above Portsmouth. The name is thought to relate to the mother goddess of the land and weather, known in Gaelic as the Cailleach. It was common for early Christians to refer to pagan beliefs as Old Lad, Old Wife or Old Woman.

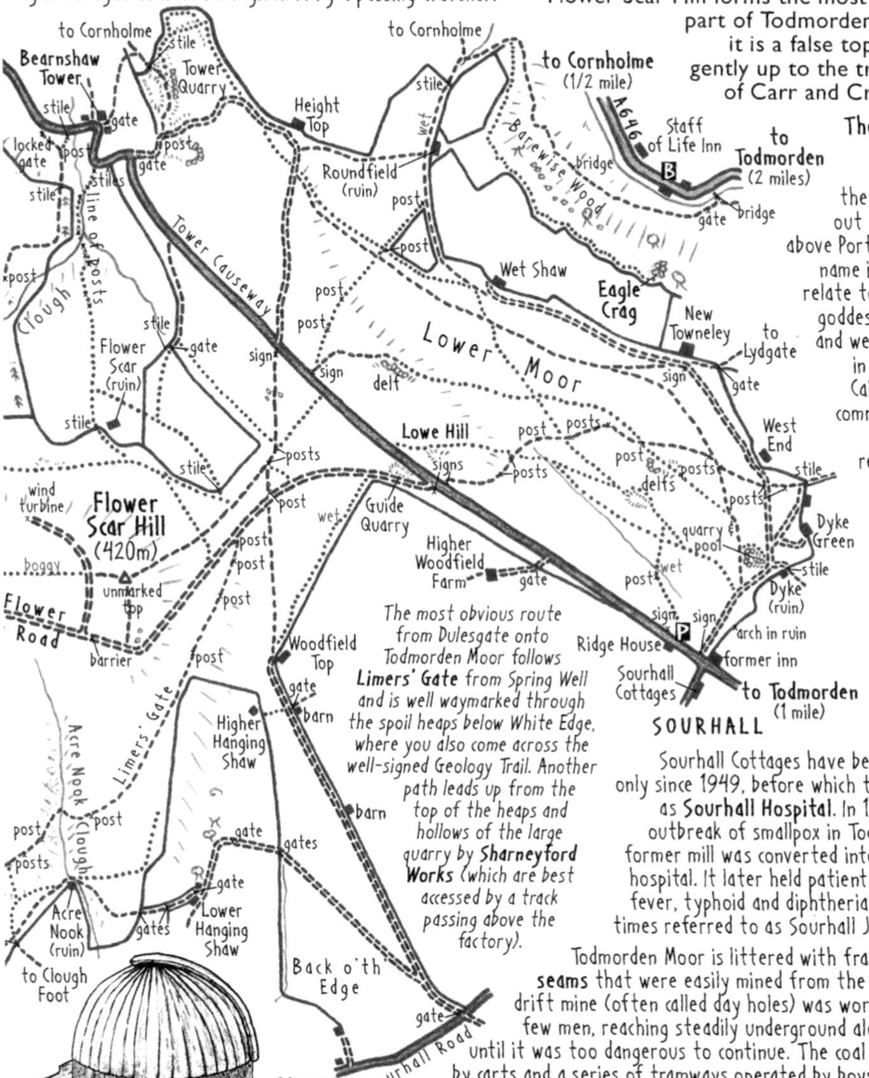

to Cornholme
Bearnshaw Tower
stile
tile
Tower Quarry
to Cornholme
stile
Height Top
Wet
to Cornholme (1/2 mile)
Bearwise Wood
A646
locked gate
post
gate
post
stile
stiles
gate
Roundfield (ruin)
post
bridge
Staff of Life Inn
B
to Todmorden (2 miles)
stile
Line of Posts
Tower Causeway
Clough
stile
post
Flower Scar (ruin)
gate
sign
sign
delf
post
Wet Shaw
gate
bridge
Eagle Crag
New Towneley
to Lydgate
Lower Moor
sign
gate
West End
stile
wind turbine
Flower Scar Hill (420m)
stile
posts
Lowe Hill
post
posts
signs
posts
post
post
delfts
posts
quarry
pool
Dyke Green
bogay
unmarked top
post
post
wet
Guide Quarry
Higher Woodfield Farm
gate
post
wet
Dyke (ruin)
stile
Flower Road
barrier
post
Woodfield Top
gate
barn
Ridge House
Sourhall Cottages
SOURHALL
P
sign
sign
arch in ruin
former inn
to Todmorden (1 mile)
Acre Nook Clough
post
Higher Hanging Shaw
barn
Limers' Gate
post
posts
gate
gates
barn
Lower Hanging Shaw
gate
Acre Nook (ruin)
gates
Back o' th Edge
gate
to Clough Foot
CLOUGH FOOT
Sourhall Road
the Astronomy Centre

The most obvious route from Dulesgate onto Todmorden Moor follows **Limers' Gate** from Spring Well and is well waymarked through the spoil heaps below White Edge, where you also come across the well-signed Geology Trail. Another path leads up from the top of the heaps and hollows of the large quarry by **Sharneyford Works** (which are best accessed by a track passing above the factory).

Sourhall Cottages have been residences only since 1949, before which they operated as **Sourhall Hospital**. In 1874, upon an outbreak of smallpox in Todmorden, this former mill was converted into an isolation hospital. It later held patients with scarlet fever, typhoid and diphtheria and is sometimes referred to as Sourhall Joint Hospital.

Todmorden Moor is littered with fragmented **coal seams** that were easily mined from the surface. Each drift mine (often called day holes) was worked by only a few men, reaching steadily underground along the seam until it was too dangerous to continue. The coal was removed by carts and a series of tramways operated by boys as young as six. Along **Dulesgate**, the presence of fire-clay also allowed for the making of bricks, with much of the coal being used to fire the brickworks. The Temperley family owned a large pipeworks making sanitary pipes in the area around the Astronomy Centre.

N

4 Crossing **Tower Clough**, the path reaches a stile; turn left before this and follow the fenceline up to another major track. Follow this left for a few yards to pick up a path continuing up the fence to the top of **Carr and Craggs Moor**. The unmarked summit is off to the left, level with the second boundary stone. Follow the high ground left here (a bearing of 150°) and hope to pick up a faint sheeptrack aiming for the marker stone at the top of **Flower Scar Road**.

3 Climb left to join the tarmac track around **Lower Moor**; follow it right only for a few yards before ascending left around the rim of a flooded quarry delf. At the back, pick up a faint path leading right across the side of the moor. Aim for a waymark post and, reaching a second post, bear left to angle up the slope on a clear path. Follow the line of posts all the way to the road (**Tower Causeway**) and head straight across to join **Flower Scar Road**, now closed to traffic. This track bends left and starts to climb up towards Flower Scar Hill. Two paths (marked by posts) cross the track; 100m beyond the second, turn sharply right onto a faint path following the line of a grassy dike around the face of Flower Scar Hill. Above the dramatic ruins of **Flower Scar Farm**, bear left and climb slightly towards the head of Tower Clough by the left corner of the plantation.

6 Crossing **Acre Nook Clough**, turn hard right down a sunken trackway past a solitary tree. The path bends round to the left and leaves the moor at a gate. Follow the wall down from here to **Lower Hanging Shaw Farm** and turn left onto a farm track that curves round this attractive valley before crossing **Back o'th' Edge**, another stretch of moorland. The track joins another shortly before Sourhall Road, where you head straight across onto another track down to **Hazel Greave**.

5 Cross **Flower Scar Road** and join a grassy path running left beyond the marker stone. Beyond the rushes at the top of **Saunder Clough**, turn right and stay above the left side of the clough until something of a path appears. This meanders down the slope towards a pylon, before which you should head off to the left to a line of waymark posts near the former **colliery spoil heaps**. Follow these left, curving around another large spoil heap before dropping down to cross a very short bridge. Immediately beyond, leave the waymarked route of Limers' Gate and fork right down the side of the rushes. Keep left to cut round to the ruins of **Acre Nook**.

7 Just before **Hazel Greave Farm**, turn left on a path above the building to reach a pair of stiles. Follow the wall down into **Mellings Clough**; beyond the stream and a stile, bear left across the field, passing a large beech tree to reach a small gate in the wall. Follow the wall along the hillside above **Stones Wood** and join a clear path straight across the fields beyond. Where the wall ascends steeply, bear right along a slight depression to reach a stile. Follow the top side of an old wall beyond and at the end bear left up a walled path above **Friths Farm**. This almost immediately opens out into a field, where you turn sharply back to the left, climbing steeply up a grassy depression to a stile into **Stones Lane**.

ROUTE 15: CARR AND CRAGGS MOOR & STONES MENHIRS FROM TODMORDEN

Distance: 7 miles (11.5km)

Ascent: 390m

Difficulty: Moderate

Parking: At Todmorden railway station or on Dobroyd Road (opposite Morrisons).

Public Transport: Todmorden is on the main Caldervale train & bus routes.

Character: Todmorden Moor is invisible from the town, but the edge of the moor is reached not far above Centre Vale Park. After heading for its high point on Carr and Craggs Moor, the return route takes in the remarkable standing stones at Stones that really ought to be better known. Some of the walking is on faint tracks (there is little else on the moor) and care is needed in navigation, but none of it is particularly rough or strenuous.

Centre Vale Park stands on the site of Centre Vale House, a mansion built by Thomas Ramsbotham in the 1820s and later owned by the Fieldens. Carr Barn was one of a number of houses along Lovers' Walk and was home to Ruth Stansfield, the weaver who captured John Fielden's heart.

❶ Head left from **Todmorden railway station** down Station Approach and, on the corner, turn left to pass under the railway. As the road bends left, ascend **Ridge Steps** straight ahead; at the top, turn soft right onto a cycleway above the houses. Passing through the woods above **Centre Vale Park**, stay on the tarmac of Lovers' Walk until you come to an open area that was the site of Carr Barn; fork left here to reach Siggett Lane.

❷ Turn left up Siggett Lane for 100m, then follow the signed path right steeply up through **Ewood Wood**. The path bends left and enters a field; follow its left-hand edge to a grassy lane climbing up to the hamlet of **Todmorden Edge**. Turn right for a short distance, then opposite the last building turn left through a scruffy gate into the field to the left. Follow a wet depression up the side of the wall and, where the wall bends, go right through a gate that is difficult to open and not waymarked. Follow the opposite side of the wall and fence to the next gate (occasionally tied), where you bear left slightly up the slope towards a gate on the edge of **Lower Moor**.

It is hard to get a glimpse of **Dobroyd Castle**, shrouded as it is by trees, yet it should be one of Todmorden's most striking buildings. It cost more than Todmorden Town Hall and was built in the 1860s by John Fielden, supposedly in response to Ruth Stansfield only agreeing to marry him if he built her a castle. Since his death, it has been used by the Home Office, as a private school, a Buddhist retreat, and most recently an activity centre.

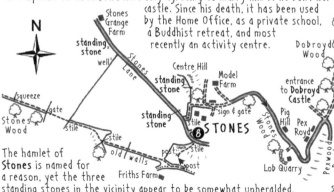

The hamlet of **Stones** is named for a reason, yet the three standing stones in the vicinity appear to be somewhat unheralded. The most prominent is a 12-foot monolith standing in a field right next to Stones Lane. Nearby a fragile finger-like stone is thrust up from a millstone on the top of Centre Hill - it is thought to have been moved here from the adjacent field to celebrate the Battle of Waterloo and used to have a weather-cock on top. The final stone is shorter and stands some 300m up Stones Lane in a field to the left. Little is known about the place, but it is a remarkable site.

❸ Turn left up Stones Lane and, before the most prominent **standing stone**, turn right to skirt around the high wall of Stones Farm. To explore the stones, head further up Stones Lane or access the fields through a couple of gates (though permission should be sought from the landowner). The route soon joins the road leading down the hill from **Stones Farm** as it winds steeply past various houses to a large junction in front of the gate to **Dobroyd Castle**. Head straight on here down a dead-end track through the woods to reach a bridge over the railway. Immediately beyond, turn left on a cycle path alongside the railway that soon emerges by **Todmorden station**.

87

TWITE

The **twite** is also known as the Pennine finch and the moors of the South Pennines are its last breeding ground in England. It is a small brown finch, closely related to the linnet and distinguished by its dark streaks and short beak. It is a partial migrant, wintering on the coast and breeding on high ground amid mature heather and bracken. There are only around a hundred pairs left in the area and their habitat is being further threatened by invasive species and moorland fires. The twite is on the red list of Birds of Conservation Concern and much work is being done to preserve and regenerate both its breeding and feeding grounds. Carr and Craggs Moor is one of the moors to have seen the twite's return in recent years.

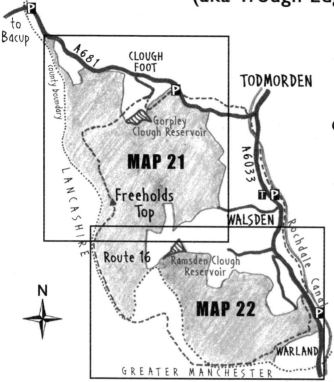

Height: 454m

Grid Ref: SD906219

Map Sheet: OL21
(South Pennines)

Access: No restrictions.

Public Transport:
Todmorden and
Walsden are on the
main Caldervale
train and bus routes.
Bus 466 runs
from Todmorden
to Bacup via
Clough Foot.

Freeholds Top stands on top of a steep escarpment visible across most of the Upper Calder Valley and offers a fine vantage point in all directions. The ridge, looking naturally to Walsden, cradles in its arms a number of impressively steep cloughs, the best-known being Gorpley Clough. There are many other corners, though, that are worth exploring on a moor that could all too easily be dismissed. It may be for this reason that it has recently been covered in windfarms, greatly changing its aspect.

Its names (it is equally often known as Trough Edge End) come from the Spodden Valley side, *freeholds* relating to the slopes above Shawforth that were enclosed from the waste in the 16th century and freed from duty to the Lords of the Manor (in this case, Lord Byron).

Freeholds Top from Sour Hall Road (before the building of the windfarms)

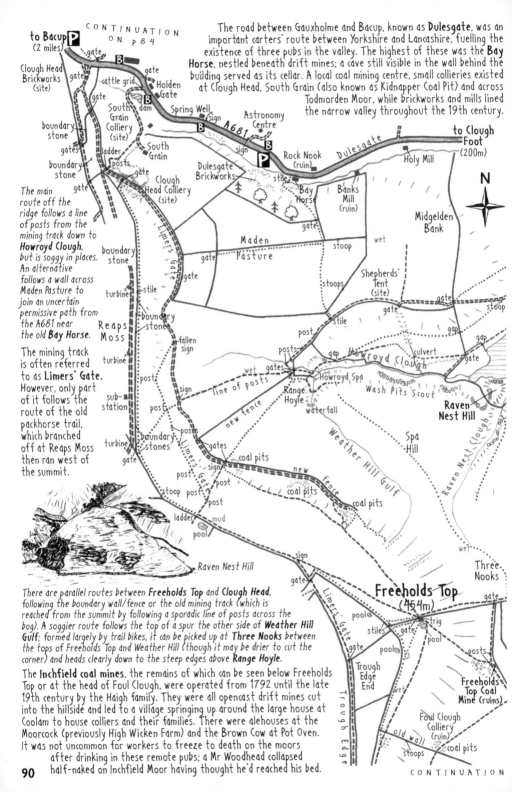

to Bacup P
(2 miles)

Clough Head
Brickworks
(site)

The road between Gauxholme and Bacup, known as **Dulesgate**, was an important carters' route between Yorkshire and Lancashire, fuelling the existence of three pubs in the valley. The highest of these was the **Bay Horse**, nestled beneath drift mines; a cave still visible in the wall behind the building served as its cellar. A local coal mining centre, small collieries existed at Clough Head, South Grain (also known as Kidnapper Coal Pit) and across Todmorden Moor, while brickworks and mills lined the narrow valley throughout the 19th century.

gate
cattle grid
Holden Gate
South Grain Colliery (site)
dam
Spring Well
sign
A681
Astronomy Centre
gate
boundary stone
gates
ladder
posts
South Grain
boundary stone
gate
Clough Head Colliery (site)
sign
Dulesgate Brickworks
P
Rock Nook (ruin)
stile
Bay Horse
Banks Mill (ruin)
Holy Mill
to Clough Foot (200m)
Dulesgate

N

*The main route off the ridge follows a line of posts from the mining track down to **Howroyd Clough**, but is soggy in places. An alternative follows a wall across Maden Pasture to join an uncertain permissive path from the A681 near the old **Bay Horse**.*

boundary stone
turbine
stile
boundary stones

Reaps Moss

fallen sign

Maden Pasture
gate
gate
stoop
wet
Midgelden Bank
gate
stoops
Shepherds' Tent (site)
gate
stile
gap
stoop
gap

*The mining track is often referred to as **Limers' Gate**. However, only part of it follows the route of the old packhorse trail, which branched off at Reaps Moss then ran west of the summit.*

turbine
post
sub-station
posts
turbine
boundary stones
gate

post
sign
line of posts
wet gates
post
new fence
posts
gates
sign
coal pits
Limers Gate
post
stoop post
post
post
ladder
mud
pool

Raven Nest Hill

post
posts
gap
Howroyd Clough
culvert
gate
Howroyd Spa
Wash Pits Scout
Range Hoyle
waterfall
Weather Hill Gulf
new fence
coal pits
coal pits
coal pits
Raven Nest Hill
Spa Hill
Raven Nest Clough
wet

sign
Three Nooks

*There are parallel routes between **Freeholds Top** and **Clough Head**, following the boundary wall/fence or the old mining track (which is reached from the summit by following a sporadic line of posts across the bog). A soggier route follows the top of a spur the other side of **Weather Hill Gulf**; formed largely by trail bikes, it can be picked up at **Three Nooks** between the tops of Freeholds Top and Weather Hill (though it may be drier to cut the corner) and heads clearly down to the steep edges above **Range Hoyle**.*

gate
Limers Gate
pool
stiles
gate
pool
gate
Freeholds Top (454m)
trig
pool
posts
gate
Trough Edge End
wet
Freeholds Top Coal Mine (ruins)

The **Inchfield coal mines**, the remains of which can be seen below Freeholds Top or at the head of Foul Clough, were operated from 1792 until the late 19th century by the Haigh family. They were all opencast drift mines cut into the hillside and led to a village springing up around the large house at Coolam to house colliers and their families. There were alehouses at the Moorcock (previously High Wicken Farm) and the Brown Cow at Pot Oven. It was not uncommon for workers to freeze to death on the moors after drinking in these remote pubs; a Mr Woodhead collapsed half-naked on Inchfield Moor having thought he'd reached his bed.

Trough Edge
old wall
Foul Clough Colliery (ruin)
stoops
coal pits

90

CONTINUATION

MAP 21: FREEHOLDS TOP NORTH (Inchfield Moor)

The northern side of Freeholds Top is dominated by Gorpley Clough, one of the finest valleys in the South Pennines. The impressive rock precipices on the southern shore of Gorpley Reservoir are in sharp contrast to the wet plateau of Inchfield Pasture and the broad ridge on which the trig point stands. The moor is easily accessed from Walsden, Gorpley Clough and Clough Head, with Freeholds Top a natural focal point for the whole moor. A striking element of the landscape here are the coal pits and black spoil heaps scattered from Foul Clough Road to Dulesgate, the remains of 19th-century drift mines that were why this moor was once far more populated than today.

If, like me, you are drawn to the rocky scars on the southern side of Gorpley Reservoir, the best route heads up the left-hand edge of the dam. After dropping down towards the water to avoid a drain, follow the shore to the bottom of Oatley Hill Scar, where you can duck under the fence and continue up the edge of the scar. A number of paths lead across the hillside from here towards Raven Nest Hill, the lower ones leading to an easy step over the fence to explore these myriad mesa-like knolls, as well as linking with a couple of worn lines that lead up to Three Nooks. The other path to Oatley Hill Scar follows the line of pylons intermittently across the hillside from Foul Clough Road.

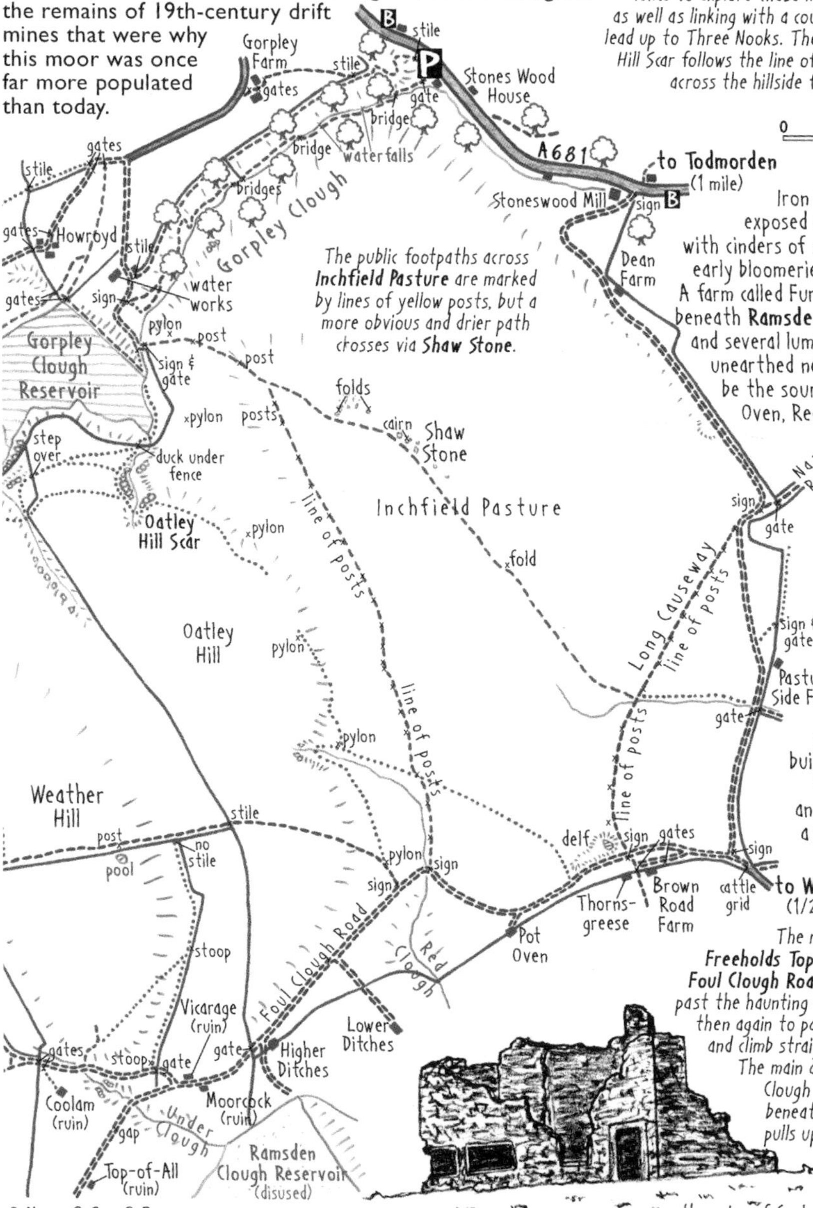

```
0        200        400
         METRES
```

Iron was extracted from exposed ore across the area, with cinders of slag iron evidence of early bloomeries in Gorpley Clough. A farm called Furnace was submerged beneath Ramsden Clough Reservoir and several lumps of cast iron were unearthed nearby. This may also be the source of the names Pot Oven, Red Clough and Reddy-shore Scout (near Summit).

Foul Clough Road was built to link the Inchfield coal mines with the turnpike, and the road down to Walsden was known as t'Coil Gate. The continuation past Top-of-All was built during the cotton famine in the 1860s and was not used until a mine was opened on Ramsden Hill in the 1920s.

The most obvious route up Freeholds Top from Walsden follows Foul Clough Road before forking right past the haunting towers of Coolam, and then again to pass the coal mine ruins and climb straight up to the summit. The main alternative leaves Foul Clough Road earlier, at a sign beneath the power lines, and pulls up the side of Weather Hill to reach the top.

The public footpaths across Inchfield Pasture are marked by lines of yellow posts, but a more obvious and drier path crosses via Shaw Stone.

the ruins of Coolam

ON p92-93

91

Ramsden Clough Reservoir was decommissioned in 2003 because there was too much peat in the water. A private company, Todmorden Water Works Company, built the reservoir in the 1880s and later sold it to the Rochdale Corporation, so Gorpley Clough had to be built to supply Todmorden.

Getting up from **Cranberry Dam** to the **Long Causeway** is not straight-forward. The easiest route follows the track up to Horsepasture's ruin, then crosses a stile to follow an angled groove across the hillside. In descent this path is easily missed, but can be joined by dropping down from a gap where the Long Causeway reaches the Long Wall. A slightly rougher alternative follows a wall along the side of a steep ravine to the north. Crossing a stile in the clough, climb straight up the steep slope to the right to join the wall; eventually cross it when the ground completely drops away.

CONTINUATION ON p90–91

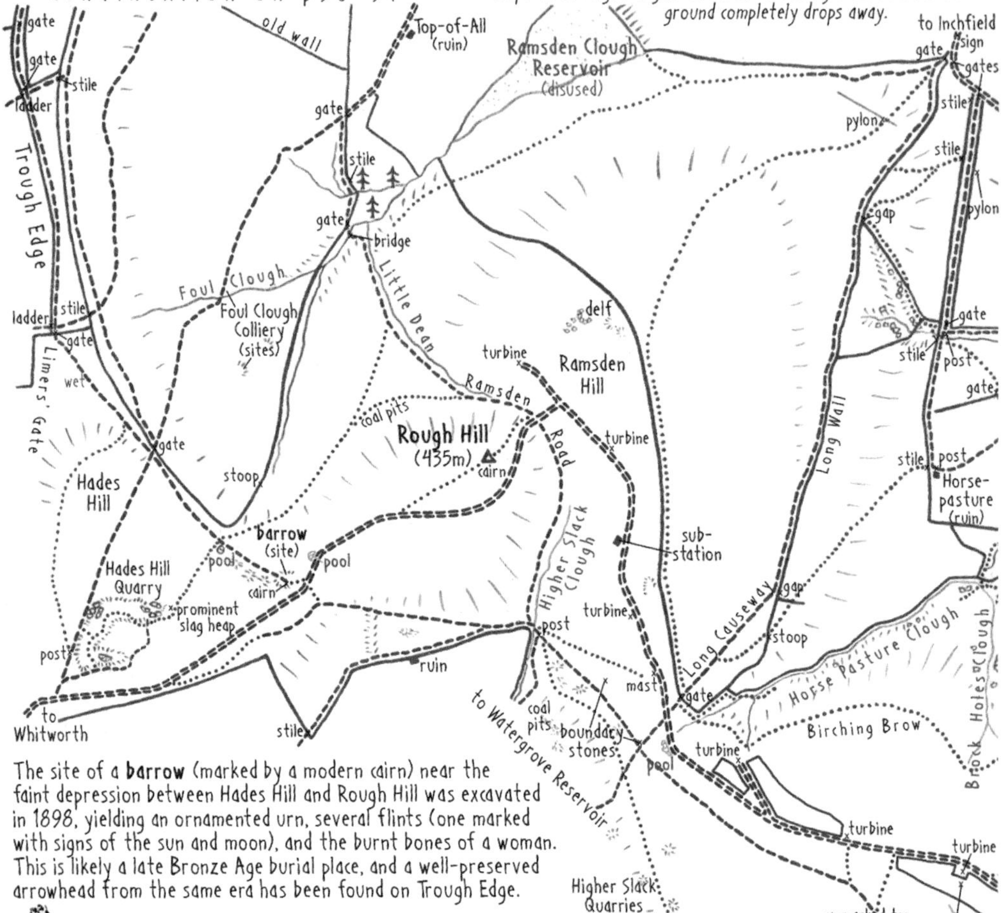

(map with labels:)

gate
gate
stile
ladder
Trough Edge
old wall
Top-of-All (ruin)
gate
stile
gate
bridge
Foul Clough
Foul Clough Colliery (sites)
Little Dean
Ramsden Clough Reservoir (disused)
to Inchfield
sign
gate
gates
stile
stile
pylon
pylon
gap
delf
turbine
Ramsden Hill
ladder
stile
gate
Limers' Gate
wet
gate
Hades Hill
stoop
Rough Hill (435m)
cairn
Ramsden Road
turbine
Long Wall
stile post
gate
stile post
Horse-pasture (ruin)
barrow (site)
pool
pool
Hades Hill Quarry
cairn
prominent slag heap
post
ruin
Higher Slack Clough
post
turbine
sub-station
stoop
Long Causeway
gap
Horse Pasture Clough
Brook Holes Clough
to Whitworth
stile
to Watergrove Reservoir
coal pits
boundary stones
mast
gate
pool
turbine
Birching Brow
turbine
turbine

The site of a **barrow** (marked by a modern cairn) near the faint depression between Hades Hill and Rough Hill was excavated in 1898, yielding an ornamented urn, several flints (one marked with signs of the sun and moon), and the burnt bones of a woman. This is likely a late Bronze Age burial place, and a well-preserved arrowhead from the same era has been found on Trough Edge.

Higher Slack Quarries

unmarked top
Crook Hill (408m)
boundary stone
coal pits
stile

White Slack Clough

The **Kemp Stone** is the largest of a cluster of rocks on the edge of Shore Moor and perhaps served as a boundary stone (kemp being suggested as a dialect word for boundary). John Billingsley, though, suggests it was also known as the Keb Stone and associated with a legend of being flung across the valley by a bilberry-loving giant called Old Chedley Redcoit. If you circle the stone nine times chanting his name, it is said he will rise.

stone shelter

Turn Slack Dam

Following **Horse Pasture Clough**, despite paths at top and bottom, is not as pleasant as it looks, but a lovely path contours round the edge of **Birching Brow** above, before descending faintly above the rock turrets of **Brock Holes**. If you stick to the high ground towards the top of **Noon Hill Clough**, another faint path can soon be picked up; this passes near the last turbine to follow the wall all the way down to a rough stile in Moorhey Clough.

to Littleborough

MAP 22: FREEHOLDS TOP SOUTH (Shore Moor)

The **Long Causeway** across Shore Moor was an important packhorse route between Wardle and Todmorden.

Shore Moor straggles messily towards Greater Manchester, the southern slopes descending to Watergrove and Littleborough. It is dominated by reservoirs, quarrying, coal mining and a new windfarm that has completely changed the face of the moor since the first edition of this book. However, this moor is not without interest, particularly in its dramatic cloughs. The large basin holding Cranberry Dam is notable, with a series of rocky scars climbing up to the tops while the shapely canyon of White Slack Clough drops away below. The moor is accessible from Ramsden Wood, Walsden and Warland.

White Slack Clough is a short but amazingly dramatic rocky cleft. Its course can be followed from a stile at the bottom of the quarry above Ramsden Wood, a faint path leading to the first of a series of waterfalls. Above this, it is a case of following the course of the stream between rocky turrets until your course is blocked by the secluded higher falls. Another faint path angles up from the lower falls to White Slack Edge with further great views.

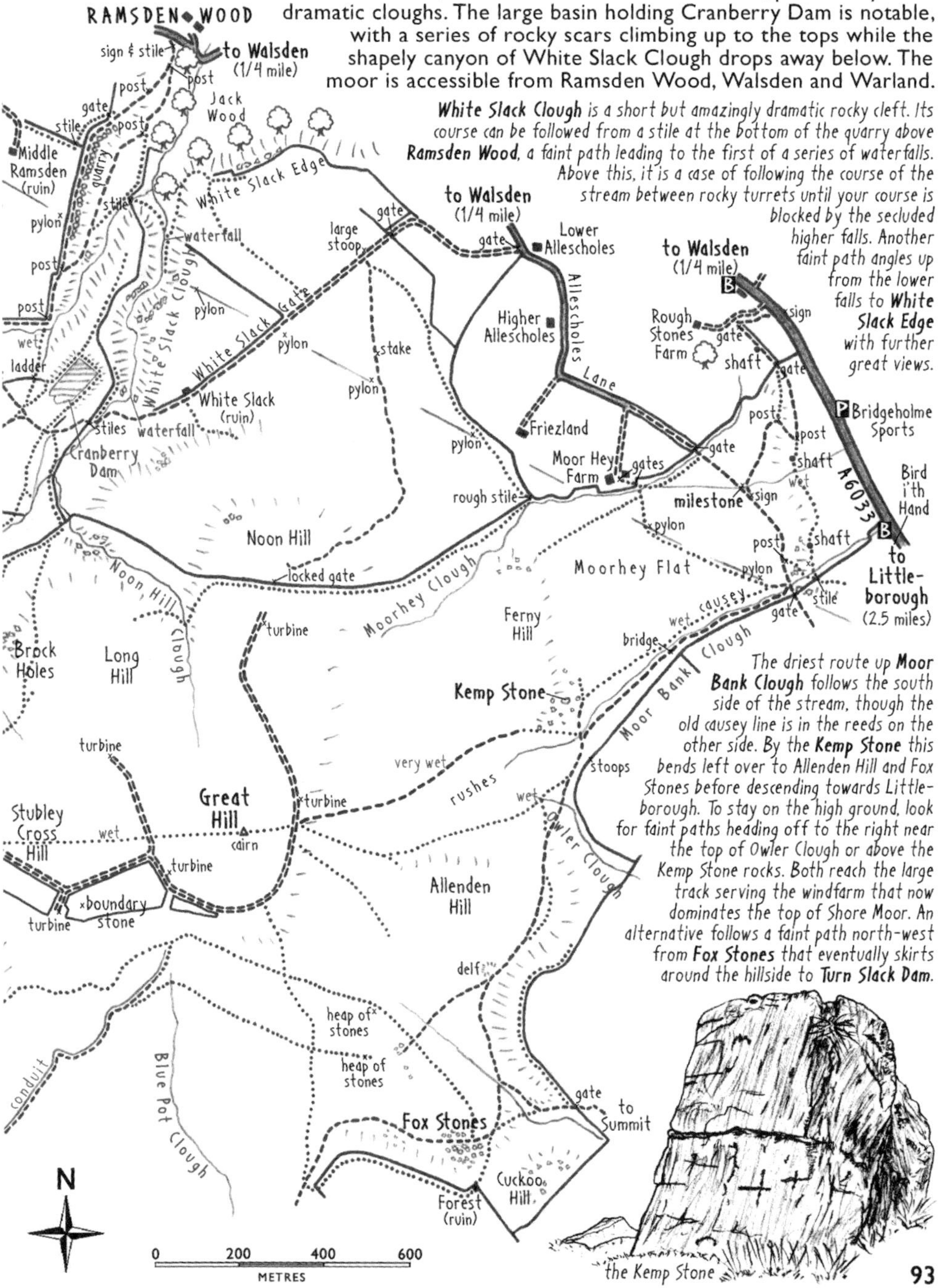

RAMSDEN✦WOOD

sign & stile
to Walsden (1/4 mile)
post
post
gate
Jack Wood
stile
post
Middle Ramsden (ruin)
quarry
stile
pylon
waterfall
post
White Slack Edge
White Slack Clough
large stoop
to Walsden (1/4 mile)
gate
gate
Lower **Allescholes**
post
pylon
White Slack Gate
pylon
stake
wet ladder
Higher Allescholes
Allescholes
to Walsden (1/4 mile)
Rough Stones Farm
sign
gate
shaft
gate
B
stiles
waterfall
White Slack (ruin)
pylon
Friezland
Allescholes Lane
post
shaft
P Bridgeholme Sports
Cranberry Dam
Moor Hey Farm
gates
gate
post
wet
Bird i'th Hand
rough stile
A6033
Noon Hill
milestone
sign
pylon
shaft
B
Noon Hill
locked gate
Moorhey Clough
Moorhey Flat
post
pylon
shaft
stile
gate
to Littleborough (2.5 miles)
turbine
Ferny Hill
bridge
wet causey
Brock Holes
Long Hill
Noon Hill Clough
Kemp Stone
Moor Bank Clough

*The driest route up **Moor Bank Clough** follows the south side of the stream, though the old causey line is in the reeds on the other side. By the **Kemp Stone** this bends left over to Allenden Hill and Fox Stones before descending towards Littleborough. To stay on the high ground, look for faint paths heading off to the right near the top of Owler Clough or above the Kemp Stone rocks. Both reach the large track serving the windfarm that now dominates the top of Shore Moor. An alternative follows a faint path north-west from Fox Stones that eventually skirts around the hillside to **Turn Slack Dam**.*

turbine
very wet
rushes
wet
stoops
Owler Clough
Stubley Cross Hill
wet
Great Hill
turbine
cairn
turbine
Allenden Hill
turbine
×boundary stone
turbine
delf
Blue Pot Clough
heap of stones
heap of stones
gate
to Summit
conduit
Fox Stones
Cuckoo Hill
N
Forest (ruin)

0   200   400   600
METRES

the Kemp Stone

93

4 Whichever path you take at the top of **Gorpley Clough**, it emerges on a track opposite the water treatment works. Follow the track right to a T-junction and turn left to Keepers Lodge at **Howroyd**. Bear right at the buildings to a gate onto the edge of the moor. On the bend after 100m bear left at an old stoop onto a faint path along a grassy level. Passing through a gap in the wall, the path contours round the hillside and aims for the waterfall at the head of **Howroyd Clough**.

5 Join another track (the line of a former tramway) to reach a small quarry at its end. Bear left across a small stream, then turn right at the top of the bank and follow the line of the stream up to a broken down wall. Head straight on, following a line of posts leading up the soggy moorland slope. Turn left at the old mining track and follow it round the hillside past a number of coal pits. Just before the last of these, fork right to skirt above the scree and join a line of sporadic posts leading across to the summit of **Freeholds Top**.

Freeholds Top (454m)

6 From **Freeholds Top** trig continue along the ridge, forking right around the end of the pool by the summit. The path follows the high ground parallel to the fenceline that marks the county boundary for some distance, before climbing slightly to reach a gate near the top of **Hades Hill**. Turn left beyond and, where the fence bends round to the left, head straight on past some slight delfs to reach a modern cairn by the site of an ancient **barrow**. Drop down to the large track beyond, following it left up onto **Rough Hill**. As it bends right, bear left up onto the summit, marked by another small cairn.

7 From **Rough Hill**, drop down to the vehicle track again, but turn right immediately on a grassy path that curves round the hillside towards Watergrove Reservoir with Greater Manchester beyond. Cross Higher Slack Clough then fork left at a waymark post, staying above the coal pits to reach a boundary stone on the **Long Causeway**. Head straight across, climbing steadily towards the unmarked top of **Crook Hill**.

Gorpley Clough Reservoir was built in the 1900s and was originally planned to have a twin above. This route joins the line of a railway that ran along the north shore, supplying stone from a quarry at the head of the clough.

3 Continue to a junction by the ruined building beyond **Frith's Farm** and head across the hillside beyond. At the next wall, bear slightly left to reach a metal kissing gate into **Stones Wood**. Reaching the road at the far end, follow it right for 200m to **Gorpley Clough** car park. Turn left through the gate here and follow a path up the steep ravine, criss-crossing the stream a number of times.

to Bacup (3 miles) — Stones Wood House

Freeholds Top summit

Distance: 10 miles (16.3km)
Ascent: 420m
Difficulty: Moderate
Parking: Car park on A6033 in Walsden, small car park by junction of A6033 and Hollins Lane in Gauxholme, or small car park on A681 at Gorpley Clough.
Public Transport: Walsden is on the main Caldervale train line and 589, 590, T6 & T8 bus routes from Todmorden or Rochdale.
Character: A very satisfying round that takes in all the tops of the Freeholds Top ridge on a long moorland yomp, as well as incorporating the subtler charms of Gorpley Clough and the Rochdale Canal. The high ground has been greatly changed by the new windfarm, so navigation is more complicated here as a result.

94

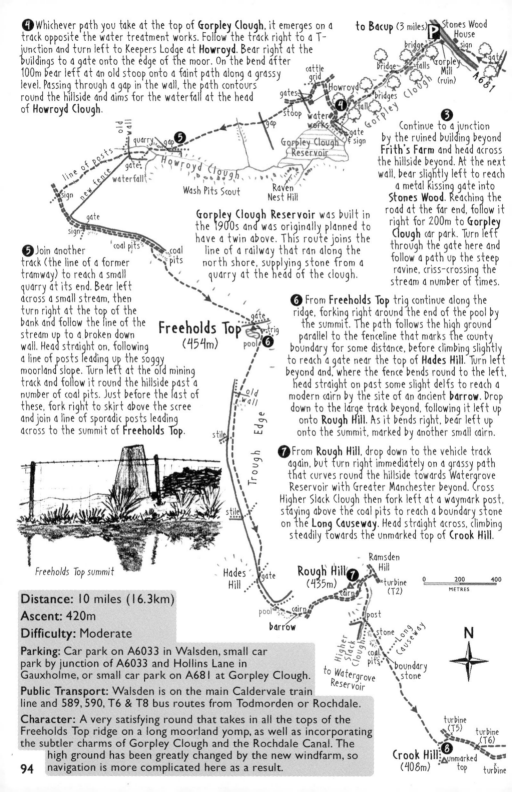

Map labels: bridge, bridge, falls, Gorpley Mill (ruin), gate, A681, cattle grid, Howroyd, bridges, lane, water works, stoop, gap, gate & sign, Gorpley Clough Reservoir, Gorpley Clough, old wall, quarry, gap, new fence, waterfall, sign, gate, sign, coal pits, coal pits, line of posts, Howroyd Clough, Wash Pits Scout, Raven Nest Hill, gate, trig, pool, old wall, stile, Trough Edge, stile, Hades Hill, gate, pool, cairn, barrow, Rough Hill (435m), cairn, Ramsden Hill, turbine (T2), post, stone, Higher Slack Clough, coal pits, Long Causeway, boundary stone, to Watergrove Reservoir, turbine (T5), turbine (T6), Crook Hill (408m), unmarked top, turbine, N, 0 200 400 METRES

ROUTE 16: FREEHOLDS TOP & GORPLEY CLOUGH FROM WALSDEN

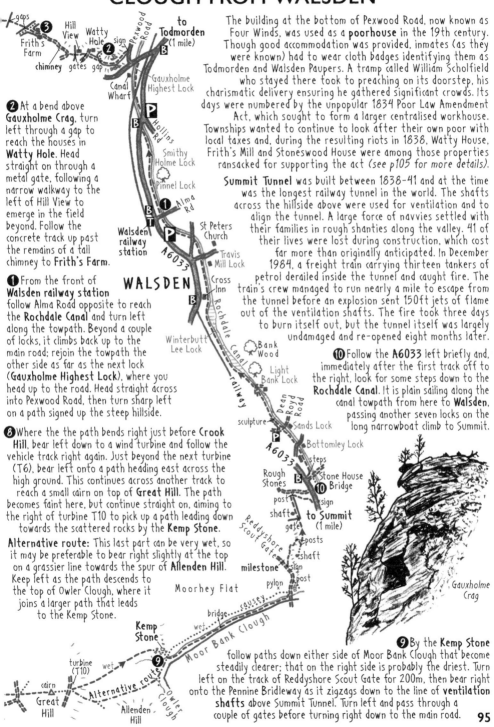

The building at the bottom of Pexwood Road, now known as Four Winds, was used as a **poorhouse** in the 19th century. Though good accommodation was provided, inmates (as they were known) had to wear cloth badges identifying them as Todmorden and Walsden Paupers. A tramp called William Scholfield who stayed there took to preaching on its doorstep, his charismatic delivery ensuring he gathered significant crowds. Its days were numbered by the unpopular 1834 Poor Law Amendment Act, which sought to form a larger centralised workhouse. Townships wanted to continue to look after their own poor with local taxes and, during the resulting riots in 1838, Watty House, Frith's Mill and Stoneswood House were among those properties ransacked for supporting the act (see p105 for more details).

Summit Tunnel was built between 1838-41 and at the time was the longest railway tunnel in the world. The shafts across the hillside above were used for ventilation and to align the tunnel. A large force of navvies settled with their families in rough shanties along the valley. 41 of their lives were lost during construction, which cost far more than originally anticipated. In December 1984, a freight train carrying thirteen tankers of petrol derailed inside the tunnel and caught fire. The train's crew managed to run nearly a mile to escape from the tunnel before an explosion sent 150ft jets of flame out of the ventilation shafts. The fire took three days to burn itself out, but the tunnel itself was largely undamaged and re-opened eight months later.

❷ At a bend above **Gauxholme Crag**, turn left through a gap to reach the houses in **Watty Hole**. Head straight on through a metal gate, following a narrow walkway to the left of Hill View to emerge in the field beyond. Follow the concrete track up past the remains of a tall chimney to **Frith's Farm**.

❶ From the front of **Walsden railway station** follow Alma Road opposite to reach the **Rochdale Canal** and turn left along the towpath. Beyond a couple of locks, it climbs back up to the main road; rejoin the towpath the other side as far as the next lock (**Gauxholme Highest Lock**), where you head up to the road. Head straight across into Pexwood Road, then turn sharp left on a path signed up the steep hillside.

❽ Where the the path bends right just before **Crook Hill**, bear left down to a wind turbine and follow the vehicle track right again. Just beyond the next turbine (T6), bear left onto a path heading east across the high ground. This continues across another track to reach a small cairn on top of **Great Hill**. The path becomes faint here, but continue straight on, aiming to the right of turbine T10 to pick up a path leading down towards the scattered rocks by the **Kemp Stone**.

Alternative route: This last part can be very wet, so it may be preferable to bear right slightly at the top on a grassier line towards the spur of **Allenden Hill**. Keep left as the path descends to the top of Owler Clough, where it joins a larger path that leads to the Kemp Stone.

❿ Follow the **A6033** left briefly and, immediately after the first track off to the right, look for some steps down to the **Rochdale Canal**. It is plain sailing along the canal towpath from here to **Walsden**, passing another seven locks on the long narrowboat climb to Summit.

❾ By the **Kemp Stone** follow paths down either side of Moor Bank Clough that become steadily clearer; that on the right side is probably the driest. Turn left on the track of Reddyshore Scout Gate for 200m, then bear right onto the Pennine Bridleway as it zigzags down to the line of **ventilation shafts** above Summit Tunnel. Turn left and pass through a couple of gates before turning right down to the main road. **95**

RING OUZEL

The **ring ouzel** is a migratory mountain thrush closely related to the blackbird (indeed ouzel is an old name for the common blackbird). The ring refers to the white band around is neck; otherwise it is largely black with a yellow bill. It tends to nest among boulders or crags and is most likely seen in steep-sided cloughs like those found around the edge of Freeholds Top, though it is a particularly shy and skittish bird.

CHAPTER 11 – STOODLEY PIKE

Height: 402m

Grid Ref: SD973241

Map Sheet: OL21
(South Pennines)

Access: No restrictions.

Public Transport:
Hebden Bridge,
Mytholmroyd and
Todmorden are on
the main Caldervale
bus and train routes.
Buses 597 & 901 run
from Hebden Bridge
to Cragg Vale, and
buses T6/T8 run
from Todmorden to
Mankinholes and
Harvelin Park.

Stoodley Pike is probably the most instantly recognisable hill in the South Pennines. This has little to do with its natural geography, but rather the 121-foot monument that gazes grimly out across half of the county. This marks a fine edge of bare scree and rock that overlooks the Upper Calder Valley, but the true summit of Stoodley Pike stands some 200m south on the flat moorland behind. Without the monument, one imagines Stoodley Pike being no more remarkable than Langfield Edge, but its hold on the consciousness of the valley is unparalleled. Stoodley Pike looks out over Todmorden, Hebden Bridge and Cragg Vale and makes a popular objective for walks. The outlying Erringden Moor was home to notorious counterfeiters, the Cragg Vale Coiners, and is separated from Stoodley Pike only by a small area of abandoned 19th-century enclosures.

The source of the name Stoodley is unclear. It has been suggested it comes from a 13th-century landowner called Harrie de Stoodley, yet his surname is likely to have been taken from a place itself. It may also derive from the Old English *stod leah* (meaning horse stud farm) and have been related to the functions of Erringden Deer Park, which covered the bulk of this moor in the Middle Ages.

Stoodley Pike from the west

97

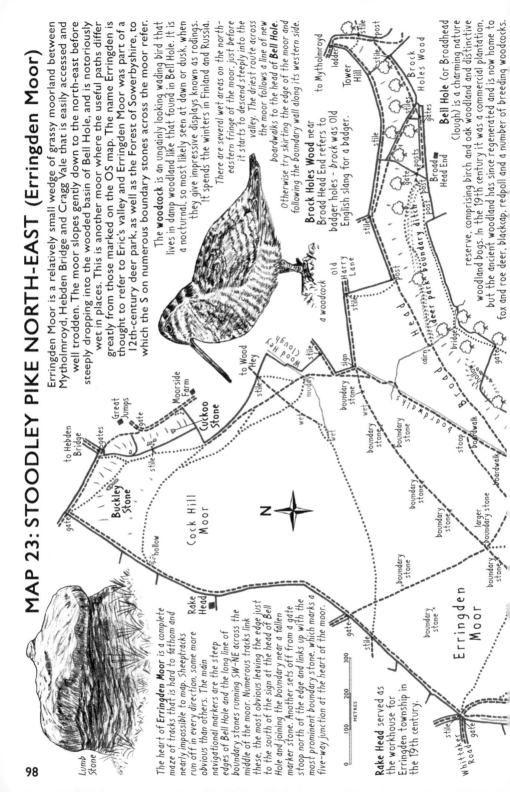

Erringden Moor is a relatively small wedge of grassy moorland between Mytholmroyd, Hebden Bridge and Cragg Vale that is easily accessed and well trodden. The moor slopes gently down to the north-east before steeply dropping into the wooded basin of Bell Hole, and is notoriously wet in places. This is another moor where the useful paths differ greatly from those marked on the OS map. The name Erringden is thought to refer to Eric's valley and Erringden Moor was part of a 12th-century deer park, as well as the Forest of Sowerbyshire, to which the S on numerous boundary stones across the moor refer.

The **woodcock** is an ungainly looking wading bird that lives in damp woodland like that found in Bell Hole. It is a nocturnal, so most likely seen at dawn or dusk, when they give impressive displays known as rodings. It spends the winters in Finland and Russia.

There are several wet areas on the north-eastern fringe of the moor, just before it starts to descend steeply into the valley. The driest route across the moor follows a line of new boardwalks to the head of **Bell Hole**.

Otherwise try skirting the edge of the moor and following the boundary wall along its western side.

Brock Holes Wood near Broad Head End refers to badger holes - brock was Old English slang for a badger.

Bell Hole (or Broadhead Clough) is a charming nature reserve, comprising birch and oak woodland and distinctive woodland bogs. In the 19th century it was a commercial plantation, but the ancient woodland has since regenerated and is now home to fox and roe deer, blackcap, redpoll and a number of breeding woodcocks.

The heart of **Erringden Moor** is a complete maze of tracks that is hard to fathom and nearly impossible to map. Sheeptracks run off in every direction, some more obvious than others. The main navigational markers are the steep edges of Bell Hole and the long line of boundary stones running SW-NE across the middle of the moor. Numerous tracks link these, the most obvious leaving the edge just to the south of the sign at the head of Bell Hole and joining the boundary near a fallen marker stone. Another sets off from a gate stoop north of the edge and links up with the most prominent boundary stone, which marks a five-way junction at the heart of the moor.

Rake Head served as the workhouse for Erringden township in the 19th century.

a woodcock

to Wood Hey

Wood Hey (Clough)

to Hebden Bridge

Great Jumps

gate

gates

gates

Moorside Farm

Cuckoo Stone

Buckley Stone

hollow

gate

stile

Cock Hill Moor

Rake Head

Lumb Stone

N

Whittaker Road

gate

stile

Erringden Moor

boundary stone

larger boundary stone

boundary stone

boundary stone

boundary stone

boundary stone

boundary stone

boundary stone

gate

stile

stile

sign

stile

muddy

wet

wet

wet

wet

boardwalks

boardwalk

boardwalk

boardwalk

stoop

Broad

Head park boundary ditch

old Harry Lane

cairn

bridge

post

post

posts

post

stile

Broad Head End

gate

gate

gate

gate

hollow

to Mytholmroyd

Tower Hill

Brock Holes Wood

ladder

stile

stile

post

stile

stiles

gates

stile

post

METRES

0 100 200 300

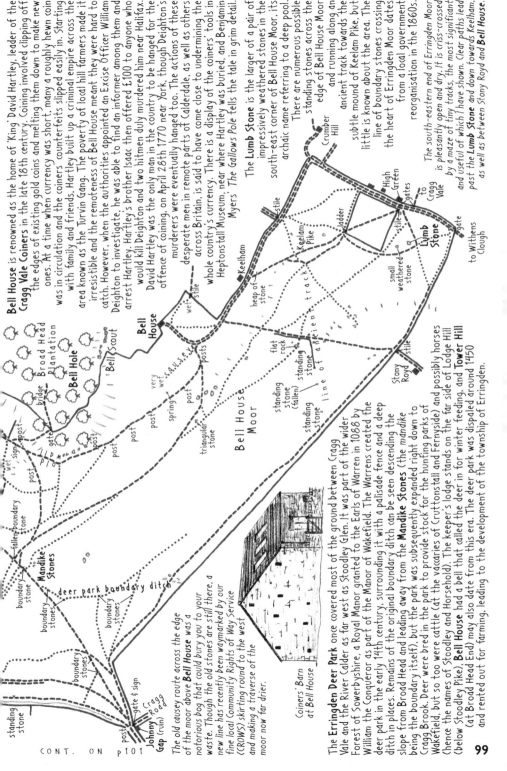

Bell House is renowned as the home of 'King' David Hartley, leader of the **Cragg Vale Coiners** in the late 18th century. Coining involved clipping off the edges of existing gold coins and melting them down to make new ones. At a time when currency was short, many a roughly hewn coin was in circulation and the coiners' counterfeits slipped easily in. Starting with family and friends, Hartley built up a criminal empire across the area known as the Turvin Gang. The poverty of local hill farmers made it irresistible and the remoteness of Bell House meant they were hard to catch. However, when the authorities appointed an Excise Officer William Deighton to investigate, he was able to find an informer among them and arrest Hartley. Hartley's brother Isaac then offered £100 to anyone who would kill Deighton and two hitmen duly murdered him near Halifax. David Hartley was the only man in the country to be hanged for the offence of coining, on April 28th 1770 near York, though Deighton's murderers were eventually hanged too. The actions of these desperate men in remote parts of Calderdale, as well as others across Britain, is said to have come close to undermining the whole country's currency. There is a display of the coiners' tools in Heptonstall Museum, near where Hartley was buried, and Benjamin Myers' The Gallows Pole tells the tale in grim detail.

The **Lumb Stone** is the larger of a pair of impressively weathered stones in the south-east corner of Bell House Moor, its archaic name referring to a deep pool. There are numerous possible standing stones across the edge of Bell House Moor and running along an ancient track towards the subtle mound of Keelam Pike, but little is known about the area. The line of boundary stones crossing the heart of Erringden Moor dates from a local government reorganisation in the 1860s.

The south-eastern end of Erringden Moor is pleasantly open and dry. It is criss-crossed by a maze of tiny tracks, the most significant and useful of which I have shown. Clear paths lead past the **Lumb Stone** and down towards Keelham, as well as between Stony Royd and **Bell House**.

*The old causey route across the edge of the moor above **Bell House** was a notorious bog that could bury you to your waist. Though the old stones are still there, a new line has recently been waymarked by our fine local Community Rights of Way Service (CROWS) skirting round to the west and making a traverse of the moor now far drier.*

Coiners' Barn at Bell House

The **Erringden Deer Park** once covered most of the ground between Cragg Vale and the River Calder as far west as Stoodley Glen. It was part of the wider Forest of Sowerbyshire, a Royal Manor granted to the Earls of Warren in 1088 by William the Conqueror as part of the Manor of Wakefield. The Warrens created the deer park in the early 14th century, surrounding it with a palisade fence and a deep ditch in places. Remains of the original boundary ditch can be seen descending the slope from Broad Head and leading away from the Mandike Stones (the *mandike* being the boundary itself), but the park was subsequently expanded right down to Cragg Brook. Deer were bred in the park to provide stock for the hunting parks of Wakefield, but so too were cattle (at the vaccaries of Cruttonstall and Ferryside) and possibly horses (hence the names of Stoodley and Horsehold). The keeper's lodge stands on the far side of Lodge Hill (below Stoodley Pike). Bell House had a bell that called the deer in for winter feeding, and Tower Hill (at Broad Head End) may also date from this era. The deer park was dispaled around 1450 and rented out for farming, leading to the development of the township of Erringden.

CONT. ON p101

99

MAP 24: STOODLEY PIKE SOUTH-WEST

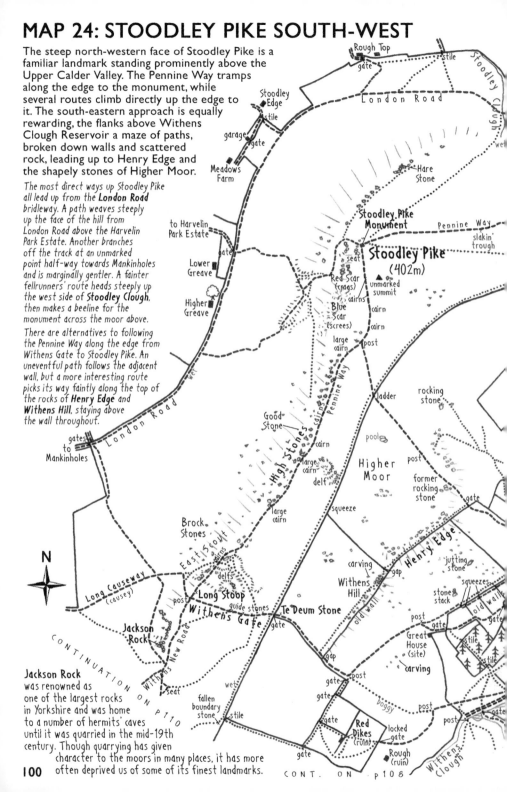

The steep north-western face of Stoodley Pike is a familiar landmark standing prominently above the Upper Calder Valley. The Pennine Way tramps along the edge to the monument, while several routes climb directly up the edge to it. The south-eastern approach is equally rewarding, the flanks above Withens Clough Reservoir a maze of paths, broken down walls and scattered rock, leading up to Henry Edge and the shapely stones of Higher Moor.

*The most direct ways up Stoodley Pike all lead up from the **London Road** bridleway. A path weaves steeply up the face of the hill from London Road above the Harvelin Park Estate. Another branches off the track at an unmarked point half-way towards Mankinholes and is marginally gentler. A fainter fellrunners' route heads steeply up the west side of **Stoodley Clough**, then makes a beeline for the monument across the moor above.*

*There are alternatives to following the Pennine Way along the edge from Withens Gate to Stoodley Pike. An uneventful path follows the adjacent wall, but a more interesting route picks its way faintly along the top of the rocks of **Henry Edge** and **Withens Hill**, staying above the wall throughout.*

Jackson Rock
was renowned as one of the largest rocks in Yorkshire and was home to a number of hermits' caves until it was quarried in the mid-19th century. Though quarrying has given character to the moors in many places, it has more often deprived us of some of its finest landmarks.

100

CONT. ON p108

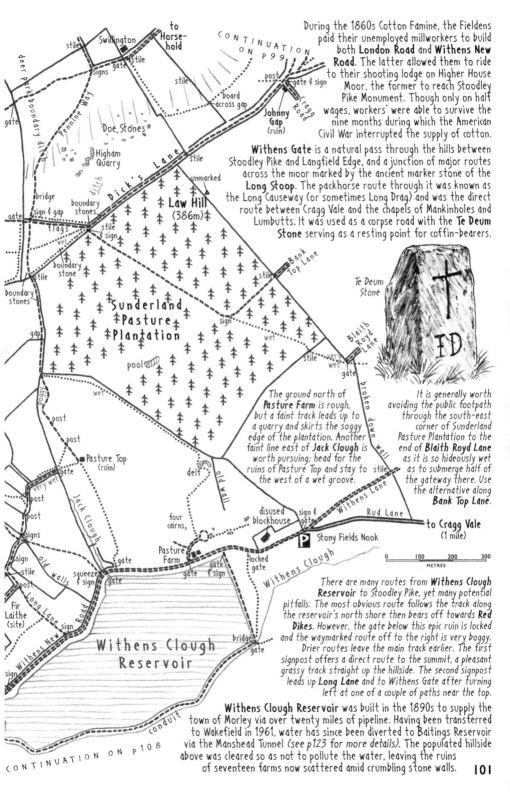

During the 1860s Cotton Famine, the Fieldens paid their unemployed millworkers to build both **London Road** and **Withens New Road**. The latter allowed them to ride to their shooting lodge on Higher House Moor, the former to reach Stoodley Pike Monument. Though only on half wages, workers' were able to survive the nine months during which the American Civil War interrupted the supply of cotton.

Withens Gate is a natural pass through the hills between Stoodley Pike and Langfield Edge, and a junction of major routes across the moor marked by the ancient marker stone of the **Long Stoop**. The packhorse route through it was known as the Long Causeway (or sometimes Long Drag) and was the direct route between Cragg Vale and the chapels of Mankinholes and Lumbutts. It was used as a corpse road with the **Te Deum Stone** serving as a resting point for coffin-bearers.

The ground north of **Pasture Farm** is rough, but a faint track leads up to a quarry and skirts the soggy edge of the plantation. Another faint line east of **Jack Clough** is worth pursuing; head for the ruins of Pasture Top and stay to the west of a wet groove.

It is generally worth avoiding the public footpath through the south-east corner of Sunderland Pasture Plantation to the end of **Blaith Royd Lane** as it is so hideously wet as to submerge half of the gateway there. Use the alternative along **Bank Top Lane**.

There are many routes from **Withens Clough Reservoir** to Stoodley Pike, yet many potential pitfalls. The most obvious route follows the track along the reservoir's north shore then bears off towards **Red Dikes**. However, the gate below this epic ruin is locked and the waymarked route off to the right is very boggy. Drier routes leave the main track earlier. The first signpost offers a direct route to the summit, a pleasant grassy track straight up the hillside. The second signpost leads up **Long Lane** and to Withens Gate after turning left at one of a couple of paths near the top.

Withens Clough Reservoir was built in the 1890s to supply the town of Morley via over twenty miles of pipeline. Having been transferred to Wakefield in 1961, water has since been diverted to Baitings Reservoir via the Manshead Tunnel (see p123 for more details). The populated hillside above was cleared so as not to pollute the water, leaving the ruins of seventeen farms now scattered amid crumbling stone walls.

Te Deum Stone

CONTINUATION ON P99

to Cragg Vale
(1 mile)

to Horse-hold

101

0   100   200   300
METRES

ROUTE 17: STOODLEY PIKE FROM HEBDEN BRIDGE

Distance: 6½ miles (10.4km) **Difficulty:** Easy

Ascent: 370m

Parking: Various pay car parks in Hebden Bridge. Limited free parking by station.

Public Transport: Hebden Bridge is on the main Caldervale train & bus routes.

Character: Although Stoodley Pike is hidden from view from the centre of Hebden Bridge, its familiar monument makes a natural target for a day's walk. There are dozens of possible routes up, but my favourite is the one used here in descent, skirting round Lodge Hill and Edge End Moor, while the ascent via Wood Hey and Erringden Moor allows for a decent tramp across the moor immediately above the town. The route is on good paths throughout.

Though the impressive ruin at **Cruttonstall** dates from the 17th century, it was included in the Domesday Book and was the site of a medieval vaccary (locally the suffix - *tonstall* indicates the existence of a cattle ranch). Cattle were enclosed during the winter by crude hedges and stock-proof ditches, the remains of which may be picked out around the fringe of Edge End Moor.

7 Keep right again as you near the elegant ruins of **Cruttonstall**: this brings you to a gate above the farm. Follow the path down the wall beyond to drop down to the vehicle track up **Beaumont Clough**.

Alternative route: Bear left down through Cruttonstall itself (via an often-wet gateway) and follow the old walls to reach a stile at the top of **Callis Woods**. Immediately beyond, bear right on a rough path hugging the fence at the top of the woods; this

8 Follow the Pennine Bridleway down to **Beaumont Clough Bridge** and keep left along the top of Horsehold Wood. This emerges on Horsehold Road, which leads left steeply down into Hebden Bridge. Near the top, a short detour left through a gate to **Horsehold Scout** offers a magnificent view of the Calder Valley. The road emerges at **Hebble End**; join the towpath on the far bank to return to Holme Street or the railway station.

1 From the traffic lights in the centre of **Hebden Bridge**, go down Holme Street past the post office. At the end, cross the canal and turn right, following a path up some steps to **Palace House Road**. Turn left, cross the railway and turn second right on to a track behind the houses. Bear left after 200m where this track forks around a house, then continue straight on to climb gently up through **Crow Nest Wood** to reach Wood Top.

Palace House Road is named after the palisade fence that ran around Erringden Deer Park in the 14th century (see p99 for more details).

HEBDEN BRIDGE

Like many of the hilltop settlements, **Wood Top** was a handloom weavers' hamlet with its own cotton mill and millpond. It made fustian, a hard-wearing cotton material that Hebden Bridge was renowned for producing.

2 Keep to the right of the buildings at **Wood Top**, joining a concrete track, before turning left into Wood Hey Lane at the bottom of the setts. Turn right over a stile just before **Wood Hey Clough** and climb steadily through youthful woodland. Turn right on to the track at the top, then go left almost immediately by some old gate stoops. Follow the right-hand side of a gully up to a stile on the edge of **Erringden Moor**.

Beaumont Clough is said to have been used during World War II for secretive pig slaughtering. Since all livestock had to be registered for redistribution, occasionally animals were killed for personal use away from prying eyes.

3 At the edge of the moor, ignore the waymarker pointing straight ahead and bear left on a faint path towards a wall on the skyline. This soon joins a larger path and crosses a boggy

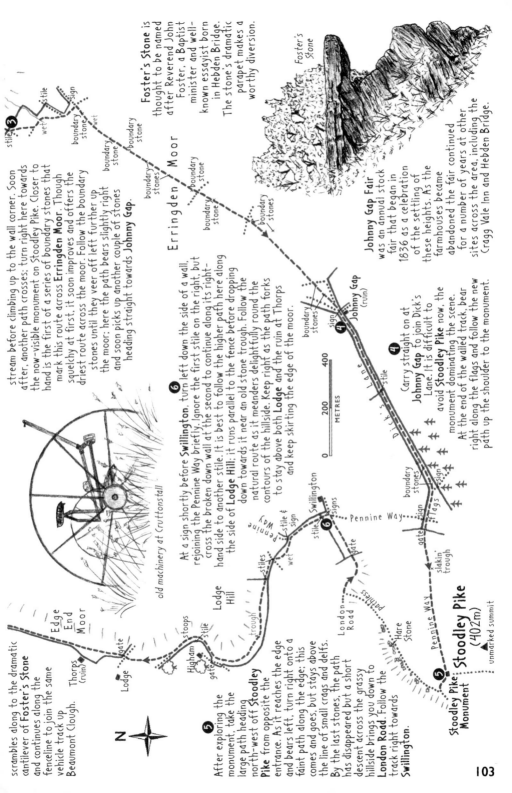

Foster's Stone is thought to be named after Reverend John Foster, a Baptist minister and well-known essayist born in Hebden Bridge. The stone's dramatic parapet makes a worthy diversion.

Foster's Stone

Erringden Moor

boundary stone
boundary stone
boundary stones
boundary stone
boundary stone
boundary stones

Johnny Gap Fair was an annual stock fair that began in 1836 as a celebration of the settling of these heights. As the farmhouses became abandoned the fair continued for a number of years at other sites across the area, including the Cragg Vale Inn and Hebden Bridge.

③ stile
wet
stile
boundary sign
wet

scrambles along to the dramatic antilever of Foster's Stone and continues along the fenceline to join the same vehicle track up Beaumont Clough.

⑤ After exploring the monument, take the large path heading north-west of Stoodley Pike from opposite the entrance. As it reaches the edge and bears left, turn right onto a faint path along the edge; this comes and goes, but stays above the line of small crags and delfs. By the last stones, the path has disappeared but a short descent across the grassy hillside brings you down to London Road. Follow the track right towards Swillington.

stream before climbing up to the wall corner. Soon after, another path crosses; turn right here towards the now-visible monument on Stoodley Pike. Closer to hand is the first of a series of boundary stones that mark this route across **Erringden Moor**. Though squelchy at first, it soon improves and offers the driest route across the moor. Follow the boundary stones until they veer off left further up the moor: here the path bears slightly right and soon picks up another couple of stones heading straight towards **Johnny Gap**.

⑥ At a sign shortly before **Swillington**, turn left down the side of a wall, rejoining the Pennine Way briefly. Ignore the first stile on the right, but cross the broken down wall at the second to continue along its right-hand side to another stile. It is best to follow the higher path here along the side of **Lodge Hill**; it runs parallel to the fence before dropping down towards it near an old stone trough. Follow the natural route as it meanders delightfully round the contours of the hillside. Keep right as the path forks to stay above both **Lodge** and the ruin at Thorps and keep skirting the edge of the moor.

④ Carry straight on at **Johnny Gap** to join Dick's Lane. It is difficult to avoid **Stoodley Pike** now, the monument dominating the scene. At the end of the walled track, bear right along the flags and follow the new path up the shoulder to the monument.

old machinery at Cruttonstall

N

Edge End Moor
Thorps (ruin)
Lodge
Higham stoops
stile
gate
gate
trough
Lodge Hill

Pennine Way
stile & sign
stiles
wet stile & sign
Swillington
signs
gate
London Road
pathless
Hare Stone
Pennine Way

Stoodley Pike Monument
Stoodley Pike (402m)
▲ unmarked summit

Pennine Way
slakin' trough
gate
sign
flags
boundary stones
⑥
sign
Dick's Lane
stile
⑦ Johnny Gap (ruin)
sign
boundary stones

0   200   400
METRES

103

ROUTE 18: STOODLEY PIKE & LANGFIELD EDGE FROM TODMORDEN

Distance: 7½ miles (11.8km)

Ascent: 380m

Difficulty: Easy

Parking: Various town centre car parks in Todmorden, including those on Lever Street and Oxford Street.

Public Transport: Todmorden is on the main Caldervale train and bus routes.

Character: Stoodley Pike is a prominent landmark from the centre of Todmorden and, along with Langfield Edge, dominates the town's southern aspect. This route makes a beeline for the towering monument, passing Lumbutts and Mankinholes, before following the edge past Gaddings Dam (and a swimming opportunity) on its return. The route is on clear and good paths throughout.

TODMORDEN

❷ Continue straight on through the hamlet of **Oldroyd** and turn right just before a collection of sheds and caravans. A path skirts above the sheds and along the edge of the field to a stile into **Bird Bank Wood**. Continue straight on through the wood and eventually drop down onto the road. Follow it right briefly, then bear left onto a path down into **Lumbutts Clough**. Carry straight on to cross a bridge and follow the clough up to **Lumbutts**.

0   200   400
METRES

❶ From the centre of **Todmorden**, pick up the **Rochdale Canal** heading east either directly from the Lever Street or Oxford Street car parks, or via a tunnel under the A6033 from the lock adjacent to the road. The towpath leads beneath Baltimore Bridge to reach **Kilnhurst Bridge**, where you join the road crossing the canal. Turn second left on Kilnhurst Mount, then go right up a narrow ginnel. At the top continue straight on up a track past **Kilnhurst Old Hall**, from which a short diversion leads to **Trigger's Grave**.

❻ Follow Moor Lane down to **Top o' Rough** and turn right just before the farm. A narrow path skirts the property and follows the wall down to **Lumbutts Road**. Head straight across and follow the edge of the field to a squeeze that leads to the top of Shoebroad Lane. The track heads down to Todmorden past the **Quaker Burial Ground** and the attractive enclave of Honey Hole. Where the road (now tarmacked) bends sharp right, head straight on into the graveyard of **Todmorden Unitarian Church** and follow a path down to the bottom entrance. This emerges by the Golden Lion, from where the main road can be followed back over the canal to the town centre.

❼ Follow the dam wall right, passing **Gaddings Dam** and its beach, and descend the first set of steps at the far end. Bear left at the bottom on a faint path crossing the grassy ground behind the edge. Join the main path down to a large cairn by the junction on **Rake End**. Head straight across and follow the path as it bends round to the right and drops down to a gate at the top of **Moor Lane**.

Lumbutts Mill wheel tower

The **Shewbread Quaker Burial Ground** is a small tidy enclosure off Shoebroad Lane where dozens of Quakers, including many of the Fieldens, are buried. Its first burials took place around the 1680s, at a time when Quakers were not allowed to mark their burial places; the few stones present are more recent additions. There was a meeting house down the lane at Shoebroad, a direct result of the 1689 Toleration Act, which allowed freedom of Christian worship for the first time. Shoebroad may be a corruption of Shewbread, which refers to the Old Testament *showbread* that was prepared for God on a specially dedicated table, but it is also a dialect word for a narrow strip of land.

The prominent Gothic building of **Todmorden Unitarian Church** was built in the 1860s by the Fielden family.

The **Harvelin Park Estate** stands on the site of the old **Todmorden Union Workhouse**, which was torn down to make way for its development. Latterly converted into Stansfield View Hospital for the Mentally Handicapped, the workhouse was built like a great house for around a hundred paupers from the various townships of Todmorden. When it was built in 1878, Todmorden was the last Union in the country to build a workhouse, due to its vehement opposition to the amendment of the Poor Law in 1834. When bailiffs arrived from Halifax on 16th November 1838 to collect taxes in Lumbutts, a large mob descended from John Fielden's mills and proceeded to burn their cart and strip them. A few days later, another mob went on a rampage through Todmorden and Gauxholme, smashing windows, destroying furniture and setting properties alight. The 5th Light Dragoons cavalry were summoned from Burnley, soon followed by infantry troops from Manchester, who became permanently stationed in the town for a while. Despite forty arrests, no-one could be found to testify against John Fielden for inciting the riot. People came to Todmorden to view the destruction and it would take forty years to force the centralised workhouse upon the people of the town.

❹ Turn left and follow **London Road** along the bottom edge of the moor. The track bends left and passes an often-wet section with a path alongside. Soon after, and some way before the building at Higher Greave, take a path climbing up the bank to the right with **Stoodley Pike** towering above. This fine path climbs steadily towards the monument before joining the main track up to the summit. You can explore the **monument** via the stairs inside.

❸ Follow the road left and, on the bend opposite the tower of **Lumbutts Mill**, turn left up the Pennine Bridleway. Turn right at the top and climb some steps to the right of the **Top Brink Inn**. Follow the edge of the field up to **Mankinholes** and head straight across the road here, following a good track (Sisley Lane) across the hillside past **Spencer House**. Turn right at the junction beyond to reach the edge of the moor.

Stoodley Pike — Monument

Stoodley Pike
(402m)

Red Scar (crags)
unmarked summit
cairn
Blue Scar (screes)
cairn
cairn
large cairn — post

HARVELIN PARK ESTATE
wet

Old Farm
Sisley — Lane
Spencer House
post
gate
❹

Lumbutts Mill
post
Top Brink Inn
sign
sign
stile
youth hostel
B

B❸ sign — Steps — **MANKINHOLES**

LUMBUTTS

large cairn

All that remains of **Lumbutts Mill** is the waterwheel tower and chimney which stands proudly over the hamlet. This was built in the early 19th century, but there was a corn mill on the site from the 16th century.

Kilnhurst Old Hall was the home of author William Holt, who wrote *Trigger in Europe* and many other titles. Billy sold his books by loading them on his famous white horse, Trigger, who outlived him by a year and is buried through a gate just off the track to Oldroyd.

High Stones
line of cairns

large cairn

East Scout
large cairn
cairns
delfs
post
delf — **Long Stoop**
Withens Gate
small cairn — seat

Long Stoop

❺ Follow the well-cairned Pennine Way south from the opposite side of the monument to its entrance – the true summit of **Stoodley Pike** is on the first slight rise along the path. Follow the cairns and stay with the edge to reach Withens Gate, marked by the massive guidestone of **Long Stoop**. Head straight on and climb up towards Coldwell Hill. By some stones on a slight crest (which marks the start of a line of flagstones), bear right off the main track. A path crosses the boggy ground adjacent to the flat top of **Coldwell Hill**, marked by a collection of huge flat stones.

N

Langfield Edge
cairn
wet

Coldwell Hill
(398m)

Noon Stone Edge
Noon Stone Hole
post
❻

Jeremy Hill

Black Clough
wet

❻ Follow the obvious path along the edge of the high ground, the start of **Langfield Edge**. After crossing Black Clough the path bends round towards the quarried faces of **Gaddings Hole**; fork left at a waymark post to stay above the edge and join the line of a dry drain that leads to the old dam wall of **Gaddings Dam East**. **105**

Gaddings Hole on Langfield Edge

STOODLEY PIKE MONUMENT

Stoodley Pike Monument is one of the most recognisable features on the West Yorkshire Moors, a great black obelisk that rears up over every horizon and muscles in on every photograph. Everything else on these moors is well proportioned, but Stoodley's monument is a gross imposition, too big and unwieldy to make sense of in a landscape where every small rock seems important.

The prominent site on Stoodley Pike has probably been important for as long as people have been living in the Upper Calder Valley. Both bones and stones were discovered when digging foundations for the first monument, possibly part of a Bronze Age burial ground. It has been suggested that a tribal chieftain was buried here with a cairn circle to mark the ground. According to legend, the owner of Stoodley Pike had to keep the cairn in perfect order or everyone in the area would be unable to sleep.

Though it looks every bit the war memorial, Stoodley Pike Monument is actually a monument to peace. The foundation stone was laid in 1814 to celebrate the surrender of Paris and the defeat of Napoleon. It would, however, take two years to complete, as work had to be suspended when Napoleon briefly escaped from Elba. That early model was a rather plain cylindrical tower; marginally lower than the existing structure, it had a room at the top with a fireplace, and its stairwell was said to climb all the way up the hollow tower without any handrail. However, having been weakened by a lightning strike, the monument collapsed on 8th February 1854, at the same time as the Russian Ambassador left London and the outbreak of the Crimean War was declared. Peace, it seemed, was reliant on the monument standing.

When peace was proclaimed in 1856 the monument was rebuilt, at a cost of £812 raised largely by public subscription. It was moved a few yards back from the edge and a design by local architect, James Green, was chosen by a committee. Thus it became vulgarly Victorian and the entrance covered with Masonic symbolism, probably at the behest of the Fieldens who subsidised the building and provided the inscription above the entrance. The thirty-nine steps up to the viewing platform were originally climbed in complete darkness, a ritual in itself, and the Freemasons conducted various other activities around the monument and the nearby public slake trough, as they had at the opening of the original tower.

Along with other repairs, a grill allowing some light into the stairwell and a lightning conductor were added in 1889. Another problem associated with the monument was vandalism. The first model was already blocked up before it collapsed and the CND symbol which is still evident was daubed high on the new monument in 1962. As for the monument itself, it has withstood the Pennine wind for over 150 years and one suspects will take some unsettling – if only our peace were as well founded as James Green's structure.

Stoodley Pike Monument

CHAPTER 12 – BLAKE MOOR
(aka Little Holder Stones)

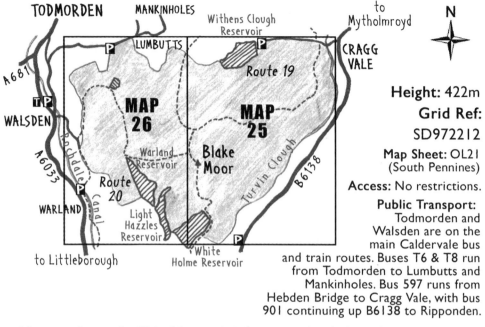

TODMORDEN

MANKINHOLES

Withens Clough Reservoir

LUMBUTTS

to Mytholmroyd

N

CRAGG VALE

Route 19

A681

WALSDEN

MAP 26

MAP 25

Rochdale Canal

A6033

Warland Reservoir

Blake Moor

Turvin Clough

B6138

WARLAND

Route 20

Light Hazzles Reservoir

to Littleborough

White Holme Reservoir

Height: 422m

Grid Ref: SD972212

Map Sheet: OL21 (South Pennines)

Access: No restrictions.

Public Transport: Todmorden and Walsden are on the main Caldervale bus and train routes. Buses T6 & T8 run from Todmorden to Lumbutts and Mankinholes. Bus 597 runs from Hebden Bridge to Cragg Vale, with bus 901 continuing up B6138 to Ripponden.

I have a soft spot for Blake Moor as it is forever in the shadow of its near neighbour Stoodley Pike, despite being some 20m higher. The name is probably unfamiliar as the trig point stands on nearby Little Holder Stones and the moorland could equally be referred to as Turley Holes and Higher House Moor or Withens Moor. Yet Blake Moor is the true high point of the fascinating moorland that stretches west from Cragg Vale, east from Walsden and south from the Calder Valley. Its summit plateau is encircled by high-level drains and reservoirs but, despite being crested by numerous intriguing outcrops, it remains a lost peak. Someone recently built a huge cairn on the plateau, yet it is still some way from the true top. While many wander across Langfield Common, or tramp along the Pennine Way, Blake Moor stands in quiet isolation.

Its name may be a corruption of either black or bleak, both of which will be familiar to anyone who has crossed the dark peat expanse of its summit plateau.

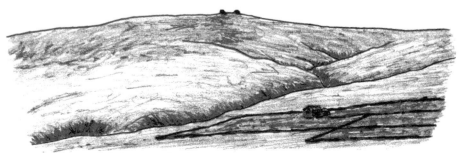

Blake Moor and Holder Stones from Stoodley Pike

107

MAP 25: BLAKE MOOR EAST (Turley Holes & Higher House Moor)

This side of the moor naturally looks towards the summit of Blake Moor, which lies within a circle of high drains. It is an enchanting warren of peat and heather strewn with interestingly sculpted stones. The twin pikes of Holder Stones stand out from the north-west and Dove Lowe Stones dominate from the south, while the Two Lads is a truly atmospheric place on the north-eastern shoulder of the moor. Before the new peat regeneration fencelines went up, it was one of my favourite areas of wild moorland; though it has been tamed a little, it is still well worth exploring from Withens Clough, Sykes Gate or near Blackstone Edge Reservoir.

The main paths from **Withens Clough Reservoir** head north-west towards Withens Gate, but a faint path from a stile at the south-west end of the reservoir allows direct access onto Blake Moor. The first section is rough but becomes more defined following a branch of **Deep Slade** up through the bracken. The path disappears upon reaching the peat wastes near the new fenceline further up, and the fence can be followed left to reach the main path along the drain. It is also possible to head straight up towards the Two Lads from the gate at the south end of the dam wall; aim for the rocks of Fletcher Downfall, though there is no path to help here. Another oddly sited large cairn on **Turley Holes Edge** is sited 50m back from the edge, invisible from anywhere below.

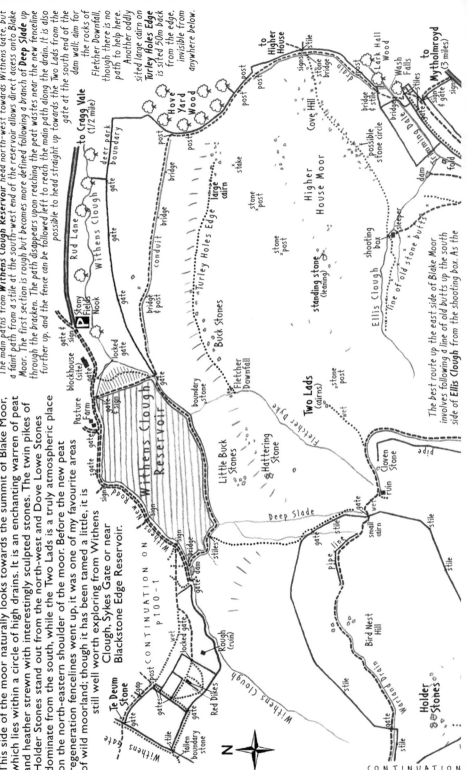

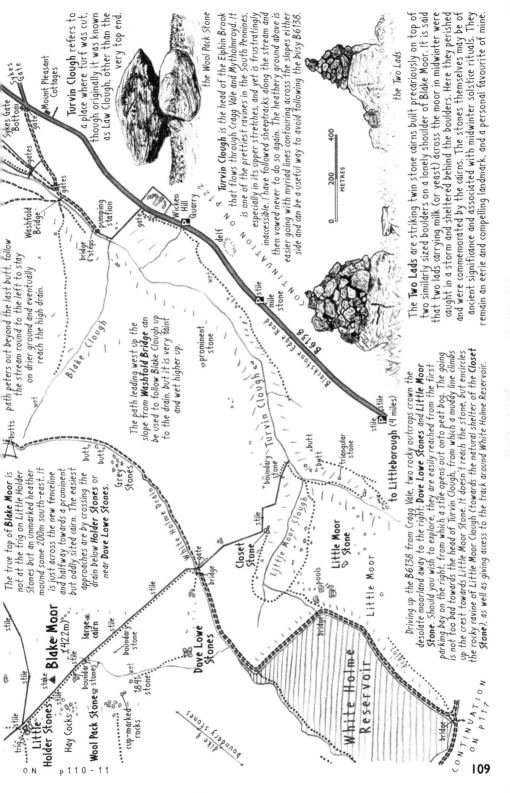

Turvin Clough refers to a place where turf was cut, though originally it was known as Law Clough, other than the very top end.

the Wool Pack Stone

Turvin Clough is the head of the Elphin Brook that flows through Cragg Vale and Mytholmroyd. It is one of the prettiest ravines in the South Pennines, especially in its upper stretches, and yet is frustratingly inaccessible. I have followed sheeptracks along the stream and then vowed never to do so again. The heathery ground above is easier going with myriad lines contouring across the slopes either side and can be a useful way to avoid following the busy B6138.

Sykes Gate

Mount Pleasant Cottages

Sykes Gate Bottom

gate

gates

gates

gates

Washfold Bridge

pumping station

bridge & steps

Wicken Hill Quarry

gate

delf

CONTINUATION ON P112

the Two Lads

The **Two Lads** are striking twin stone cairns built precariously on top of two similarly sized boulders on a lonely shoulder of Blake Moor. It is said that two lads carrying milk (or yeast) across the moor in midwinter were caught in a storm and sheltered behind the boulders. Here they perished and were commemorated by the cairns. The stones themselves may be of ancient significance and associated with midwinter solstice rituals. They remain an eerie and compelling landmark, and a personal favourite of mine.

0   200   400
METRES

path peters out beyond the last butt, follow the stream round to the left to stay on drier ground and eventually reach the high drain.

butts

Blake Clough

wet

The path leading west up the slope from **Washfold Bridge** can be used to follow Blake Clough up to the drain, but it is very faint and wet higher up.

prominent stone

B6138

Blackstone Edge Road

stile

mile stone

stile

to Littleborough (4 miles)

Driving up the B6138 from Cragg Vale, two rocky outcrops crown the desolate moorland away to the right, **Dove Lowe Stones** and **Little Moor Stone**. Should you wish to explore, they are easily reached from the first parking bay on the right, from which a stile opens out onto peat bog. The going is not too bad towards the head of Turvin Clough, from which a muddy line climbs up the crest towards Little Moor Stone. It doesn't reach the stone, but encircles the rocky ravine of Little Moor Clough (towards the natural shelter of the **Closet Stone**), as well as giving access to the track around White Holme Reservoir.

butt

butt

Grey Stones

The true top of **Blake Moor** is not at the trig on Little Holder Stones but an unmarked heather mound some 200m south-east. It is just across the new fenceline and halfway towards a prominent but oddly sited cairn. The easiest approaches are by crossing the drain below **Holder Stones** or near **Dove Lowe Stones**.

boundary stone

Turvin Clough

stile

"boundary" stone

butt

triangular stone

White Holme Drain

stile

gate

bridge

Closet Stone

Little Moor Clough

Little Moor Stone

pools

stile

Blake Moor (422m)

stake

large cairn

stile

boundary stones

184ft stone

cup-marked rocks

Dove Lowe Stones

bridge

Little Moor

bridge

White Holme Reservoir

drains

Little Holder Stones

trig

stile

stile

stile

stile

Hay Cocks

Wool Pack Stones

boundary stones

wet

dike & boundary stones

ON   p110-11

CONTINUATION ON P117

109

MAP 26: BLAKE MOOR WEST (Langfield Common & Walsden Moor)

This varied and fascinating area of moorland is part of Blake Moor only because it lacks a natural high point. Coldwell Hill is as close as it gets; a rounded summit at 398m covered in giant flat boulders. The moor is well trodden because of its accessibility from Lumbutts and the Shepherd's Rest, and because of the dramatic edge it presents to the north, which forms a natural arc from Rake End round to Stoodley Pike. Above the edge, a broad plateau stretches south-east from the popular swimming spot at Gaddings Dam towards the slopes of Blake Moor itself.

*A number of routes lead up to Langfield Common from the **Shepherd's Rest**. The main track skirts beneath the impressive crags of **Langfield Edge**, while a more direct route ascends the flank to **Gaddings Dam**. An interesting alternative weaves through **Jail Hole**'s maze of outcrops and hollows; a grassy quarry path leaves the main track near the stone ruin and winds up to the quarry. A faint path then bears left and ascends the arête (of sorts) to skirt along the edge above and join the path up to Gaddings Dam.*

The current **Gaddings Dam** was originally Gaddings Dam West, built in the 1830s by the Fielden Brothers. It is said to have been built using convict labour from Manchester, which may explain the existence of **Jail Hole** nearby. Immediately adjacent was Gaddings Dam East, built thirty years earlier to supply the Rochdale Canal, but now lying breached and empty.

The **Shepherd's Rest** only became a pub in 1859. Before that it had been a museum, filled with James Greenwood's collection of curios. The museum's popularity undoubtedly inspired William Butterfield to turn it into a pub.

The dam was bought in 2001 by the Gaddings Dam Group to protect its status as 'the highest beach in England' and is an increasingly popular swimming spot.

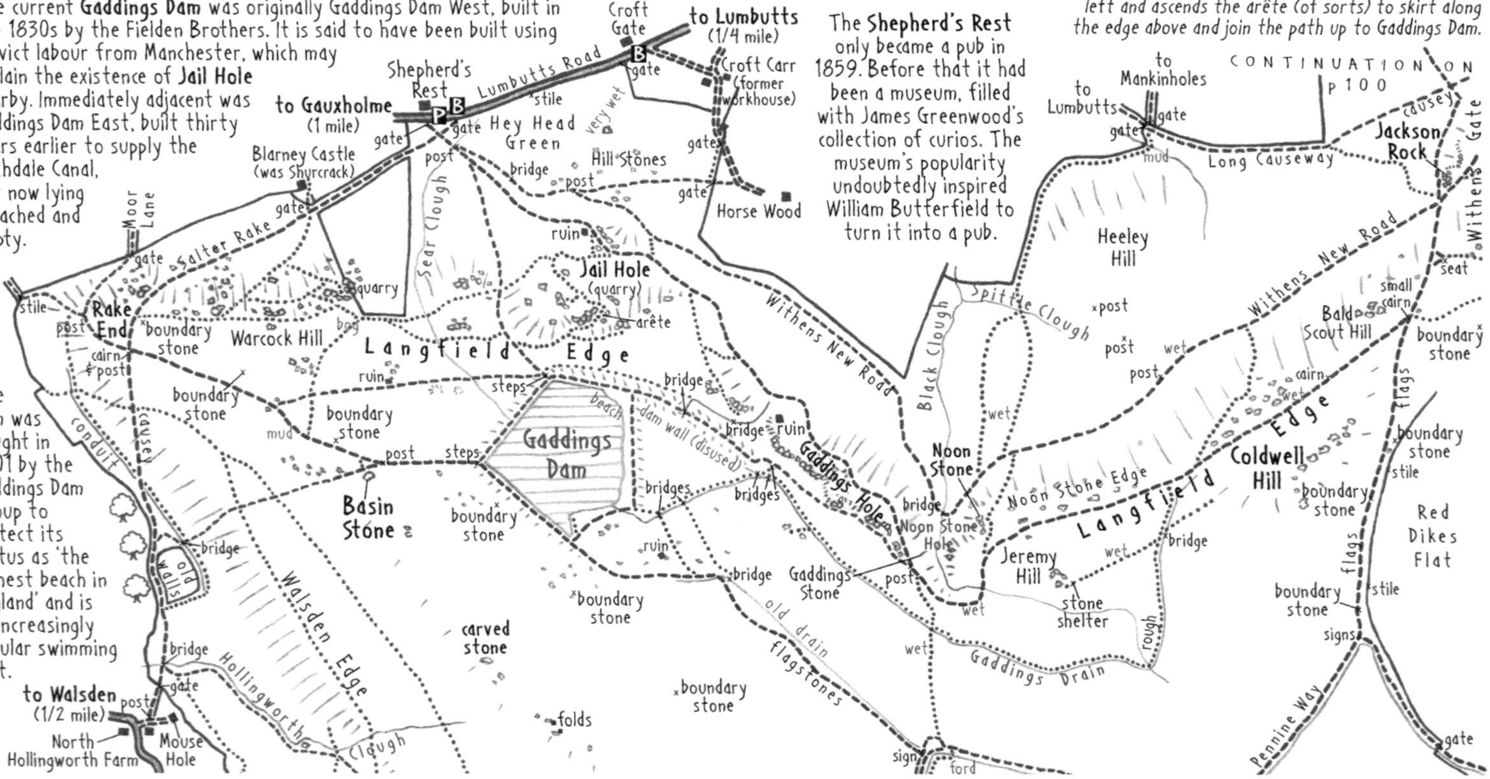

to Lumbutts
(1/4 mile)
Croft Gate
Lumbutts Road
Shepherd's Rest
to Gauxholme
(1 mile)
Blarney Castle
(was Shurcrack)
Croft Carr
(former workhouse)
Horse Wood
Hey Head Green
Hill Stones
very wet
Salter Rake
Moor Lane
Rake End
Warcock Hill
quarry
Sear Clough
Jail Hole
(quarry)
arête
Langfield Edge
Withens New Road
Gaddings Dam
dam wall (disused)
beach
Basin Stone
carved stone
boundary stone
Walsden Edge
Hollingworth Clough
old walls
conduit
causey
to Walsden
(1/2 mile)
North Hollingworth Farm
Mouse Hole
folds
Gaddings Hole
Gaddings Stone
old drain
flagstones
Noon Stone
Noon Stone Hole
Noon Stone Edge
Black Clough
Spittle Clough
Heeley Hill
Jeremy Hill
stone shelter
Gaddings Drain
Coldwell Hill
Langfield Edge
Bald Scout Hill
small cairn
Red Dikes Flat
Pennine Way
to Mankinholes
to Lumbutts
Long Causeway
Jackson Rock
Withens Gate
seat
flags
signs
ford
CONTINUATION ON P100

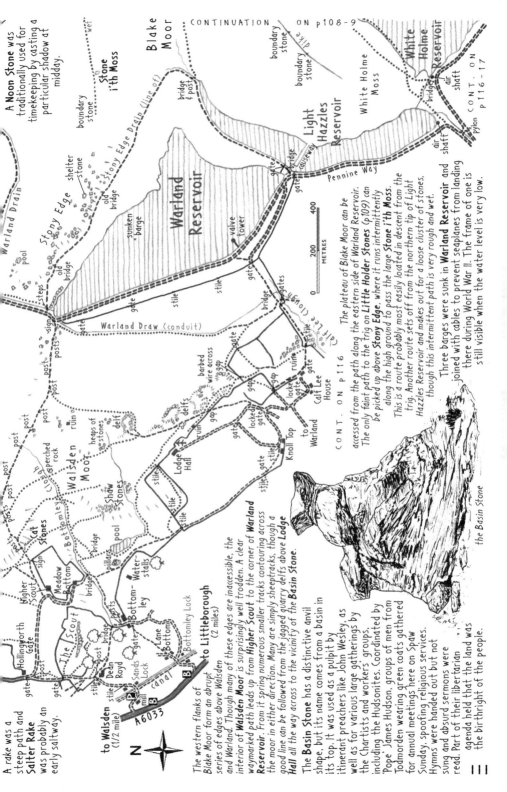

A **Noon Stone** was traditionally used for timekeeping by casting a particular shadow at midday.

A rake was a steep path and **Salter Rake** was probably an early saltway.

Blake Moor

Stone i'th Moss

boundary stone

boundary stone

White Holme Reservoir

boundary stone

White Holme Moss

CONT. ON p116-17

air shaft

pylon

bridge

Light Hazzles Reservoir

bridge & post

Stony Edge Drain (line of)

Warland Drain

Stony Edge

shelter stone

old bridge

old bridge

pool

step

sunken barge

Warland Reservoir

valve tower

gate

gate bridge

causeway

Pennine Way

air shaft

0 200 400
METRES

sign

gate

posts

post

post

Warland Draw (conduit)

gate

stile

stile

stile

bridge

gates

stile

Calf Lee Clough

post

posts

post

post

post

post

post

barbed wire across

gap

gate

ruin

Walsden Moor

heaps of stones

delf

delfs

gap

gap

gate

locked gate

locked gate

ruin

Calf Lee House

Knoll Top to Warland

perched rock

Shaw Stones

stile

stile

pool

Lodge Hall

stile

stile

stile

gate

stile

Cat Stones

pillars

bridge

Water-stalls

Meadow Bottom

Higher Scout

sign

sign

Bottomley

bridge

bridge

Bottomley Lock

to Littleborough (2 miles)

posts

Hollingworth Gate

post

post

gate

stile

The Scout

post

bridge

gate

gate

Dean Royd

Sands Lock

stile

stile

gates

Lane Bottom

mill

canal

A6033

to Walsden (1/2 mile)

N

CONT. ON P 116   The plateau of Blake Moor can be accessed from the path along the eastern side of Warland Reservoir. The only faint path to the trig on **Little Holder Stones** (p109) can be picked up above **Stony Edge**, where it runs intermittently along the high ground to pass the large **Stone i'th Moss**. This is a route probably most easily located in descent from the trig. Another route sets off from the northern tip of Light Hazzles Reservoir and makes out for a loose cluster of stones, though this intermittent path is very rough and wet.

Three barges were sunk in **Warland Reservoir** and joined with cables to prevent seaplanes from landing there during World War II. The frame of one is still visible when the water level is very low.

The western flanks of Blake Moor form an abrupt series of edges above Walsden and Warland. Though many of these edges are inaccessible, the interior of **Walsden Moor** is surprisingly well trodden. A clear waymarked path leads up from **Higher Scout** to the corner of **Warland Reservoir**. From it spring numerous smaller tracks contouring across the moor in either direction. Many are simply sheeptracks, though a good line can be followed from the jagged quarry delfs above **Lodge Hall** all the way across to the vicinity of the **Basin Stone**.

The **Basin Stone** has a distinctive anvil shape, but its name comes from a basin in its top. It was used as a pulpit by itinerant preachers like John Wesley, as well as for various large gatherings by the Chartists and workers' groups, including the Hudsonites. Coordinated by 'Pope' James Hudson, groups of men from Todmorden wearing green coats gathered for annual meetings here on Spaw Sunday, spoofing religious services. Hymns were handed out but not sung and absurd sermons were read. Part of their libertarian agenda held that the land was the birthright of the people.

the Basin Stone

111

ROUTE 19: HOLDER STONES & STOODLEY PIKE

Distance: 8 miles (13km)

Ascent: 320m

Difficulty: Moderate

Parking: On the roadside near Hinchliffe Arms or on B6138 through Cragg Vale.

Public Transport: Cragg Vale is served by the 597 bus from Hebden Bridge and Mytholmroyd, and 900 Hebden Bridge-Huddersfield bus.

Character: A high-level circuit around Withens Clough that takes in the summits of both Blake Moor and Stoodley Pike. The first section, from Higher House up to the Two Lads, is pathless across rough heather moor and navigation is not straightforward (a compass should be carried). Blake Moor's wild nature though contrasts nicely with the well-trodden paths of Stoodley Pike.

The new fenceline around the summit plateau of Blake Moor is part of a large-scale peat restoration project, with brash being spread across areas of bare peat.

Holder Stones were originally known as Alder or Alderman Stones, probably referring to the tree found on wet slopes. It has been suggested as the site of ancient remains by a 19th-century archaeologist, T. James.

(map labels)
Pennine Way
Stoodley Pike Monument
Stoodley Pike (402m)
gate
sign flags
stile & sign
cairns
Sunderland
cairn
unmarked summit
cairns
post
large cairn
ladder
post
High Stones
alternative route
old wall
gap
Henry Edge
Long Stoop
Te Deum Stone
Withens Gate
gate
gap
seat
small cairn
stile
fallen boundary stone
new fenceline
Coldwell Hill
boundary stone
Pennine Way
stile
boundary stone
Red Dikes Flat
boundary stone
sign
N
0   200   400   METRES
Bird Nest Hill
Warland Drain
Pipeline
Deep Slade
wet
cairn gate
shooting box (ruin)
Cloven Stone
drain
gate
new fenceline
pathless
Holder Stones
Holder Stones
trig
stile
Little Holder Stones
stile
stake
Blake Moor (422m)

6 Turn right and follow the main path east from **Stoodley Pike Monument** to a gate. Where the Pennine Way turns left, continue straight on along the flags to a stile leading into **Sunderland Pasture Plantation.** Turn left at a sign in the middle of the plantation to reach a stile leading onto **Bank Top Lane.**

The **Te Deum Stone** stands at the top of Withens Gate and is carved with a cross and an inscription 'Te Deum Laudamus', meaning 'We praise thee, o Lord'. Also known as The Cross or Lord's Stone, it is thought to have been erected in the 1680s by Robert Sutcliffe of Withens. Coffin-bearers heading from Cragg Vale or Withens to the chapels at Mankinholes and Lumbutts are thought to have rested the coffin on the stone and prayed. Part of the stone has since been chipped off, possibly by a quarryman aiming to damage the cross.

5 Beyond the low ramparts of **Coldwell Hill**, a path arrives from the left just before a small rocky outcrop. The **alternative route** (identical to part of Route 18, see p105) continues straight on to join the main path along the edge to Stoodley Pike but, to stick to our circuit of Withens Clough, turn right here down a fainter path. This aims for the corner of the wall ahead and follows the left side of the wall to the main track across **Withens Gate**. Turn right through the gate, passing the **Te Deum Stone** and descending to the next wall. Turn left before the wall and pick up a faint sheeptrack climbing along the shallow edge above it. Through a gap in the next wall, the rocks of Henry Edge can be followed to meet a large path heading up the hill. Turn left here to reach the summit of **Stoodley Pike**, its giant monument already obvious ahead.

4 Retrace your steps to **Warland Drain** and rejoin the path along its side. At a sharp kink in the drain, turn right along the flagstoned Pennine Way across **Red Dikes Flat.**

3 Turn left up the shoulder from the **Two Lads** and pick up a faint line leading to the path along the drain that encircles Blake Moor. Follow this right, passing a small ruin and joining the line of an exposed pipeline. The towers of **Holder Stones** soon loom ahead; to reach them, cross Warland Drain where you can, and climb up the rough slope (if the drain is full, using the fence to cross may be the best bet). A faint path leads across the worn peat between Holder Stones and Little Holder Stones, but the true summit of Blake Moor stands by a stake to the south-east back across the new fenceline.

112

FROM CRAGG VALE

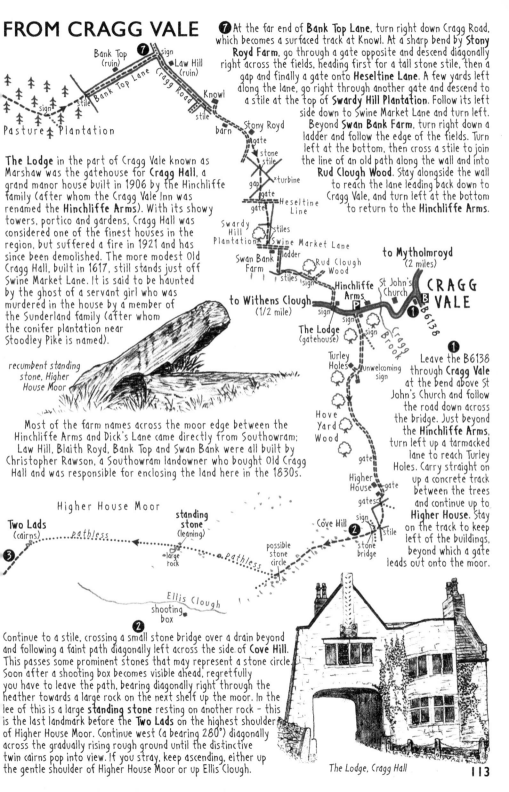

7 At the far end of **Bank Top Lane**, turn right down Cragg Road, which becomes a surfaced track at Knowl. At a sharp bend by **Stony Royd Farm**, go through a gate opposite and descend diagonally right across the fields, heading first for a tall stone stile, then a gap and finally a gate onto **Heseltine Lane**. A few yards left along the lane, go right through another gate and descend to a stile at the top of **Swardy Hill Plantation**. Follow its left side down to Swine Market Lane and turn left. Beyond **Swan Bank Farm**, turn right down a ladder and follow the edge of the fields. Turn left at the bottom, then cross a stile to join the line of an old path along the wall and into **Rud Clough Wood**. Stay alongside the wall to reach the lane leading back down to Cragg Vale, and turn left at the bottom to return to the **Hinchliffe Arms**.

The Lodge in the part of Cragg Vale known as Marshaw was the gatehouse for **Cragg Hall**, a grand manor house built in 1906 by the Hinchliffe family (after whom the Cragg Vale Inn was renamed the **Hinchliffe Arms**). With its showy towers, portico and gardens, Cragg Hall was considered one of the finest houses in the region, but suffered a fire in 1921 and has since been demolished. The more modest Old Cragg Hall, built in 1617, still stands just off Swine Market Lane. It is said to be haunted by the ghost of a servant girl who was murdered in the house by a member of the Sunderland family (after whom the conifer plantation near Stoodley Pike is named).

recumbent standing stone, Higher House Moor

Most of the farm names across the moor edge between the Hinchliffe Arms and Dick's Lane came directly from Southowram; Law Hill, Blaith Royd, Bank Top and Swan Bank were all built by Christopher Rawson, a Southowram landowner who bought Old Cragg Hall and was responsible for enclosing the land here in the 1830s.

1 Leave the B6138 through **Cragg Vale** at the bend above St John's Church and follow the road down across the bridge. Just beyond the **Hinchliffe Arms**, turn left up a tarmacked lane to reach Turley Holes. Carry straight on up a concrete track between the trees and continue up to **Higher House**. Stay on the track to keep left of the buildings, beyond which a gate leads out onto the moor.

2 Continue to a stile, crossing a small stone bridge over a drain beyond and following a faint path diagonally left across the side of **Cove Hill**. This passes some prominent stones that may represent a stone circle. Soon after a shooting box becomes visible ahead, regretfully you have to leave the path, bearing diagonally right through the heather towards a large rock on the next shelf up the moor. In the lee of this is a large **standing stone** resting on another rock – this is the last landmark before the **Two Lads** on the highest shoulder of Higher House Moor. Continue west (a bearing 280°) diagonally across the gradually rising rough ground until the distinctive twin cairns pop into view. If you stray, keep ascending, either up the gentle shoulder of Higher House Moor or up Ellis Clough.

The Lodge, Cragg Hall

113

OMBROGENOUS BOG: Moors for the Future?

Ombrogenous bogs have dominated large parts of the Pennine uplands for thousands of years. Peat is formed of partially decomposed vegetation, particularly mosses, and the high rainfall and flat plateaus of the West Yorkshire Moors provide the perfect conditions for this process. The word *ombrogenous* refers to these plants, which thrive in wet conditions but rely entirely on rainfall for their water. The result is a very acidic and specialised microclimate in which only a few (often rare) species thrive. Because of this, and the fact that peat is essentially a living organism, the blanket bogs are very sensitive to changes in climate, hydrology, air pollution, grazing and burning.

Peat erosion is now widespread in the South Pennines, possibly an inevitable consequence of climate change. Every time you scramble up a peat hag and the surface gives way, it is obvious just how easy it is to erode peat. In part the erosion of the peat surface is due to its natural ageing, but the rate of degradation has accelerated significantly. The smoke from mills in neighbouring industrial towns, overgrazing and the popularity of walking on the moors have destroyed many plants, particularly the sphagnum mosses that regenerate the peat.

But help is at hand. These blanket bogs are a surprising hive of activity these days, with new fences, pathways, helicopter bags and jute netting appearing all the time. Though this may go against the grain for those who value these moors for their open spaces and solitude, it is all an essential part of protecting and restoring this fragile landscape. Currently the South Pennines are considered to be botanically poor and the Moors for the Future project was launched in 2002 to counter this. Across Blake Moor and Black Hill, many steep peat slopes have been covered with netting to prevent peat from being washed away, and reseeded to encourage surface vegetation to regenerate. The fences are to keep sheep from grazing any new growth that develops and are designed to be only a temporary feature of the moorlands.

CHAPTER 13 – **BYRON EDGE**

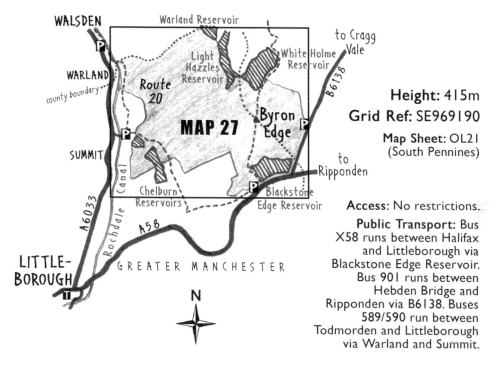

Height: 415m

Grid Ref: SE969190

Map Sheet: OL21
(South Pennines)

Access: No restrictions.

Public Transport: Bus X58 runs between Halifax and Littleborough via Blackstone Edge Reservoir. Bus 901 runs between Hebden Bridge and Ripponden via B6138. Buses 589/590 run between Todmorden and Littleborough via Warland and Summit.

Byron Edge is a gentle rise on the reservoir-studded moor north of the A58 at the White House, its unmarked summit straddling the county boundary like any true Pennine top. Byron Edge is likely named after the Barony of Rochdale whose manor it would have fallen under. They went by the name Lord Byron, the most famous being the renowned romantic poet.

Sandwiched between Blackstone Edge Reservoir, White Holme Reservoir and a series of drains, Byron Edge is largely unspectacular and a series of power lines crossing the moor does little to improve matters. It is easily bypassed on the Pennine Way, but its western flank has its moments, particularly where Leach Hill Rocks and the shapely outlier of Snoddle Hill overlook the Chelburn Reservoirs. Despite being part of Greater Manchester, these slopes are easily reached climbing out of Walsden and Warland and offer the most interesting approach to Byron Edge.

Byron Edge from Blackstone Edge Reservoir

MAP 27: BYRON EDGE

CONTINUATION ON p111

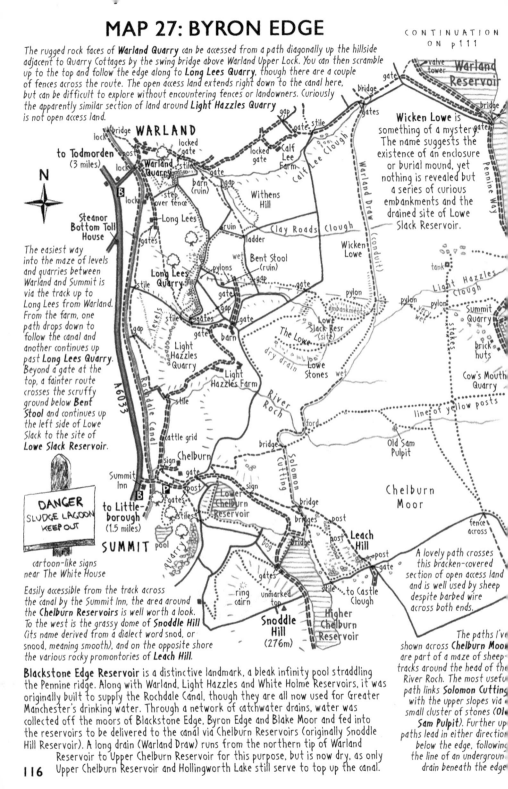

The rugged rock faces of **Warland Quarry** can be accessed from a path diagonally up the hillside adjacent to Quarry Cottages by the swing bridge above Warland Upper Lock. You can then scramble up to the top and follow the edge along to **Long Lees Quarry**, though there are a couple of fences across the route. The open access land extends right down to the canal here, but can be difficult to explore without encountering fences or landowners. Curiously the apparently similar section of land around **Light Hazzles Quarry** is not open access land.

Wicken Lowe is something of a mystery. The name suggests the existence of an enclosure or burial mound, yet nothing is revealed but a series of curious embankments and the drained site of Lowe Slack Reservoir.

The easiest way into the maze of levels and quarries between Warland and Summit is via the track up to Long Lees from Warland. From the farm, one path drops down to follow the canal and another continues up past **Long Lees Quarry**. Beyond a gate at the top, a fainter route crosses the scruffy ground below **Bent Stool** and continues up the left side of Lowe Slack to the site of **Lowe Slack Reservoir**.

DANGER
SLUDGE LAGOON
KEEP OUT

cartoon-like signs near The White House

Easily accessible from the track across the canal by the Summit Inn, the area around the **Chelburn Reservoirs** is well worth a look. To the west is the grassy dome of **Snoddle Hill** (its name derived from a dialect word snod, or snood, meaning smooth), and on the opposite shore the various rocky promontories of **Leach Hill**.

A lovely path crosses this bracken-covered section of open access land and is well used by sheep despite barbed wire across both ends.

The paths I've shown across **Chelburn Moor** are part of a maze of sheep-tracks around the head of the River Roch. The most useful path links **Solomon Cutting** with the upper slopes via a small cluster of stones (**Old Sam Pulpit**). Further up paths lead in either direction below the edge, following the line of an underground drain beneath the edge.

Blackstone Edge Reservoir is a distinctive landmark, a bleak infinity pool straddling the Pennine ridge. Along with Warland, Light Hazzles and White Holme Reservoirs, it was originally built to supply the Rochdale Canal, though they are all now used for Greater Manchester's drinking water. Through a network of catchwater drains, water was collected off the moors of Blackstone Edge, Byron Edge and Blake Moor and fed into the reservoirs to be delivered to the canal via Chelburn Reservoirs (originally Snoddle Hill Reservoir). A long drain (Warland Draw) runs from the northern tip of Warland Reservoir to Upper Chelburn Reservoir for this purpose, but is now dry, as only Upper Chelburn Reservoir and Hollingworth Lake still serve to top up the canal.

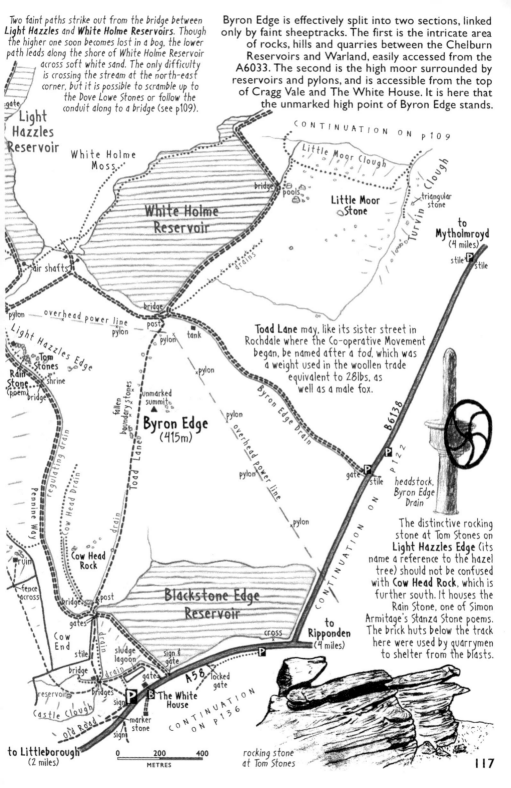

Two faint paths strike out from the bridge between **Light Hazzles** and **White Holme Reservoirs**. Though the higher one soon becomes lost in a bog, the lower path leads along the shore of White Holme Reservoir across soft white sand. The only difficulty is crossing the stream at the north-east corner, but it is possible to scramble up to the Dove Lowe Stones or follow the conduit along to a bridge (see p109).

Byron Edge is effectively split into two sections, linked only by faint sheeptracks. The first is the intricate area of rocks, hills and quarries between the Chelburn Reservoirs and Warland, easily accessed from the A6033. The second is the high moor surrounded by reservoirs and pylons, and is accessible from the top of Cragg Vale and The White House. It is here that the unmarked high point of Byron Edge stands.

Light Hazzles Reservoir

White Holme Moss

CONTINUATION ON p109

Little Moor Clough

bridge   pools

Little Moor Stone

Turvin Clough

triangular stone

to **Mytholmroyd** (4 miles)

stile   stile

White Holme Reservoir

air shafts

drains

bridge

pylon   overhead power line   pylon   post

tank

pylon

Toad Lane may, like its sister street in Rochdale where the Co-operative Movement began, be named after a tod, which was a weight used in the woollen trade equivalent to 28lbs, as well as a male fox.

Light Hazzles Edge

Tom Stones

Rain Stone (poem)   shrine

bridge

fallen boundary stones

unmarked summit

Byron Edge (415m)

pylon

pylon

Byron Edge Drain

B6138

overhead power line

pylon

pylon

gate   stile

P122

headstock, Byron Edge Drain

regulating drain

Cow Head Drain

drain

Pennine Way

Cow Head Rock

Blackstone Edge Reservoir

ruin

fence across

bridge   post

gates

Cow End

stile

sludge lagoon

sign & gate

cross

to **Ripponden** (4 miles)

P

CONTINUATION ON P122

The distinctive rocking stone at Tom Stones on **Light Hazzles Edge** (its name a reference to the hazel tree) should not be confused with **Cow Head Rock**, which is further south. It houses the Rain Stone, one of Simon Armitage's Stanza Stone poems. The brick huts below the track here were used by quarrymen to shelter from the blasts.

bridge   drain   gates

reservoir   bridges

Castle Clough

old Road

A58   locked gate

P

B **The White House**

sign

marker stone

sign

CONTINUATION ON P136

to **Littleborough** (2 miles)

0   200   400
METRES

rocking stone at Tom Stones

117

ROUTE 20: BYRON EDGE & BLAKE MOOR FROM WARLAND (OR WALSDEN)

Distance: 9½ miles (15.3km)

Ascent: 370m

Difficulty: Strenuous

Parking: Lay-by on A6033 by Bellholme Sports Club between Walsden and Warland, or a small parking area down Deanroyd Lane on the edge of Walsden.

Public Transport: Warland is on the 589/590 bus routes between Halifax and Rochdale. Walsden is on the main Caldervale train line.

Character: A fine circuit taking in two tops, several reservoirs, the Basin Stone and a stretch of the Rochdale Canal. Navigation is largely straightforward except for the rough section across Blake Moor's plateau. Care is needed here, especially in bad weather, but there are still plenty of useful landmarks.

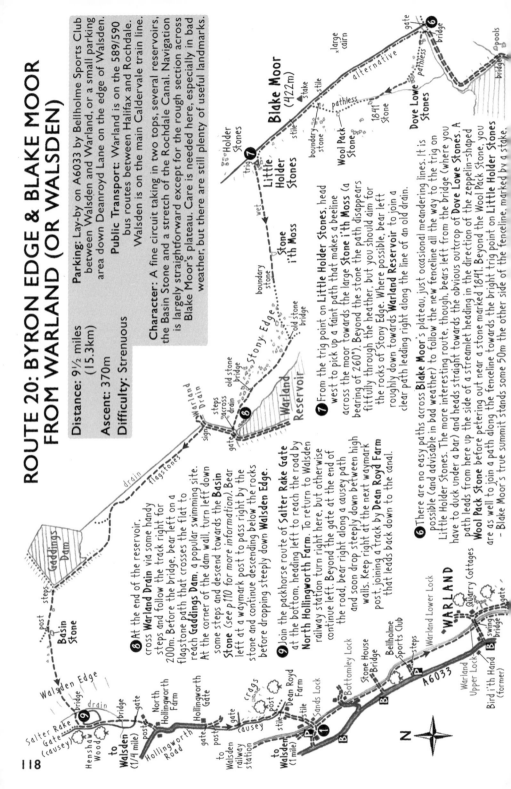

8 At the end of the reservoir, cross **Warland Drain** via some handy steps and follow the track right for 200m. Before the bridge, bear left on a flagstone path that crosses the flat to reach **Gaddings Dam**, a popular swimming site. At the corner of the dam wall, turn left down some steps and descend towards the **Basin Stone** (see p110 for more information). Bear left at a waymark post to pass right by the stone and continue descending below the rocks before dropping steeply down **Walsden Edge**.

9 Join the packhorse route of **Salter Rake Gate** at the bottom, heading left to reach the road by **North Hollingworth Farm**. To return to Walsden railway station turn right here, but otherwise continue left. Beyond the gate at the end of the road, bear right along a causey path and soon drop steeply down between high walls. Keep right at the next waymark post, joining a track by **Dean Royd Farm** that leads back down to the canal.

7 From the trig point on **Little Holder Stones**, head west to pick up a faint path that makes a beeline across the moor towards the large **Stone i'th Moss** (a bearing of 260°). Beyond the stone the path disappears fitfully through the heather, but you should aim for the rocks of Stony Edge. Where possible, bear left roughly down towards **Warland Reservoir** to join a clear path leading right along the line of an old drain.

6 There are no easy paths across **Blake Moor**'s plateau, just occasional meandering lines. It is possible (and advisable in bad weather) to follow the new fenceline all the way to the trig on Little Holder Stones. The more interesting route, though, bears left from the bridge (where you have to duck under a bar) and heads straight towards the obvious outcrop of **Dove Lowe Stones**. A path leads from here up the side of a streamlet heading in the direction of the zeppelin-shaped **Wool Pack Stone** before petering out near a stone marked 1841. Beyond the Wool Pack Stone, you are as well to join a path along the fenceline towards the bright trig point on **Little Holder Stones** – Blake Moor's true summit stands some 50m the other side of the fenceline, marked by a stake.

118

to Walsden (1 mile)

to Walsden (¼ mile)

N

4 Reaching the lower car park below the **White House**, turn left and follow a path down across the stream. Across the drain beyond, turn right immediately in front of a small building and follow a path along the new fenceline to reach the corner of **Blackstone Edge**.

White Holme Reservoir

pylon

bridge

5 **Byron Edge** ▲ unmarked summit (415m)

Toad Lane

× fallen × boundary stones

5 Toad Lane continues down to **White Holme Reservoir**, where you turn right and follow a track around the shallow dam wall. Continue until the first bridge across the drain beyond the reservoir, just before a new fenceline crosses it.

Blackstone Edge Reservoir. Head straight across the main track here and pick up another path by an open access land post some 20m beyond. This is **Toad Lane**, which follows the line of an old drain over the top of **Byron Edge** – the true top is some 20m off to the right of the track just beyond a cluster of stones.

Cow Head Rocks

gate

bridges

post

Blackstone Edge

to Ripponden (4 miles)

3 Emerging on the track beyond Leach, follow it left all the way to **Castle Clough**.

Soon after crossing the stream, double back left at the next junction. Where the track crosses back over the clough, bear right to a gate and climb steeply up the slope to join the line of the Old Road leading up to **The White House**.

The White House

P 4 sign drain marker stone

A58 old Road

Castle Clough

to Littleborough (2 miles)

gate bridge

barn

cattle grid & post sign & stile

bridge

sign & gate gate gate sign & gate

Leach Hill

Leach

3

Higher Chelburn Reservoir

drain bridge post post

sign

bridge

Lower Chelburn Reservoir

gates

sign gate

0 200 400 600
METRES

Steanor Bottom Toll House, Warland

The Bird i'th Hand, then known as the Bird at Calf Holes, was originally built on the old Calderbrook Road over to Littleborough. When the new turnpike road was opened in 1825 along the line of today's A6033, landlord Henry Rogers had it taken down and rebuilt at its current location.

One of the original proposals for the route of a trans-Pennine canal was a route linking Chelburn and Ripponden via a 4.8-mile tunnel. In the end a competing company built the **Rochdale Canal**, though it too was planned to have a significant tunnel between Walsden and Sladen. When this was by-passed by a series of locks, it necessitated the building of several reservoirs to supply them with water: Chelburn, Blackstone Edge, White Holme, Light Hazzles, Warland, and Hollingworth Lake (from which water was pumped by steam up 45 feet to a 4-mile conduit that linked to Summit Locks).

1 Join the **Rochdale Canal** (either opposite Walsden railway station, from the small car park down Deanroyd Lane, or behind Bellholme Sports Club) and follow it right as far as **Warland**. Above Warland Upper Lock, cross the canal via a swing bridge and turn immediately right. Follow the track up to **Long Lees Farm** and fork right through a gate between the buildings. Follow the rough canal side to a stile and, beyond a broken down wall, climb away from the canal a little. At a new fenceline, skirt round it to the left to find a stile onto a track that leads down to **Chelburn**.

Long Lees Farm
gate
Long Lees Mill (site)
stile
gap wall old
Withens Hill
stile
cattle grid
Chelburn
signs gate
2
P B
Summit Inn
SUMMIT
alternative route
Rochdale Canal

to Littleborough (1.5 miles)

Alternative route: As is evident from this map, it is entirely possible to follow the canal all the way to the Summit Inn, but I've tried to break up the route and make it more interesting. Turn left before the pub to rejoin the main route.

2 The track reaches a junction below the hamlet of **Chelburn**; follow the sign along a path that continues opposite. It bends round to the left and joins the track up from the Summit Inn; follow this left up through a gate onto the open moor. Past **Lower Chelburn Reservoir** bear left at a signpost and fork left again to stay on the waymarked Pennine Bridleway across a drain and up over **Leach Hill**. This drops down to a gate and follows a fenced route around the farm at Leach (home to the Field of Dreams animal sanctuary).

rocks below Leach Hill

EMPEROR MOTH

The **Emperor Moth** is found on moorland and heath on the West Yorkshire Moors in the spring, though it is far from common. It is distinctive for the peacock eyes on each of its four wings (the hawk moth has them only on the hind wings), yet my only sighting of one was in the heather near Byron Edge. This sketch is of the female, which is up to 10cm in span and a bluish-brown colour with red patches on the tips of her wings. The male is smaller with feathered antennae and brighter colours, and is the only one likely to be seen during the day, as the females fly only at night.

CHAPTER 14 – MANSHEAD HILL

Height: 417m

Grid Ref: SD997197

Map Sheet: OL21 (South Pennines)

Access: No dogs during nesting bird season (1st March to 31st July) except on the permissive path along summit ridge.

Public Transport: Ripponden is served by various bus routes from Halifax. The X58 runs to Littleborough via Blackstone Edge Reservoir, and the 901 from Hebden Bridge to Ripponden via Cragg Vale and Blackstone Edge Reservoir. Bus 597 runs from Hebden Bridge to Cragg Vale.

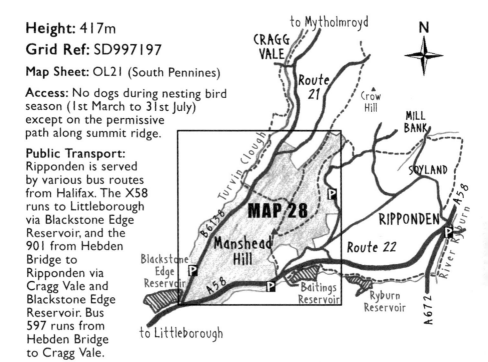

Manshead Hill is a graceful ridge of soft grassland rising between the Ryburn Valley and Cragg Vale. The trig point at Crow Hill above Sowerby village marks the culmination of this ridge of high ground that juts out eastwards from the main Pennine ridge, though it is separate from the bulk of the moor. Manshead is one of the most defined hills in West Yorkshire, its summit the only obvious target on the moor, with great views across Calderdale. All of the ground is easily accessible from both the A58 and B6138 and there is lots of scope to create short circular walks, particularly from Baitings Reservoir or Coal Gate Road above Cotton Stones.

Manshead Hill's name may derive from the Celtic word *maen* (meaning stone), though it is marked on some older maps as Mons Head, possibly referring to the Latin word for a mountain.

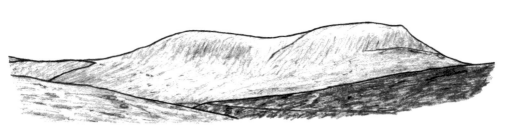

Manshead Hill from the head of Turvin Clough

121

Manshead Hill, a ridge with two distinctive humps, is one of the most shapely hills in Calderdale. It is also remarkably smooth, thanks to its covering of parched yellow-orange grass, particularly striking when compared with the rough, scarred peat the other side of the B6138. Rather than a barren moorland waste, Manshead is a gentle and welcoming hill, though this appearance is due to intensive farming across the hillsides, a process that is now in reverse. Manshead Hill is most frequently climbed from Baitings Reservoir in the south, where a permissive path allows access up Greenwood Clough, but the ridge walk from the north-east is probably the most satisfying route and allows you to take in the well-preserved World War II decoy bunker on Slate Delfs Hill.

In areas of rough, tussocky grassland like that which covers Manshead Hill, the **wheatear** is a common summer visitor. Seen between March and October, it is a small ground-dwelling bird distinguished by a black T shape on its tail and white flash on its underside - indeed the name wheatear is a corruption of 'white arse' (though locally it was known as a smattie). The sighting of a wheatear was considered to bring bad luck in some areas, particularly if it was sitting on a stone.

Old Bar House Delf marks the original location of the toll bar at the top end of the Cragg Road Turnpike, which opened in 1816. It was home to Turvin Jim, a man with a famously voracious appetite, including for grass and live fish. Within a few years, the bar was moved down the road to the marginally more secluded Mount Pleasant.

The dry grassy slopes of Manshead Hill might appeal from the **B6138** above Cragg Vale, but it is a frustrating hillside. Despite a number of lay-bys and stiles, none gives access to any sort of path. Only the path along Cold Laughton Drain from the top lay-by provides an easy route to the summit, and links to the track to White Holme Reservoir.

Encircled by Black Castle Drain is an area called **Hassock**, which is a term that refers to the thick tussocks of mat-grass that cover Manshead Hill. Though gentle-looking, it is unabashed ankle-twisting ground. Other Hassocks are found near the summit of Way Stone Edge, and the word gave its name to kneelers used in churches, which were originally stuffed with dried grass or straw.

MAP 28: MANSHEAD

The disused brick bunker near Slate Delfs Hill was a **World War II Starfish Bombing Decoy** control centre. Across the moor towards Manshead Hill there would have been a series of decoy lights, simulated fires and shadow buildings controlled from this bunker. These decoys utilised special effects from film studios and were designed to draw German bombers away from their intended targets - in this case, Greetland Station and Marshalling Yard, as well as the urban areas of Leeds and Manchester. This site was unsuccessful, but is one of the best preserved of the 235 Starfish sites around the country. An earthen blast screen surrounds the two small rooms, the control centre on the left with an escape hatch and a generator room on the right.

a wheatear

The name **Collin Hill** (like Collon Flat on Wadsworth Moor) refers to collin-bobs, dead or burnt heather shoots which were gathered for kindling.

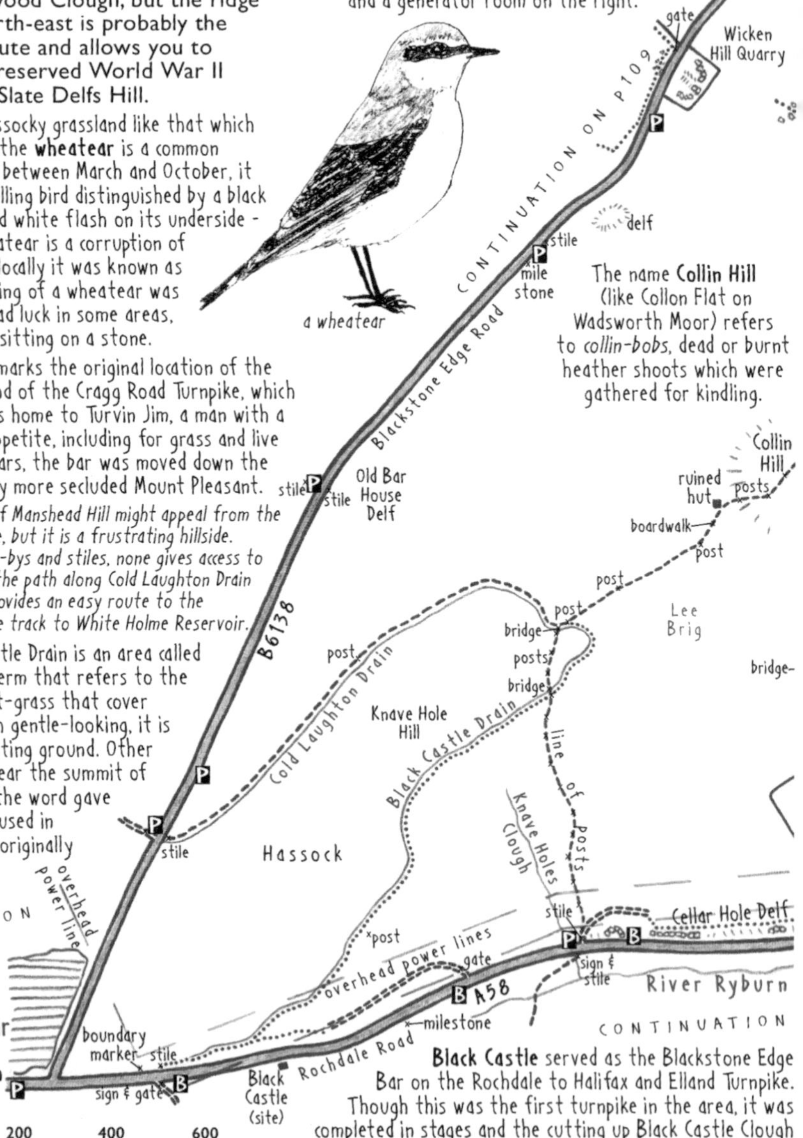

Black Castle served as the Blackstone Edge Bar on the Rochdale to Halifax and Elland Turnpike. Though this was the first turnpike in the area, it was completed in stages and the cutting up Black Castle Clough was one of the last sections to be constructed in the 1820s.

Wicken Hill Quarry

CONTINUATION ON P109

delf

stile

mile stone

Old Bar House Delf

CONTINUATION ON P117

Blackstone Edge Road

Blackstone Edge Reservoir

to Littleborough (3 miles)

Hassock

B6138

Cold Laughton Drain

Knave Hole Hill

Black Castle Drain

boundary marker

overhead power lines

Black Castle (site)

Rochdale Road

milestone

Collin Hill

ruined hut   posts

boardwalk

post

post

Lee Brig

bridge

posts

bridge

line of posts

Knave Holes Clough

stile

Cellar Hole Delf

A58

sign & stile

River Ryburn

CONTINUATION

0   200   400   600
METRES

122

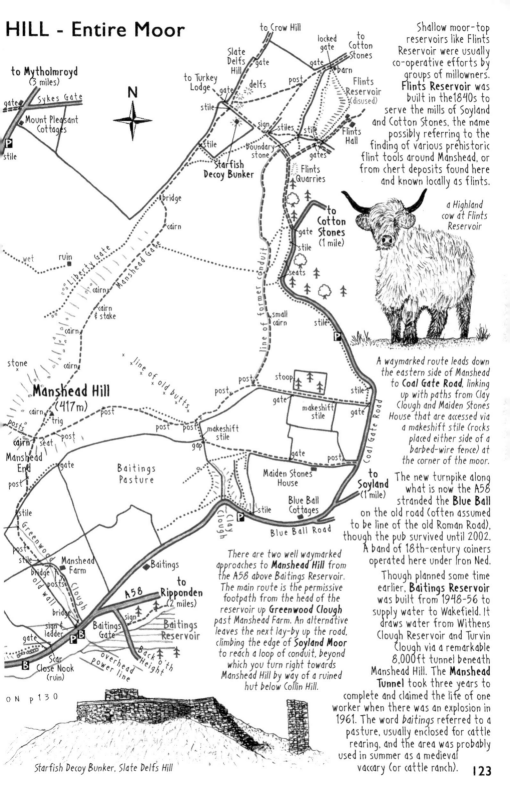

HILL - Entire Moor

Shallow moor-top reservoirs like Flints Reservoir were usually co-operative efforts by groups of millowners. **Flints Reservoir** was built in the1840s to serve the mills of Soyland and Cotton Stones, the name possibly referring to the finding of various prehistoric flint tools around Manshead, or from chert deposits found here and known locally as flints.

a Highland cow at Flints Reservoir

A waymarked route leads down the eastern side of Manshead to **Coal Gate Road**, linking up with paths from Clay Clough and Maiden Stones House that are accessed via a makeshift stile (rocks placed either side of a barbed-wire fence) at the corner of the moor.

The new turnpike along what is now the A58 stranded the **Blue Ball** on the old road (often assumed to be line of the old Roman Road), though the pub survived until 2002. A band of 18th-century coiners operated here under Iron Ned.

Though planned some time earlier, **Baitings Reservoir** was built from 1948-56 to supply water to Wakefield. It draws water from Withens Clough Reservoir and Turvin Clough via a remarkable 8,000ft tunnel beneath Manshead Hill. The **Manshead Tunnel** took three years to complete and claimed the life of one worker when there was an explosion in 1961. The word *baitings* referred to a pasture, usually enclosed for cattle rearing, and the area was probably used in summer as a medieval vaccary (or cattle ranch).

There are two well waymarked approaches to **Manshead Hill** from the A58 above Baitings Reservoir. The main route is the permissive footpath from the head of the reservoir up **Greenwood Clough** past Manshead Farm. An alternative leaves the next lay-by up the road, climbing the edge of **Soyland Moor** to reach a loop of conduit, beyond which you turn right towards Manshead Hill by way of a ruined hut below Collin Hill.

Map labels

to Crow Hill
locked gate
to Cotton Stones
Slate Delfs Hill
gate
gate
barn
to Mytholmroyd (3 miles)
to Turkey Lodge
gate
delfs
post
Flints Reservoir (disused)
gate
Sykes Gate
N
stile
sign
stiles
stile
Flints Hall
Mount Pleasant Cottages
P
stile
boundary stone
stiles
gates
Starfish Decoy Bunker
Flints Quarries
bridge
cairn
to Cotton Stones (1 mile)
gate
stile
wet
ruin
Liberty Gate
Manshead Gate
seats
cairn
cairn & stake
small cairn
stile
cairn
P
stone
cairn
line of old butts
line of former conduit
post
stoop
stile
Manshead Hill (417m)
post
gate
makeshift stile
gate
Coal Gate Road
cairn
trig
post
post
post
makeshift stile
posts
cairn
seat
post
gap
gate
post
Manshead End
gate
Baitings Pasture
Maiden Stones House
to Soyland (1 mile)
post
Blue Ball Cottages
stile
stile
Greenwood Clough
Clay Clough
P
Blue Ball Road
post
stile
Manshead Farm
Baitings
to Ripponden (2 miles)
bridge
old posts
old wall
A58
sign
Baitings Reservoir
bridge
sign & ladder
P
Baitings Gate
Back o' th' Height
overhead power line
gate
B
Scar Close Nook (ruin)

ON p130

Starfish Decoy Bunker, Slate Delfs Hill

ROUTE 21: MANSHEAD HILL & CRAGG VALE FROM MYTHOLMROYD

Distance: 10 miles (15.8km)

Ascent: 390m

Difficulty: Moderate

Parking: Car parks at Mytholmroyd Community Centre and St Michael's Church.

Public Transport: Mytholmroyd is on the main Caldervale train & bus routes.

Character: A very satisfying round that combines the beautiful wooded valley of Cragg Vale with the broad ridge of high ground extending all the way down from Manshead Hill to Blackwood Common. Though there is a very rough section at the head of the clough, an alternative is provided and the long steady descent thereafter is very much simpler.

Nab End Quarries is a small delf surrounded by ugly barbed wire fences, but it houses a surprising sculpture garden in one of its nooks. Go right to the far end from the stile to find the **Lawrence Millennium Garden**, where carved stone faces and stunted trees lend a surreal atmosphere to this windswept hilltop.

sculpture in Nab End Quarries

① From the main road in **Mytholmroyd**, head south on the B6138. Under the railway and just beyond the Shoulder of Mutton pub, turn left into Scout Road and then first right into Hall Bank Lane. Climb the hill and turn right on the bend up Stubbings Close. At the end of which a footpath continues into the wood beyond. At a pair of stone stoops, fork right and descend to the old **Hoo Hole Dye Works**. Bear right over the bridge and turn left onto Cragg Road.

② Just before **Dauber Bridge**, follow a track off to the right (signed 'Parrock Clough & Frost Hole'). After a few hundred metres, another sign takes you right down to a bridge over **Parrock Clough** (also known here as Wriggles Bottom). From here a good path follows the right bank of Cragg Brook for nearly a mile. At the first road across head left for a few metres to rejoin the route, and by **Cragg Spa** follow the road right briefly. The path climbs through **Paper Mill Wood** before rejoining the stream at the mill ruins by Papermill Cottage. Turn left here across the bridge, then immediately right to climb up to **Castle Gate**.

③ Turn right along **Castle Gate** and pass the millpond (either on the track or a path that skirts around it). On the corner before New Bridge, head straight on alongside the stream. This emerges on the road by **St John's Church**; turn right over the bridge and soon after the Hinchliffe Arms turn left up a track signed towards Higher House Moor.

④ The path over Blackwood Common emerges by **Nab End Quarries**, where you follow the old stone track left past Nab End Farm. If you have the energy to explore the sculptures of the **Millennium Garden**, bear right into the quarries, but the route continues straight on around the perimeter fence. Beyond a path signed off to the left, follow an open fenced path down off the common. Through a gate at the bottom, head straight on, joining a track down to **Bent**, where the onward path is waymarked through the garden and down the soggy edge of the field beyond.

⑤ Arriving at a stile at the top of **Hollin Hey Bank**, the onward path is not immediately obvious but heads diagonally down to the right the other side of a large bush. Following yellow stakes, the path picks its way down through further thickets before doubling back to reach a gate into **Stake Lane**. Turn left down the old lane to join the tarmac of Hall Bank Lane and follow it all the way back down into **Mytholmroyd**.

⑨ Turn right on **High Stones Road** for just a few yards before following a sign left over a stile and along the side of a small wood. The mud can be avoided to the right before rejoining the path along the wall to pass a pond and emerge on another road. Follow it right for 100m and look for an unsigned path which leads left across the heart of **Blackwood Common**.

MYTHOLMROYD

(map labels:)

to Hebden Bridge (1 mile)

to Halifax (6 miles)

Dusty Miller

Shoulder of Mutton

Mytholmroyd railway station

Scout Road

Hall Bank Lane

New House (Sweet & Maxwell)

Stake Lane

posts

Hollin Hey Bank

gate

sign

stiles

wet

Bent

cattle grid

gate

sign

stile

Millenium Garden (sculptures)

Nab End Quarries

Nab End

Blackwood Common

gate

dairy

post

pond

Pitts Farm

Water mud Stalls

High Stones Road

sign & stile

Cragg Road

stoops

Top Land Farm

Hoo Hole Dye Works

Dauber Bridge

sign

Wriggles Bottom

bridge

stile

sign

stable

B6138

Clough Foot Bridge

sign

Cragg Spa

Spa Bridge

Cragg Brook

Spa Laithe Farm

gates

post

Paper Mill Wood

gate & sign

Papermill Cottage

New Bridge Pond

posts

gate

CRAGG VALE

gap & sign

Castle

gate

St John's Church

Marsh Grove

sign

Hinchliffe Arms

The small swimming pool below **Wash Falls** was apparently created by airmen stationed at the nearby Starfish Decoy site during World War II.

4 After 200m fork left (towards 'Green Bank') and follow a path that heads back towards the river. It doesn't matter which route you take through **Higher House Wood**, though the smaller path along the river may be drier at times. All routes lead to a stile at the far end of the wood. Soon after, the path reaches the lovely clapper bridge at **Dog Bridge**, where the main route turns right to climb up a long set of steps. Reaching a path near **Higher House**, turn left to a stile on the edge of the moor.

5 Once on the moor, join a path left along the edge of a drain to reach a stile. The path continues down to a large bridge in **Trimming Dale** and climbs steeply to a stile beyond. After another stile you reach a tall waymarker; continue straight along the higher of two grassy tracks above the clough. At the end continue straight on past **Washfold Bridge** (not as picturesque as it sounds) and cross a metal bridge by the pumping station. Follow the stream for 100m, then re-cross it and follow the **B6138**. If the stream is high you can stay on the left bank and scramble over the short section of wooden fence that bars your way on this side of the stream.

Cragg Spa is a small spring that was a 19th-century attraction, its sulphurous waters thought to have healing properties, particularly for skin ailments. On Spaw Sunday the spa was dressed in a ceremony often linked to a religious gathering; this tradition has recently been resurrected.

6 Cross straight over the road and climb up to the back left corner of **Wicken Hill Quarry**, where you can climb over the fence (unfortunately the stiles off the road here are all some distance away). This side of Manshead Hill is a warren of tussocks and rushes, but you can try to pick up a faint line that aids progress by aiming slightly to the right of a ruin visible below Great Manshead Hill. After a particularly wet section of tussock hopping it bends left and makes straight for the lonely ruin. From here the best bet is to head straight up the slope, a rough but short assault. At the top join the main path near one of the cairns and follow it right for half a mile to reach the **Manshead Hill** trig, safe in the knowledge that the rough going is firmly behind you.

7 You may wish to wander on past the summit to **Manshead End**, where there is a seat and an excellent view. Otherwise retrace your steps back along the ridge and begin the long steady descent. The path drops down to a small wooden bridge and follows the wall towards the prominent WW2 **Starfish Decoy Bunker** on Slate Delfs Hill (see p122) for more information.

8 Continue straight on along the ridge to reach a walled path that heads up towards **Little Crow Hill**. After crossing a field it becomes a surfaced track (Water Stalls Road) to descend steadily past **Crow Hill Farm**, where a tarmacked road is joined, dropping down to **High Stones Road**.

Alternative route: To avoid the rough section from Washfold Bridge to Manshead Hill, you can cross **Dog Bridge** and climb up to the **B6138** through one of the gardens of Green Bank. Follow the road right to Moorland Cottages, then turn left behind them and pick up a path up the side of the fields. Head straight across the next road and fork right where the track splits, continuing up past **Slate Delfs Farm** to reach the moor by the **Starfish Decoy bunker**.

cairn on Manshead End

125

ROUTE 22: MANSHEAD HILL FROM RIPPONDEN

Distance: 9 miles (14.5km)

Ascent: 370m

Difficulty: Easy

Parking: Free car park in Ripponden on Royd Lane and Mill Fold Way (off the B6113). There are also smaller car parks off the A58 by Ryburn Reservoir and Baitings Reservoir.

Public Transport: Ripponden is on various bus routes from Halifax and the 901 bus between Hebden Bridge and Huddersfield.

Character: A simpler route to Manshead Hill from the Ryburn Valley side, this walk also takes in Ryburn and Baitings Reservoirs of the Upper Ryburn Valley and the charming woods around Mill Bank. The paths are largely easy to follow and the ground is generally good.

4 Just beyond Blue Ball Lane, turn right off the A58 over a ladder stile and follow a path up the right side of **Greenwood Clough**. This recrosses the stream above Manshead Farm and turns right over a stile to continue up the clough. A clear path leads over another fenceline and up onto the steep dome of Manshead End. At the prominent cairn, continue straight on to reach the trig point on **Manshead Hill**.

5 From **Manshead Hill** trig, turn right and cross the rough grass on the summit to reach another good path. Follow this left along a line of posts, until it forks not far before a small plantation. Bear left along the line of an **old conduit** that leads all the way round the east side of the hill. Eventually reaching a larger track, head straight across to reach a stile near the site of **Flints Reservoir**. Bear right along the fence, then turn left on the track at the end. Passing the buildings of **Flints Hall**, bear right to a gate and follow a grassy track along the edge of the field beyond.

Despite the **Old Bridge Inn** claiming to be 'probably Yorkshire's oldest hostelry' from 1307, the current building is thought to date from the 16th century. Although an inn is recorded in the vicinity in 1307, the first reference to this pub is in 1754. It was renamed the Old Waterloo Inn for a time after Wellington's victory.

Manshead Hill
(417m)

Ripponden Old Bridge (also known as Waterloo Bridge) was built in 1752, though there was a bridge at the site as early as 1307.

Ripponden Old Bridge

3 At a bridge by the curious **Spewing Well**, stay on the right bank of the stream through a series of gates to join a fenced path leading up to the car park by **Baitings** Reservoir. Follow the A58 left for 100m, then bear left onto a signed path though the thin trees along the reservoir shore. At the far end, turn right up **Baitings Gate Road**, then left on the main road again.

Beeston Hall Rocks take their name from the farm just up the hillside, which was originally Thrum Hall (after the loose ends of a warp when cloth is cut) and the rocks appear to have been renamed at the same time.

6 Reaching a track, turn hard right along a walled path through what was once known as **Jacob Park**. Turn right at the end, then follow Ash Hall Lane left. Turn right at the next junction and follow **Eccles Parlour** down to the end, where you head straight across into Gough Lane. Where the track bends sharp right, turn left onto a path down through Gough Wood to **Mill Bank**.

Ripponden is an attractive if rather slight town strung out along arterial roads. Its name is a contraction of Ryburn-Dean and it is thought to have been the site of a Roman ford. The original settlement was on the south-east side of the river

MILL BANK

Soyland Mill (ruin)

Severhills Dam

7 Head straight across the road in **Mill Bank**, following a path along the stream and into **Fiddle Wood**. Follow the main path through the heart of the wood until a pair of stoops, then turn right up the steps. By the curious ruin at the top, head straight across Clapgate Lane towards **Delf Field**. Go straight on through a gate to pass above a barn and cross the fields via further gates. At the next lane head straight on, passing in front of the cottages at **Myrtle Grove**. On the bend turn left through a squeeze and follow the top of the field to join another old lane leading down to **Birks**. Bear right in front of the buildings here and follow a path across the hillside, joining a flagstone line to descend to Royd Lane, which leads back down into **Ripponden**.

Soyland Mill ruins

The elegant ruins of **Soyland Mill** rise through the dense larch trees at the foot of Severhills Clough. It was just one of a large complex of mills built on the site of the original 13th-century Soyland corn mill between here and Lower Soyland Mill by Mill Bank Bridge. There were as many as seven mills in this small valley at one time.

2 Follow the main road right over **Slitheroe Bridge**, then immediately turn left along **Bar Lane**. This leads all the way up the valley, where mills have been replaced by new housing developments. Where the (now rough) track eventually bends sharply right, head straight on past a ruined garage and climb up steps to the small car park by **Ryburn Reservoir**'s dam wall. Turn left opposite the car park, crossing a field to enter the woods along the reservoir shore. A good path continues all the way to its end, passing **Beeston Hall Rocks**.

Ryburn Reservoir, like the reservoirs at Baitings and Booth Dean, was built by the Wakefield Corporation. It may originally have been named Bogden Reservoir after the clough and mill it inundated. On the slopes above, Hanging Lee Mill (known as Little Britain long before the TV series) was used as a hostel during the reservoir's construction.

RIPPONDEN

Old Bridge Inn

1 From the bottom of Royd Lane in **Ripponden**, head straight across the A58 and down the cobbles to the **Old Bridge Inn**. Across the old packhorse bridge, double back to the right on Mill Fold, which leads beneath the road. Follow a path on through the park (alongside the Mill Fold Way car park) and join the road along the **River Ryburn**. Stay on the river bank past Ellis Bottom Farm, heading up some steps near the bridge. Bear right at some signs to rejoin the river bank and turn right at the end to reach the main road by **Slitheroe Mills**. **127**

0   250   500   750
METRES

N

STONECHAT

The **stonechat** is a small bird found in undisturbed vegetation, often around moorland reservoirs. It has a black head, white collar and orange breast, and is named for its call, a clack reminiscent of stones being knocked together. It is a partial migrant, generally remaining in the UK through the winter, and so is more rotund than the whinchat.

WHINCHAT

The **whinchat** is a small migratory bird that breeds on the Pennine moors in the summer months before returning to sub-Saharan Africa. It is closely related to the more common stonechat, but has longer wings and a more slender body, and is most easily distinguished by its paler orange breast and distinctive white stripe above the eyes. Unlike the stonechat its presence is becoming increasingly rare, possibly because of changes in its winter habitat in Africa. It is most likely found near patches of bracken, where it prefers to nest, though its name refers to gorse (from the word *whin*).

CHAPTER 15 – DOG HILL

Height: 435m

Grid Ref: SE003171

Map Sheet: OL21
(South Pennines)

Access: No
restrictions.

**Public
Transport:**
Ripponden is
served by various
bus services
from Halifax, with
the 560 continuing
to Rishworth. Bus
901 runs from
Ripponden to
Hebden Bridge via
Blackstone Edge
Reservoir, and the
X58 from Halifax
to Littleborough via
Blackstone Edge
Reservoir.

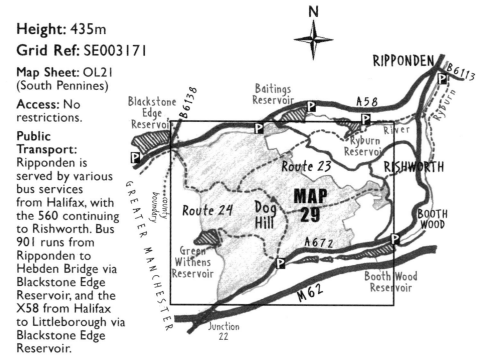

Dog Hill is an outlying eastward spur from neighbouring Blackstone Edge, but forms a satisfying twin with Manshead Hill, the two trigs facing each other across the Upper Ryburn Valley. Both hills are pleasing ascents, with Dog Hill having more varied approaches and being easily accessible from any direction, particularly Rishworth and along the A672. The moor is dominated by reservoirs and their drains, which encircle the summit plateau, though the quarried knoll of Pike End and the impressive buttresses of Castle Dean Rocks ensure that there is plenty of interest.

Its obvious sounding name may refer to one of the black dogs of legend, like the Barguest or Gabriel's Hounds (known as Gabble Ratchets in the Calder Valley), or simply the more domesticated kind – certainly ours always seem at home on its summit *(see sketch at the front of the book)*.

Dog Hill and Green Withens Reservoir from Blackstone Edge

Cat Stones is an intriguing site, made up of an array of hollows and low heaped stones. Though visually disappointing, it may be the site of a number of unexcavated round barrows and cairns. Identifying the burial chambers is confused by the presence of quarry remains (which make up most of the stones here) and an adjacent stone circle. The latter is almost certainly a modern creation, but nonetheless highlights the important associations of the site. A number of Bronze Age and Neolithic arrowheads and tools have been found in the area and it has been suggested the Cat Stones mark the tomb of an important local figure who died fighting at this spot (*Cath* referring to a battle in Gaelic). Cat Stones are also found on Ickornshaw Moor (p18), above Shipley Glen and on Harden Moor near Keighley, the latter thought to be associated with a battle between the Celtic people of Elmet and the invading Angles.

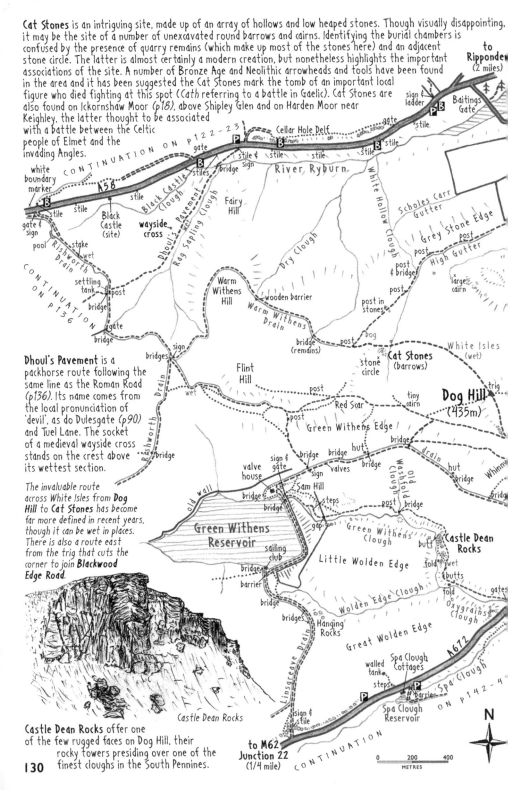

Dhoul's Pavement is a packhorse route following the same line as the Roman Road (p136). Its name comes from the local pronunciation of 'devil', as do Dulesgate (p90) and Tuel Lane. The socket of a medieval wayside cross stands on the crest above its wettest section.

The invaluable route across White Isles from **Dog Hill** to **Cat Stones** has become far more defined in recent years, though it can be wet in places. There is also a route east from the trig that cuts the corner to join **Blackwood Edge Road**.

Castle Dean Rocks offer one of the few rugged faces on Dog Hill, their rocky towers presiding over one of the finest cloughs in the South Pennines.

130

MAP 29: DOG HILL

Dog Hill is the shapely eastward extension of Blackstone Edge, with slopes overlooking Ripponden, Rishworth, Baitings and Booth Dean. There are no Rights of Way between Blackwood Edge in the east and Rag Sapling Clough in the west, which is particularly curious as there are several old packhorse routes crossing the moor; Blackwood Edge Road, Pike End Gate, Dog Hill Road and Henley Road can all still be traced (even if not always walked). There are however plenty of paths, the clearest following the drains to the north and south of the high ground or leading up from Oxygrains Old Bridge, all of which are permissive routes. There are smaller tracks across the heart of the moor, but the rough tussocky flanks are best avoided if you value your ankles.

*The jumbled shapes of **Lench Holes** (lench is a dialect word for a ledge of rock) form one of the more interesting sides of Dog Hill, yet remain largely inaccessible. From the north-east, a faint track follows an old level towards them, but crosses a very wet depression. You're probably better cutting across from High Gutter towards a large cairn on the shoulder opposite. From **Blackwood** or **Nook End** ruins, there are also faint tracks up the hillside. One of these follows the zigzag depression of the old **Dog Hill Road** and can be recognised in descent by an abandoned sink alongside it*

*Rish is an old form of rush and, considering the extent of the squelchy rush-strewn fields below Nook End, Blackwood and Lench House, **Rishworth** seems well named.*

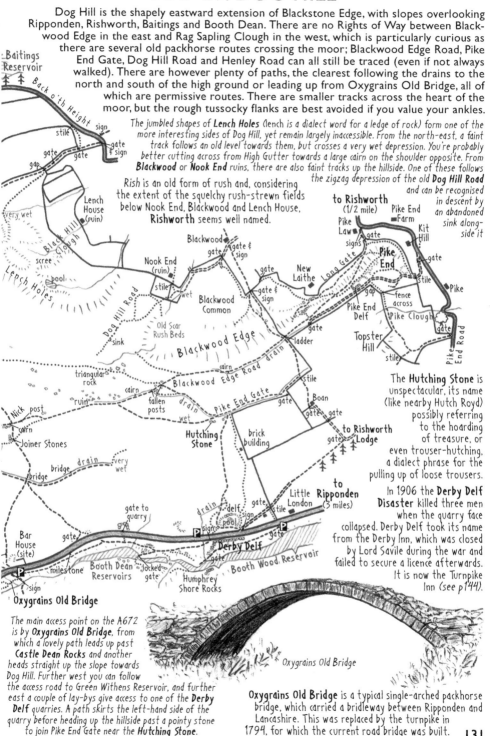

The **Hutching Stone** is unspectacular, its name (like nearby Hutch Royd) possibly referring to the hoarding of treasure, or even trouser-hutching, a dialect phrase for the pulling up of loose trousers.

In 1906 the **Derby Delf Disaster** killed three men when the quarry face collapsed. Derby Delf took its name from the Derby Inn, which was closed by Lord Savile during the war and failed to secure a licence afterwards. It is now the Turnpike Inn (see p144).

Oxygrains Old Bridge

The main access point on the A672 is by **Oxygrains Old Bridge**, from which a lovely path leads up past **Castle Dean Rocks** and another heads straight up the slope towards Dog Hill. Further west you can follow the access road to Green Withens Reservoir, and further east a couple of lay-bys give access to one of the **Derby Delf** quarries. A path skirts the left-hand side of the quarry before heading up the hillside past a pointy stone to join Pike End Gate near the **Hutching Stone**.

Oxygrains Old Bridge

Oxygrains Old Bridge is a typical single-arched packhorse bridge, which carried a bridleway between Ripponden and Lancashire. This was replaced by the turnpike in 1794, for which the current road bridge was built.

ROUTE 23: DOG HILL & RYBURN RESERVOIR FROM RIPPONDEN

Distance: 8½ miles (13.5km)

Ascent: 370m

Difficulty: Moderate

Public Transport: Ripponden is on various bus routes from Halifax and the 901 Hebden Bridge-Huddersfield bus.

Parking: Free car park in Ripponden on Mill Fold Way (off the B6113).

Character: Dog Hill overlooks the upper Ryburn Valley and makes a natural objective from Ripponden or Rishworth. The valley itself is beautifully verdant, especially around Ryburn Reservoir, yet also dense with the mills, ponds and railways of its industrial heritage. The route follows the valley out to Rishworth Mill then ascends Dog Hill via Pike End before returning via Ryburn Reservoir. The ground and navigation is generally easygoing, though it can be very overgrown around Upper Arkin Royd.

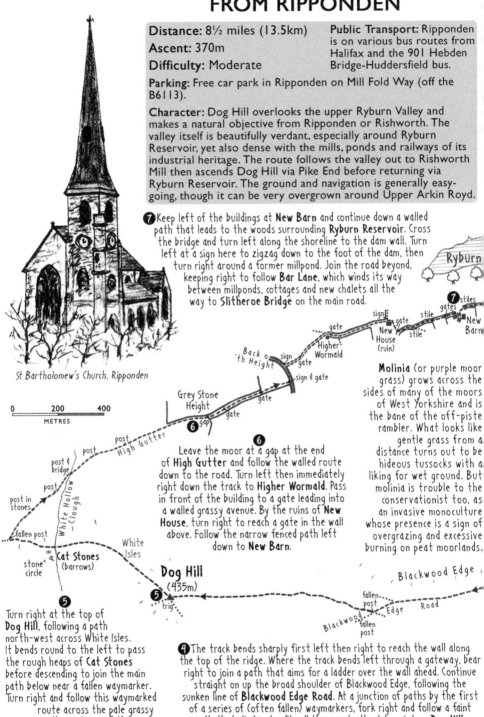

St Bartholomew's Church, Ripponden

7 Keep left of the buildings at **New Barn** and continue down a walled path that leads to the woods surrounding **Ryburn Reservoir**. Cross the bridge and turn left along the shoreline to the dam wall. Turn left at a sign here to zigzag down to the foot of the dam, then turn right around a former millpond. Join the road beyond, keeping right to follow **Bar Lane**, which winds its way between millponds, cottages and new chalets all the way to **Slitheroe Bridge** on the main road.

Ryburn

0   200   400
METRES

6 Leave the moor at a gap at the end of **High Gutter** and follow the walled route down to the road. Turn left then immediately right down the track to **Higher Wormald**. Pass in front of the building to a gate leading into a walled grassy avenue. By the ruins of **New House**, turn right to reach a gate in the wall above. Follow the narrow fenced path left down to **New Barn**.

Molinia (or purple moor grass) grows across the sides of many of the moors of West Yorkshire and is the bane of the off-piste rambler. What looks like gentle grass from a distance turns out to be hideous tussocks with a liking for wet ground. But molinia is trouble to the conservationist too, as an invasive monoculture whose presence is a sign of overgrazing and excessive burning on peat moorlands.

Dog Hill
(435m)

5 Turn right at the top of **Dog Hill**, following a path north-west across White Isles. It bends round to the left to pass the rough heaps of **Cat Stones** before descending to join the main path below near a fallen waymarker. Turn right and follow this waymarked route across the pale grassy northern slopes of the moor.

4 The track bends sharply first left then right to reach the wall along the top of the ridge. Where the track bends left through a gateway, bear right to join a path that aims for a ladder over the wall ahead. Continue straight on up the broad shoulder of Blackwood Edge, following the sunken line of **Blackwood Edge Road**. At a junction of paths by the first of a series of (often fallen) waymarkers, fork right and follow a faint path that climbs steadily all the way to the trig point on Dog Hill.

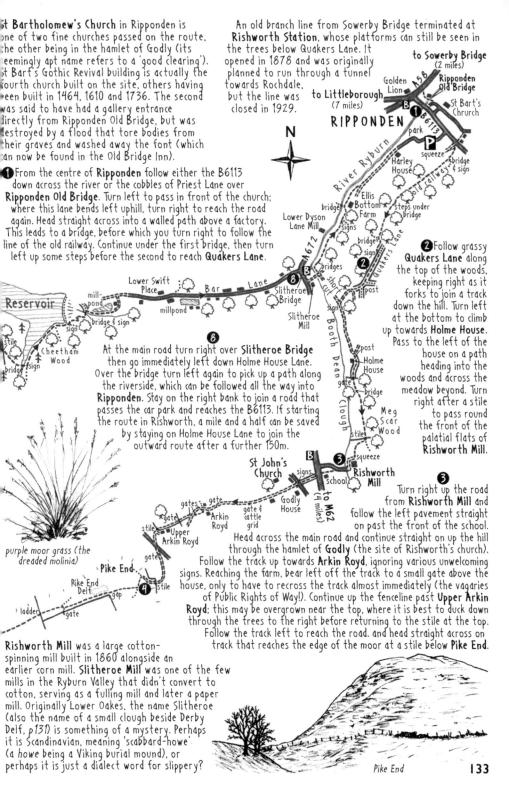

St Bartholomew's Church in Ripponden is one of two fine churches passed on the route, the other being in the hamlet of Godly (its seemingly apt name refers to a 'good clearing'). St Bart's Gothic Revival building is actually the fourth church built on the site, others having been built in 1464, 1610 and 1736. The second was said to have had a gallery entrance directly from Ripponden Old Bridge, but was destroyed by a flood that tore bodies from their graves and washed away the font (which can now be found in the Old Bridge Inn).

❶ From the centre of **Ripponden** follow either the B6113 down across the river or the cobbles of Priest Lane over **Ripponden Old Bridge**. Turn left to pass in front of the church; where this lane bends left uphill, turn right to reach the road again. Head straight across into a walled path above a factory. This leads to a bridge, before which you turn right to follow the line of the old railway. Continue under the first bridge, then turn left up some steps before the second to reach **Quakers Lane**.

An old branch line from Sowerby Bridge terminated at **Rishworth Station**, whose platforms can still be seen in the trees below Quakers Lane. It opened in 1878 and was originally planned to run through a tunnel towards Rochdale, but the line was closed in 1929.

RIPPONDEN

to Sowerby Bridge (2 miles)

to Littleborough (7 miles)

Golden Lion

Ripponden Old Bridge

St Bart's Church

park

P

squeeze

Harley House

bridge & sign

River Ryburn

old railway

Ellis Bottom Farm

steps under bridge

bridge

Lower Dyson Lane Mill

signs

bridge sign

A672

bridges

B

Short cut

post

sign

❷ Follow grassy **Quakers Lane** along the top of the woods, keeping right as it forks to join a track down the hill. Turn left at the bottom to climb up towards **Holme House**. Pass to the left of the house on a path heading into the woods and across the meadow beyond. Turn right after a stile to pass round the front of the palatial flats of **Rishworth Mill**.

Lower Swift Place

Bar Lane

mill-pond

millpond

Slitheroe Bridge

Slitheroe Mill

Reservoir

bridge & sign

sign

stile

Cheetham Wood

bridge sign

❽ At the main road turn right over **Slitheroe Bridge** then go immediately left down Holme House Lane. Over the bridge turn left again to pick up a path along the riverside, which can be followed all the way into **Ripponden**. Stay on the right bank to join a road that passes the car park and reaches the B6113. If starting the route in Rishworth, a mile and a half can be saved by staying on Holme House Lane to join the outward route after a further 150m.

post

Holme House

gate

bridge

Booth Dean Clough

Meg Scar Wood

stile

squeeze

St John's Church

signs

B

❸

School

Rishworth Mill

❸ Turn right up the road from **Rishworth Mill** and follow the left pavement straight on past the front of the school. Head across the main road and continue straight on up the hill through the hamlet of **Godly** (the site of Rishworth's church). Follow the track up towards **Arkin Royd**, ignoring various unwelcome signs. Reaching the farm, bear left off the track to a small gate above the house, only to have to recross the track almost immediately (the vagaries of Public Rights of Way!). Continue up the fenceline past **Upper Arkin Royd**; this may be overgrown near the top, where it is best to duck down through the trees to the right before returning to the stile at the top. Follow the track left to reach the road, and head straight across on track that reaches the edge of the moor at a stile below Pike End.

gates

gate

gate

gate & cattle grid

Godly House

to M62 (4 miles)

Arkin Royd

stile

Upper Arkin Royd

gate

purple moor grass (the dreaded molinia)

Pike End

Rike End Delf

❹

stile

ladder

gate

gap

Rishworth Mill was a large cotton-spinning mill built in 1860 alongside an earlier corn mill. **Slitheroe Mill** was one of the few mills in the Ryburn Valley that didn't convert to cotton, serving as a fulling mill and later a paper mill. Originally Lower Oakes, the name Slitheroe (also the name of a small clough beside Derby Delf, p131) is something of a mystery. Perhaps it is Scandinavian, meaning 'scabbard-howe' (a howe being a Viking burial mound), or perhaps it is just a dialect word for slippery?

Pike End

TWENTY THINGS IT'S FORBIDDEN TO DO ON ACCESS LAND

1) Drive or ride any vehicle other than an invalid carriage.

2) Use a vessel or sailboard on any non-tidal water.

3) Have with you any animal other than a dog.

4) Commit any criminal offence.

5) Light or tend a fire or do any act which is likely to cause a fire.

6) Intentionally or recklessly take, kill, injure or disturb any animal, bird or fish.

7) Intentionally or recklessly take, damage or destroy any eggs or nests.

8) Feed any livestock.

9) Bathe in any non-tidal water.

10) Engage in any operations connected with hunting, shooting, fishing, trapping, snaring, taking or destroying of animals, birds or fish, or have with you any engine, instrument or apparatus used for hunting, shooting, fishing, trapping, snaring, taking or destroying animals, birds or fish.

11) Use or have with you any metal detector.

12) Intentionally remove, damage or destroy any plant, shrub, tree or root or any part of a plant, shrub, tree or root.

13) Obstruct the flow of any drain or watercourse, or open, shut or otherwise interfere with any sluice-gate or other apparatus.

14) Without reasonable excuse, interfere with any fence, barrier or other device designed to prevent accidents to people or to enclose livestock.

15) Neglect to shut any gate or to fasten it where any means of doing so is provided, except where it is reasonable to assume that a gate is intended to be left open.

16) Affix or write any advertisement, bill, placard or notice.

17) In relation to any lawful activity which persons are engaging in or are about to engage in on that or adjoining land, do anything which is intended by you to have the effect:

(i) of intimidating those persons so as to deter them or any of them from engaging in that activity,

(ii) of obstructing that activity, or

(iii) of disrupting that activity.

18) Without reasonable excuse, do anything which (whether or not intended by him to have the effect mentioned in paragraph 17) disturbs, annoys or obstructs any persons engaged in a lawful activity on the land.

19) Engage in any organised games, or in camping, hang-gliding or para-gliding.

20) Engage in any activity which is organised or undertaken for any commercial purpose.

(Taken from the Countryside and Rights of Way Act 2000)

CHAPTER 16 – BLACKSTONE EDGE

Height: 472m

Grid Ref: SD972163

Map Sheet: OL21 (South Pennines)

Access: No restrictions.

Public Transport: Littleborough is on the main Caldervale train route. Bus X58 runs from Halifax to Littleborough via Blackstone Edge Reservoir. Bus 901 runs from Hebden Bridge to Huddersfield via Ripponden and Blackstone Edge Reservoir.

Blackstone Edge is a fine summit, its trig perched on one of the rocky castellations that peer down on the A58. Lancastrians will justifiably claim this peak as their own, as its imposing wall of rock looks west over Littleborough and Rochdale, yet its summit stands atop the Pennines and it cradles the basin of Green Withens Reservoir on its Yorkshire flank. The proximity of Dog Hill and Byron Edge means Blackstone Edge is hemmed in tightly, yet its small surface area is generally covered in shattered rock. The quantity of stone hereabouts is demonstrated by the line of cairns along the Pennine Way and the fact that monoliths and stone circles on the hill are almost impossible to distinguish. With main roads crossing the Pennines either side, Blackstone Edge is easily accessed and rarely quiet, though when Daniel Defoe crossed Blackstone Edge in his *Tour Through the Whole Island of Great Britain* in 1727, he likened the Pennines to the Andes and feared for his life in inclement weather.

Blackstone Edge is a name that appears on some of the earliest maps of the Pennines, and as Blakestone Edge on Saxton's sixteenth century map of Yorkshire. It has been suggested that the name referred to a boundary marker no longer present rather than the natural rock itself (which is only black thanks to industrial pollution), but it could also derive from *bealach*, a Celtic word for a pass or way from one district to another.

Blackstone Edge from the north

135

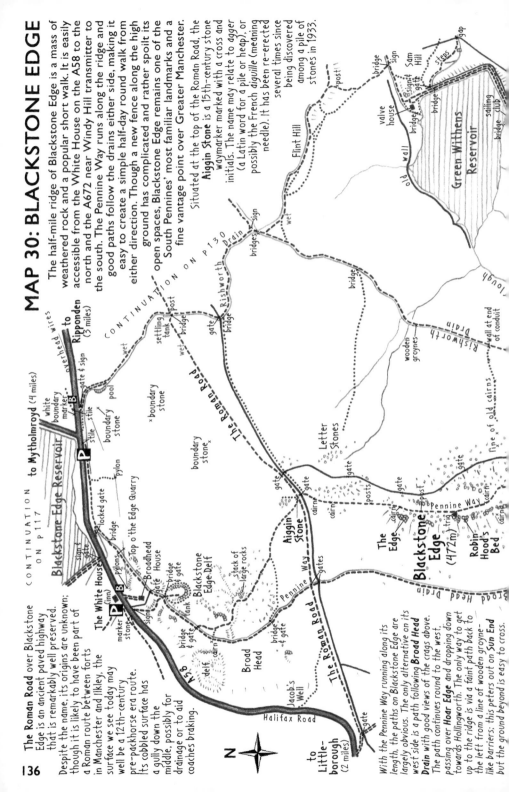

MAP 30: BLACKSTONE EDGE

The half-mile ridge of Blackstone Edge is a mass of weathered rock and a popular short walk. It is easily accessible from the White House on the A58 to the north and the A672 near Windy Hill transmitter to the south. The Pennine Way runs along the ridge and good paths follow the drains either side, making it easy to create a simple half-day round walk from either direction. Though a new fence along the high ground has complicated and rather spoilt its open spaces, Blackstone Edge remains one of the South Pennines' most familiar landmarks and a fine vantage point over Greater Manchester.

Situated at the top of the Roman Road, the **Aiggin Stone** is a 15th-century stone waymarker marked with a cross and initials. The name may relate to *agger* (a Latin word for a pile or heap), or possibly the French *aiguille* (meaning needle). It has been re-erected several times since being discovered among a pile of stones in 1933.

The **Roman Road** over Blackstone Edge is an ancient paved highway that is remarkably well preserved. Despite the name, its origins are unknown; though it is likely to have been part of a Roman route between forts in Manchester and Ilkley, the surface we see today may well be a 12th-century pre-packhorse era route. Its cobbled surface has a gully down the middle, possibly for drainage or to aid coaches braking.

With the Pennine Way running along its length, the paths on Blackstone Edge are largely obvious. The only alternative on its west side is a path following **Broad Head Drain** with good views of the crags above. The path continues round to the west, passing over **Hoar Edge** and dropping down towards Hollingworth. The only way to get up to the ridge is via a faint path back to the left from a line of wooden groyne-like barriers: this peters out on **Sun End** but the ground beyond is easy to cross.

CONTINUATION ON P117

CONTINUATION ON P130

to Ripponden (3 miles)

to Mytholmroyd (4 miles)

to Little-borough (2 miles)

Green Withens Reservoir

Blackstone Edge Reservoir

The White House (inn)

Blackstone Edge (472m) trig

Robin Hood's Bed

The Edge

Aiggin Stone

Blackstone Edge-Delf

Broad Head

Jacob's Well

Halifax Road

The Roman Road

Pennine Way

Rishworth Drain

Broad Head Drain

Flint Hill

Sam Hill

Letter Stones

Top o' the Edge Quarry

Broadhead House

CONTINUATION ON p130

Hanging Rocks

bridge

bridge

bridge

bridge

to Rishworth (4 miles)

to Ripponden

stile

sign

Linsgrave Drain

The eastern flank of Blackstone Edge is less dramatic than its west side, but its grassy slopes are crossed by some smaller paths. A couple of faint paths head up the edge from the new fenceline below the summit in the right place; one heads towards the **Letter Stones**, and another follows a line of old cairns, a route now cut off by the new fenceline.

Rocking Stone

depot

Lads Grave Clough

bridge

Redmires

wet

gate

very wet

gate

gate

tiny cairn

Redmires Moss

Pennine Way

Slippery Moss

gate

gate

cairn

cairn

cairn

gate

cairn

sign

Lads Grave (site)

pool

M62 (Junction 22)

A672

footbridge

CONTINUATION

Longden End Brook

stone shelter

gate

cairn

line of cairns

Sun End

tiny cairn

groyne-like barriers

bridge

to Hoar Edge

Redmires Moss, marked on older maps as *stakes* in the Moss, was once renowned for being the boggiest stretch of the Pennine Way – some feat indeed! It is now a straightforward tramp to the motorway, where the Pennine Way continues south past the mast on **Windy Hill**. Another useful path follows the motorway down to a conduit in Lads Grave Clough.

In 2007 the *Rochdale Observer* featured an article on the witches of Blackstone Edge. Groups of white-robed women had been seen clambering up Blackstone Edge from The White House on a number of occasions. It was suggested there might be a fertility stone or some other such mystical site hidden amid the scattered rocks where they performed rituals, but the group's intentions remained a mystery.

Rook Stones Hill

flags

post

sign

mast

Windy Hill Transmitter

sign

P sign

to Denshaw (2.5 miles)

to Hollingworth Lake

0   200   400

METRES

The names of **Blackstone Edge** and **Robin Hood's Bed** tend to be used interchangeably to refer to the rough rocks scattered across the crest of the ridge. Blackstone Edge itself is the wall of vertical black rock rearing up at the northern end of the ridge, while Robin Hood's Bed is the cloven hoof of towering rock just south of the parapet on which the trig point stands. This higher rock tower is riven with great cracks that make it hard to reach; perhaps Robin was thought to have lain in the natural cradle on top, which is eroded rather like a paw. It is most likely that he replaced earlier folklore about a character who was said to have hurled a rock now known as Robin Hood's Quoit from here across the other side of Littleborough.

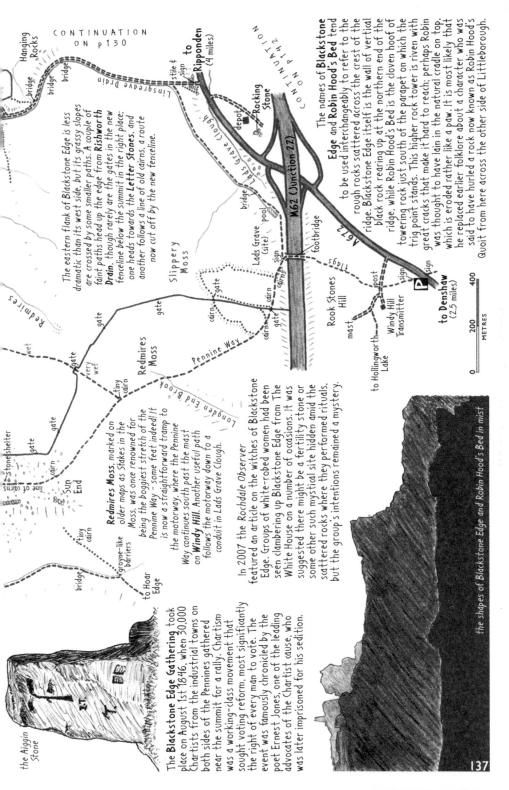

the shapes of Blackstone Edge and Robin Hood's Bed in mist

the Aiggin Stone

The **Blackstone Edge Gathering** took place on August 1st 1846, when 30,000 Chartists from the industrial towns on both sides of the Pennines gathered near the summit for a rally. Chartism was a working-class movement that sought voting reform, most significantly the right of every man to vote. The event was famously chronicled by the poet Ernest Jones, one of the leading advocates of the Chartist cause, who was later imprisoned for his sedition.

137

ROUTE 24: BLACKSTONE EDGE & DOG HILL

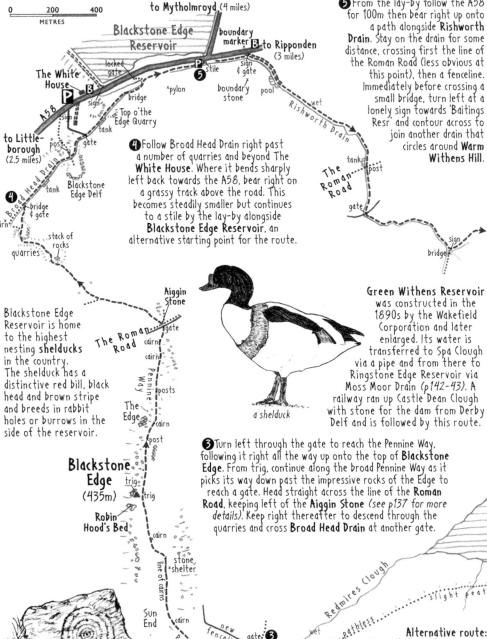

0 200 400
METRES

to Mytholmroyd (4 miles)

Blackstone Edge
Reservoir

boundary
marker **B** to Ripponden
(3 miles)

The White
House **B**
P
sign
A58
sign
to Little-
borough
(2.5 miles)

locked
gate

P
5

stile

sign
& gate

bridge

Top o'the
Edge Quarry

tank

post

gate

tank

*pylon

boundary
stone

pool

wet

Rishworth Drain

❺ From the lay-by follow the A58
for 100m then bear right up onto
a path alongside **Rishworth
Drain**. Stay on the drain for some
distance, crossing first the line of
the Roman Road (less obvious at
this point), then a fenceline.
Immediately before crossing a
small bridge, turn left at a
lonely sign towards 'Baitings
Resr' and contour across to
join another drain that
circles around **Warm
Withens Hill**.

tank
post

The
Roman
Road

gate

sign

bridge

Blackstone
Edge Delf

❹

bridge
& gate

cairn

stack of
rocks

quarries

❹ Follow Broad Head Drain right past
a number of quarries and beyond The
White House. Where it bends sharply
left back towards the A58, bear right on
a grassy track above the road. This
becomes steadily smaller but continues
to a stile by the lay-by alongside
Blackstone Edge Reservoir, an
alternative starting point for the route.

Aiggin
Stone

The Roman
Road

gate

cairn

cairn

Pennine Way

posts

The
Edge

cairn

post

Green Withens Reservoir
was constructed in the
1890s by the Wakefield
Corporation and later
enlarged. Its water is
transferred to Spa Clough
via a pipe and from there to
Ringstone Edge Reservoir via
Moss Moor Drain (p142-43). A
railway ran up Castle Dean Clough
with stone for the dam from Derby
Delf and is followed by this route.

Blackstone Edge
Reservoir is home
to the highest
nesting **shelducks**
in the country.
The shelduck has a
distinctive red bill, black
head and brown stripe
and breeds in rabbit
holes or burrows in the
side of the reservoir.

a shelduck

❸ Turn left through the gate to reach the Pennine Way,
following it right all the way up onto the top of **Blackstone
Edge**. From trig, continue along the broad Pennine Way as it
picks its way down past the impressive rocks of the Edge to
reach a gate. Head straight across the line of the **Roman
Road**, keeping left of the **Aiggin Stone** (see p137 for more
details). Keep right thereafter to descend through the
quarries and cross **Broad Head Drain** at another gate.

**Blackstone
Edge**
(435m)

trig

trig

Robin
Hood's Bed

cairn

stone
*shelter

Sun
End

cairn

line of cairns

new
fenceline

gate **❸**

wet

Redmires Clough

slight peat

pathless

Alternative route:
To avoid the pathless section
up Redmires Clough, continue along the track
from the sailing club. After half a mile, turn
right where the drain veers off, following it to its
end by the M62. Continue alongside the motorway
to reach the Pennine Way, which is followed right
for half a mile to rejoin the main route.

Pennine Way

wet

tiny
cairn

Alt route

Redmires
Moss

carved stone at the centre
of the modern stone
circle at Cat Stones

138

FROM OXYGRAINS BRIDGE/THE WHITE HOUSE

Distance: 8 miles (12.7km)
Ascent: 250m
Difficulty: Moderate

Parking: Lay-bys on A671 by Oxygrains Bridge or on A58 by Blackstone Edge Reservoir. Free car park below The White House.

Public Transport: Blackstone Edge Reservoir is on X58 (Halifax-Rochdale) and 901 (Hebden Bridge-Huddersfield) bus routes.

Character: Beginning and ending on the moor, this relatively short walk links the natural neighbours of Blackstone Edge and Dog Hill via Green Withens and Blackstone Edge Reservoirs and their many drains. The route can be started from either Oxygrains Bridge or the White House, though the former offers the more natural starting point in the valley bottom. Much of the walking is straightforward and a pathless section above Green Withens Reservoir can be avoided.

6 The path along **Warm Withens Drain** continues beyond the end of the drain to reach a junction before an old waymarker post. Keep right to climb slightly past **Cat Stones**, the heaped quarried stones here marking the site of a series of burial chambers (see p130 for more details). Continue across the moor, initially aiming left of the trig point, before the path bends round to ascend the low rise to the bright white trig of **Dog Hill**. A clear path leads straight on from the top of **Dog Hill**. Continue straight on at a junction marked by a cairn and descend past **Joiner Stones**. Cross another drain and continue down the grassy hillside to emerge at a gate just above the lay-by at **Oxygrains Bridge**.

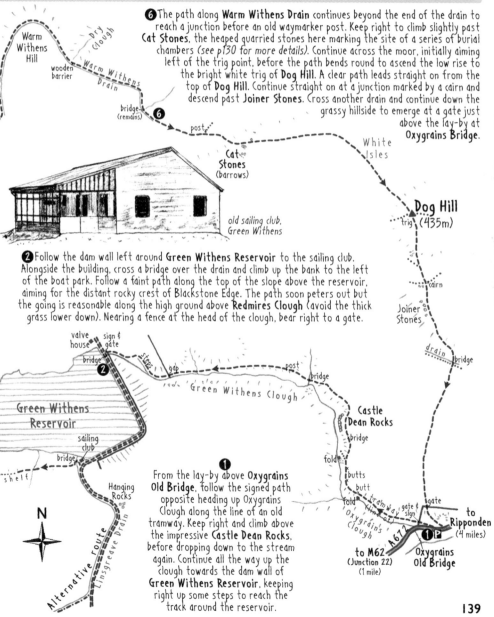

old sailing club, Green Withens

2 Follow the dam wall left around **Green Withens Reservoir** to the sailing club. Alongside the building, cross a bridge over the drain and climb up the bank to the left of the boat park. Follow a faint path along the top of the slope above the reservoir, aiming for the distant rocky crest of Blackstone Edge. The path soon peters out but the going is reasonable along the high ground above **Redmires Clough** (avoid the thick grass lower down). Nearing a fence at the head of the clough, bear right to a gate.

1 From the lay-by above **Oxygrains Old Bridge**, follow the signed path opposite heading up Oxygrains Clough along the line of an old tramway. Keep right and climb above the impressive **Castle Dean Rocks**, before dropping down to the stream again. Continue all the way up the clough towards the dam wall of **Green Withens Reservoir**, keeping right up some steps to reach the track around the reservoir.

to M62 (Junction 22) (1 mile)

to Ripponden (4 miles)

139

THE CIVIL WAR IN THE SOUTH PENNINES

The English Civil War reached all corners of the country and the hills of West Yorkshire were no exception. It is often assumed that when the war broke out in 1642, most of the manufacturing towns on both sides of the Pennines signed up with the Roundheads. Though they often provided men for the Parliamentary cause, support was far from unanimous and much of the north was still in thrall to the gentry. Rochdale, for example, was divided equally, with the Lord of the Manor being rewarded for his services to the King with the title Baron Byron. Given the opportunity, the Puritan populace generally supported the Parliamentarians, but neighbours fought each other on both sides right up to the Battle of Marston Moor.

Initially much of the fighting in the county took place around Leeds, control of which changed hands more than once. After a West Yorkshire Parliamentarian force was defeated at Adwalton Moor (near Drighlington) in June 1643, a Royalist base was established in Halifax under Sir Francis Mackworth. The rebels fled over the hills to Rochdale, where by now there was a Parliamentary garrison of 800 troops guarding the routes across the Pennines. There were cannons positioned at Blackstone Edge and a sentry station at Bleakedgate to the south. When the Royalist cavalry under the Marquis of Newcastle tried to advance on Manchester, the charge floundered in the heather and they beat a hasty retreat.

By the autumn of 1643 the Parliamentarians had established a garrison at Heptonstall; though considerably smaller than Sir Francis Mackworth's force at Halifax, they regularly harassed them and raided outposts at Sowerby Bridge and Warley. A skirmish is thought to have taken place on the moorland fringe at Slaughter Gap near Mixenden, while the Roundheads were returning over the moors from a raid. Gun barrels, locks and flints have been recovered in the area and the site is sometimes referred to as Bloody Field (though it may be that the name Slaughter originally referred to a sloe tree).

After one sortie Mackworth responded with a night-time assault on Heptonstall, but in bad weather they were repelled in the Battle of Heptonstall, during which stones were rolled down the Buttress upon the attackers. However, the Heptonstall base was soon abandoned and a large Royalist force burned part of the village in revenge. Haworth suffered similar retaliation for rebel allegiance. Within nine days, though, the Royalists lost Halifax when a force was dispatched from Rochdale, and Mackworth abandoned the area to deal with the advance of the Scots. Royalists were gradually pushed out of West Yorkshire, and York was under siege, so relief was sent for. A large Royalist army marched into the area, pillaging as it went, and the decisive battle took place at Marston Moor near York in July 1644. The Parliamentarian victory there effectively ended any Royalist presence in the north of England, though Skipton Castle was surrendered only in 1645, after a three-year siege, and Pontefract Castle (the last northern bastion of the Royalists) was finally destroyed in 1649.

the Parliamentary ensign

CHAPTER 17 – WAY STONE HILL

Height: 482m

Grid Ref: SE001140

Map Sheet: OL21 (South Pennines)

Access: No restrictions.

Public Transport: Regular bus and train services to Marsden and Slaithwaite from Huddersfield. Bus 184 runs from Marsden to Oldham via A62. Deanhead is on the twice-daily 900 bus from Hebden Bridge and Ripponden

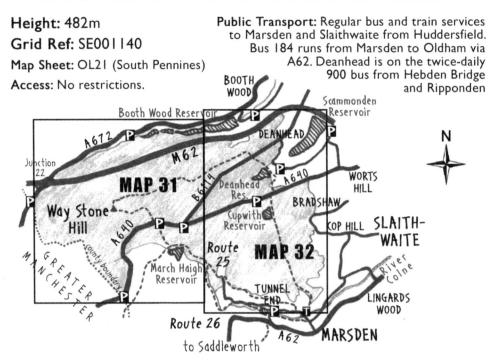

Way Stone Hill is the highest point in the borough of Calderdale and stands on a striking shelf overlooking the M62. This unremarkable summit plateau is bypassed by the Pennine Way and A640 Buckstones Road and could equally go by the name of Moss Moor, Buckstones Moss or White Hassocks (the latter is the first recorded name on Jefferys' map but has shifted south on maps in the intervening years).

Though the moor is dominated by the motorway across its northern flank, it retains a sense of barren solitude especially when the cloud descends (which in my experience is fairly often). Apart from the busy basin around March Haigh Reservoir, Way Stone Hill often feels like a forgotten moor and it is rare to meet another soul. Even Deanhead's charming basin is overlooked, but is just one of the corners of this moor worth seeking out.

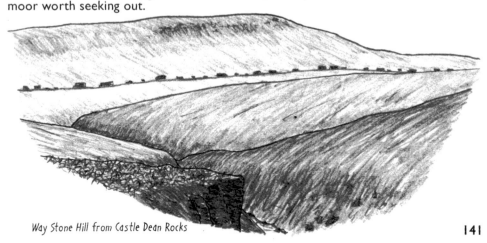

Way Stone Hill from Castle Dean Rocks

MAP 31: WAY STONE HILL WEST (Moss Moor

Way Stone Hill and Moss Moor appear as barren spaces on the OS Map, featureless and cut off by the M62 to the north. There would appear little cause for straying from the Pennine Way across White Hill, which is crowned by the moor's only trig point, despite being over 15m lower than Way Stone Hill. However, there is more here than meets the eye; the busy basin of March Haigh Reservoir is the most obvious area to explore, with Buckstones Edge and March Hill towering above, but Moss Moor Edge and Way Stone Hill offer more unexplored features.

*The **M62** yields just once to allow the pedestrian to pass, via a tunnel along the line of the conduit that skirts the northern fringe of **Moss Moor**. The conduit can be accessed at its end by Spa Clough Cottage, or from a path by Oxygrains Bridge, where a line of posts leads up the opposite side of **Spa Clough** from the lay-by.*

The **Rocking Stone** by Junction 22 (which is known as the Rockingstones Interchange) cuts a rather sad profile amid the tarmac slip roads. The rocking stone fell long before the motorway arrived, but was said to be associated with nearby **Booth Dean Spa** (Reverend Watson suggests both were sacred sites). The Spa Inn stood just down the road and served beer made using spa water.

*The clear path along the foot of Way Stone Edge suddenly disappears upon reaching **Linsgreave Clough**. From there you can continue up the other side of the clough, following a faint path to **Wicken Clough**, which can be followed up towards the summit of White Hill and the Pennine Way. Alternatively follow **Linsgreave Clough** down to Junction 22; rough at first, you soon pick up a path that leads down from the fenceline.*

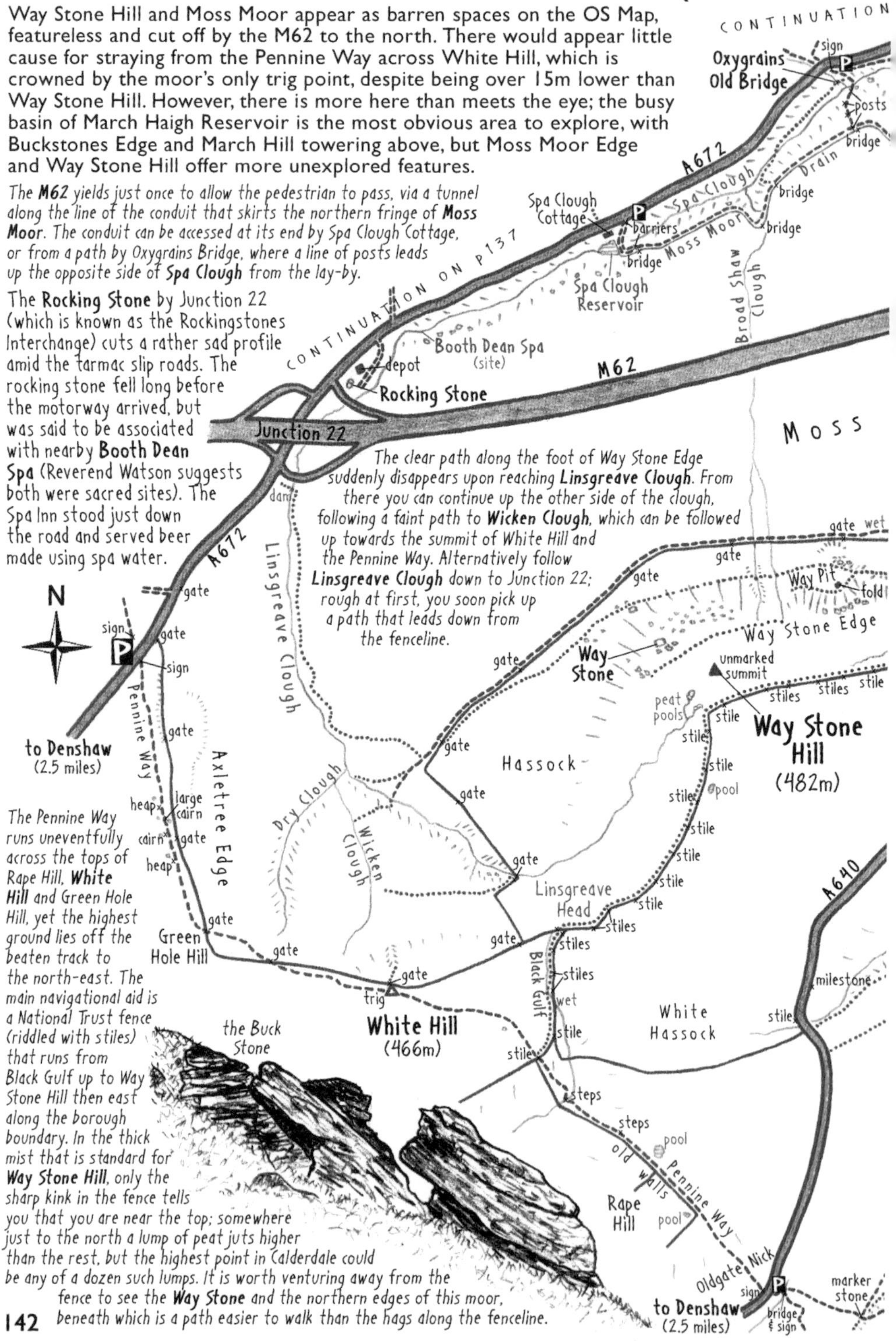

CONTINUATION
sign
Oxygrains Old Bridge
P
posts
bridge
Drain
A672
Spa Clough
bridge
Spa Clough Cottage
P
barriers
bridge
Moss Moor
bridge
Broad Shaw Clough
Spa Clough Reservoir
CONTINUATION ON P137
Booth Dean Spa
(site)
depot
Rocking Stone
M62
Junction 22
Moss
dam
A672
Linsgreave Clough
gate
wet
gate
gate
Way Pit
fold
Way Stone Edge
N
gate
sign
P
gate
sign
gate
Way Stone
unmarked summit
peat pools
stiles
stiles
stile
stile
stile
Way Stone Hill
(482m)
to Denshaw
(2.5 miles)
Pennine Way
gate
Axletree Edge
Hassock
gate
stile
pool
stile
Dry Clough
Wicken Clough
heap
large cairn
cairn
gate
heap
gate
stile
stile
Linsgreave Head
stile
A640
gate
Green Hole Hill
gate
gate
stiles
stiles
Black Gulf
stiles
gate
trig
wet
White Hill
(466m)
milestone
White Hassock
stile
the Buck Stone
stile
stile
steps
steps
old walls
pool
Pennine Way
Rape Hill
pool
Oldgate Nick
sign
P
marker stone
to Denshaw
(2.5 miles)
bridge & sign

*The Pennine Way runs uneventfully across the tops of Rape Hill, **White Hill** and Green Hole Hill, yet the highest ground lies off the beaten track to the north-east. The main navigational aid is a National Trust fence (riddled with stiles) that runs from Black Gulf up to Way Stone Hill then east along the borough boundary. In the thick mist that is standard for **Way Stone Hill**, only the sharp kink in the fence tells you that you are near the top; somewhere just to the north a lump of peat juts higher than the rest, but the highest point in Calderdale could be any of a dozen such lumps. It is worth venturing away from the fence to see the **Way Stone** and the northern edges of this moor, beneath which is a path easier to walk than the hags along the fenceline.*

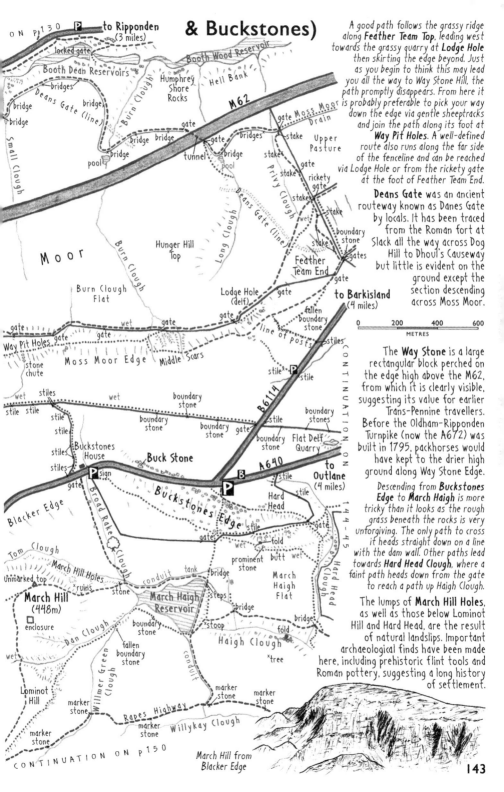

& Buckstones)

to Ripponden
(3 miles)

Booth Wood Reservoir

Booth Dean Reservoirs

locked gate

Humphrey
Shore
Rocks

Hell Bank

M62

Burn Clough

Small Clough

bridges

Deans Gate (line)

bridge

bridge

bridge

bridge

bridge

pool

tunnel

bridge

bridge

bridge

gate

gate

bridges

pool

Moss Moor
Drain

gate

stake

Upper
Pasture

stake

Privy Clough

gate

rickety
gate

stake

stake

Deans Gate (line)

Long Clough

wet

boundary
stone

stake

gates

Feather
Team End

Moor

Hunger Hill
Top

Burn Clough

gate

to Barkisland
(4 miles)

Burn Clough
Flat

Lodge Hole
(delf)

gate

gate

gate

gate

gate

fallen
boundary
stone

line of Posts

stiles

gate

Way Pit Holes

gate

gate

wet

stone
chute

Moss Moor Edge

Middle Scars

stile

P

stile

B6114

CONTINUATION

wet

stiles

wet

stile

stile

stile

boundary
stone

boundary
stone

boundary
stone

boundary
stone

gate

boundary
stones

stile

boundary
stone

Flat Delf
Quarry

Buckstones
House

stiles

stiles

stiles

Buck Stone

Buckstones Edge

A640

B

P

to
Outlane
(4 miles)

ON P.144-45

P

sign

gate

Broad Rake Clough

Blacker Edge

stile

stile

Hard
Head

gate

stile

Hard Head Clough

Tom Clough

March Hill Holes

ruins

conduit

tank

bridge

gate

wet

fold

prominent
stone

butt

wet

March
Haigh
Flat

Unmarked top

stone

March Haigh
Reservoir

steps

bridge

bridge

March Hill
(448m)

enclosure

Dan Clough

boundary
stone

fallen
boundary
stone

stoop

fold

Haigh Clough

conduit

wet

Willmer Green Clough

Lominot
Hill

marker
stone

marker
stone

conduit

tree

marker
stone

marker
stone

marker
stone

Rapes Highway

marker
stone

Willykay Clough

CONTINUATION ON P.150

March Hill from
Blacker Edge

A good path follows the grassy ridge along **Feather Team Top**, leading west towards the grassy quarry at **Lodge Hole** then skirting the edge beyond. Just as you begin to think this may lead you all the way to Way Stone Hill, the path promptly disappears. From here it is probably preferable to pick your way down the edge via gentle sheeptracks and join the path along its foot at **Way Pit Holes**. A well-defined route also runs along the far side of the fenceline and can be reached via Lodge Hole or from the rickety gate at the foot of Feather Team End.

Deans Gate was an ancient routeway known as Danes Gate by locals. It has been traced from the Roman fort at Slack all the way across Dog Hill to Dhoul's Causeway but little is evident on the ground except the section descending across Moss Moor.

The **Way Stone** is a large rectangular block perched on the edge high above the M62, from which it is clearly visible, suggesting its value for earlier Trans-Pennine travellers. Before the Oldham-Ripponden Turnpike (now the A672) was built in 1795, packhorses would have kept to the drier high ground along Way Stone Edge.

Descending from **Buckstones Edge** to **March Haigh** is more tricky than it looks as the rough grass beneath the rocks is very unforgiving. The only path to cross it heads straight down on a line with the dam wall. Other paths lead towards **Hard Head Clough**, where a faint path heads down from the gate to reach a path up Haigh Clough.

The lumps of **March Hill Holes**, as well as those below Lominot Hill and Hard Head, are the result of natural landslips. Important archaeological finds have been made here, including prehistoric flint tools and Roman pottery, suggesting a long history of settlement.

143

HILL EAST (Slaithwaite & Deanhead Moors)

Crossing the **M62** from Booth Wood Reservoir, various routes open up onto the long ridge of **Feather Team** and **Moselden Height**, as well as along Moss Moor Drain (which eventually ducks back under the motorway on p143).

Way Stone Hill's peat massif sprawls eastward towards Booth Wood, Deanhead, Slaithwaite and Marsden, but it is a difficult area of moorland to get to know. There are few paths across the moor, and accessing the enticing Park Clough and Deanhead Clough is awkward. Though there are few landmarks, the moors here are riddled with the scars of its past uses; old tracks, marker stones, quarries and ruined lodges.

The mast on **Cow Gate Hill** marks the end of the open moorland. A cow gate was an area of moor or common allotted to one cow: commoners paid a rent for each cow gate.

Deanhead Clough is awkward to explore. A faint path follows Deanhead Reservoir's southern shore but falters in the rough ground beyond, while several tracks cross the maze of old walls on the northern shore. The best onward route continues most of the way up the east side of **Great Clough** to emerge near a lay-by on the A640 below Cupwith Hill.

Deanhead Reservoir is much older than its neighbour just downstream, Scammonden Reservoir, which largely drowned the village of Deanhead in the 1960s. (see p.148 for more details).

The A640 began as the **Huddersfield & New Hey Turnpike**. Built in 1806, it remained a major Trans-Pennine Route until the M62 was built in the 1960s (see p.148).

Originally the Coach & Horses Inn, **Nont Sarah's** was renamed by the landlord in the 1870s to thank his aunt for a loan to keep the pub going. In 1939 a sun lounge was added at the rear in the shape of a liner's bridge, modelled on RMS Mauretania.

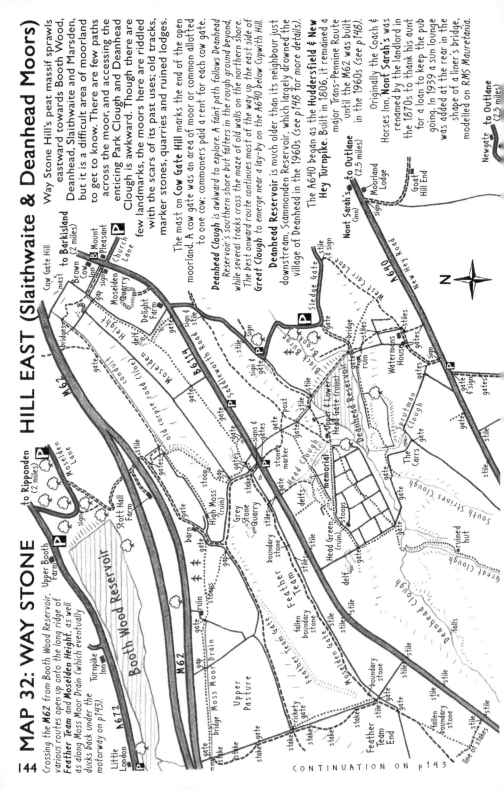

CONTINUATION ON p143

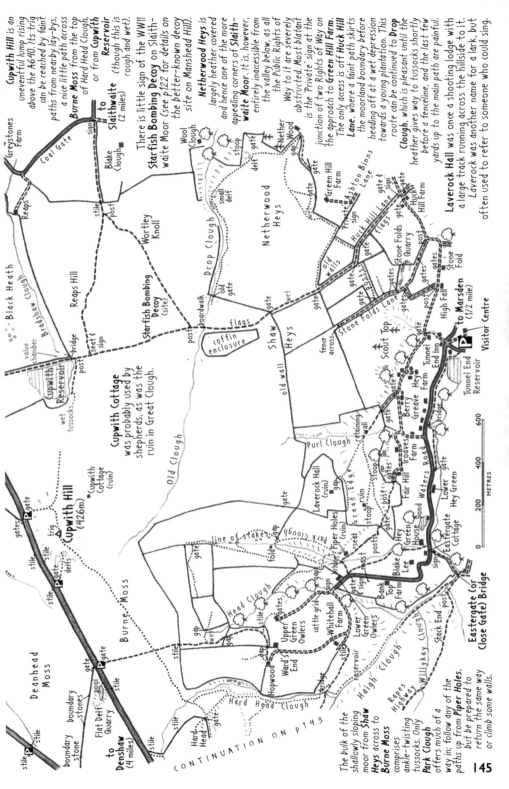

ROUTE 25: WAY STONE HILL & DEANHEAD

Distance: 10 miles (16.1km)

Ascent: 470m

Difficulty: Strenuous

Parking: Various street parking in Marsden. Lay-bys on A640 at Buckstones House or Cupwith Reservoir, or along B6114 above Deanhead Reservoir.

Public Transport: Regular trains to Marsden between Huddersfield and Manchester and buses 182, 183 & 184 from Huddersfield. Buses 185/186 continue to Dirker (by the station).

Character: Way Stone Hill is awkward to reach, but this route provides a satisfactory yomp across the moors north of Marsden. The section across the summit is necessarily rough and pathless but, thanks to the various fences, navigation is never too complicated. Otherwise I've resisted the temptation to stray too far from the clearer paths around March Haigh, Deanhead and Cupwith Reservoirs, which provide great variety to the route.

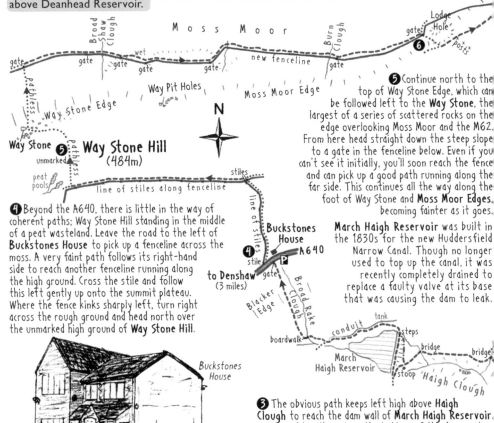

⑤ Continue north to the top of Way Stone Edge, which can be followed left to the **Way Stone**, the largest of a series of scattered rocks on the edge overlooking Moss Moor and the M62. From here head straight down the steep slope to a gate in the fenceline below. Even if you can't see it initially, you'll soon reach the fence and can pick up a good path running along the far side. This continues all the way along the foot of Way Stone and **Moss Moor Edges**, becoming fainter as it goes.

March Haigh Reservoir was built in the 1830s for the new Huddersfield Narrow Canal. Though no longer used to top up the canal, it was recently completely drained to replace a faulty valve at its base that was causing the dam to leak.

④ Beyond the A640, there is little in the way of coherent paths; Way Stone Hill standing in the middle of a peat wasteland. Leave the road to the left of **Buckstones House** to pick up a fenceline across the moss. A very faint path follows its right-hand side to reach another fenceline running along the high ground. Cross the stile and follow this left gently up onto the summit plateau. Where the fence kinks sharply left, turn right across the rough ground and head north over the unmarked high ground of **Way Stone Hill**.

③ The obvious path keeps left high above **Haigh Clough** to reach the dam wall of **March Haigh Reservoir**. Turn right, either along the bottom of the dam or its top, and cross the overflow channel at the far end of the dam. A path bears left round the reservoir, beyond which you fork right. After crossing Broad Rake Clough on some boardwalk, climb steeply up towards the dark silhouette of **Buckstones House**.

Buckstones House served as the Buckstones Inn and earlier the Buck Inn on the Huddersfield and New Hey Turnpike. Indeed the Saddleworth side of the pack-horse road had long been known as the Buck Road. In the early 19th century it was home to a gang of thieves who held up coaches and travellers and raided villages in the area (a possible source of the name Thieves Bridge across Close Moss, p151). When one of their number informed, they were arrested and many were transported for their crimes. It later served as a gamekeeper's house and is now a private residence.

the Way Stone

RESERVOIR FROM MARSDEN

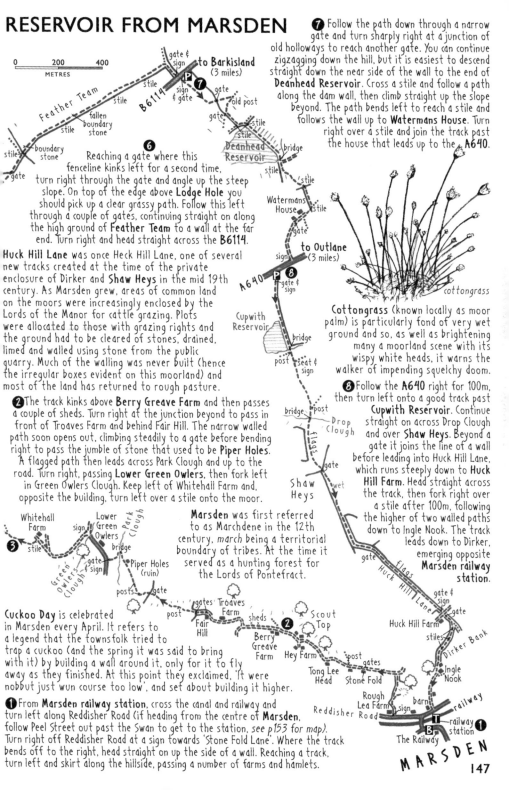

7 Follow the path down through a narrow gate and turn sharply right at a junction of old holloways to reach another gate. You can continue zigzagging down the hill, but it is easiest to descend straight down the near side of the wall to the end of **Deanhead Reservoir**. Cross a stile and follow a path along the dam wall, then climb straight up the slope beyond. The path bends left to reach a stile and follows the wall up to **Watermans House**. Turn right over a stile and join the track past the house that leads up to the **A640**.

6 Reaching a gate where this fenceline kinks left for a second time, turn right through the gate and angle up the steep slope. On top of the edge above **Lodge Hole** you should pick up a clear grassy path. Follow this left through a couple of gates, continuing straight on along the high ground of **Feather Team** to a wall at the far end. Turn right and head straight across the **B6114**.

Huck Hill Lane was once Heck Hill Lane, one of several new tracks created at the time of the private enclosure of Dirker and **Shaw Heys** in the mid 19th century. As Marsden grew, areas of common land on the moors were increasingly enclosed by the Lords of the Manor for cattle grazing. Plots were allocated to those with grazing rights and the ground had to be cleared of stones, drained, limed and walled using stone from the public quarry. Much of the walling was never built (hence the irregular boxes evident on this moorland) and most of the land has returned to rough pasture.

2 The track kinks above **Berry Greave Farm** and then passes a couple of sheds. Turn right at the junction beyond to pass in front of Troaves Farm and behind Fair Hill. The narrow walled path soon opens out, climbing steadily to a gate before bending right to pass the jumble of stone that used to be **Piper Holes**. A flagged path then leads across Park Clough and up to the road. Turn right, passing **Lower Green Owlers**, then fork left in Green Owlers Clough. Keep left of Whitehall Farm and, opposite the building, turn left over a stile onto the moor.

Cuckoo Day is celebrated in Marsden every April. It refers to a legend that the townsfolk tried to trap a cuckoo (and the spring it was said to bring with it) by building a wall around it, only for it to fly away as they finished. At this point they exclaimed, 'It were nobbut just wun course too low', and set about building it higher.

1 From **Marsden railway station**, cross the canal and railway and turn left along Reddisher Road (if heading from the centre of **Marsden**, follow Peel Street out past the Swan to get to the station, see p153 for map). Turn right off Reddisher Road at a sign towards 'Stone Fold Lane'. Where the track bends off to the right, head straight on up the side of a wall. Reaching a track, turn left and skirt along the hillside, passing a number of farms and hamlets.

Cottongrass (known locally as moor palm) is particularly fond of very wet ground and so, as well as brightening many a moorland scene with its wispy white heads, it warns the walker of impending squelchy doom.

8 Follow the **A640** right for 100m, then turn left onto a good track past **Cupwith Reservoir**. Continue straight on across Drop Clough and over **Shaw Heys**. Beyond a gate it joins the line of a wall before leading into Huck Hill Lane, which runs steeply down to **Huck Hill Farm**. Head straight across the track, then fork right over a stile after 100m, following the higher of two walled paths down to Ingle Nook. The track leads down to Dirker, emerging opposite **Marsden railway station**.

Marsden was first referred to as Marchdene in the 12th century, *march* being a territorial boundary of tribes. At the time it served as a hunting forest for the Lords of Pontefract.

Map labels

- 0 200 400 METRES
- gate & sign
- **to Barkisland** (3 miles)
- stile
- Feather Team
- stile
- B6114
- P sign & gate
- old post
- gate
- fallen boundary stone
- stile
- gate
- boundary stone
- stile
- **Deanhead Reservoir**
- bridge
- stile
- stile
- Watermans House
- stile
- gate
- **to Outlane** (3 miles)
- sign
- A640 P **8** gate & sign
- Cupwith Reservoir
- bridge
- post Seat & sign
- cottongrass
- bridge post
- Drop Clough
- slabs
- gate wet
- **Shaw Heys**
- Whitehall Farm
- sign
- Lower Green Owlers
- Park Clough
- bridge
- stile
- Green Owlers Clough
- gate & sign
- Piper Holes (ruin)
- posts gate
- post
- gates Troaves Farm
- sheds
- Fair Hill
- Berry Greave Farm
- **2**
- Scout Top
- Hey Farm
- post gates
- Tong Lee Head
- Stone Fold
- Rough Lea Farm sign
- Reddisher Road
- barn
- The Railway
- gate & sign
- gate
- Huck Hill Farm
- stiles
- Dirker Bank
- Ingle Nook
- Huck Hill Lane
- flags
- railway
- railway station **1**

MARSDEN
147

THE M62 & SCAMMONDEN RESERVOIR

Plans for a trans-Pennine motorway had been discussed since the 1930s, but the first route was not proposed until 1952. Questions were raised about its high altitude crossing and the fact that it did not cater for many of the major towns in the area. Although it now reaches 1,220ft at its highest point, the motorway would have been 150ft higher had it run along the exposed height of Buckstones Edge as was initially suggested. A new route was devised in 1961 and became known as the Lancashire-Yorkshire motorway (the order decided by a coin toss on Windy Hill by the two surveyors). A full-scale mock-up of a half-mile stretch of the motorway was constructed near the Brown Cow to see how it coped with the elements, and various other blasting, fencing and vegetation tests took place.

Construction began in 1964 by cutting through 150ft of hillside near Dean Head and dumping it in the adjacent valley to form the 200ft-high dam for Scammonden Reservoir. This feat of engineering had never been tried before, nor indeed since. The motorway severed the Blackburn valley in two and the reservoir drowned much of the village of Dean Head, leaving its church stranded on the hillside above. Scammonden Cotton Mill is the only mill whose ruins remain (just below the dam), which is ironic given that this is 'the mill that never was' – the six-storey building was constructed in the 1860s just before the Cotton Famine and never made a stitch.

Work on the Moss Moor section began in 1966, but there were notable problems. The weather was hideous – even the summers were some of the wettest on record – and once vegetation was removed from the peat the surface became impassable. A horse called Peggy was initially used to lay out the line of the road, yet she too sank into the peat; a frame had to be erected around her and Peggy was heaved out using a sling. In all, 500,000 cubic metres of peat was excavated to allow this section of the road to be laid. The peat was dumped on the adjacent moor and material from the Windy Hill cutting used to form the embankment across Moss Moor.

The M62 opened to traffic on December 20th 1970 and was officially inaugurated by the Queen the following year. When it was built, the 625ft bridge carrying the A6025 was the longest single span in Europe, and Scammonden Dam is still the largest earth-filled dam in Europe. The motorway used mesh fencing and a wire central reservation designed to prevent snow drifts building up; it was claimed that it would never be closed as a result of snow. Closures in the past have been blamed on gritters' strikes or incompetency (for example, an occasion when both Yorkshire and Lancashire gritters turned round on Junction 22, with neither gritting the junction itself), but it succumbed to the weather for the first time in April 2012.

It is sometimes suggested that the road divides around Stott Hill Farm because of its owner's refusal to move out, but it was actually due to the underlying geology that the carriageway had to be split, as the bedrock couldn't take the weight of the whole road. The eighteenth-century farmhouse has since earned the nicknames the Island and Little House on the Prairie. In fact individuals in these communities had little power to hinder development due to powers of compulsory purchase. Just ask Wilfred Dyson, whose farm was lost beneath Scammonden Reservoir; he challenged the compensation he was being offered even as the bulldozers were moving in on his land, and was nearly buried in clay.

CHAPTER 18 – STANDEDGE
(aka Millstone Edge)

Height: 448m

Grid Ref: SE012104

Map Sheet: OL21 (South Pennines)

Access: No restrictions.

Public Transport: Regular bus and train services to Marsden from Huddersfield. Bus 184 runs from Huddersfield and Marsden to Oldham via the A62.

Standedge (like Stanage in the Peak District, which it is pronounced the same as) was originally 'stone edge' and refers to the long rocky escarpment that stretches most of the way between the A62 and A640. Standedge straddles the county boundary, its face lifted west towards Greater Manchester. On its Yorkshire side it is somewhat overshadowed by Pule Hill, its lower but sleeker neighbour. Hidden from Marsden, Standedge is revealed from the A62 only as a vast peat massif, though on closer inspection it is riven by a series of attractive ravines. The Pennine Way runs north along the edge from Millstone Edge, where there is a trig point, but the true summit lies a short distance to the north.

I've used the name Standedge for this whole area of moorland, but it is also often used to refer to the cutting where the A62 crosses the tops, as well as the canal and railway tunnels cut deep beneath the moor. It is just outside the Peak District National Park but part of the National Trust's Marsden Moor estate.

Standedge, Lominot Hill and March Hill above March Haigh Reservoir

149

MAP 33: STANDEDGE

The main route from Marsden to Oldgate Nick (also known as Badger Slack) follows a former packhorse road called **Rapes Highway**. It is marked by a series of stones engraved 'PH Road', erected in 1907 by Marsden Urban District Council after improving the whole route. Prior to this the landowners had threatened users and tried to assert that the route over Oldgate had never existed, despite obvious evidence to the contrary.

Standedge has a simple topography and its paths follow suit; hugging the escarpment in the west and following ancient highways down towards Marsden at both north and south ends. In between, the great waste of Close Moss puts off most visitors, though it hides some rocky cloughs that are worth exploring. Redbrook Clough is a particular favourite, with the impressive engine house looming at its head.

A clear path follows **Redbrook Clough** south from **Eastergate Bridge**, but becomes harder to follow as the ravine closes in. Criss-cross the stream as necessary to reach a point where the wall on your left first allows you to clamber up the bank. A faint path can be picked up the other side of the wall, which eventually drops back down to the ravine below Far Owlers. Through a gap in the wall, climb immediately back up the bank on your left to follow the top of the ravine the rest of the way, a very faint line persisting to reach the spoil heaps.

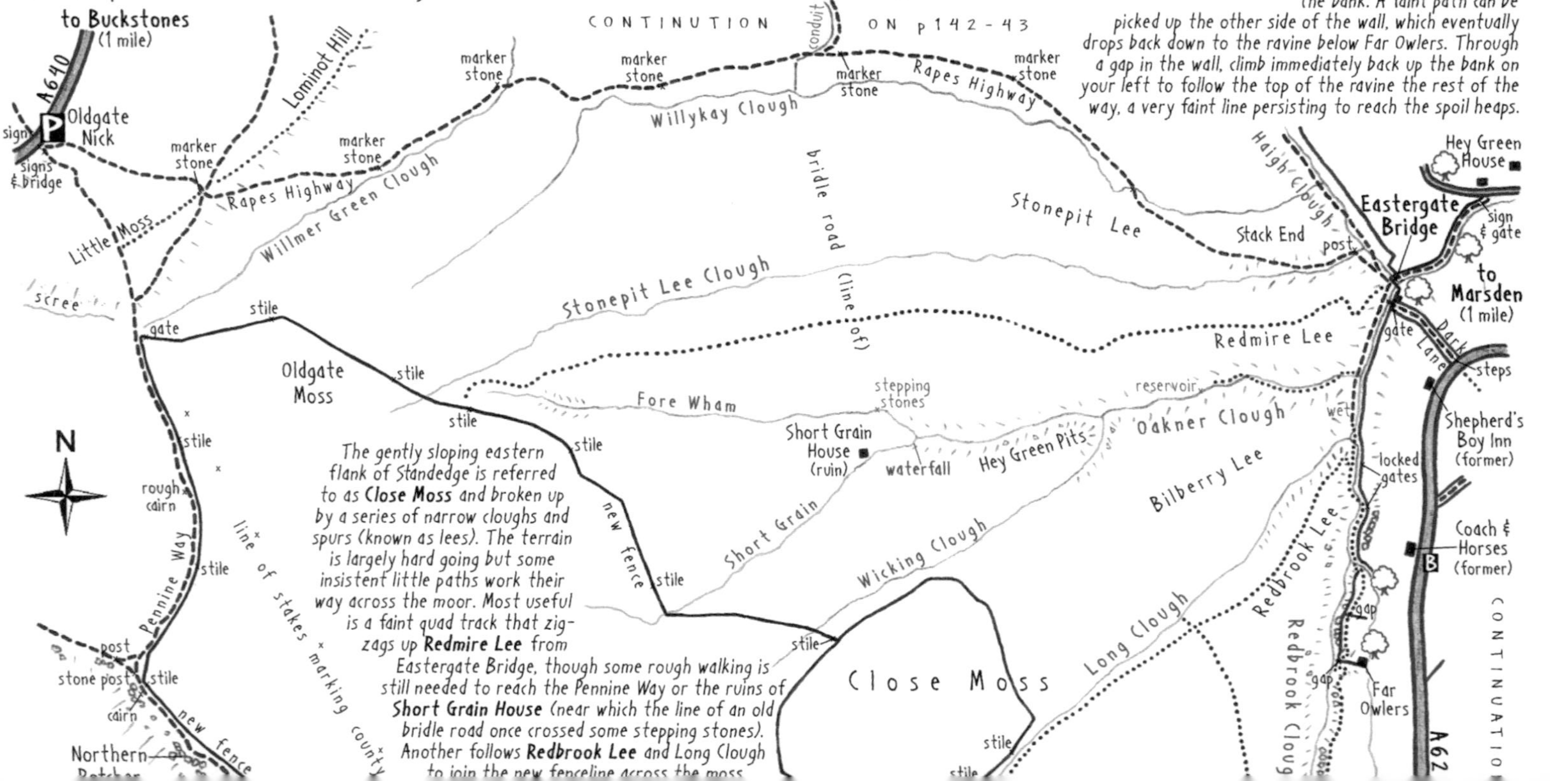

The gently sloping eastern flank of Standedge is referred to as **Close Moss** and broken up by a series of narrow cloughs and spurs (known as lees). The terrain is largely hard going but some insistent little paths work their way across the moor. Most useful is a faint quad track that zig-zags up **Redmire Lee** from Eastergate Bridge, though some rough walking is still needed to reach the Pennine Way or the ruins of **Short Grain House** (near which the line of an old bridle road once crossed some stepping stones). Another follows **Redbrook Lee** and **Long Clough** to join the new fenceline across the moss.

to Buckstones
(1 mile)

to Marsden
(1 mile)

CONTINUATIO[N]

A62

Hey Green House
sign & gate
Dark Lane
Steps
Shepherd's Boy Inn (former)
Coach & Horses (former)

Eastergate Bridge
gate post
locked gates
west
Far Owlers
Map

Redbrook Clou[gh]

Haigh Clough
Stack End
Redmire Lee
Oakner Clough
Bilberry Lee
Long Clough

Stonepit Lee
reservoir
Hey Green Pits
Wicking Clough

CONTINUATION ON p.142–43

marker stone
marker stone
Rapes Highway
conduit
marker stone

bridle road (line of)
stepping stones
Short Grain House (ruin)
waterfall
Short Grain

C l o s e   M o s s

stile
stile
stile

Willykay Clough
Stonepit Lee Clough
Fore Wham
new fence
stile
stile

marker stone
Lominot Hill
Willmer Green Clough
Rapes Highway
marker stone

Oldgate Moss
stile
stile
stile
line of stakes marking county
Pennine Way
stile
new fence
Northern

to Buckstones
(1 mile)
signs & Bridge
A640
Oldgate Nick
Little Moss
scree
gate
gate
rough cairn
stone post
cairn
stile
post

N

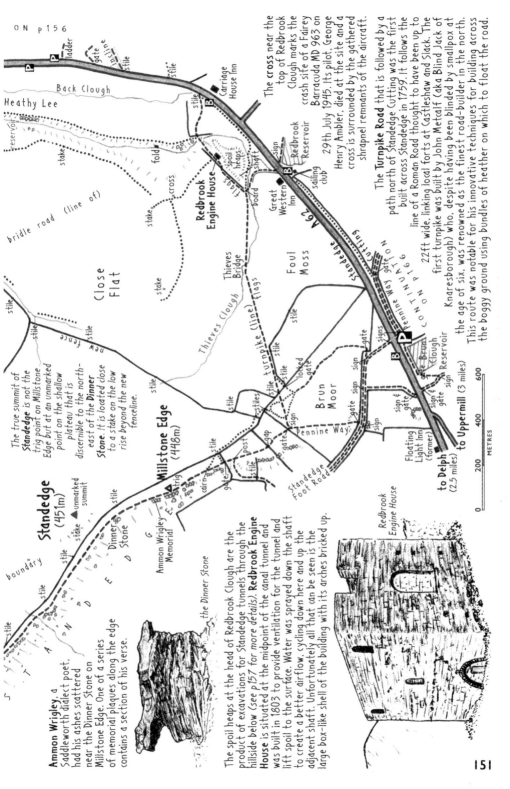

ON p156

Back Clough

Heathy Lee

reservoir · sip · stake · cross

ladder · gate · stile · gate · stile · fold line · stile · Carriage House Inn · B · stile

The cross near the top of Redbrook Clough marks the crash site of a Fairey Barracuda MD 963 on 29th July 1945. Its pilot, George Henry Ambler, died at the site and a cross is surrounded by the gathered shrapnel remnants of the aircraft.

The **Turnpike Road** that is followed by a path north of Standedge Cutting was the first built across Standedge in 1759. It follows the line of a Roman Road thought to have been up to 22ft wide, linking local forts at Castleshaw and Slack. The first turnpike was built by John Metcalf (aka Blind Jack of Knaresborough) who, despite having been blinded by smallpox at the age of six, was renowned as the finest road-builder in the north. This route was notable for his innovative techniques for building across the boggy ground using bundles of heather on which to float the road.

bridle road (line of) · stake · cross · stake × · stake ×

Redbrook Engine House · spoil heaps · board · shaft · sign · **Redbrook Reservoir** · sailing club · B

Great Western Inn · A62 · Standedge · Pennine Way gate · CONTINUED p166 · P · B · de Brun Clough Reservoir

Close Flat

Thieves Bridge · Thieves Clough · turnpike (line) · flags

Foul Moss

stile · new fence · stile · stile · boundary · stile · stile · stile · stile

The true summit of **Standedge** is not the trig point on Millstone Edge but at an unmarked point on the shallow plateau that is discernible to the north-east of the **Dinner Stone**. It is located close to a stake on the low rise beyond the new fenceline.

Standedge (451m) · stake · ▲ unmarked summit

Millstone Edge (448m) · Dinner Stone · trig · Ammon Wrigley Memorial

Brun Moor · Pennine Way · sign · gate · signs · gate · sign · locked gate · stile · stiles · stile · Post · cairn · gate · trig

Floating Light Inn (former) · Standedge Foot Road

to Delph (2.5 miles) · **to Uppermill** (3 miles)

METRES 0 200 400 600

Ammon Wrigley, a Saddleworth dialect poet, had his ashes scattered near the Dinner Stone on Millstone Edge. One of a series of memorial plaques along the edge contains a section of his verse.

the Dinner Stone

The spoil heaps at the head of Redbrook Clough are the product of excavations for Standedge tunnels through the hillside below *(see p157 for more details).* **Redbrook Engine House** is situated at the midpoint of the canal tunnel and was built in 1803 to provide ventilation for the tunnel and lift spoil to the surface. Water was sprayed down the shaft to create a better airflow, cycling down here and up the adjacent shaft. Unfortunately all that can be seen is the large box-like shell of the building with its arches bricked up.

Redbrook Engine House

151

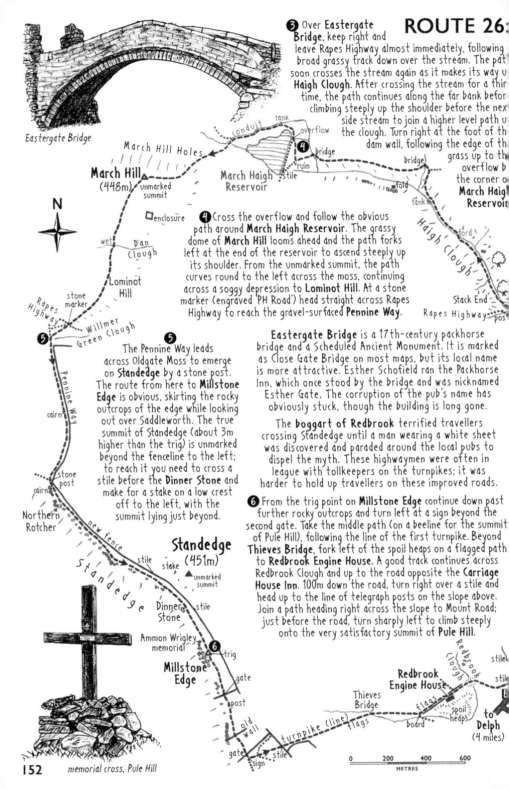

ROUTE 26:

❸ Over **Eastergate Bridge**, keep right and leave Rapes Highway almost immediately, following broad grassy track down over the stream. The pat soon crosses the stream again as it makes its way u **Haigh Clough**. After crossing the stream for a thir time, the path continues along the far bank befor climbing steeply up the shoulder before the nex side stream to join a higher level path u the clough. Turn right at the foot of th dam wall, following the edge of th grass up to th overflow b the corner o **March Haig Reservoir**

Eastergate Bridge

March Hill Holes

March Hill (448m) unmarked summit

conduit tank overflow ❹ bridge ruin bridge

March Haigh Reservoir stile fold tank

❹ Cross the overflow and follow the obvious path around **March Haigh Reservoir**. The grassy dome of **March Hill** looms ahead and the path forks left at the end of the reservoir to ascend steeply up its shoulder. From the unmarked summit, the path curves round to the left across the moss, continuing across a soggy depression to **Lominot Hill**. At a stone marker (engraved 'PH Road') head straight across Rapes Highway to reach the gravel-surfaced **Pennine Way**.

enclosure

wet Dan Clough

Lominot Hill

stone marker

Rapes Highway

Willmer Green Clough

Haigh Clough ford

Stack End

Rapes Highway pos

❺

❺ The Pennine Way leads across Oldgate Moss to emerge on **Standedge** by a stone post. The route from here to **Millstone Edge** is obvious, skirting the rocky outcrops of the edge while looking out over Saddleworth. The true summit of Standedge (about 3m higher than the trig) is unmarked beyond the fenceline to the left; to reach it you need to cross a stile before the **Dinner Stone** and make for a stake on a low crest off to the left, with the summit lying just beyond.

Pennine Way

cairn

stone post

cairn

Northern Rotcher

new fence

Standedge

stile stake

Standedge (451m) ▲ unmarked summit

Dinner Stone stile

Ammon Wrigley memorial ❻ trig

Millstone Edge gate

post

old wall

gate stile sign

Eastergate Bridge is a 17th-century packhorse bridge and a Scheduled Ancient Monument. It is marked as Close Gate Bridge on most maps, but its local name is more attractive. Esther Schofield ran the Packhorse Inn, which once stood by the bridge and was nicknamed Esther Gate. The corruption of the pub's name has obviously stuck, though the building is long gone.

The **boggart of Redbrook** terrified travellers crossing Standedge until a man wearing a white sheet was discovered and paraded around the local pubs to dispel the myth. These highwaymen were often in league with tollkeepers on the turnpikes; it was harder to hold up travellers on these improved roads.

❻ From the trig point on **Millstone Edge** continue down past further rocky outcrops and turn left at a sign beyond the second gate. Take the middle path (on a beeline for the summit of Pule Hill), following the line of the first turnpike. Beyond **Thieves Bridge**, fork left of the spoil heaps on a flagged path to **Redbrook Engine House**. A good track continues across Redbrook Clough and up to the road opposite the **Carriage House Inn**. 100m down the road, turn right over a stile and head up to the line of telegraph posts on the slope above. Join a path heading right across the slope to Mount Road; just before the road, turn sharply left to climb steeply onto the very satisfactory summit of **Pule Hill**.

Redbrook Clough stile

Redbrook Engine House stile

Thieves Bridge flags spoil heaps board **to Delph** (4 miles)

turnpike (line) flags

0 200 400 600
METRES

152 *memorial cross, Pule Hill*

N

STANDEDGE & PULE HILL FROM MARSDEN

Distance: 9½ miles (15km)

Ascent: 400m

Difficulty: Moderate

Parking: Small free car park at Standedge Visitor Centre. Various on-street parking in Marsden or at the far end of Waters Lane.

Public Transport: Regular trains to Marsden between Huddersfield and Manchester and buses 182, 183 & 184 from Huddersfield. Buses 185/186 continue to Dirker (by the station).

Character: A lovely route up the valley from Marsden that takes in the three tops of March Hill, Standedge and Pule Hill and avoids the long trudge of Rapes Highway. It follows clear paths throughout, so is not difficult even when visibility is poor, though it is a shame to miss the impressive views both east and west.

A large corn mill stood opposite **Lower Hey Green**, with Hey Green House the millowner's house. It was owned in the late 19th century by Joseph Crowther, who built the **Hey Green Generator** to provide the house with water-powered electricity. It was the first in the area to have electricity and people used to walk up from Marsden to watch the lights being turned on. It is also said he used it to heat the water in the pond for his Polynesian wife to swim in – the modern cast iron gate depicting an aquatic goddess makes reference to this.

❶ The **Mechanics Hall** dominates the centre of **Marsden**; go down the street opposite (Market Place) and over the bridge at the end. Follow the river round to the right; reaching a road, head straight across into Clough Lea. After 100m, cross **Mellor's Bridge** and turn left to reach a footway leading up the hill. At the top, turn right to reach a gap in the fence opposite and join **Huddersfield Narrow Canal** heading back to the left not far from the **railway station**.

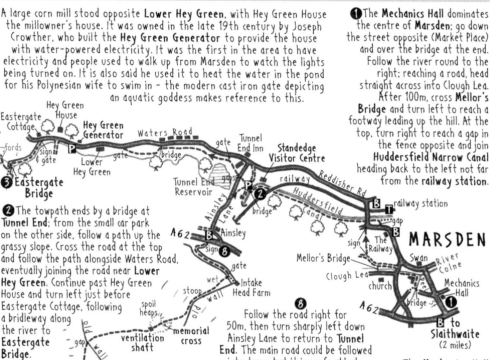

❸ **Eastergate Bridge**

❷ The towpath ends by a bridge at **Tunnel End**; from the small car park on the other side, follow a path up the grassy slope. Cross the road at the top and follow the path alongside Waters Road, eventually joining the road near **Lower Hey Green**. Continue past Hey Green House and turn left just before Eastergate Cottage, following a bridleway along the river to **Eastergate Bridge**.

❽ Follow the road right for 50m, then turn sharply left down Ainsley Lane to return to **Tunnel End**. The main road could be followed into town, but it is preferable to rejoin the canal back into **Marsden**.

❼ Follow the path along the edge of the crags from the top of **Pule Hill**. Well beyond the quarries the path bends right through a broken down wall to reach a square **ventilation shaft** for the Standedge Tunnels. A **memorial cross** stands on the crest beyond and the path descends to its left to join the line of a wall down the hillside. Where the ground becomes wet above Intake Head Farm, head for a gate in the fence below and follow the fenced path left down to the **A62**.

Pule Hill (437m)

❶ to **Slaithwaite** (2 miles)

The **Mechanics Hall** was built by the Marsden Mechanics Institution in 1861 as an educational centre. In the days before universal education, volunteers from such institutions offered elementary education to young working men.

Tunnel End is self-explanatory, being where Standedge Tunnels disappear into Pule Hill (see p157 for more information). An aqueduct carries the River Colne over the railway and canal from Tunnel End Reservoir, which used to be much larger, but has silted up and is generally kept low due to weaknesses in the dam wall. This was the case with many of those built to supply the canals; Tunnel End Reservoir burst in 1799 flooding Marsden and beyond. A large warehouse has been restored as the **Standedge Visitor Centre** (free entry) with boat trips possible into the canal tunnel. Tunnel End Cottages were built to house tunnel keepers and the large stone blocks alongside were used to weigh weigh down unladen boats going into the tunnel to make sure they fitted.

BOGBEAN

Bogbean (or buckbean) is found in particularly wet
areas of bog, its star-like white flowers growing on long
stems from the water. It has groups of three shiny
leaves whose similarity to the leaves of various beans
has given the plant its common name. The bitter leaves
have long been held to have medicinal properties and
were traditionally being used to cure ailments like
rheumatism, tuberculosis, ague and scurvy. In times of
hardship the roots were also used in many places as a
flour to make missen bread (famine bread). It is still
prescribed by modern herbalists and has also been known
as 'bog hop' because of its occasional use in brewing.

CHAPTER 19 – PULE HILL

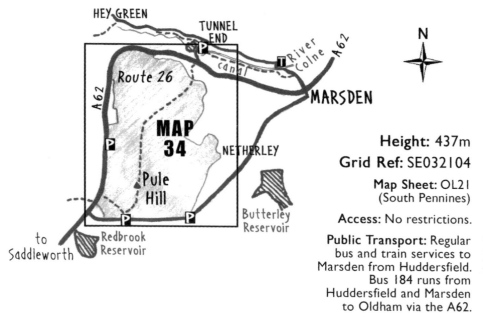

Height: 437m

Grid Ref: SE032104

Map Sheet: OL21
(South Pennines)

Access: No restrictions.

Public Transport: Regular bus and train services to Marsden from Huddersfield. Bus 184 runs from Huddersfield and Marsden to Oldham via the A62.

Pule Hill is unique among West Yorkshire's summits in being a pure hill, rising steeply on all sides to a pointed peak. It is surrounded by expanses of peat moorland, yet forms a tiny oasis in their midst and a welcome view from almost any direction. The dramatic quarried face of Pule Edge looks west and dominates the moor, along with the shafts of the Standedge Tunnel that cut below the hillside on their way across the Pennines. Pule Hill is an easy climb, especially from the lay-bys on the roads below, but even from Marsden, which lies on the gentlest side of the hill.

Pule Hill is a corruption or local version of *pool* (or probably the Celtic equivalent *pwll*), one of which used to lie either on the hill's summit or on its north shoulder.

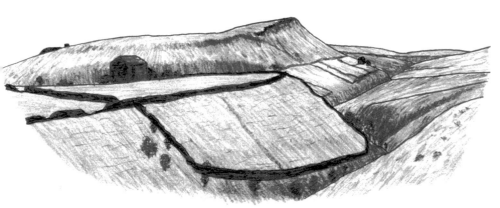

Pule Hill from Green Owlers Clough

155

MAP 34: PULE HILL

Pule Hill is a fine peak that covers only a very small area, squeezed between the A62 and Old Mount Road. Given its obvious aesthetic appeal and proximity to Marsden, one would expect it to be busy and covered in paths. In fact Pule Hill is surprisingly difficult to access from Marsden, its main routes climbing up from lay-bys on the roads to the west and south. Elsewhere faint paths meander across the steep flanks of the hill, leading from one large quarry delf to the next. The hill is dominated by ventilation shafts, engine houses, spoil heaps and marker stones for the numerous Standedge Tunnels that run 300m below the moor as they make for nearby Tunnel End.

A site below **Worlow Quarry** has been suggested to be that of a Roman fortlet or signal station. It stands on the likely earliest route of a Roman Road between Castleshaw Fort (near Delph) and Slack Fort (near Outlane), later supplanted by one further north roughly along the line of the A640. Fragments of Roman pottery similar to those at Castleshaw were found here in a series of excavations by Huddersfield & District Archaeological Society in the 1980s.

*Pule Edge Quarry is easily reached from a large lay-by on the A62 and is surrounded by all manner of industrial remains. The simplest route to the edge is to pick up the main track running diagonally up past both of the ventilation shafts. It is also possible to scramble up from the loading bay at the top of the tramway incline, skirting round the edge of the quarry. Pule Edge's dramatic rock arch at **Trog 'Ole** is reached from here by staying on a faint sheeptrack below the edge.*

The flat summit area of **Pule Hill** was the site of a Bronze Age cemetery, which was discovered and excavated in the 1890s by George Marsden. Though there was no obvious burial mound, four urns containing human remains were found in rock cavities on the site, along with a number of food vessels and pots. An arrowhead and other flint chippings have also been found here, thought to represent the workshops of Mesolithic hunter-gatherers who camped on the high ground of the South Pennines during the summer months. These finds are similar to dozens of others across this area's moorland, representing the greatest density of Mesolithic sites anywhere in the country.

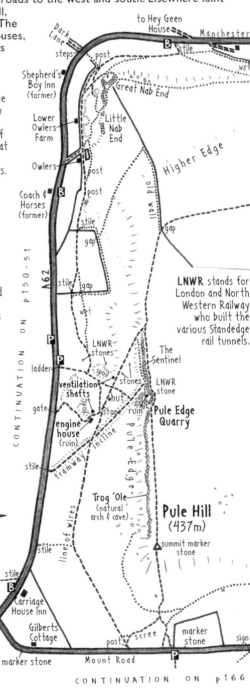

LNWR stands for London and North Western Railway who built the various Standedge rail tunnels.

Pule Hill
(437m)

N

The Standedge Tunnels represent a collection of remarkable engineering feats, transporting narrow boats and trains the three miles between Marsden and Diggle. The first, the canal tunnel, was built between 1794 and 1811 at a cost of £123,804 and is still the longest, deepest and highest canal tunnel in the country. There were many complications as the two separate ends were constructed simultaneously and with differing alignments and heights, so that bends had to be built into the design and the initial work had to be undermined at one end. The need to remove spoil via 500ft shafts resulted in the deaths of fifty workers and in one particular year just 150ft of the tunnel was dug. There are just four passing places on the route and no towpath. Professional leggers propelled the boats through the tunnel using its walls at a speed of roughly 1-2 mph while the horses and crew crossed the hill by road. The canal was abandoned in 1944 and only reopened in 2001 after £5 million of restoration work by the Huddersfield Canal Society.

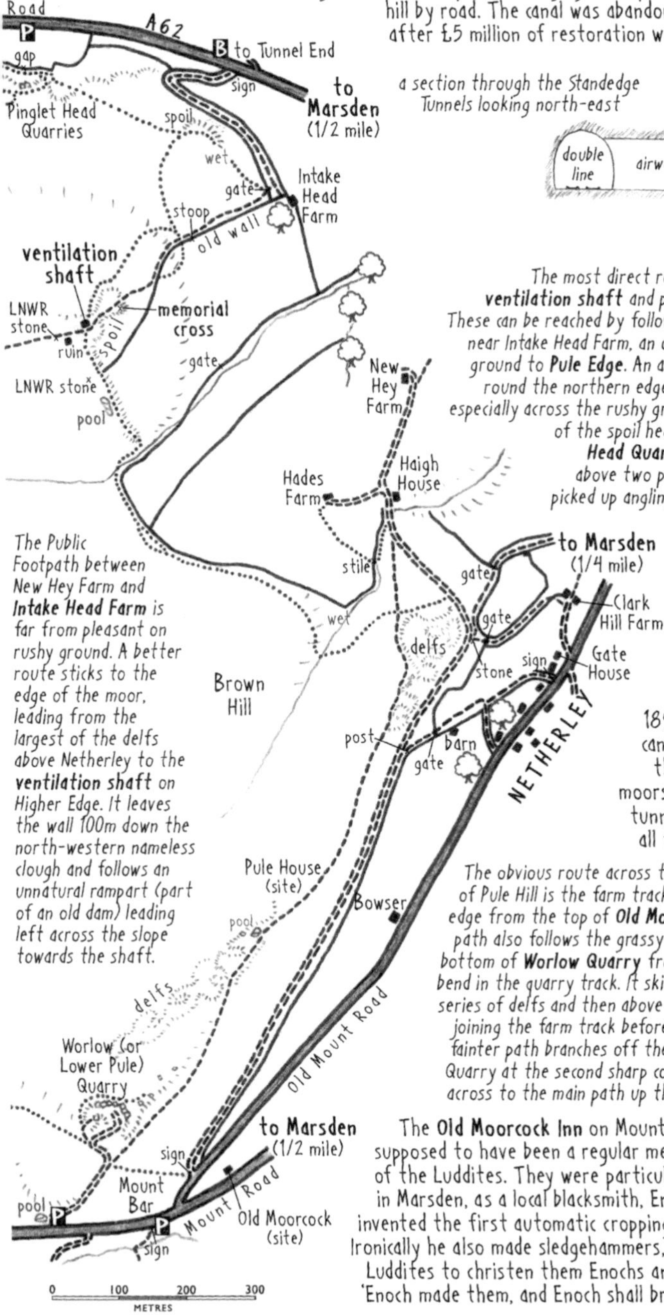

Road

A62

P
gap

B to Tunnel End

sign

to Marsden (1/2 mile)

Pinglet Head Quarries

spoil

wet

gate

stoop

old wall

Intake Head Farm

ventilation shaft

LNWR stone

memorial cross

ruin

spoil

gate

LNWR stone

pool

New Hey Farm

Hades Farm

Haigh House

a section through the Standedge Tunnels looking north-east

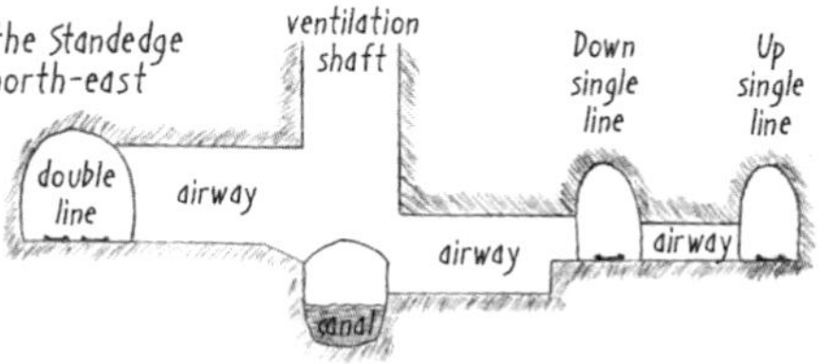

ventilation shaft

double line   airway

airway

canal

Down single line

Up single line

airway

The most direct route from Marsden to Pule Hill is past the **ventilation shaft** and prominent **memorial cross** on Higher Edge. These can be reached by following the line of an old wall up from a gate near Intake Head Farm, an obvious track then running across the high ground to **Pule Edge**. An alternative is to follow the public footpath round the northern edge of the hill. The route is not always clear, especially across the rushy ground near Intake Head Farm. From the top of the spoil heap, a faint path contours across to **Pinglet Head Quarries**, from where the fenceline is followed above two properties. A faint grassy track can then be picked up angling across the slope towards Great Nab End.

The Public Footpath between New Hey Farm and **Intake Head Farm** is far from pleasant on rushy ground. A better route sticks to the edge of the moor, leading from the largest of the delfs above Netherley to the **ventilation shaft** on Higher Edge. It leaves the wall 100m down the north-western nameless clough and follows an unnatural rampart (part of an old dam) leading left across the slope towards the shaft.

stile

Wet

delfs

Brown Hill

post

gate

barn

stone   sign

to Marsden (1/4 mile)

Clark Hill Farm

Gate House

NETHERLEY

The first **railway tunnel** (the Down single line) was constructed between 1845-48, while its twin (the Up single line) was not constructed until 1868-70 and was the first to be dead straight. The double-line tunnel, which is the only one still in regular use today, was built from 1890-94 and crosses narrowly above the canal tunnel near each end. All but one of the seven ventilation shafts across the moors overhead are directly above the canal tunnel, with a series of airways connecting all the other tunnels (see diagram above).

Pule House (site)

pool

Bowser

The obvious route across the eastern side of Pule Hill is the farm track along the moor edge from the top of **Old Mount Road**. A good path also follows the grassy level around the bottom of **Worlow Quarry** from the first sharp bend in the quarry track. It skirts below the first series of delfs and then above the second, before joining the farm track before **Haigh House**. A fainter path branches off the track to Worlow Quarry at the second sharp corner and contours across to the main path up the end of Pule Hill.

delfs

Worlow (or Lower Pule) Quarry

Old Mount Road

pool

P

Mount Bar

sign

P

Old Moorcock (site)

to Marsden (1/2 mile)

sign

Mount Road

The **Old Moorcock Inn** on Mount Road is supposed to have been a regular meeting place of the Luddites. They were particularly active in Marsden, as a local blacksmith, Enoch Taylor, invented the first automatic cropping machines. Ironically he also made sledgehammers, leading the Luddites to christen them Enochs and exclaim, 'Enoch made them, and Enoch shall break them!'

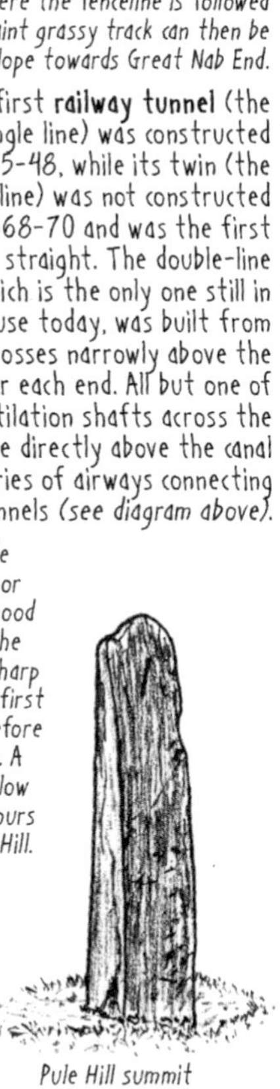

Pule Hill summit marker

0   100   200   300
METRES

MEADOW PIPIT

The **meadow pipit** is the most common bird on the moors of the South Pennines, its familiar sharp song a soundtrack to any day out during the warmer months. It looks fairly undistinctive; small and mostly brown, with mottled streaks on its back and white underneath its wings. It calls when in flight, particularly during the breeding season, when it performs its trademark parachute dives. Despite its prevalence here, the meadow pipit is in decline due to a loss of its winter habitat of rough pasture and broad hedgerows.

CHAPTER 20 – WEST NAB
(including Shooters Nab)

Height: 500m

Grid Ref: SE077088

Map Sheets:
OL1 (The Dark Peak) &
OL21 (South Pennines)

Access: No public access to shooting range and large Danger Area around Shooters Nab *(see p164 for more details)*. No dogs east of fenceline around summit of West Nab.

Public Transport: Regular bus and train services to Marsden, Slaithwaite and Meltham from Huddersfield. Buses 335 & 389 run from Slaithwaite to Meltham via Holt Head, with the 335 continuing to Holmfirth.

West Nab and Shooters Nab form a distinctive anvil-shaped hunk of moorland jutting out north-eastwards from the Black Hill massif. It stands out from across most of Huddersfield, with Shooters Nab dominating the southern skyline of Marsden and Slaithwaite and the sharp peak of West Nab becoming more pronounced as you near Meltham. Both are peaks in their own right, but are dealt with here as one single chapter because of the issues surrounding access to the summit of Shooters Nab (which is very rarely legally possible) and half of the moorland in between the two.

The access exclusion zone for the rifle range near Shooters Nab sadly rips the heart out of the moor and means it is explored far less than it deserves. Other than the busy moorland fringes, West Nab is usually accessed from the road immediately below the summit, a route that hardly does the peak justice. However, access is possible to far more of the moor, most of which is surrounded by rocky ramparts and rarely disappoints the ambitious moorland tramper.

West Nab and Shooters Nab from White Moss

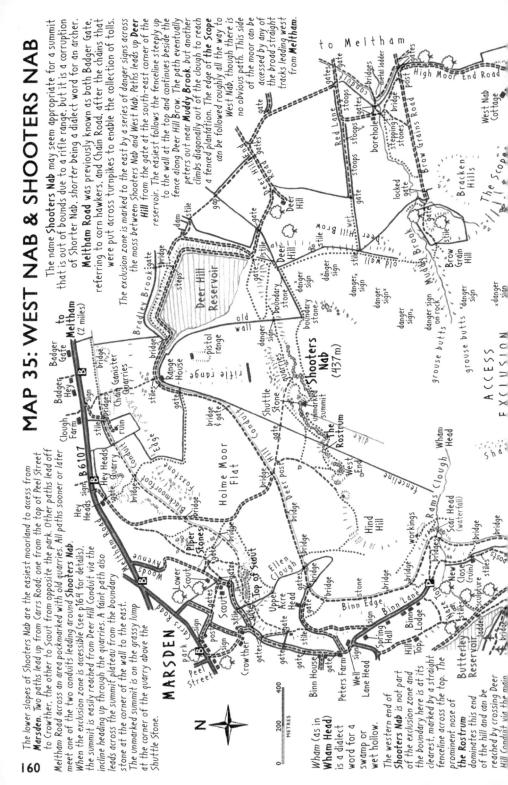

MAP 35: WEST NAB & SHOOTERS NAB

The name **Shooters Nab** may seem appropriate for a summit that is out of bounds due to a rifle range, but it is a corruption of Shorter Nab, shorter being a dialect word for an archer.

Meltham Road was previously known as both Badger Gate, referring to corn hawkers, and Chain Road, after the chains that were put across turnpikes to enable the collection of tolls.

The exclusion zone is marked by a series of danger signs across the moss between Shooters Nab and West Nab. Paths leads up **Deer Hill** from the gate at the south-east corner of the reservoir. The easiest follows the fenceline steeply up to the wall at the top and continues beside the fence along Deer Hill Brow. The path eventually peters out near **Muddy Brook**, but another climbs diagonally out of the clough to reach a fenced plantation. The edge of **the Scope** can be followed roughly all the way to West Nab, though there is no obvious path. This side of the moor can be accessed by any of the broad straight tracks leading west from **Meltham**.

The lower slopes of Shooters Nab are the easiest moorland to access from **Marsden**. Two paths lead up from Carrs Road; one from the top of Peel Street to Crowther, the other to Scout from opposite the park. Other paths lead off Meltham Road across an area pockmarked with old quarries. All paths sooner or later meet one of the two conduits leading around **Shooters Nab**. When the exclusion zone is accessible (see p164 for details), the summit is easily reached from Deer Hill Conduit via the incline heading up through the quarries. A faint path also leads across the summit plateau from the boundary stone at the corner of the wall to the east. The unmarked summit is on the grassy lump at the corner of the quarry above the Shuttle Stone.

Wham (as in **Wham Head**) is a dialect word for a swamp or wet hollow.

The western end of **Shooters Nab** is not part of the exclusion zone and the boundary here is at its clearest, marked by a straight fenceline across the top. The prominent nose of **the Rostrum** dominates this end of the hill and can be reached by crossing Deer Hill Conduit via the main

Map labels

to Meltham

High Moor End Road

West Nab Cottage

The Scope

Bracken Hills

gate

Brow Grdin Hill

Muddy Brook

old wall

stile

danger sign

danger sign × on rock

grouse butts

Deer Road

Red Lane

stoops gates

stoops

borehole

stepping stones

bridge

locked gate

Deer Hill

Deer Hill Brow

Deer Hill

boundary stone

danger sign

boundary stone

Shooters Nab (437m)

The Rostrum

West End

Wham Head

Rams Clough

Sha

Deer Hill End

gate

gate

stile

dam

Deer Hill Reservoir

steps

Bradley Brook gate

bridge

old wall

pistol range

Range House

rifle range

Shuttle Stone

quarries

unmarked summit

Deer post

dike

fenceline

Hill

Hind Hill

workings

Scar Head (waterfall)

New Close (ruin)

Binn Lane

bridge

to Meltham (2 miles)

Badger Gate

Badger Hey

Clough Farm

Hey Heads Road

Hey sign Heads

B6107

Chain Ganister Quarries

ruin

Edge

Quarry

Meltham Road

Conduit

Blackmoorfoot

Foxstone

Piper Stones

Holme Moor Flat

Lower Scout

Scout

Top of Scout

Upper Acre Head

Ellen Clough

Binn Edge

Spring Hall

Binn Top Lodge

Hill Lodge

MARSDEN

Meltham Avenue

Woods

Park Carrs Road

Peel Street

Crowther

Binn House

Peters Farm

Well Lane Head

Butterley Reservoir

Maze stile

Fox stile

sculpture ladder

Scale

N

0   200   400
METRES

Access

ACCESS
EXCLUSION

the Cock Crowing Stone

COCK CROWING STONE

Map labels

to Meltham (1 mile)

to Holmfirth (3 miles)

to Greenfield (5 miles)

Kinsley quarry

quarry

sign & gate

locked gate

boundary stone

locked gate

Cock Crowing Stone

West Nab Brow

West Nab Head Road

West Nab (500m)

gate, stile

P

Wessenden

boundary stone

Bellman Castle (ruin)

marker stone

fold

boundary stone

marker stone

hurdle

Higher Wicken Stones

Lower Wicken Stones

Scope Moss

B17 plane wreckage

danger x sign

danger signs

danger x signs x

West Nab Moss

hurdle

danger x signs x

Raven Stones

step over fence

heap of stones

fold

stile

stile

wet

Leyzing Clough

Winter Clough

bridge

bridge

bridge

hut

Wessenden Head Reservoir

Wessenden Head (site)

Navvy village (site)

boundary stone

delfs

sign & gate

P

stile

stile

stile

stile

ladder

sign

A635 Isle of Skye Inn (ruin)

P sign & gate

B

Holly Bank Moss

Little West Nab

danger x sign

Scotling Stone

danger sign

ZONE

Rigg Top

old wall

Great Clough

bridge

Near New Close (ruin)

Far New Close (ruin)

gate posts stiles

locked gate

Blakeley Reservoir

Smaley Bank

danger x signs x

Great Hey Sike Clough

Little Hey Sike Clough

Hey Brinks

Round Hills

Wessenden Brook

CONTINUATION ON P 167

bridge

bridge

bridge

bridge

Horseley Head

gate

bridge

post

post

gap

stile

Hey Green (ruin)

Wessenden Lodge

post

sign

Wessenden Reservoir

bridge

mast

the Rostrum on Shooters Nab

Right column text

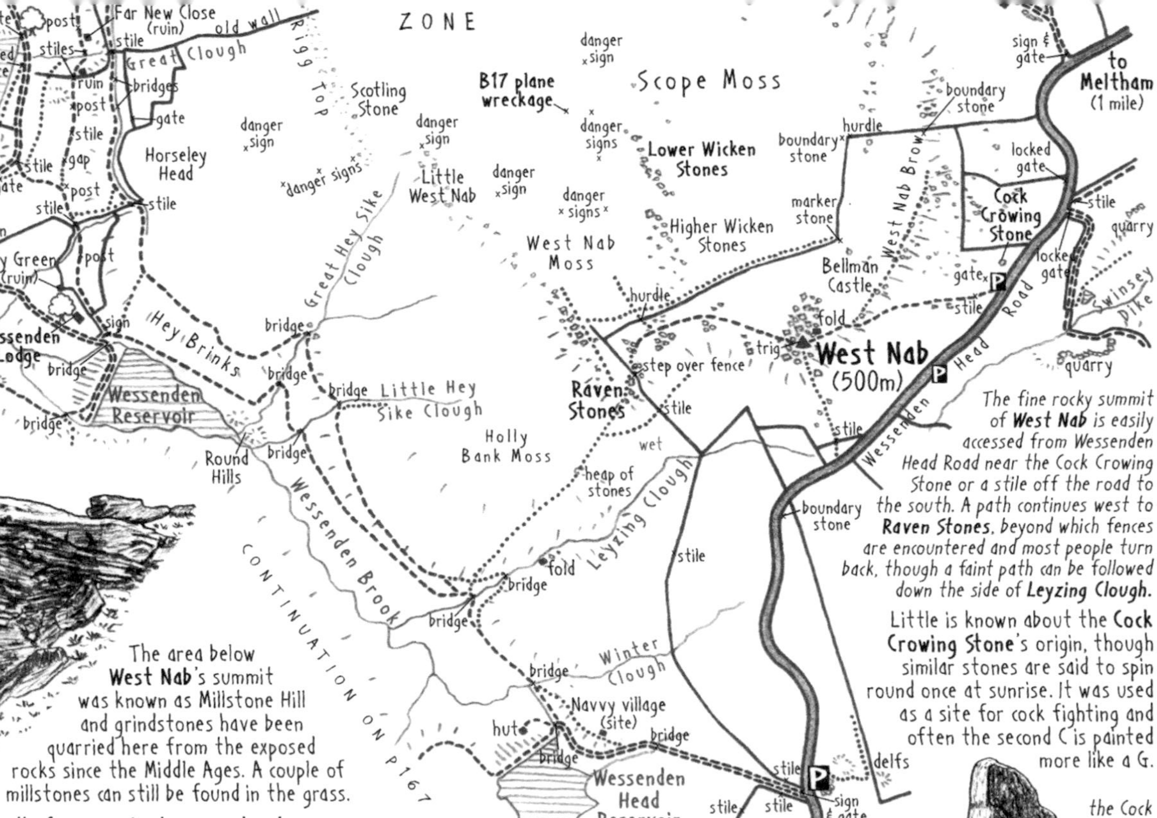

The fine rocky summit of **West Nab** is easily accessed from Wessenden Head Road near the Cock Crowing Stone or a stile off the road to the south. A path continues west to **Raven Stones**, beyond which fences are encountered and most people turn back, though a faint path can be followed down the side of **Leyzing Clough**.

Little is known about the **Cock Crowing Stone**'s origin, though similar stones are said to spin round once at sunrise. It was used as a site for cock fighting and often the second C is painted more like a G.

Left / bottom text

incline and following the way-markers right, then bearing left up to the edge. A fainter alternative climbs **Hind Hill** from a bridge over the conduit at the top of **Ellen Clough**.

The plane wreckage

on Scope Moss is that of Barbara Jane, a B17 Flying Fortress that crashed in bad weather in 1945. The crew survived, but the rear gunner had to crawl off the moor to raise the alarm.

At the far end of **Lower Wicken Stones** there used to be a rocking stone until a Whit Monday in the 1820s, when a group of stonemasons decided to move it by blasting it with gunpowder, then drilling into the stone and levering it off. Another rocking stone near Raven Stones was toppled by a gamekeeper to prevent folk trespassing to it. Neither stone is evident today, but there are several obvious drill marks across the Wicken Stones.

Bottom paragraph

The area below **West Nab**'s summit was known as Millstone Hill and grindstones have been quarried here from the exposed rocks since the Middle Ages. A couple of millstones can still be found in the grass.

West Nab and Shooters Nab naturally form a single moorland expanse, despite looking away from each other. The lower part of Shooters Nab is the busiest part of the moor and, along with the Wessenden Valley, a popular excursion from Marsden. The exclusion of public access from the summit of Shooters Nab and the mosses beyond makes it hard to explore the heart of this moor, but there is plenty to discover around the edges, even on the less-trodden eastern slopes where rocky outcrops lead all the way from West Nab to Deer Hill.

161

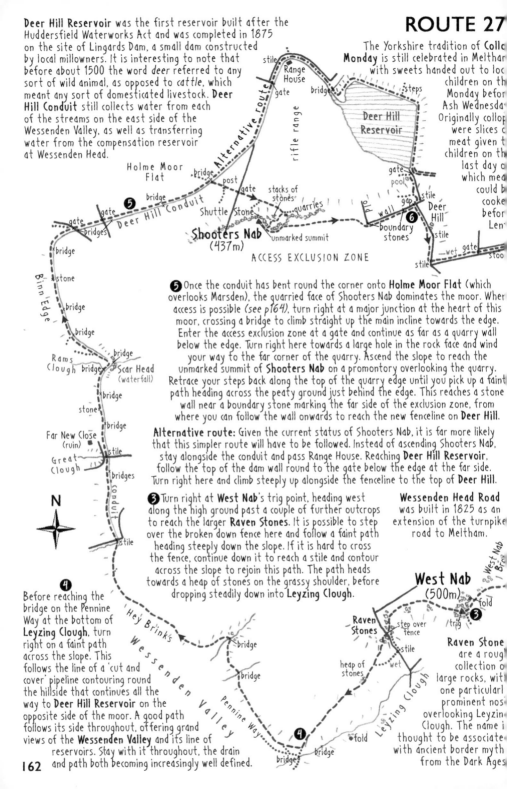

Deer Hill Reservoir was the first reservoir built after the Huddersfield Waterworks Act and was completed in 1875 on the site of Lingards Dam, a small dam constructed by local millowners. It is interesting to note that before about 1500 the word *deer* referred to any sort of wild animal, as opposed to *cattle*, which meant any sort of domesticated livestock. **Deer Hill Conduit** still collects water from each of the streams on the east side of the Wessenden Valley, as well as transferring water from the compensation reservoir at Wessenden Head.

The Yorkshire tradition of Collo **Monday** is still celebrated in Meltham with sweets handed out to loc children on th Monday befor Ash Wednesda Originally collop were slices c meat given t children on th last day o which mea could b cooke befor Len

❺ Once the conduit has bent round the corner onto **Holme Moor Flat** (which overlooks Marsden), the quarried face of Shooters Nab dominates the moor. Wher access is possible *(see p164)*, turn right at a major junction at the heart of this moor, crossing a bridge to climb straight up the main incline towards the edge. Enter the access exclusion zone at a gate and continue as far as a quarry wall below the edge. Turn right here towards a large hole in the rock face and wind your way to the far corner of the quarry. Ascend the slope to reach the unmarked summit of **Shooters Nab** on a promontory overlooking the quarry. Retrace your steps back along the top of the quarry edge until you pick up a faint path heading across the peaty ground just behind the edge. This reaches a stone wall near a boundary stone marking the far side of the exclusion zone, from where you can follow the wall onwards to reach the new fenceline on **Deer Hill**.

Alternative route: Given the current status of Shooters Nab, it is far more likely that this simpler route will have to be followed. Instead of ascending Shooters Nab, stay alongside the conduit and pass Range House. Reaching **Deer Hill Reservoir**, follow the top of the dam wall round to the gate below the edge at the far side. Turn right here and climb steeply up alongside the fenceline to the top of **Deer Hill**.

❸ Turn right at **West Nab**'s trig point, heading west along the high ground past a couple of further outcrops to reach the larger **Raven Stones**. It is possible to step over the broken down fence here and follow a faint path heading steeply down the slope. If it is hard to cross the fence, continue down it to reach a stile and contour across the slope to rejoin this path. The path heads towards a heap of stones on the grassy shoulder, before dropping steadily down into **Leyzing Clough**.

Wessenden Head Road was built in 1825 as an extension of the turnpike road to Meltham.

❹ Before reaching the bridge on the Pennine Way at the bottom of **Leyzing Clough**, turn right on a faint path across the slope. This follows the line of a 'cut and cover' pipeline contouring round the hillside that continues all the way to **Deer Hill Reservoir** on the opposite side of the moor. A good path follows its side throughout, offering grand views of the **Wessenden Valley** and its line of reservoirs. Stay with it throughout, the drain and path both becoming increasingly well defined.

West Nab
(500m)

Raven Stone are a roug collection o large rocks, wit one particularl prominent nos overlooking Leyzin Clough. The name i thought to be associate with ancient border myth from the Dark Ages

N

Map labels: stile, Range House, gate, bridge, steps, Deer Hill Reservoir, rifle range, Alternative route, Holme Moor Flat, bridge, post, gate, stacks of stones, quarries, gate, pool, stile, gap, wall, Deer Hill, Shuttle Stone, Deer Hill Conduit, gate, gate, bridges, bridge, Shooters Nab (437m), unmarked summit, boundary stones, stile, wet gate, stoo, ACCESS EXCLUSION ZONE, stile, Binn Edge, stone, bridge, bridge, Rams Clough bridge, Scar Head (waterfall), bridge, stone, bridge, Far New Close (ruin), stile, Great Clough, bridges, Hey Brinks, Wessenden Valley, bridge, bridge, Pennine Way, Wessenden conduit, stile, Raven Stones, step over fence, trig, stile, heap of stones, wet, Leyzing Clough, fold, West Nab Brig, fold, bridge

WEST NAB & SHOOTERS NAB FROM MELTHAM

Distance: 9½ miles (15.1km)

Ascent: 410m

Difficulty: Moderate

Parking: Clarke Lane and Carlisle Street car parks and other street parking in Meltham, or lay-by on Wessenden Head Road.

Public Transport: Buses 321/324/335 run from Huddersfield to Meltham.

Note: No dogs allowed on this route.

Character: West Nab's rocky tor makes a pleasing objective from Meltham and this route combines it with the beautiful Wessenden Valley and an ascent of neighbouring Shooters Nab. Though this can only be crossed on certain days and times *(see p164 for more details)*, a simple alternative circles the access exclusion zone. There are a couple of short rough sections, but navigation is not particularly difficult.

❽ Turn left down the road, then first left again into Leygards Lane. Almost immediately turn right down **Colders Lane** and follow the grassy track into Meltham, passing a couple of terraces before it turns into a tarmac road. Turn right at the end, skirting round St **Bartholomew's Church** to reach the crossroads at the heart of **Meltham** again.

❼ Through the gate by the **borehole**, turn left and cross the large conduit. Immediately over the bridge, turn right across a metal sluice and drop down a short metal ladder to continue along the conduit's side. Cross **Brow Grains Road**, rejoining the conduit over a stile and continuing alongside it until you reach the road near Wentworth Farm. At the second farm bridge, look right to see the outline of an **Iron Age enclosure** on Oldfield Hill.

❻ Turn right alongside the fence on top of **Deer Hill**, following a path past a large unnamed stone and on along the edge. Where the fence bends sharply left, cross a stile and follow a fence steeply down to a gate at the end of **Red Lane**. Follow the walled path down until it reaches a track, where you turn right to reach the red brick building at **Brow Grains Road Borehole**.

The remains of two **Iron Age enclosures** are evident above Meltham, one on Royd Edge and the other on Oldfield Hill. Evidence of smelting has been uncovered and the earthen ramparts are particularly clear at the latter, which was originally mistaken for a Roman camp.

❷ Continue along the field edge past **Orleans Lodge** towards West Nab's rocky crown, eventually reaching Wessenden Head Road. Turn left for 250m and turn right just beyond the painted **Cock Crowing Stone**. Follow the path diagonally up towards the ridge, crossing the fenceline via a stile (not the nearby gate) and following the obvious line to the summit of **West Nab**.

❶ From the crossroads at the centre of **Meltham** (by the Swan Inn), head out along Holmfirth Road. Pass the fire station, before turning second right up Tinker Lane. Turn left on the bend onto a footpath between houses; after crossing Heather Road this reaches Calmlands Road. Turn right up past the cemetery and continue straight on along the top of **Royd Edge**. Reaching a gate and stile, bear right over a second stile and follow the wall up the hill to the right of the barn. Over the wall is the faint outline of an **Iron Age enclosure**.

Meltham was recorded in the Domesday Book, its name thought to be Scandinavian in origin, possibly referring to a bog covered in cloudberry. Alternatively, Joseph Hughes has suggested it meant 'honey hamlet', referring to the practice of laying beehives across the moorland when the heather was in bloom.

the old cairn on the summit of West Nab

SHOOTERS NAB ACCESS RESTRICTIONS

paint daubed on a rock near West Nab

The quarried face of Shooters Nab constitutes one of the higher tops in West Yorkshire – at 437m, it should warrant a chapter of its own. However, the presence of a rifle range on Deer Hill Moss and its associated exclusion zone means the opportunity to access it is rare. Even on West Nab at the opposite end of the moor, paint is daubed on rocks like the one illustrated above; however, this part of the moor is now designated as open access land so these warnings no longer carry any weight.

The same is not true on Shooters Nab. The rifle range there is home to Lydgate Rifle and Pistol Club, but it is the MoD who license them, having set up the range in the 1930s. The MoD paid compensation to farmers, but still allowed grazing around the range. The extent of the current access land exclusion zone is defined by the potential 'fall of shot', based on the calibre and velocity of the firearms used on the range, something that is reassessed with each new set of regulations. No-one has ever been harmed by stray shot on the moor, but club members are required to stop shooting if they are aware of anyone within the exclusion zone, even though it stretches for more than a mile over the top of Shooters Nab. The current boundary is clearly marked by a new fence along its western edge and a series of danger signs to the south and east. Access is permitted to the western end of Shooters Nab (around the overhanging rock of the Rostrum), but not the summit itself.

The matter is complicated by the existence of Public Rights of Way alongside the range and up into the quarries beneath Shooters Nab. While there has been talk of extinguishing these, they remain on Ordnance Survey maps, potentially luring unwitting walkers up the crag. Though the legal right of access exists here, these routes are probably best avoided when the crackle of gunfire can be heard.

The British Mountaineering Council have negotiated a number of weekend days each year when climbing is permitted on the whole crag, along with Friday evenings after 6pm. It would be safe to assume that the moor is fully accessible at these times, but it is recommended to check up-to-date details first with the BMC. All these agreements are fragile and at the behest of the club; access was withdrawn in 2006 when a shooting competition was interrupted by a group of climbers. Very occasional walks on Shooters Nab may also be organised by the Ramblers' Association and the Peak District National Park, but it is unlikely that individual groups will be able to negotiate access with the club.

one of the danger signs on Shooters Nab

CHAPTER 21 – BLACK HILL

Height: 582m

Grid Ref: SE078047

Map Sheet: OL1
(The Dark Peak)

Access: No dogs on Cook's Study Hill and Snailsden Pike (east of South Yorkshire boundary fence) at any time.

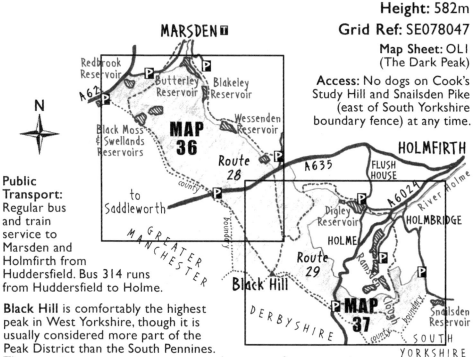

Public Transport: Regular bus and train service to Marsden and Holmfirth from Huddersfield. Bus 314 runs from Huddersfield to Holme.

Black Hill is comfortably the highest peak in West Yorkshire, though it is usually considered more part of the Peak District than the South Pennines. The name is very apt, as its vast peaty plateau was famous as a bane of Pennine Way walkers for many years. These days stone walkways cross the peat, but Black Hill retains its formidable air. The summit crests a massive expanse of moorland that starts above Marsden and continues round to Ramsden Clough, while also taking in large sections of moorland in Greater Manchester, Derbyshire and South Yorkshire.

The whole of the moor is within the Peak District National Park, the only part of West Yorkshire that is, so it is very accessible and popular. The valleys around Digley, Ramsden Clough and the Wessenden Reservoirs are the busiest, but elsewhere people tend to disappear into the endless mosses of Black Hill.

Ramsden Clough, Ruddle Clough Knoll and the Black Hill massif

165

A well-waymarked route has been created around **Butterley Reservoir**, though it offers little chance to explore further. 'Walking the Wild Wood' can be joined in **Netherley** by dropping down from the playing fields and following a path along the edge of the plantation. The promising looking path along the reservoir shore itself has a fence across its line.

A circuit of **Swellands Reservoir** is possible using faint paths. A faint path also strikes off north-west across **Good Hill** from the end of the dam to reach the old coach road above **Carr Clough**. Another follows the old drain around the hillside, but is very wet at the dam end.

Floating Light Inn (former)

to **Delph** (2 miles)

to **Diggle** (1 mile)

An alternative to following the Pennine Way from **Black Moss Reservoir** down to the Brun Clough car park heads left just beyond the north end of the dam, following a broad grassy depression (and occasional vehicle track) around the hillside. It is muddy in places, but drops down to a track near the Standedge Tunnel ventilation shaft below **Brun Clough Reservoir**.

ruined game-keeper's house, Brun Clough

Black Moss Reservoir, originally called Diggle Moss and later Blakely Moss, was built to supply the Huddersfield Narrow Canal and had dams at both ends so that it could be used to supply the canal in either direction. **Swellands Reservoir** (or Swillers as it was originally known) was built alongside on the advice of the canal's engineer, Thomas Telford, who expressed regret that such small dams as that at Brun Clough had been built. On a November night in 1810, just before Swellands' completion, the 'Black Flood' swept down the valley towards Marsden, killing six people and damaging several mills. Though Diggle Moss is sometimes blamed for this event, it was actually Swellands' dam that burst after being undercut by seepage despite there being only 2m of water present.

The original route of the **Pennine Way** ran along the watershed from Black Hill to Standedge via Dean Head, Featherbed, White and Black Mosses, but that was changed in 1990 to avoid further damaging the peat. The route was moved to what had previously been the Wessenden Alternative, a more pleasant but less pure Pennine Way, following **166** the valley rather than the moor tops.

MAP 36: BLACK HILL NORTH
(Wessenden Moor)

to **Netherley** (1/4 mile)

to **Marsden** (2 miles)

CONT. ON p156-57

Gilberts Cottage

Great Western Inn

Redbrook Reservoir

sailing club

Floating Light Inn

Brun Clough Reservoir

ventilation shaft

quarry

Higher Knoll

Black Moss Reservoir

Warcock Hill

Old Bridge House (site)

Good Hill

Swellands Reservoir

Black Moss Reservoir

Round Hill

Little Black Moss Reservoir

Black Moss (or Blakely Moss)

Diggle Edge

North Clough

cairn

stake

White Moss

0 — 250 — 500 — 750
METRES

A broad pair of straight lines crosses Featherbed Moss, the route of a **Cotton Famine Road** constructed in the 1860s. Like the Fieldens' roads above Todmorden, it was built to help unemployed cotton mill workers during the American Civil War, when imported cotton dried up. The road was never completed or surfaced, but the ditches either side remain.

South Clough

N

The **curlew** is probably the most easily identifiable moorland bird, thanks to its long bill and eerie rising call. The largest of Europe's waders, the curlew spends most of the year on river estuaries, but is common across the moors of West Yorkshire when nesting in late spring and early summer.

a curlew

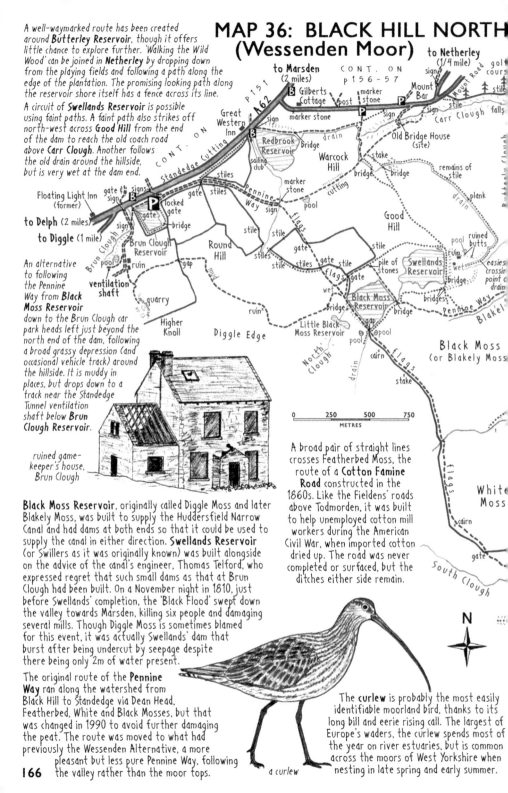

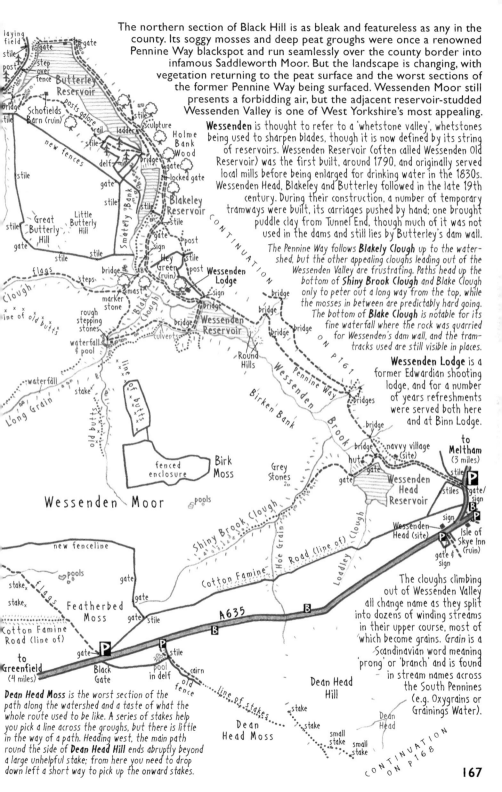

The northern section of Black Hill is as bleak and featureless as any in the county. Its soggy mosses and deep peat groughs were once a renowned Pennine Way blackspot and run seamlessly over the county border into infamous Saddleworth Moor. But the landscape is changing, with vegetation returning to the peat surface and the worst sections of the former Pennine Way being surfaced. Wessenden Moor still presents a forbidding air, but the adjacent reservoir-studded Wessenden Valley is one of West Yorkshire's most appealing.

Wessenden is thought to refer to a 'whetstone valley', whetstones being used to sharpen blades, though it is now defined by its string of reservoirs. Wessenden Reservoir (often called Wessenden Old Reservoir) was the first built, around 1790, and originally served local mills before being enlarged for drinking water in the 1830s. Wessenden Head, Blakeley and Butterley followed in the late 19th century. During their construction, a number of temporary tramways were built, its carriages pushed by hand; one brought puddle clay from Tunnel End, though much of it was not used in the dams and still lies by Butterley's dam wall.

The Pennine Way follows **Blakely Clough** up to the watershed, but the other appealing cloughs leading out of the Wessenden Valley are frustrating. Paths head up the bottom of **Shiny Brook Clough** and Blake Clough only to peter out a long way from the top, while the mosses in between are predictably hard going. The bottom of **Blake Clough** is notable for its fine waterfall where the rock was quarried for Wessenden's dam wall, and the tram-tracks used are still visible in places.

Wessenden Lodge is a former Edwardian shooting lodge, and for a number of years refreshments were served both here and at Binn Lodge.

The cloughs climbing out of Wessenden Valley all change name as they split into dozens of winding streams in their upper course, most of which become grains. Grain is a Scandinavian word meaning 'prong' or 'branch' and is found in stream names across the South Pennines (e.g. Oxygrains or Grainings Water).

Dean Head Moss is the worst section of the path along the watershed and a taste of what the whole route used to be like. A series of stakes help you pick a line across the groughs, but there is little in the way of a path. Heading west, the main path round the side of **Dean Head Hill** ends abruptly beyond a large unhelpful stake; from here you need to drop down left a short way to pick up the onward stakes.

Map labels: laying field, gate, gate, stile, post, step over fence, Butterley Reservoir, bridge, stile, Schofields Barn (ruin), posts galore, rail, ladder, sculpture, Holme Bank Wood, new fences, delf, bridge, gate, locked gate, stile, gate, Blakeley Reservoir, stile, stile, stile, Smatley Bank, Little Butterly Hill, Great Butterly Hill, gate, stile, stile, gate, sign, Hey Green (ruin), post, stile, post, Wessenden Lodge, flags, Clough, line of old butts, marker stone, rough stepping stones, Blake Clough, bridge, steps, mast, sign, bridge, bridge, bridge, Wessenden Reservoir, bridge, culvert, CONTINUATION ON P.161, waterfall & pool, Round Hills, waterfall, stake, line of butts, Long Grain, old butts, fenced enclosure, Birk Moss, Wessenden Moor, pools, Birken Bank, Wessenden Brook, Pennine Way, Grey Stones, navvy village (site), huts, gate, bridges, bridge, bridge, gate, Wessenden Head Reservoir, Wessenden Head (site), sign, to Meltham (3 miles), stile, gate/sign, P, B, P, Isle of Skye Inn (ruin), gate & sign, new fenceline, pools, stake, flags, stake, gate, gate, Featherbed Moss, gate, stile, Cotton Famine Road (line of), A635, B, B, to Greenfield (4 miles), P, Black Gate, P, pool in delf, stile, cairn, old fence, line of stakes, Shiny Brook Clough, Hoe Grain, Loddley Clough, Cotton Famine Road (line of), Dean Head Hill, Dean Head, stake, stake, Dean Head Moss, small stake, small stake, CONTINUATION ON P.168

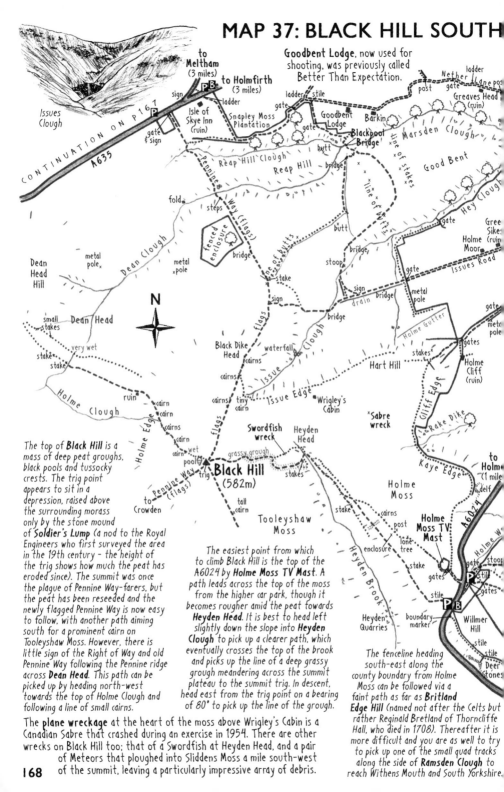

Goodbent Lodge, now used for shooting, was previously called Better Than Expectation.

to **Meltham** (3 miles)

to Holmfirth (3 miles)

sign

Isle of Skye Inn (ruin)

Snapley Moss Plantation

ladder
gate
ladder stile
gate

Goodbent Lodge

Barkin

Blackpool Bridge

ladder
Nether Lane post
post gate
Greaves Head (ruin)

Marsden Clough

line of stakes

Good Bent

Hey Clough

Gree Sike (ruin)

Holme Moor

Issues Road

Issues Clough

CONTINUATION ON P167

A635

gate & sign

Reap Hill Clough

Reap Hill

butt

bridge

line of butts

fold

steps

bridge

fenced enclosure

line of butts

butt

bridge

stoop

sign
bridge

Pennine Way (flags)

metal pole×

Dean Clough

metal ×pole

stake

sign

drain bridge

metal pole

gate

gate

mete pole

Dean Head Hill

Dean Head

small stakes

very wet

stake×
stake

Holme Clough

ruin

cairn
cairn
cairns
cairn
cairn
cairn
wet pool

Black Dike Head

cairns

cairns

cairns tiny
cairn

flags

waterfall

Issue Clough

Issue Edge

bridge

Hart Hill

stakes

gates

Holme Guffer

Holme Cliff (ruin)

gate

metc pole

Cliff Edge

Rake Dike

•Wrigley's Cabin

*Sabre wreck

Kaye Edge

to Holm (1 mile delf

N

Swordfish wreck

Heyden Head

grassy grough

stakes

Holme Moss

Holme Moss TV Mast

A6024

Holme W

Holme Edge

Pennine Way (flags)

trig **Black Hill** (582m)

to Crowden

tall cairn

Tooleyshaw Moss

stake

cairns

post

lone tree

enclosure

stake

gates

Heyden Brook

Heyden Quarries

boundary marker

gate stoop

P Stil

P B gates

Willmer Hill

stile

stile

Deer stones

The top of **Black Hill** is a mass of deep peat groughs, black pools and tussocky crests. The trig point appears to sit in a depression, raised above the surrounding morass only by the stone mound of **Soldier's Lump** (a nod to the Royal Engineers who first surveyed the area in the 19th century – the height of the trig shows how much the peat has eroded since). The summit was once the plague of Pennine Way-farers, but the peat has been reseeded and the newly flagged Pennine Way is now easy to follow, with another path aiming south for a prominent cairn on Tooleyshaw Moss. However, there is little sign of the Right of Way and old Pennine Way following the Pennine ridge across **Dean Head**. This path can be picked up by heading north-west towards the top of Holme Clough and following a line of small cairns.

The easiest point from which to climb Black Hill is the top of the A6024 by **Holme Moss TV Mast**. A path leads across the top of the moss from the higher car park, though it becomes rougher amid the peat towards **Heyden Head**. It is best to head left slightly down the slope into **Heyden Clough** to pick up a clearer path, which eventually crosses the top of the brook and picks up the line of a deep grassy grough meandering across the summit plateau to the summit trig. In descent, head east from the trig point on a bearing of 80° to pick up the line of the grough.

The fenceline heading south-east along the county boundary from Holme Moss can be followed via a faint path as far as **Britland Edge Hill** (named not after the Celts but rather Reginald Bretland of Thorncliffe Hall, who died in 1708). Thereafter it is more difficult and you are as well to try to pick up one of the small quad tracks along the side of **Ramsden Clough** to reach Withens Mouth and South Yorkshire.

The **plane wreckage** at the heart of the moss above Wrigley's Cabin is a Canadian Sabre that crashed during an exercise in 1954. There are other wrecks on Black Hill too; that of a Swordfish at Heyden Head, and a pair of Meteors that ploughed into Sliddens Moss a mile south-west of the summit, leaving a particularly impressive array of debris.

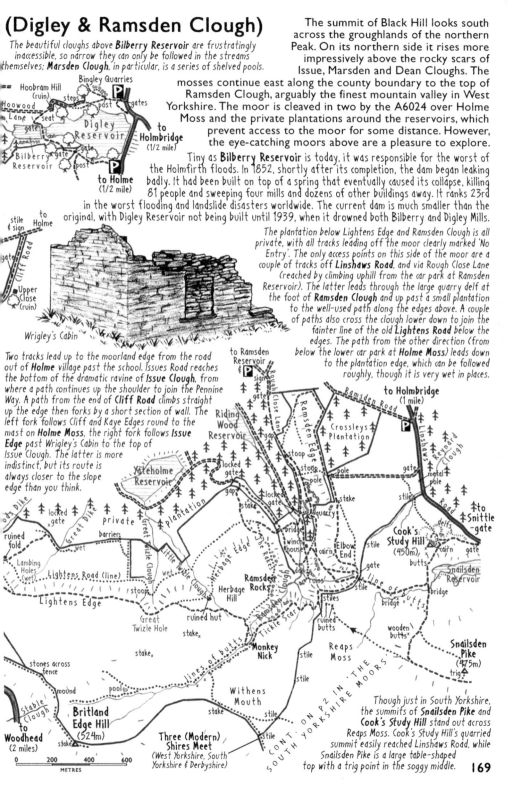

(Digley & Ramsden Clough)

*The beautiful cloughs above **Bilberry Reservoir** are frustratingly inaccessible, so narrow they can only be followed in the streams themselves; **Marsden Clough**, in particular, is a series of shelved pools.*

The summit of Black Hill looks south across the groughlands of the northern Peak. On its northern side it rises more impressively above the rocky scars of Issue, Marsden and Dean Cloughs. The mosses continue east along the county boundary to the top of Ramsden Clough, arguably the finest mountain valley in West Yorkshire. The moor is cleaved in two by the A6024 over Holme Moss and the private plantations around the reservoirs, which prevent access to the moor for some distance. However, the eye-catching moors above are a pleasure to explore.

Tiny as **Bilberry Reservoir** is today, it was responsible for the worst of the Holmfirth floods. In 1852, shortly after its completion, the dam began leaking badly. It had been built on top of a spring that eventually caused its collapse, killing 81 people and sweeping four mills and dozens of other buildings away. It ranks 23rd in the worst flooding and landslide disasters worldwide. The current dam is much smaller than the original, with Digley Reservoir not being built until 1939, when it drowned both Bilberry and Digley Mills.

*The plantation below Lightens Edge and Ramsden Clough is all private, with all tracks leading off the moor clearly marked 'No Entry'. The only access points on this side of the moor are a couple of tracks off **Linshaws Road**, and via Rough Close Lane (reached by climbing uphill from the car park at Ramsden Reservoir). The latter leads through the large quarry delf at the foot of **Ramsden Clough** and up past a small plantation to the well-used path along the edges above. A couple of paths also cross the clough lower down to join the fainter line of the old **Lightens Road** below the edges. The path from the other direction (from below the lower car park at **Holme Moss**) leads down to the plantation edge, which can be followed roughly, though it is very wet in places.*

Two tracks lead up to the moorland edge from the road out of **Holme** village past the school. Issues Road reaches the bottom of the dramatic ravine of **Issue Clough**, from where a path continues up the shoulder to join the Pennine Way. A path from the end of **Cliff Road** climbs straight up the edge then forks by a short section of wall. The left fork follows Cliff and Kaye Edges round to the mast on **Holme Moss**, the right fork follows **Issue Edge** past Wrigley's Cabin to the top of Issue Clough. The latter is more indistinct, but its route is always closer to the slope edge than you think.

Though just in South Yorkshire, the summits of **Snailsden Pike** and **Cook's Study Hill** stand out across Reaps Moss. Cook's Study Hill's quarried summit easily reached Linshaws Road, while Snailsden Pike is a large table-shaped top with a trig point in the soggy middle.

169

ROUTE 28: BLACK HILL & WESSENDEN VALLEY FROM MARSDEN

Distance: 13½ miles (21.9km)

Ascent: 500m

Difficulty: Strenuous

Parking: Various street parking in Marsden. Free car parks at Black Gate or Wessenden Head.

Public Transport: Regular trains and buses from Huddersfield to Marsden.

Character: A long tramp across Wessenden Moor to the Black Hill plateau that utilises both the old and new routes of the Pennine Way. While the path across the mosses is boggy and indistinct in places, it is a far easier going that it used to be, and on a good day offers a fine high level circuit of the moor. From the summit the descent is on firm paths throughout, winding its way down the delightful Wessenden Valley back to Marsden.

Bank Bottom Mills form a giant complex of weaving sheds along the bottom end of Wessenden Brook and are Marsden's most dominant landmark. Bank Bottom originally referred to two older mills slightly upstream; the higher mill (known locally as Top Bonk) was lost beneath Butterley's dam wall and the lower mill demolished soon after. Under the Crowther Family, the present site of Bank Bottom developed in the early 20th century, covering fourteen acres and employing nearly 2,000 people. During World War I it was a major source of troops blankets and George V visited in 1918 in recognition of this service.

In 1931, the mills' philanthropic owner John Edward Crowther shot himself at the height of the Depression and the whole village is said to have mourned. Bank Bottom Mills only closed down in 2003, when the last 244 jobs at the site went.

a black rabbit by Holme Bank Wood

① Following the A62 west out of **Marsden**, turn left into Fall Lane, signed 'Marsden Golf Club' – from the railway station, head left down through the village centre to reach the A62 by the New Inn. Continue straight on at the mini roundabout, starting to climb up Binn Road. After less than 100m bear right before the Marsden Industrial Society building on a track heading between (and in places under) the towering buildings of **Bank Bottom Mills**.

② Where the track emerges below **Butterley Reservoir**, head straight on across the overflow channel, keeping left of the trees before climbing some steps (which also look like a spillway). Turn right at the top to reach Mount Road in **Netherley**. Head straight across into Netherley Drive (unsigned), then bear right up a tarmac track past Spout Ing. Reaching **Old Mount Road** at a signpost, turn left then go immediately right up a narrow path that follows a wall up to the edge of the moor just beyond a large barn.

③ Turn left upon reaching the large track across the hillside. This rejoins **Old Mount Road** near the junction with Mount Road. Head straight across the junction, following a signed path down into Carr Clough. Follow a broad path the other side along the line of the old Coach Road across the moss.

The **Coach Road** is another name for the second turnpike road across Warcock Hill and Standedge. It was built in two stages, in 1791 and 1815, replacing an earlier route across the foot of Pule Hill. When the third turnpike road was built in 1839, along what is now the A62 through Standedge Cutting, the Coach Road was intentionally damaged to prevent its use.

⑦ Where the vehicle track ends by **Wessenden Head Reservoir**'s dam wall, continue straight on along a path down the east side of Wessenden Valley. It is a beautiful route past **Wessenden, Blakeley** and **Butterley Reservoirs**, as open moorland gives way to rhododendrons

MARSDEN

to Huddersfield (7 miles)

New Inn, fire station, Marsden Industrial Society, Binn Road, A62, Marsden Sports Hall, Bank Bottom Mills, signs, gate, barrier, signpost, Gate House, Spout Ing, sign, signs, Old Mount Road, Mount Road, NETHERLEY, Warcock Hill, Carr Clough, sign, Bank Top Farm, Butterley Reservoir, sculpture, gate, former rocking stone, Blakeley Reservoir, sign, Holme Bank Wood, Wessenden Lodge, gate, Wessenden Road, Wessenden Reservoir, bridge, Round Hills, bridge, Leyzing Clough, bridge, Good Hill, Black Moss Reservoir, Little Black Moss Reservoir, Good Hill, market stone, spool, flags, gate, stile, bridge

to Meltham (3 miles)

to Holmfirth (4 miles)

barrier · **P** · gate & sign · sign · **A635** · gate & sign · **B**

Reap Hill Clough · Dean Clough · flags · bridge · sign

Black Hill (582m) · flags · line of cairns · trig · pool

Holme Edge · cairns · ruin · stake

7 bridge · hut · Wessenden Brook · Wessenden Head Reservoir

N

4 Reaching the Pennine Way beyond a small stream, double back left to ascend **Good Hill** via the flagstones. After a couple of gates the Pennine Way flags bend sharply left; continue straight on to cross the low dam wall of **Black Moss Reservoir**. A muddy stretch lies ahead, following a path parallel to the fenceline across Black Moss, but you soon rejoin the flagstones that continue all the way across White Moss and Featherbed Moss to reach the **A635**.

6 Turn left at the trig point on **Black Hill** and join the flagstoned Pennine Way heading off the plateau. Be assured that the going is all straightforward from here. Indeed the Pennine Way is flagged most of the way to the A635 as it bounds across both **Dean Clough** and **Reap Hill Clough** before climbing up to the road. Turn right here, then fork left towards Meltham. Leave the road just before the car park, turning left down a large track towards **Wessenden Head Reservoir**.

0 · 200 · 400 · 600
METRES

Black Moss · White Moss · Long Grain · flags · cairn · new fenceline · gate · flags · Cotton Famine Road (line) · Featherbed Moss · gate · **P** posts · **A635** · pool & stile · Black Gate · cairn · old fence

to Greenfield (4 miles) · **5**

Dean Head Moss · line of stakes · stake · small stake · small stake · Dean Head Hill · Holme Clough · very wet stake · small stake · Holme Edge · stake

5 Follow the **A635** left for 300m to a path leading right by a couple of posts. Over a stile, follow the fenceline until it stops abruptly on the edge of **Dean Head Moss**. The path from here to Holme Clough is rather unclear, guided only by a series of stakes that often appear to contradict each other (guiding you first on one path, then another). Continue straight on from the end of the fenceline to find the first of the line of stakes. Where these stop abruptly, continue ahead (aiming roughly for Holme Moss mast) until another stake is visible to the left. A faint path is picked up heading across the side of **Dean Head Hill**. Ignore a couple of small stakes off to the left and continue right to reach a couple more stakes near Holme Clough. Across the wet gulch, pick up the obvious pathline heading straight up onto **Holme Edge**. Cairns begin soon after you pass a ruin, leading you nicely across the plateau to the trig point on **Black Hill**.

The A635 between Holmfirth and Greenfield is still often referred to as the Isle of Skye Road, a reference to the now ruined pub at the top of the road. The Isle of Skye Inn was closed in the 1950s as part of the clearances in the Digley Reservoir catchment. The Peak District and Northern Counties Footpaths Preservation Society lamented its imminent closure in 1952, suggesting pollution concerns can easily be met by sewage diversion on a small scale. It is the first inn on the Four Inns Walk, a Scout-run event that has been held in March every year since 1957; its 45-mile route continues south to the Snake Pass Inn, Nag's Head and Cat & Fiddle on the way to Buxton.

Bank Bottom Mills

ROUTE 29: BLACK HILL & RAMSDEN CLOUGH FROM HOLMBRIDGE

Distance: 11 miles (17.5km)

Ascent: 550m

Difficulty: Moderate

Parking: Limited street parking in Holmbridge. Free car parks at Digley Reservoir and Holme Moss.

Public Transport: Bus 314 runs from Huddersfield/Holmfirth to Holmbridge and bus H7 runs from Holmfirth only.

Character: A beautiful route and possibly the finest circuit of West Yorkshire's highest peak. Despite crossing Black Hill's barren peat mosses by less popular routes, there are clear paths throughout and only the section from Holme Moss to Black Hill needs any real care. Elsewhere the route takes in the drama of Ramsden and Marsden Cloughs and the charms of Digley Reservoir.

Blackpool Bridge is a popular picnic spot, though the bridge itself is not the ancient crossing one might imagine. It is probably named after one of Marsden Clough's dark, peaty pools.

Bent is used for an area of coarse grass, so I'm not sure how you can have a Good Bent.

❻ Having forded Hey Clough the track arcs clearly around Good Bent and drops down to Blackpool Bridge at the junction of three picturesque cloughs. Follow the waymarked track up the other side to reach Nether Lane via a couple of gates. Turn right and follow the track across the hillside for some distance. Eventually turn right at a junction of tracks beyond Greaves Head, the third abandoned farm (the hillsides above these reservoirs were all cleared to keep Huddersfield's drinking water clean).

❺ At the summit of Black Hill, turn right along the flagstoned Pennine Way. After dropping steeply down Black Dike Head the flags resume and the path bends left. Turn right at a sign down to a ford across the bottom of Issue Clough, which boasts an impressive waterfall halfway up. Beyond the stream look for a broken down wall crossing the track and follow it down to the left to cut the corner and join a large track down into Hey Clough (if you miss it you'll soon reach a sign at the junction beyond).

❹ Follow the main road left up to the summit car park, then cross the stile to the right and follow a path out across Holme Moss. This kinks left then largely follows the left edge of the plateau. Beyond a broad peat grough, the path drops down slightly towards Heyden Brook near a wooden stake. It continues above the stream and eventually crosses the clough just before Heyden Head (a brief diversion up the stream leads past one of Black Hill's many plane wrecks). Soon after, you join the line of a grassy grough meandering across the summit plateau of Black Hill; an increasingly well-worn path leads to the trig point.

Map labels:
post, stile, Nether Lane, gate, Greaves Head (ruin), Goodbent Lodge, Barkin (ruin), gate, Marsden Clough, Blackpool Bridge, Good Bent, bridge, stoop, Hey Clough, sign, broken wall, sign, bridge, flags, waterfall, Issue Clough, Black Dike Head, cairns, cairns, Black Hill (582m), pool, trig, flags, grassy grough, plane wreck, Heyden Head, stakes, Heyden Brook, stake, grough, Holme Moss, Holme Moss TV Mast, P, gate, stake, gate, grough, stile, P, B, A6024, to Woodhead (2 miles), Holme Moss TV Mast, N

172

Holmbridge was recorded in the Middle Ages, with a bridge referred to in the 1430s. St David's Church was built in 1839 only to have its floor torn up in the flood of 1852. Inside is the Flood Bible, which was rescued intact after the flood, despite its owner's house and belongings all being washed away.

HOLMBRIDGE

to Holmfirth (1 mile)

to Holme (1 mile)

A *hoo* (found in Hoowood Lane and Hoobram Hall near Digley Reservoir) is an Old English word for a spur of land.

7 Follow Hoowood Lane round above the reservoirs, dropping into the woods by **Digley Reservoir**. Keep left up a set of metal steps and join a walled track that reaches the car park in **Bingley Quarries**. Keep right to avoid the road until you have to join it. Continue straight on past the end of the dam and, shortly after a small building, follow a path right through a small gate. It angles down through the woods to join Digley Road, which leads back into **Holmbridge**.

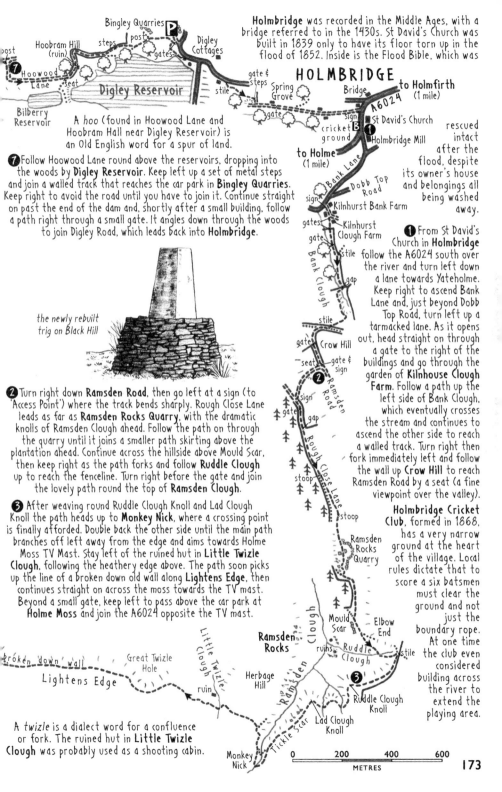

the newly rebuilt trig on Black Hill

1 From St David's Church in **Holmbridge** follow the A6024 south over the river and turn left down a lane towards Yateholme. Keep right to ascend Bank Lane and, just beyond Dobb Top Road, turn left up a tarmacked lane. As it opens out, head straight on through a gate to the right of the buildings and go through the garden of **Kilnhouse Clough Farm**. Follow a path up the left side of Bank Clough, which eventually crosses the stream and continues to ascend the other side to reach a walled track. Turn right then fork immediately left and follow the wall up **Crow Hill** to reach Ramsden Road by a seat (a fine viewpoint over the valley).

Holmbridge Cricket Club, formed in 1868, has a very narrow ground at the heart of the village. Local rules dictate that to score a six batsmen must clear the ground and not just the boundary rope. At one time the club even considered building across the river to extend the playing area.

2 Turn right down **Ramsden Road**, then go left at a sign (to 'Access Point') where the track bends sharply. Rough Close Lane leads as far as **Ramsden Rocks Quarry**, with the dramatic knolls of Ramsden Clough ahead. Follow the path on through the quarry until it joins a smaller path skirting above the plantation ahead. Continue across the hillside above Mould Scar, then keep right as the path forks and follow **Ruddle Clough** up to reach the fenceline. Turn right before the gate and join the lovely path round the top of **Ramsden Clough**.

3 After weaving round Ruddle Clough Knoll and Lad Clough Knoll the path heads up to **Monkey Nick**, where a crossing point is finally afforded. Double back the other side until the main path branches off left away from the edge and aims towards Holme Moss TV Mast. Stay left of the ruined hut in **Little Twizle Clough**, following the heathery edge above. The path soon picks up the line of a broken down old wall along **Lightens Edge**, then continues straight on across the moss towards the TV mast. Beyond a small gate, keep left to pass above the car park at **Holme Moss** and join the A6024 opposite the TV mast.

A *twizle* is a dialect word for a confluence or fork. The ruined hut in **Little Twizle Clough** was probably used as a shooting cabin.

0   200   400   600
METRES

173

CLOUDBERRY

The **cloudberry** (or dwarf mulberry) is a type of raspberry found on northern acid uplands. Though it is not common in this country, it can occasionally be found as a ground-hugging mat of crinkly green leaves, particularly around Black Hill. Leo H. Grindon describes the Isle of Skye Road in 1882, 'It is hereabouts that the cloudberry, that most artistic of northern fruits, never seen and unable to exist upon lower levels is, for our own neighbourhood, so plentiful. When ripe, so thick is the spread of rosy amber that the spectacle is most bright and pretty, the ground seeming strewed with white-heart cherries'.

When it blooms, the cloudberry has small white flowers, after which it develops a distinctive edible orange fruit that is particularly high in Vitamin C. Across West Yorkshire, the names of Cloud Berry Farm, Cloudberry Way and Cloudberry Knoll demonstrate its proliferation in the past. It was also known as knotberry or knoutberry (see Knotberry Moor in Derbyshire and Great Knoutberry Hill in North Yorkshire).
There is some debate as to the origins of this name, which may refer to a *knott* (as in a crag), to King Cnut (who is said to have been saved by eating cloudberries), or simply to the knotted nature of the fruit itself.

BIBLIOGRAPHY

Armitage, Harry – 'Dam It! - The Building of the Halifax Reservoirs 1830-1914' in *Transactions of the Halifax Antiquarian Society* (1977)

Armitage, Harry – *Dawson City, Heptonstall* (1980)

Askwith, Richard – *Feet in the Clouds* (London: Aurum, 2004)

Baines, Edward – *History of the County Palatine and Duchy of Lancashire* (London: Fisher, Co and Son, 1836)

Barley, M.W. (ed) – *The Buildings of the Countryside 1500-1750* (Cambridge: Cambridge University Press, 1990)

Baumber, Michael – *A History of Haworth from Earliest Times* (Lancaster: Carnegie, 2009)

Bennett, Paul – *The Old Stones of Elmet* (Milverton: Capall Bann, 2001)

Bibby, Andrew – *The Backbone of England* (London: Frances Lincoln, 2011)

Billingsley, John – *Folk Tales from Calderdale: Volume 1* (Mytholmroyd: Northern Earth, 2007)

Binns, Jack – *Yorkshire in the Civil Wars* (Pickering: Blackthorn Press, 2004)

Bishop, Reginald William Snowden – *My Moorland Patients* (London: John Murray, 1922)

Bowtell, Harold D – *Reservoir Railways of the Yorkshire Pennines* (Oakwood Press, 1979)

Brown, Alfred J. – *Moorland Tramping in West Yorkshire* (London: Country Life Ltd, 1931)

Brunskill, R.W. – *Houses and Cottages of Britain: Origins and Development of Traditional Buildings* (London: Orion, 1997)

Campbell, Marie – *Curious Tales of West Yorkshire* (Wilmslow: Sigma Leisure, 1999)

Campbell, Marie – *Strange World of the Brontës* (Wilmslow: Sigma Leisure, 2001)

Cary, John – *A New Map of Yorkshire* (1808)

Clark, E. Kitson – 'Excavation at Pule Hill near Marsden' in *Yorkshire Archaeological and Topographical Journal, Vol 16* (1902)

Clay, J.W. – 'The Savile Family' Marsden' in *Yorkshire Archaeological and Topographical Journal, Vol 25* (1923)

Collins, Herbert Cecil – *The Roof of Lancashire* (London: Dent, 1950)

Comfort, Arthur – *Ancient Halls in and about Halifax* (Halifax: Halifax Courier, 1913)

Cowling, Eric T. – *Rombalds Way: A Pre-history of Mid-Wharfedale* (Otley: William Walker, 1946)

Craven, Joseph – *A Brontë Moorland Village and its People: A History of Stanbury* (Keighley: The Rydal Press, 1907)

Crossland, C – 'Some Place Names In The Parish Of Halifax' in *Transactions of the Yorkshire Dialect Society Part IV* (Ilkley: 1902)

Crump, W.B. – 'Dialect on the Map – Some Calder Valley Placenames' in *Transactions of the Halifax Antiquarian Society* (1931)

Crump, W.B. – *Huddersfield Highways Down The Ages* (Huddersfield: S. R. Publishers, 1949)

Crump, W.B. – 'The Little Hill Farm' in *Transactions of the Halifax Antiquarian Society* (1938)

Dawson, Alan – *The Relative Hills of Britain* (Milnthorpe: Cicerone, 1992)

Dawson, T – *The Todmorden and Hebden Bridge Historical Almanack for 1877 & 1890* (Todmorden: T. Dawson)

Dearne, Martin J – *The Economy of the Roman South Pennines with Particular Reference to the Lead Extraction Industry in Its National Context* (Sheffield: University of Sheffield, 1990)

Dixon, Mike – *History and Guide: Ilkley* (Stroud: Tempus, 2002)

Dyson, Taylor – *The History of Huddersfield and District from the earliest times down to 1951* (Huddersfield: Alfred Jubb & Son, 1951)

Eccles, Robert. – 'Local Pinfolds' in *Transactions of the Halifax Antiquarian Society* (1936)

Ekwall, Eilert – *The Place-Names of Lancashire* (Manchester: University Press, 1922)

English, Barbara – *Yorkshire Enclosure Awards* (Hull University Press, 1985)

Faull, M.L. & Moorhouse, S.A. (eds) – *West Yorkshire: An Archaeological Survey to AD1500* (Wakefield: West Yorkshire County Council, 1981)

Fielding, Alan & Haworth Paul F – *Upland Habitats* (London: Routledge, 1999)

Fletcher, J.S. – *A Picturesque History of Yorkshire* (General Books, 2010)

Fletcher, John C. – 'Flints Reservoir, 1834-1929' in *Transactions of the Halifax Antiquarian Society* (2004)

Fleure, Herbert John & Davies, Margaret – *A Natural History of Man in Britain* (London: Collins, 1970)

Folley, E.W. – *Romantic Wycoller* (Nelson: Coulton & Co, 1949)

Forrest, Charles and Grainge, William – *A Ramble on Rombalds Moor* (Wakefield: W.T. Lamb, 1868)

Gee, H.L. – *Folk Tales of Yorkshire* (Edinburgh: Thomas Nelson & Sons, 1960)

Gledhill, B – 'Cragg Road: A Turnpike Trust' in *Transactions of the Halifax Antiquarian Society* (1987)

Gledhill, Mrs H. – 'Lost Homes of Dean Head and Scammonden' in *Transactions of the Halifax Antiquarian Society* (1978)

Goodhall, Armitage – *Place-names of South-west Yorkshire* (Cambridge: Cambridge University Press, 2012)

Greenough, George Bellas – *Memoir of a Geological Map of England* (London: The Geological Society of London, 1840)

Grindon, Leo Hartley – *Country Rambles, And Manchester Walks And Wild Flowers: Being Rural Wanderings in Cheshire, Lancashire, Derbyshire, & Yorkshire* (Manchester: Palmer & Howe, 1882)

Haigh, Donald – 'Local History from World War II: The 'Starfish' Sites at Cragg Vale and Clifton' in *Transactions of the Halifax Antiquarian Society* (1993)

Hannon, Paul – *Ilkley Moor* (Keighley: Hillside, 1994)

Hanson, T.W. – 'Cattle Ranches of Sowerbyshire' in *Transactions of the Halifax Antiquarian Society* (1949)

Hanson, T.W. – 'The Cragg Coiners' in *Transactions of the Halifax Antiquarian Society* (1909)

Hardwick, C – 'Traditions' in *Yorkshire Folk-lore Journal* (1888)

Harland, John & Wilkinson, T.T. – *Lancashire Folklore* (London: Frederick Warne, 1867)

Harwood, H.W. – 'Four Midgley Farms' in *Transactions of the Halifax Antiquarian Society* (1939)

Heginbottom, J.A. – 'Early Christian Sites in Calderdale' in *Transactions of the Halifax Antiquarian Society* (1988)

Heginbottom, J.A. – 'Fences and Fields: The Evolution of the Calderdale Rural Landscape from Prehistoric Times to the Present Day' in *Transactions of the Halifax Antiquarian Society* (1993)

Heginbottom, J.A. – 'The Early Bridges of Calderdale' in *Transactions of the Halifax Antiquarian Society* (1986)

Heginbottom, J.A. – 'The Landscape History of Erringden Park for the 12th to the 20th Century' in *Transactions of the Halifax Antiquarian Society* (2006)

Heginbottom, J.A. – 'The Stoodley Pike Obelisk: A Commemoration Monument' in *Transactions of the Halifax Antiquarian Society* (1995)

Hewitt, Peggy – *These Lonely Mountains: A Biography of the Brontë Moors* (Huddersfield: Springfield Books, 1985)

Heywood, Malcolm, Heywood, Freda & Jennings, Bernard – *A History of Todmorden* (Skipton: Dalesman, 1996)

Hill, Howard – *Freedom to Roam* (Ashbourne: Moorland, 1980)

Hindley, R – *Oxenhope: The Making of a Pennine Community* (Cleckheaton: Amadeus, 2004)

Hindley, Reg – *Exploring Oxenhope* (Cleckheaton: Amadeus, 2006)

Historic Society of Lancashire and Cheshire – *Transactions of the Historic Society of Lancashire and Cheshire, Volume 5* (Liverpool: Adam Holden, 1861)

Historic Society of Lancashire and Cheshire – *Transactions of the Historic Society of Lancashire and Cheshire, Volume 18* (Richard Gill, 1900)

Historic Society of Lancashire and Cheshire – *Transactions of the Historic Society of Lancashire and Cheshire, Volume 17* (Adam Holden, 1865)

Holden, Joshua – *A Short History of Todmorden with Some Account of the Geology and Natural History of the Neighbourhood* (Manchester: Sherratt & Hughes, 1912)

Holdsworth, Alfred – *A Poet Passed: The Poems of Alfred Holdsworth* (Ridings, 1968)

Hone, William – *The Table Book* (London: William Tegg, 1827)

Hudson, David – *Grouse Shooting* (Shrewbury: Quiller, 2008)

Hughes, Joseph – *The History of the Township of Meltham* (Huddersfield: J. Crossley & Co, 1866)

Hughes, Ted – *Remains of Elmet* (London: Faber & Faber, 1993)

Jacobi, R.M, Tallis, J.H. & Mellars, P.A. – *The Southern Pennine Mesolithic and the Ecological Record* (1976)

James, T. – 'On Antiquities of the South Western Part of the County of York' in *Huddersfield Archaeological and Topographical Association Papers* (1867)

Jefferys, Thomas – *Map of Yorkshire* (Woodbridge: Harry Margary, 1973)

Jennings, B – *Pennine Valley: A History of Upper Calderdale* (Skipton: Dalesman, 1992)

Jepson, Boel – *English Place-Name Elements Relating to Boundaries* (Lund University, 2011)

Keevil, Graham – *Standedge Guide* (Kirklees Metropolitan Council Huddersfield, 1986)

Keighley, Jack – *South Pennine Walks: Thirty Circular Walks* (Milnthorpe: Cicerone, 2004)

Keighley, William – *Keighley: Past and Present* (Keighley: A. Hey, 1879)

Kendall, H.P. – 'The Civil War as affecting Halifax and the Surrounding Towns' in *Transactions of the Halifax Antiquarian Society* (1911)

Kendall, H.P. – 'Tom Bell's Cave: A Heptonstall Legend' in *Transactions of the Halifax Antiquarian Society* (1902)

Kendall, Hugh P – 'The Forest of Sowerbyshire' in *Transactions of the Halifax Antiquarian Society* (1926)

King, Robert E. – *Petroleum Exploration and Production in Europe in 1963* (AAPG, 1964)

Langdale, Thomas – *A Topographical Dictionary of Yorkshire* (Northallerton: J. Langdale, 1809)

Lawrence, A – *A History of Menston and Hawksworth* (Otley: Smith Settle, 1991)

Le Patourel, Jean, Long, Moira H. and Pickles, May F. – *Yorkshire Boundaries* (Leeds: Yorkshire Archaeological Society, 1993)

Lunn, Norman – *The Romans Came This Way* (Huddersfield & District Archaeological Society, 2008)

Manley, Gordon – 'Saxton's Survey of Northern England' in *The Geographical Journal Vol 83* (Blackwell Publishing, 1934)

March, Dr H.C. – *East Lancashire Nomenclature and Rochdale Names* (London: Simpkin, 1880)

Massey, Gerald – *Book of the Beginnings, Part 1* (Whitefish, MT: Kessinger, 2002)

McMillan, Ian – *T'Olympics* (Skipton: Dalesman, 2011)

Midgley History Group – *Pennine Perspectives: Aspects of the History of Midgley* (Midgley: Midgley Books, 2007)

Midgley, Samuel & Bentley, William – *A History of the Town and Parish of Halifax* (Halifax: E. Jacobs, 1789)

Minter, Gordon & Enid – *Discovering Old Huddersfield* (Huddersfield Local History Society, 2010)

Moule, Thomas – *The English Counties Delineated: Vol II* (London: George Virtue, 1837)

Newell, Abraham – 'Long Causeway Crosses' in *Transactions of the Halifax Antiquarian Society* (1911)

Newell, Abraham – 'Primitive Iron Industry in Upper Calder Dale' in *Transactions of the Halifax Antiquarian Society* (1918)

Newell, Abraham – *A Hillside View of Industrial History* (Todmorden: Newell, 1925)

Northern Earth Magazine, Issue 123 (Mytholmroyd: Northern Earth, 2010)

Ogden, J.H. – 'A Moorland Township: Wadsworth in Ancient Times' in *Transactions of the Halifax Antiquarian Society* (1904)

Orton, Richard – *The Story of Meltham* (Meltham Town Council, 1977)

Peak District & Northern Counties Footpaths Preservation Society – *Annual Report for 1952* (Manchester: A. Spooner, 1952)

Pearson, E. Irene – *Marsden Through the Ages* (Marsden: E. Irene Pearson, 1984)

Priestley, J.B. – *Bright Day* (London: Penguin, 1951)

Priestley, J.H. – 'Mills of the Ryburn Valley' in *Transactions of the Halifax Antiquarian Society* (1933-4)

Priestley, J.H. – 'Ryburn Inns' in *Transactions of the Halifax Antiquarian Society* (1942)

Priestley, J.H. – 'The Rochdale to Halifax and Elland Turnpike' in *Transactions of the Halifax Antiquarian Society* (1952-53)

Radford, George – *Walks and Drives from Ben Rhydding* (Leeds: Richard Jackson, 1881)

Raistrick, Dr A. – 'The Bronze Age in West Yorkshire' in *Yorkshire Archaeological Journal* (1929)

Raistrick, Arthur – *Yorkshire Maps and Map-makers* (Skipton: Dalesman, 1969)

Redfern, Roger – *Country Diary: Wessenden'* (published in *The Guardian*, Sauturday 14th July 2001)

Redmonds, Dr. George – *Slaithwaite Places and Place Names* (Huddersfield: GR Books, 1988)

Samuels, David – *The Ripple of a Chinese Feather* (Keighley: Samuels, 2000)

Samuels, David et al – *A Brief History of Oxenhope* (Keighley: Samuels, 1996)

Savage, E.M. – *Stoodley Pike* (Todmorden Antiquarian Society, 1974)

Savage, Mrs E.M. – *Stoodley Pike* (Todmorden Antiquarian Society, 1974)

Sellers, Gladys – *Walking in the South Pennines* (Milnthorpe: Cicerone Press, 1991)

Senior, A – 'Bell House Farm and Erringden Park' in *Transactions of the Halifax Antiquarian Society* (1952)

Shepherd, David – 'Prehistoric Activity in the Central South Pennines' in *Transactions of the Halifax Antiquarian Society* (2003)

Shepherd, David – 'Prehistoric Standing Stones in the South Pennines' in *Transactions of the Halifax Antiquarian Society* (2009)

Shires, David and King, Sheila – *The Halifax Cavaliers and the Heptonstall Roundheads* (Hollis, NH: Puritan Press, 1993)

Simmons, Prof Ian – *The Moorlands of England and Wales* (Edinburgh University Press, 2003)

Slack, Margaret – *Portrait of West Yorkshire* (London: Robert Hale, 1984)

Smith, Albert Hugh – *The Place-names of the West Riding of Yorkshire* (Cambridge: The University Press, 1959)

Smith, Nigel – 'The Location and Organisation of Demesne Cattle Farms in Sowerby Graveship Circa 1300' in *Transactions of the Halifax Antiquarian Society* (2007)

Smith, Nigel – 'The Medieval Park of Erringden' in *Transactions of the Halifax Antiquarian Society* (2009/2011)

Smith, William – *Old Yorkshire Volume IV* (London: Longmans, Green, 1883)

Speight, Harry – *Chronicles and Stories of Bingley and District* (London: Elliot Stock, 1904)

Speight, Harry – *Upper Wharfedale - Being a Complete Account of the History, Antiquities and Scenery of the Picturesque Valley of the Wharfe from Otley to Langstrothdale* (1900)

Spikins, P.A. – *Prehistoric People of the Pennines* (West Yorkshire Archaeology Service, 2002)

Spikins, Penny – *Prehistoric People of the Pennines: Reconstructing the Lifestyles of Mesolithic Hunter-gatherers on Marsden Moor* (Wakefield: West Yorkshire Archaeology Service, 2002)

Stephens, J.V, Mitchell, G.H. & Edwards, Wilfrid – *Geology of the Country Between Bradford and Skipton* (London: HMSO, 1953)

Stephenson, Tom – *Forbidden Land: The Struggle for Access to Moorland and Mountain* (Manchester University Press, 1989)

Stirling, A.M.W. – *Annals of a Yorkshire House from the Papers of a Macaroni & his Kindred* (London: John Lane, 1911)

Sugden, John – *Slaithwaite Notes Past and Present* (Manchester: John Heywood, 1905)

Summers, Montague – *Werewolf* (Whitefish, MT: Kessinger Publishing, 2003)

Sutcliffe, Halliwell – *By Moor and Fell: Landscapes and Lang-Settle Lore from West Yorkshire* (London: T. Fisher Unwin, 1899)

Sutcliffe, T – 'Castle Carr' in *Transactions of the Halifax Antiquarian Society* (1921)

Sykes, D.F.E. – *The History of Huddersfield and its Vicinity* (Huddersfield: The Advertiser Press, 1898)

Sykes, D.F.E. – *The History of the Colne Valley* (Slaithwaite: F. Walker, 1906)

Tallis, J.H. – *Forest and Moorland in the South Pennine Uplands in the Mid-Flandrian Period: III The Spread of Moorland - Local, Regional and National* (Journal of Ecology Vol. 79, 1991)

Teal, Alfred – *West Yorkshire Pioneer* (1902)

Thompson, Dennis – *Stanbury: A Pennine Country Village* (Calgary: Two Margarets, 2002)

Thornber, Titus – *A Pennine Parish: The History of Cliviger* (Burnley: Rieve Edge Press Limited, 1987)

Toomey, J.P. – *An Iron Age Enclosure at Oldfield Hill, Meltham* (Huddersfield: Brigantian, 1976)

Trigg, W.B. – 'The Industrial Water Supply of Ovenden' in *Transactions of the Halifax Antiquarian Society* (1933)

Trueman, A.E. - *Geology and Scenery in England and Wales* (London: Pelican, 1961)

Turner, Whiteley – *A Spring-time Saunter Round and About Brontë Land* (Wakefield: S.R. Publishers, 1913)

Wainwright, Alfred – *Pennine Way Companion: A Pictorial Guide* (Kendal: Westmorland Gazette, 1975)

Watson, E.W. & Gledhill, G – 'Wadsworth Highways' in *Transactions of the Halifax Antiquarian Society* (1951-55)

Watson, Revd John – *The History and Antiquities of Halifax* (Manchester: F.J.Morten, 1973)

Whitehead, Lewis Buckley – *Bygone Marsden* (Manchester: Percy Brothers, 1942)

Wild, Jack – 'Castle Carr & the Abergele Disaster' in *Transactions of the Halifax Antiquarian Society* (1976)

Wilkinson, T.T. – 'On the Druidical Rock Basins in the Neighbourhood of Burnley', in *Transactions of the Historic Society of Lancashire and Cheshire, Volume 5* (Liverpool: Adam Holden, 1861)

Wilkinson, Tattershall – 'Local Folklore' in *Transactions of the Halifax Antiquarian Society* (1904)

Wilkinson, Tattershall and Tattershall, J. F. – *Memories of Hurstwood, Burnley, Lancashire* (Burnley: J & A Lupton, 1889)

Williams, Eileen – *Holmfirth: From Forest to Township* (Huddersfield: The Advertiser Press, 1975)

Wood, Alec (ed) – *Cowling: A Moorland Parish* (Cowling Local History Society, 1980)

Wood, Alec (ed) – *Sutton-in-Craven: The Old Community* (Driffield: The Ridings, 1973)

Wood, Steven & Palmer, Ian – *Oxenhope and Stanbury Through Time* (Stroud: Amberley, 2009)

Woodhead, T.W. – *History of the Huddersfield Water Supplies* (Huddersfield: The Tolson Museum, 1939)

WEBSITES

Charlestown History Group (*www.charlestownhistory.org.uk*)
Cotton Town (*www.cottontown.org*)
Countryside and Rights of Way Act 2000
    (*www.legislation.gov.uk/ukpga/2000/37/contents*)
Cowling Web (*www.cowlingweb.co.uk*)
Forgotten Relics of an Enterprising Age (*www.forgottenrelics.co.uk*)
Friends of Ilkley Moor (*www.ilkleymoor.org*)
From Weaver to Web (*www.calderdale.gov.uk/wtw*)
Haworth Village (*www.haworth-village.org.uk*)
Hebden Bridge Local History Society (*www.hebdenbridgehistory.org.uk*)
Hebden Bridge Web (*www.hebdenbridge.co.uk*)
Internet Archive: Digital Library (*www.archive.org*)
Jim Jarrett (*www.jimjarratt.co.uk*)
Mytholmroyd Net (*www.mytholmroyd.net*)
One Guy From Barlick (*www.oneguyfrombarlick.co.uk*)
Pennine Prospects (*www.pennineprospects.co.uk*)
Power in the Landscape (*www.powerinthelandscape.co.uk*)
Scammonden Wardens (*www.scammondenwardens.co.uk*)
Stoodley Pike West Yorkshire (*stoodleypike.blogspot.com*)
The Cricket History of Calderdale and Kirklees (*www.ckcricketheritage.org.uk*)
The Megalithic Portal (*www.megalithic.co.uk*)
The Modern Antiquarian (*www.themodernantiquarian.com*)
The Moorland Association (*www.moorlandassociation.org*)
The Northern Antiquarian (*megalithix.wordpress.com*)
The Ramblers Association (*www.ramblers.org.uk*)
The Rombalds Moor Project (*therombaldsmoorproject.wordpress.com*)
Todmorden and Walsden History
    (*freepages.genealogy.rootsweb.ancestry.com/~todmordenandwalsden*)
Todmorden.org (*www.todmorden.org*)
Treasures Revealed in West Yorkshire (*www.treasuresrevealed.co.uk*)
Wild West Yorkshire Nature Diary (*www.wildyorkshire.co.uk*)

INDEX / GAZETTEER

191

THE WEST YORKSHIRE WOODS

Part 1: The Calder Valley

a hand-drawn guide to walking and exploring
the woodlands in the borough of Calderdale

Christopher Goddard

THE SOUTH YORKSHIRE MOORS

a hand-drawn guide to walking and
exploring the moorlands of South Yorkshire
and northern Derbyshire, covering
large parts of the Dark Peak

Christopher Goddard

All books, as well as maps, prints and posters, are available from
my website. I would also welcome your feedback, queries and
any suggestions or corrections you may have.

www.christophergoddard.net